Our Journey to Corporate Sanity

Transformational Stories from the Frontiers of 21st Century Leadership

Ayelet Baron

Advance Copy – Do Not Cite

This is an Advance Copy. Please do not cite.
Formatting and text revisions forthcoming.
All suggestions and reviews may be emailed to
editor@parammedia.com.
Thank you for your support!

PARAM MEDIA INC.
Vancouver, BC

ISBN: 978-0-9950302-4-4

Cover design by Param Media

AyeletBaron.com
ParamMedia.com

ADVANCE ACCLAIM

'Historically speaking, the modern business world is in its infancy. Therefore, it is not too late to mold it and breathe a new spirit into it. Ayelet Baron's *Our Journey to Corporate Sanity* is a mirror to reflect and a tool to redefine the purpose and responsibility of the business world. Moreover, it helps corporate leaders to redirect its journey towards an era of a new corporate culture.'

Rami Kleinmann
President & CEO of the Canadian Friends of the Hebrew University
and Founder of the Einstein Legacy Project.

'Why are leaders fixated on empathy and authenticity? Because we humans—customers, users, employees, stakeholders, the public et al—want more of it. And the supply is just not keeping up with demand. Ayelet Baron sees a future where organizations can be healthier, saner and simpler and shares the underlying wisdom with us in a way that is transformative.'

Julie Anixter
Executive Director, AIGA, the professional association for design,
Co-founder, Think Remarkable
and Co-founder, Innovation Excellence

“The world is all gates, —all opportunities, —strings of tension waiting to be struck."

Ralph Waldo Emerson

Acknowledgements

This creation of this book has been my biggest teacher in life. It has brought me closer to new and ancient teachings, as well as deep relationships that have forever transformed who I am. What this means is that I am on a journey of identifying my limiting beliefs and un-conditioning my life from how I was told I was supposed to live. I started trusting my intuition more and listened to the calling I heard deep in the Ecuadorian Amazon rainforest, finding others who can help humanity re-imagine the nature of business, work, and life. On this path, I have connected with many pioneers who have joined forces in sharing their stories with grace, vulnerability, and authenticity. This journey has opened my heart and mind to what is possible when we adopt a 21st century mindset.

I am forever grateful to my family, friends, and community who continue to support me on my journey; there are too many amazing people to mention by name. You know who you are and the role you play in my life. I also want to thank the many people who supported my crowdfunding campaign.

Life always provides us with opportunities to grow—if we choose to embrace those opportunities—and I am grateful for the lessons I have learned by facing the challenging people and situations that have shown up on my path, lessons that allowed me to experience the full spectrum of emotions that make us human.

I am thankful for the openness, generosity, and love that I have received as I continue on this road to do my life's work of opening hearts and minds and creating a healthier and saner world, a world where people matter and business is a holistic part of our lives. I have come to understand that it requires a shift in how we each think, how we behave, and how we act. As I have discovered, it starts with a journey within ourselves to explore how we transform and begin living our purpose, while connecting with others around a higher shared purpose—with a vivid imagination, strength of conviction, and the curiosity of an adventurer.

Most importantly, I want to acknowledge you, the reader, for joining me in exploring new possibilities, and for starting this important conversation in your own communities wherever you are on the planet. I look forward to hearing from and connecting with you as we experience and co-create a world where cooperation and dialogue allow us to thrive in this century and beyond.

Our Itinerary

Third Leg of the Journey: Creating the 21st Century Organization on the Edge

Foreword: Embarking on a New Path

John H Spencer, PhD
author of the multiple award winning book
The Eternal Law: Ancient Greek Philosophy, Modern Physics, and Ultimate Reality

There is so much beauty and good in the world, but it is equally true that humanity has made quite a horrific mess of the great gift of existence we have been given. We have polluted our air, water, and soil, created unnecessary starvation, homelessness, and war, and continue to suppress and oppress our innate drive for freedom. The list goes on, but grasping at superficial platitudes, or naively asserting that everything will somehow magically be okay without us having to do the work ourselves, has contributed to bringing us to an unprecedented breaking point in human history.

It is—or at least it should be—completely obvious that polluting the environment that sustains our existence is not a very wise thing to do. In fact, it is quite stupid. Financial sustainability is vital in our current economic system, and it is foolish to think otherwise, but it is also insanity to prioritize profit at the expense of poisoning ourselves. And we don't just poison our bodies, whether through eating too much unhealthy food or breathing polluted air—we also pollute our minds. It is the mind pollution, the acceptance of false and harmful beliefs, that most urgently needs our attention. We need a revolution in the mindset of humanity, which begins with each of us.

Why do we perpetuate behaviors that make no sense, that actually harm us, whether such behaviors play out on the global stage or within the spheres of our own private lives? There are many contributing factors, but at least one important aspect has to do with fear. We fear what we do not know, and we cling to what we do know – even if clinging to something known is actually destroying us. It is quite astonishing that we would rather destroy ourselves than admit that we have been wrong about something. It is easy to tell people "step out of your comfort zone" or to talk about going through a process of "transformation"—but genuine transformation, and completely stepping outside of your comfort zone, can be quite frightening. It can also be temporarily painful when we suddenly find ourselves face to face with our own previously unconscious false beliefs, fears, and harmful habits of thought.

The good news is that a growing number of people are starting to recognize that the fear of the unknown is not as great as the fear of the obvious self-destruction we face on our current trajectory. More of us are starting to see that we need to make many significant changes, and fast—especially changes in our own mindset and in the collective mindset of humanity. One of the most urgent practical expressions of such changes needs to occur in business. We often spend more time at work than with our families, and business is one of the most dominant collective forces on the planet. Businesses can bring us great products and extraordinary opportunities for our personal and universal development, but they can also destroy our environment, feed us harmful chemicals, and crush the spirit of far too many individuals.

Our Journey to Corporate Sanity offers much needed guidance to better ways of living and doing business; in fact, as Ayelet Baron makes clear, life and work should be seen as an integrated whole, rather than as fragmented parts. The numerous examples of 21st century leadership, although varied in their unique forms of expression, are actually united by common principles. But rather than being read as a "how to" manual, their stories are meant to act more as inspiring guides to help you find your own unique path. The many reflective questions and exercises can also help you to gain a better understanding of how you too can become a 21st century leader, or become an even better leader if you are already on this path.

One particularly important thing to note about this book is that its basic ideas of wholeness and integration, which seem to be relatively new insights and goals for business, are not simply the latest fad. These ideas are so powerful precisely because they are true. They form part of our best understanding of reality. In fact, the recognition of the integrated wholeness of all reality is a key idea stemming from several of the pioneers in quantum physics during the last century. But modern science has been relatively slow to come to these realizations. Many ancient Greek philosophers, and those from various cultures and traditions who have been part of what is known as the "perennial philosophy" (a term popularised by Aldous Huxley), have recognized the wholeness of reality. (And I am not talking about the often dry, arcane, jargon-filled, boring academic type of philosophy, which is often nothing more than a skeleton of the great ancient tradition of philosophy as a way of life.)

Another important aspect of this book is its emphasis on self-knowledge, which is also one of the main goals of the ancient philosophers and sages. While it may seem unusual to talk of philosophy and physics in a Preface to a book on business, that unusualness does not invalidate the truth that those with greater self-knowledge are far more likely to succeed in business, and in any other area of life. If you are in a business negotiation where the other party is planning a hostile takeover, or is in some way trying to take unfair advantage of you, and if that other party is more self-aware of their own weaknesses than you are of your own hidden weaknesses, then it is likely that they will be better able to push your buttons and manipulate you. One of the greatest defences to being deceived and bullied is to have deep knowledge of yourself; armed with this self-knowledge, you are less likely to unconsciously react in ways that would be to your own disadvantage. This practice of self-knowledge has been an intrinsic part of many ancient philosophical/spiritual teachings throughout history, and it is time for business to start catching up.

Several years ago I was running a seminar for management in one the largest tech companies in the world. They too did not initially understand how philosophy could have anything to with their goals in business. The opening conversation with the group started off something like this:

"All things being equal, which person is most likely to make a sale or succeed in a business negotiation: a wise person or an unwise person?"

"The wise person, obviously. Unwise people tend to make poor decisions."

"And do wise people have more wisdom than unwise people?"

"Yes." (I could see some quizzical faces wondering why I would ask such an obvious question.)

"So, in order to increase your chances of being successful in business, you would agree that it is better to have wisdom than not to have wisdom?"

"Yes."

"Then wisdom is something that we should desire to have?"

"Yes."

"And the more successful we want to be, the wiser we should desire to be?"

"Yes."

"Do you know what the literal meaning of the word *philosophy* is?"

"No."

"It comes from the Greek word *philosophia*, which literally means the *love of wisdom*."

--

Enjoy your own journey to greater wisdom with *Our Journey to Corporate Sanity.*

JHS

Introduction: Preparing for Our Journey

The thought of a journey can get our adrenaline rushing. We spend hours researching and reading reviews of the places we want to see, checking prices, dreaming. There is great excitement in the planning process. But what if *this* is our greatest journey? What if we genuinely experience life as one big adventurous trek—or better yet, many beautiful excursions? It may sound cliché to call life our greatest journey, but what if it is true? What if we engage all the preparatory energy and excitement we would normally devote to a holiday and instead use that energy and excitement to explore our own purpose—our deep, fundamental purpose?

This book takes us on an excursion that requires imagination and a desire to find our own pathways in the 21st century. It explores our vast opportunities when it comes to what is possible in business right now and why we need to find our bold voice in a world that constantly tries to mold us into someone else's story. We can wait for others to pave our path forward or we can realize that it's our time, both personally and collectively, to go on this journey to becoming whole again as individuals and organizations. One path my story has taken me on is the realization that when it comes to being human, there is not much new in the fundamental sense, as we still face the similar types of basic challenges as previous generations have faced. I have also learned that even though we may have more technology available to us than previous generations, to connect deeply with other people what we need is more curiosity, purpose, and a vivid imagination of the world we want to live in and co-create.

For a big part of my life, like many of my friends and colleagues, I defined myself by what I did for a living and measured my success or failure by the external metrics that surrounded me every day. The story we were sold was that a solid education with numerous degrees would open many doors. It would allow us to move up the ranks, and by outperforming everyone else we would be on the path to a successful career. It is the narrative of our times, and what no one tells us is that there is a high personal cost to being very successful as that term is usually defined, and there is a deep difference between achieving our personal best and being the best in the world. What you learn as you move up the coveted corporate ladder and get exposed to the top of the corporation is that you may not want to be part of the top rung. An increasing number of people are starting to re-define what success means to them, and it no longer includes the corporation's insatiable appetite for growth in profits and shareholder value.

The current business model, which demands constant growth, productivity, and a parochial version of efficiency, no longer serves the vast majority of humanity—and never really served any of us, in a deeper sense. Business is at the edge of a major crisis that is slowly unfolding and reminding us that we cannot continue on the current trajectory for much longer. While the media endlessly celebrates successful corporations for their profitability, there is a growing human toll that ranges from increased burnout of people to an epidemic of busyness, where people are not able to find the time to live outside the confines of their career and pursuit of "making a living." There is also the often horrible and senseless destruction of our environment in the pursuit of maximizing profit at any cost, which is basically like dumping toxic waste into our own living room. We wouldn't put harmful chemicals in the gas tank of our expensive car, so why do we put them in our own bodies? There are people within the corporate structures who are becoming increasingly aware of the cracks that are starting to show in how corporations are run, but not many people have any idea of how to address them.

One might think this only holds true of the private sector but in essence many governmental and non-profit organizations are focused on growing, and accumulating more power as well. A typical annual report for major non-profit organizations provides an account of their increased fundraising and span of influence. Some well-known non-profit organizations that focus on preventing diseases, for example, have been known to take public donations from the very corporations that cause the diseases they are fighting.

While this may sound bleak to some, it is actually one of our biggest opportunities to bring sanity back within the corporate walls. It is up to us to recognize that we can chart a new course for business and for ourselves. It requires pausing and rethinking our way forward as global citizens, both as individuals and corporations—like The Body Shop, who uses safe ingredients instead of animal tests for their cosmetics, or Petco and PetSmart, who have transformed the traditional pet store model by forswearing puppy mill suppliers in favor of shelter dogs.

Ultimate Software, a leader in HR software, has been introducing people-centered principles into the basic fabric of how they do business since being founded in 1990. When you talk to one of their employees, they will share with you how their purpose is aligned with that of the corporation's. They focus on the future of people as part of their holistic and integrated strategy. Putting people first encompasses not only how they treat their employees, but how they partner with customers, the community, and even their shareholders. Those businesses that truly value people—not as mere consumers, or as liabilities or resources, but as fellow human beings on our shared journey—are more likely to succeed in the 21st century. When we feel genuinely valued, we are more eager to bring our talents and hearts to our work, and that can only benefit all stakeholders.

We are entering some very exciting times in human history, which includes people being able to connect across the world in instantaneous ways. It is a reminder to each of us as inventors and architects on this journey of discovery of our responsibility to more wisely navigate the future course of business. Information inside the corporate walls can no longer be controlled the way it used to be, as the world is now opening up in front of us in new ways. We are still regulated in large organizations by a code of business conduct policy, but at the same time, our access to people and information is flowing in new and previously untapped ways. And we are starting to recognize that we have more choices, and that there are many new and exciting paths we can take on this journey where people matter deeply and are the heart of business.

The organizations that are best able to re-invent themselves as needed are the ones that are moving to the edges with purpose. They no longer see their opportunities through the lens of mainstream assumptions, or measure how close or far they are from the normal distribution of the famous bell curve. They are focused on the edges and outlier opportunities where they can conduct their business in a human-to-human way. They don't need to focus on looking around at what others are doing to see how they can outshine them; rather, they can focus on bringing their business to the people who care about what they produce for the world. Their leaders value dialogue and understand that deep relationships are foundational to building thriving organizations. It is a world where we learn to trust ourselves and each other. In this era, we are the leaders at the forefront of a human-to-human, purpose-driven experience.

There is also no need to follow blindly when we learn to listen to our internal compass. In 21st century pioneering organizations, people don't have to wait for the annual performance review to share their ideas on how the corporation can thrive. When we encourage people to make suggestions for improvements in the moment that they have an insight, we are much more likely to ignite innovation. We can't wait for someone else to take action or spend our lives complaining about how broken the system is. It is up to each of us to drive our own journey to a saner world, where business creates genuine value for people and for society at large.

By infusing wisdom from transformational stories of 21st century leadership, you will discover in this book how the old is becoming new again in business, and discover why community, trust, and relationships are at the heart of the 21st century. Our fellow passengers on this journey are people from around the world who are co-creating paths for business as a force of good in the 21st century. These are leaders who care about the planet while also creating financially viable businesses. They are doing what their hearts are telling them and tapping into their purpose, driving forward in directions that speak to their vision of the world they want to live in.

Please Leave Your Limiting Beliefs Behind

A vital part of achieving corporate sanity in the 21st century requires us to find the courage to challenge our beliefs and ask ourselves whether they are truly ours. We have been told to aim for success, and we've been instructed on what success itself looks like, feels like, tastes like, and even what it smells like. We may have checked almost everything off the list: education, career, family, home, cars, vacations, promotions, friends, awards. Yet many of us find ourselves questioning what we truly want to achieve, and we find we need to redefine what success really means to us. There is an increasing yearning for deeper experiences alongside the awareness that continually numbing ourselves with superficial achievements and acquiring more and more possessions does not actually fulfill us. In the frenzy to achieve success on this materialistic and achievement-driven road, we have lost vital pieces of ourselves.

We live in a world that tells us more is better, where there is only one winning team, one promotion, one award, and one best organization to work for. We are taught and conditioned to compete to be the best in the world. But a higher common sense prevails when we realize that we don't have to crush everyone else in order to be the only "winner", an alternative mindset I witnessed in many young people I had the privilege to connect with during my career at the networking company Cisco Systems. I met people who lived in slums, and yet they inspired me with their hope and courage to pursue possibilities. One young man, an aspiring poet, would slip one of his poems under his pillow at night when he knew he would be facing a great challenge the next day, describing his anguish. After I shared with a group of youth in Kibera how to use social media tools to get their voice into the world, this young poet started posting his poetry online, where no one needed to know that he was living in a slum. He then started getting feedback and connecting with other poets, and also began getting invited to read his poetry in public, for which he would sometimes get paid. All he needed was his imagination, connectivity, and a deep purpose to open new doors for his life.

This is our opportunity to tap into a new way of doing business by shedding the theories, practices, and mindsets that no longer serve us. We do not need to follow the latest fad; rather, we can start listening more closely to our intuition and combine it with our rational knowledge to guide us to make better decisions. Let's leave our limiting beliefs behind. They don't need to be on our packing list for this new journey.

1) Fear is as Deep as the Mind Allows

Some of us may feel that we cannot pursue our dreams in life. I have spoken to so many people who started on a life path they wanted to follow, but then succumbed to the fear of failure or the pressure to take a job just to pay the bills. Unfortunately, this is often considered honorable in our society.

Our society conditions us to fear. We are taught that danger is everywhere, especially if we are entering into the space of the unknown. We have been conditioned to embrace predictability and routine, while fearing that we won't get everything on our "to do" list done. We too often come together in business to solve pending problems simply out of fear that the competition will outperform or out-innovate us. We tend to spend more time simply protecting and surviving than creating with pure joy and curiosity.

After one of my recent keynotes on 21st century leadership, one participant shared the following insight: "I am so focused on this notion of fear as the biggest cause of failure and why people don't live to their full potential. People sitting in their cubes, hating their jobs, are afraid to make the leap, afraid to take a chance, to do what they love because they fear so many things...things that almost never come true." And it is true—most of what we fear or worry about never actually happens.[1]

---

[1] Robert Leahy, Ph.D., The Worry Cure, 2006.

A year ago I was invited to join a journey I never could have imagined taking. A group of sixteen women known as the Jungle Mamas were heading into the Amazon to learn about maternal health. I was busy working as an innovator-in-residence with a large pharmaceutical company, and did not think I had the time to go. I had to sit with the idea for a while before replying. Eventually, I came to see it as an opportunity to address my fears, and I decided to take a leap and accept the invitation. That decision literally changed my life. When our small plane took off from Puyo to head into the jungle, I turned my head and saw my old self waving goodbye, knowing that when I returned, I would be leaving a lot of my worries, doubts, and fears composting in the heart of the rainforest.

I faced some scary moments during my time in the rainforest, and I looked my fears straight in the eye. I discovered there is a whole other side to fear. Sure, there were scary snakes and bugs, but there was also immense beauty and tranquility. I realized I had dealt with bigger snakes in the business world throughout my career, and by taking a break from the daily noise of news and media, I understood that by facing my fears, I could tap into possibility, simplicity, and my ability to believe in and love myself. When you dig deep down and uncover the origins of your fears, you can start facing them head on by naming them and acknowledging them. Once you start on the journey of addressing these fears, you will find you no longer need to allow them to control your life or your business.

2) The (Often False) Sense of Safety

We have been conditioned to believe that we always need to be safe and careful, which on the surface makes sense. After all, we don't want to drive our car at high speeds on wet roads. But this conditioning then gets taken much too far, and we then become overly fearful, which keeps us caged. Danger is everywhere, we are told. But what if that is nothing more than a limiting belief? What if being too safe is actually too risky? Being "safe" can also be dangerous when our safety means locking ourselves in a cage, disconnected from our potential to fly. To open the cage door, we need to listen to our own internal compass.

We don't have to experience the world in ways dictated by someone else. Gaining approval doesn't always make us feel like we are living with purpose. More of us are spending our lives pushing back on boundaries, battling the rules, and trying to find ways that work for us. This is part of the great shift. We can choose to follow the status quo or we can break away. So much of it comes down to how we define success and failure. If our success is determined simply by comparing ourselves to everyone else, we will always be slaves to other peoples' standards and needs.

3) The Culture of Sameness

It's fascinating how the most memorable line in Nora Ephron's script for *When Harry Met Sally* (dir. Rob Reiner, 1989) is not spoken by either Harry or Sally. Instead, it's an unnamed character who reacts to Sally's fake orgasm in Katz's Deli by saying, "I'll have what she's having."

We have been conditioned to look outside ourselves for guidance on what we need in our lives. We always seem to want what others are having, even when what they appear to have is purely fake, just like Sally's fake orgasm.

We don't need to adopt someone else's best practices to have a fulfilling life. Cookie cutters only work when we are baking. In business and in life, we need to break the culture of sameness so that we can come into our own as creators, makers, and doers. It's time to break the tyranny of being like everyone else and remember the unique and beautiful voices that our souls whisper to us when we dream.

4) Making a Living and Supporting Myself—Even at the Expense of Myself

What allows us to tap into deeper meaning in our lives? We may be getting a monthly salary, but at what cost? We all talk about how we must have the material basics, like a roof over our heads and food to fuel us, and too often we mention Maslow's hierarchy of needs as our model of self-actualization. But what if there is a better model out in the world waiting for each of us to discover?

Whose story do you want to live? Is money a tool for you, or is it a way of life? What drives your existence? Do you ascribe to limiting beliefs, or do your beliefs open up new possibilities? What is it that you need to live your purpose fully? I bet when you truly invest the time in yourself to answer these questions and use your own metrics, you will make different choices about how you spend your time and what's truly important in your life.

5) What If They Find Out I am a Fraud?

There was little pressure to write before the 1940s; it was a passion. But now there is a growing pressure to generate content, even for companies that have nothing to do with publishing or writing content as part of their business. This pressure to write can also cause fear, and then we can believe we have fallen into writer's block. But isn't it interesting that we don't say, "I have chef's block"? As Seth Godin shared on his well-known blog, he believes that many of us hold the belief that writers get blocked from practicing their art.[2] When rock star novelists were born and prestige was assigned to writers, much changed. People who experience writer's block may see their work as inferior, and fear someone may discover that they are supposedly frauds, instead of recognizing that going through the struggle of writing well actually shows commitment to the craft. But this struggle can be quite challenging, and our fear of being a failure helped provoke us to invent this ailment as a way to stop us from writing. Famed literary agent Bill Gladstone (who represents Eckhart Tolle, Shari Arison, and many more) puts it this way: "I don't believe in writer's block; you just have to sit down and write, period. You're not inspired; so what? You're tired; so what? You've made a commitment to write, and it's the universe writing the book through you, ultimately."[3]

You'd be surprised at how many successful people have considered themselves frauds or fakes at one stage of their lives or another. Why does this happen? One key reason is that we have been conditioned to compare ourselves with others, to seek out very limiting metrics that

---

[2] http://sethgodin.typepad.com/seths_blog/2011/09/talkers-block.html

[3] Gladstone in Blackie and Spencer, 2015, p. 242.

are supposed to prove our worth. And that moment when we feel most vulnerable? That's when all our doubts flood our minds and often we become paralyzed by fear.

Instead of fighting this monster that tells you that you are a fraud, invite it in. Discover what it means to you and how you can play with it to develop and grow on your journey. Let go of the fear of being found out. Once you realize you are in the storytelling business, you can befriend the monster and focus on the stories you want to tell.

6) Waiting to be Chosen

Rejection is a gift. Sure, our feelings may be a bit hurt when a person or organization doesn't choose us. But rejection creates space for something else that is more meaningful. It's not about winning that award or getting that job. It's about our own journey and making our way in the world in the best way possible, and moving away from seeking permission and safety and trusting that someone else will take care of us. We can harness the courage to experiment and learn how to choose ourselves. Choosing ourselves—which really means that we stop waiting for someone else to discover us, like a recruiter who has the perfect job for us or the client with the perfect project—can be one of the hardest things to do for many reasons. This is especially difficult when the common story about rejection being a sign of failure is the story we continue to tell ourselves.

For me, waiting to be chosen was a limiting belief. Why did I need to wait for someone else to pick me for what I wanted to create with my life and my work? I had falsely assumed that someone else knew what I needed better than I knew for myself. I started thinking more and more about why this was happening. Why were we even talking about who deserved that promotion at work? The 20th-century business model (what I call "command central") tries to keep us competing against each other and ourselves. No one wants to be the last kid picked.

So much can shift when we change our mindsets and move away from common definitions of success and failure. To me, being safe is often risky, as it means that I have not explored my deepest dreams. Being courageous means stepping outside of our comfort zones and letting go of the fear of failure that we have been conditioned by. I keep firing myself from situations and stories that no longer serve me, that are not aligned with my deeper purpose. I am learning what it means to be true to myself, and it's definitely not an easy road. But I have decided to choose myself by listening to my intuition, and you can choose yourself, too.

7) Hanging on to Our Baggage

The road to knowing what is truly in your own heart takes courage—the courage to face and relinquish the limiting beliefs that have gotten in your way of living the life your soul desires. You may think a business book should be written in a certain way, filled with quotes from all of the right authors. You may have other beliefs that can get in the way of your enjoyment of this journey. Whatever those beliefs are, write them down for yourself and then find a way to remove them from your baggage. Where we are going, you won't need them.

The Path Ahead

We are at the intersection of the present moment and future possibilities. I invite you to join in the journey of the 21st century leader who wants to create a new path for business as a force of good in the world.

We have billions of people on this journey, each at their own intersection. It all starts with the conscious decisions we make about our own path, and the most important one is not buying into the notion that what we do for a living defines who we are. Let's recognize that change is constant and that we do not need to rush, and that we do not need to be the best or have the most.

Remember that what got you to where you currently are may no longer be useful to you on your journey forward. And don't forget to look out the window during the journey; you may see something new and spectacular that you want to experience, or something you are passionate about changing.

We are entering a world where individual and corporate sanity and wellbeing matter more than profits or competition, where your imagination can take you into a world of opportunities to explore the inherent beauty of business when it is aligned with a higher purpose.

Since we are on this journey together, I'd like to share a little more about myself.

I first started writing down my thoughts and impressions in a small orange notebook when I was seven years old. My father's job took us from Israel to Canada, and writing became my key to having a safe place to share the transitions I was undergoing and the new world I was being exposed to. I haven't stopped writing since.

To my father's horror, when I was applying for university at age 17, I auditioned for the best theatre school in Canada and I was accepted. My dream was to be a playwright. After a year, to my father's delight, I transferred to a more acceptable major and ended up completing my undergraduate degree in two years. Academic writing did not feel very inspiring, as I was pushed into formats of sameness, and this unpleasant experience only increased during my PhD studies. So I fired myself from academia, even though I was so close to getting that coveted doctoral degree. My father, who was distraught with my decision, died suddenly soon after.

When I started my corporate career, I was rewarded for my writing, and I started loving it again—although I was largely unaware that I now excelled at corporate speak, and my mark upon it was that I knew how to make it more "chatty" and personal. But it was only when I fired myself from corporate America three years ago that I unleashed my voice in my writing and public speaking.

I was shocked when I discovered that I was one of the top one hundred flyers for United Airlines in San Francisco. This one fact changed my entire perspective on my life, and I fired myself from corporate America. My boss at the time tried hard to convince me to stay, reminding me that I always continued to play the corporate game even when hurt. And he was correct. After a decade of working together, he knew me as someone who was tough enough to put my work first, and no injury, illness, or even a painful divorce had ever gotten in my way of getting the job done. That was the defining moment that set me on this new path, and I am forever grateful to him for making it so clear to me that I had been prioritizing my work, at all costs, over my own wellbeing and my own life. He meant it as a compliment, but I now saw that it was insane. There is not enough material stuff in the universe to pay the price for our physical and mental health.

Throw Away the Rule Book: Un-Conditioning for Our Journey

As we prepare to embark on our journey, we have to decide whether or not we will let go of what no longer serves us. It's our choice to continue playing a part in someone else's manual about how our life is supposed to be lived, or to discover a new direction. The opportunity is to regain our sanity and focus on unlearning and un-conditioning those things that are now (or perhaps have always been) harmful for us.

Un-conditioning #1 – Be mindful about your life and where you invest your energy. Who do you spend time with, where do you work, what do you consume, how much do you play, and are you aligned with your purpose?

Un-conditioning #2 – As we experienced in the Introduction, we need to check in with our limiting beliefs. We don't have to allow them to weigh us down. What are you leaving behind?

Un-conditioning #3 – Remind yourself that you don't necessarily have to follow instruction manuals. It can be very helpful to receive suggestions and guidelines, such as I am offering in this book, but there can be no set manual universally applicable to all people in all the details, and that is what so many so-called experts keep trying to sell us.

Un-conditioning #4 – Give more appropriate attention to your feelings. Much of our communication happens through feelings, not just words. Getting in touch with our feelings and our interconnectedness is part of our journey to sanity, where we (re)learn how to tap into our heart as well as our mind.

We have been conditioned to wear mental armor and project various masks to hide what we are feeling; to hide who we really are. We have been told that emotions have no place in business, and, ironically, some people who assert this view can get very angry when you disagree with them. The obvious but often forgotten fact is that organizations are made up of people, and people have emotions. Advertisers prefer to appeal to emotions over facts and reasoning, precisely because people often make decisions based on emotions. How odd, then, to repeat the outdated business mantra that emotions have no place in business. But at the same time, we cannot be ruled by our emotions. They must be balanced with reason, data, and analysis. But we certainly cannot deny our emotions, as they will work through us and affect our decisions whether or not we are even aware that they are doing so.

Un-conditioning #5 – Open yourself to exploration. This journey is very personal and takes many twists and turns when we open ourselves up. It is about becoming whole, asking questions, and connecting with others.

Un-conditioning #6 – In *The Eternal Law*, Dr. John H Spencer shares an important insight from Albert Einstein:

> "Einstein, for example, was not simply born a genius. He had to work extremely hard to develop his depth of mind, passion, and creative intelligence, and he was especially critical of the educational system he had endured along the way. In contrast to the overemphasis on specialization found in this system, he believed that students must aim to 'acquire a vivid sense of the beautiful and of the morally good.' This noble goal is something that he himself lived by. He writes that 'the ideals which have lighted my way, and time after time have given me new courage to face life cheerfully, have been Kindness, Beauty, and Truth.'"[4]

Let your conscience, inner voice, and intuition guide you. We can allow ourselves to dedicate time and energy to drop the mechanical habits we have learned so that we can tap into our creativity and genius. Ask yourself what is blocking you from letting your creativity flow.

Un-conditioning #7 – Ask questions and challenge current practices that no longer serve you on your path. Our systems are

---

[4] Einstein quoted in Spencer, 2012, p. 11.

starting to crack and there is opportunity for new bridges to be built to take us into a saner world. We need to (re)learn how to ask questions like a curious young child.

When our entire system is broken, it is far saner to focus on the opportunity instead of being stuck in the pattern of trying to fix the problem while working from the same assumptions, and within the same system, that created the so-called problem in the first place. I am not saying we need to ignore our problems. I am saying that when we recognize a problem, we shouldn't simply try to "fix" it, but rather allow this crack to show you potential new opportunities that you may not otherwise have seen.

Catch yourself every time you start a sentence with "The problem is..." or "The trouble is ..." and see if you can tap into what the opportunity is instead. What questions can you ask to bring forth a new birth of a healthier, more humane, and saner world?

A Message from Your Co-Pilot

We are each on a journey that is truly as unique as we are. If we can each heal ourselves before we try to fix someone else or a broken system, we can transform the bigger systems that are cracking. We first need to figure out our purpose, and then find the other leaders, architects, and organizations share that purpose with us. We can also decide to practice our art on our own and connect with unexpected partners to create something bigger than ourselves.

As 21st century leaders, we welcome discernment because we know that this era is about bringing people together around purpose and co-creating meaningful experiences. The ongoing business separation we experience today in our siloed organizations, for example, does not have to break us or define us; it is an opportunity for integration, wholeness, and unity. We know the current business paradigm is crumbling right in front of us, and it is time for a re-birth.

I hope you will embrace this new journey to sanity, in business and in daily life, and I am excited about what is possible when we each open our hearts, overcome our limiting beliefs and unnecessary fears, and become 21st century leaders. This is the beginning of a very long and beautiful conversation.

The best is yet to come,

Ayelet
San Francisco, 2016

First Leg of the Journey
Planning with Purpose

"Our present economic, social and international arrangements are based, in large measure, upon organized lovelessness...we try to dominate and exploit, we waste the earth's mineral resources, ruin its soil, ravage its forests, pour filth into its rivers and poisonous fumes into its air."

Aldous Huxley, *The Perennial Philosophy*

Expedition 1
Welcome to the Human-to-Human Purpose and Experience Driven Adventure

Some History to Kick Off This Expedition

The documentary film The Corporation (winner of the 2004 Sundance Film Festival Audience Award for Best Documentary), takes us on a journey of the evolution of corporations as the dominant force in society. It is based on the non-fiction book by law professor Joel Balcan, The Corporation: *The Pathological Pursuit of Profit and Power* (2003). Both the book and the film contend that today's corporation is a pathological institution that wields power, not unlike monarchies and religious institutions at their worst, over the course of the very essence of how people and societies live. They focus on three observations of the modern corporation: 1) The legal mandate of the corporation is to pursue its own economic self-interest without exception, regardless of the harmful consequences it might cause to others or the planet; 2) Corporations have become solely self-interested entities that have a singular purpose, and that is to provide value and profits to its shareholders while relentlessly continuing on the path of growth. Many Wall Street scandals throughout our history have revealed how corporations can self-destruct and take down people, shareholders, and even society; and 3) Governments allow the corporation to be free from many legal constraints through deregulation, and have granted them ever greater authority over society through privatization.

It is not just the traditional corporate world that is broken. The questions this book poses go into the opportunity of addressing the breakdown of all types of organizations. Having been a Cisco

Leadership Fellow, where I stepped out of my corporate role for over a year, I worked with over 20 of the largest non-profits in the world. During that time, I experienced firsthand that even though many of these non-profits had noble purposes, they didn't actually live up to them or become better organizations to work for, something I found to be true with several government agencies as well. People in many professions are leaving all types of organizations in droves because of the organization's soulless nature. There is much growing disillusionment over our current leadership practices, which more and more people are finally acknowledging while finding the courage to explore new pathways.

Let us take a brief look at some of the biggest corporate scandals that unfortunately mostly report the financial loss of their fraud, and do not pay enough attention to what these scandals have meant for the lives of millions of people, either as employees or as people who buy products that the corporations know are harmful to human life or our environment. All this is done in the name of the current goal of corporations to survive and thrive by generating profits and the infamous shareholder value, at all costs. Ironically, one of the biggest collective financial scandals is the credit crisis of 2007 and 2008, where Lehman Brothers and the Royal Bank of Scotland were deemed "incompetent victims of events."[5]

We may have a horrible boss who stresses us out to the point where it impacts our health, yet we still need to put food on the table for our family to survive. We may feel helplessly controlled by a system that forces us to sacrifice our health and wellbeing just to eat. Should we be deemed incompetent victims of events? Is there no other way?

This has to make us wonder if some people simply feel that the events unfolding on their television, computer, or mobile device screens are occurring on a different plane of reality. It's as though we simply watch these events unfold in horror, and then discuss them in online forums or at dinner gatherings, but do not actually connect with

---

[5] https://www.theguardian.com/business/2015/jul/21/the-worlds-biggest-accounting-scandals-toshiba-enron-olympus

them in any meaningful way or even recognize them as real. Yes, many of us feel the pain of a senseless shooting that takes human life or an economic scandal that wipes out individuals' life savings. But then we just seem to move on to the latest atrocity that is being reported in the media, and the fear only perpetuates, leaving us feeling outraged but helpless. It almost feels like we have somehow become addicted to disasters.

We can choose to remain as spectators and commentators of these events, or we can take small or big actions that change this game to reflect our humanity in profound ways.

A Trip Down Memory Lane

Fortune Magazine named Enron "America's Most Innovative Company" for six years in a row prior to thousands of employees losing their livelihoods and retirement funds, and shareholders losing $74 billion in 2001 in one of the biggest corporate scandals in history. Arthur Andersen was found guilty of misrepresenting Enron's accounts.[6]

In 2002, WorldCom inflated its assets by $11 billion, which led to 30,000 people losing their jobs and $180 billion in losses for shareholders. Over a six-year period, the company made 63 acquisitions, the largest of which was MCI in 1997. When WorldCom filed for bankruptcy, it admitted that it had inappropriately booked the losses from its acquisitions from 1999 to 2002.[7]

In 2003, US federally backed mortgage-financing giant Freddie Mac intentionally misstated and understated $5 billion in earnings. A year later, Fannie Mae, the other federally backed mortgage financing company, was caught up in a similar scandal.[8]

Multinational American Insurance Group (AIG) was caught in a massive accounting fraud of $4 billion, along with stock price manipulation, in 2005. While they settled with the US Securities and

[6] https://hbr.org/product/the-fall-of-enron/109039-PDF-ENG

[7] https://hbr.org/product/accounting-fraud-at-worldcom/104071-PDF-ENG

[8] http://www.nytimes.com/2013/03/24/business/fannie-mae-freddie-mac-and-the-same-old-song.html?_r=0

Exchange Commission (SEC) CEO Hank Greenberg was fired and has never faced criminal charges. After being bailed out by taxpayers following their posting of the largest quarterly corporate loss in history in 2008 at $62 billion, AIG executives rewarded themselves with $165 million in bonuses.[9]

Global financial services corporation Lehman Brothers hid $50 billion in loans disguised as sales in the financial crisis of 2008. It was ranked by Fortune Magazine as the #1 "Most Admired Securities Firm" in 2007. They were forced into the largest bankruptcy in US history, but the SEC never prosecuted due to lack of evidence. Their auditor was Ernst & Young, who agreed to pay $10 million to New York state to settle the lawsuit for overlooking accounting gimmicks.[10]

Bernard L. Madoff's Securities LLC tricked investors out of $65 billion through the largest Ponzi scheme ever, which was uncovered in 2008. Investors were paid high returns out of their own money or that of others rather than profits. Madoff was sentenced to 150 years in prison and a few years later his son committed suicide. While over $11 billion has been recovered, with lawyers taking over $800 million of their share, the victims feel that no matter how much is recovered, their lives will never fully be the same.[11]

The Libor (London Interbank Offered Rate) scandal broke in the middle of 2012, when Barclays admitted manipulating interest rate benchmarks used to price trillions of dollars of global financial products. Barclays and other big banks have paid penalties of $9 billion. A jury was unable to reach a verdict on whether Ryan Reich and Stylianos Contogoulas had been guilty of rigging the global bank interest rate between 2005 and 2007.[12]

Toshiba admitted in 2015 that it had overstated its earnings by nearly $2 billion over seven years. Investigators reported that Toshiba

---

[9] https://www.thenation.com/article/aig-bailout-scandal/

[10] http://som.yale.edu/sites/default/files/files/001-2014-3A-V1-LehmanBrothers-A-REVA.pdf

[11] https://www.sec.gov/news/press/2008/2008-293.htm

[12] http://www.nytimes.com/interactive/2015/04/23/business/dealbook/db-libor-timeline.html#/#time370_10902

had a corporate culture in which management decisions could not be challenged.[13]

It was revealed in 2015 that Volkswagen, the world's biggest automaker, had cheated on diesel emissions tests. It had installed software on millions of cars to make the Environmental Protection Agency's emissions testers believe the cars were environmentally friendly. A settlement required Volkswagen to spend $14.7 billion to compensate vehicle owners and invest in pollution mitigation and green vehicle technology. Regardless, there are over 475,000 Volkswagen vehicles with excess emissions still on US roads, which will have an ongoing impact on the environment if owners don't bring in their vehicles to be repaired.[14]

Soccer's international governing body, FIFA, is not a traditional corporation, and yet it was part of the big business scandals of 2015 when it was found to be plagued by corruption. Investigators revealed that FIFA officials were taking millions of dollars in bribes to influence contracts, the FIFA presidential elections, and the selection process for the World Cup.[15]

In the words of Machiavelli, "The reason there will be no change is because the people who stand to lose from change have all the power. And the people who stand to gain from change have none of the power."[16] Isn't it time for us to change this story? Don't we have enough evidence and proof that our systems are dying? Isn't this an opportunity to rebuild a saner and more humane experience for all of us?

But I am not simply calling out corporations, as that is too easy. We all share in the responsibility to some degree, as many of us have uncritically accepted the mantra of materialism, that whoever dies with the most possessions and the fattest bank account wins, and that is part

---

[13] http://www.wsj.com/articles/toshiba-accounting-scandal-draws-record-fine-from-regulators-1449472485

[14] http://www.bbc.com/news/business-34324772

[15] http://guardian.ng/sport/fifa-scandal-deepens-with-16-indicted-for-corruption/

[16] The Prince by Nicolo Machiavelli Written c. 1505, published 1515

of the fuel of all these scandals. Corporations are owned and operated by people. Consumers are people. When corporate executives pollute the environment to make a bit more profit, they lose, too. They and their friends and family, whether now or later, directly or indirectly, also suffer from poor air quality, poor water quality, and so on. There is only one planet, and we are all on it together. These events are impacting each of us beyond what we see reported on our technological screens.

You will find that many of the stories shared in this book can spark conversations about the opportunities we have to rethink business and its impact on our planet and our human spirit. We should not continue to replace one fragmented and broken system with another fragmented and broken system. This is a time of discovering and integrating many relevant truths and possible directions, with diverse approaches and new (and very old) values coming into the foreground.

We can either continue to report on these and other scandals that are spurred by harmful assumptions that no longer serve greater society, or we can start a journey to examine the root of these false assumptions to create a new path. This is the time for corporations to fulfill a vitally important role in society, by bringing people together toward one common goal and shared purpose beyond the unsustainable parochialism of greed.

It's time to rethink the role of the corporation in society. Corporate influence and interests are running our world, and there are so many further examples that will remain hidden and unexposed. Talking about this can make some people uncomfortable. Apparently, some people believe that someone else will take care of these issues, while they hide their heads in the sand. But that reaction is no longer sustainable. It is time for us to dismantle this monolithic structure called the corporation and regain our sanity.

Our Business Evolution

This is the history of our business evolution over the last 200 years. Like many others who have (for a while) thrived insides the walls of corporations, I know that we can do business in much healthier, saner, and more beautiful ways. In some respects, smaller businesses collectively are exerting increasing influence, and therefore have increasing responsibility for implementing such transformational shifts in society as well.

We are born to venture into unchartered territories in search of possibilities. It's a voyage of purpose and courage. Business is becoming much more obviously personal in the 21st century, because it's becoming increasingly clear that people are the foundation of business. It's time for us to be whole as individuals and organizations.

You may have been led to believe that this era is about "things," "big data"[17] or even "robots", and such things are getting a lot of widespread coverage. We may have been led to believe that this is the Business-to-Business (B2B) or Business-to-Consumer (B2C) era, but there is no business without the involvement of people. We are becoming aware that we are actually in the human-to-human era, where people matter more and more when it comes to business. People always should have mattered, but we lost our way, and now have to find it again. We have a new breed of leaders emerging who lead with deep purpose, and know how to build relationships and have more meaningful conversations that lead to implementing better options.

Creating a healthy, humane world requires more than new organizational models that shift the deck chairs on a sinking ship. It takes entirely rethinking the nature of business, work, and life. We can no longer afford to separate work and life into two neat boxes, or segment our organizations into distinct internal functions that fight each other for budgets and resources. While many antiquated business practices still exist, it's becoming more and more urgent to leave them behind and discover new and better paths forward. We can choose to stop believing the myth that change can only come from the top of the corporation, because we live in a more open and connected world where there is an increase in transparency of communication.

---

[17] According to Gartner, big data is high-volume, high-velocity and/or high-variety information assets that demand cost-effective, innovative forms of information processing that enable enhanced insight, decision making, and process automation.

A Brief Peek into Scarcity

Think back to the last few centuries, where many believed they did not have enough, and lived in a world of scarcity driven by economic depression and war. People had to take what they needed away from others to survive. Competition was fierce and it produced a mindset of not having enough resources. It was a time when management practices were based on notions of scarcity.

There are now many views and stories surfacing in non-traditional media channels about how a concentrated economic elite have shaped modern sociopolitical structures to further their own ends, without concern for anyone else, further distorting the already grossly unjust distribution of income and wealth. As more independent media sources sprout on the Internet—many finally reporting stories of people and businesses who are doing good in society—people will have access to different types of information coming directly from people experiencing an event.[18]

With a 21st-century mindset, we can discover unique opportunities to create new markets, products, services, and, most importantly, purpose-driven experiences for people. As more people start working for gigs rather than for corporations, we will uncover new paths to living and working. As less of us follow the noise of what is expected of us and instead follow our purpose, we will trust our intuition to guide us in new ways.

Imagine for one minute if we stopped talking about "big data" and the "Internet of things" and instead talked about how we can make the world better by embracing human connectivity. Business is so obsessed with how smart we are to create all these new technologies that somehow we forgot the human who uses them, and instead call a human nothing more than the "User Interface (UI)." The dehumanization we are seeing comes from us, so we are the ones who can change it.

One serious concern is that so many of us are far too busy and often overwhelmed, and we are somehow meant to feel proud about it. But

---

[18] http://www.ithaca.edu/rhp/independentmedia/usindymedialist/

why do we accept this as normal? In America. more than fifty-two billion vacation-pay dollars are squandered because of the fear people have of taking time off[19], and all the mostly useless systems and processes, like performance management and annual surveys, have taken away our abilities to have open two-way conversations. Americans have less job security than most Europeans who are not governed by "at will" employment contracts.[20] Over 72% of Chinese workers have not taken a paid vacation in the last three years.[21] The top three reasons why Chinese workers don't take vacation are that they simply don't dare, don't have the time, or don't want to because it would affect their future development and employment.[22]

Even the people at the "top" of large organizations who have had to do massive layoffs over the last decade have lost their way. Ask any of them in private and they will show you their scars. They may have their millions or billions of dollars and their boats and private jets that create an illusionary bar of happiness for everyone else, but they are on the same journey as the rest of us in the cycle of life and death. We may put business icons like Steve Jobs on a pedestal, but we never know what someone else's journey is despite how beautifully it is played out in the media. When you talk to people who have been close to these icons—and I have—you find out that while they may be driven, money doesn't buy anyone happiness or guarantee good health. Each successful leader still has to face their own demons as they reflect on how they actually achieved what we currently call "success" and "growth." Many of these leaders at the top invested a lot of resources to bring the best talent on board, and then discarded them when they no longer reconciled with their financial statements.

---

[19] http://blogs.wsj.com/atwork/2015/03/04/the-cost-of-unused-vacation-time-224-billion/

[20] At will employment means that an employee can be dismissed by an employer for any reason without "just cause" for the termination and without any warning.

[21] http://www.marketwatch.com/story/americans-only-take-half-of-their-paid-vacation-2014-04-03

[22] http://sinosphere.blogs.nytimes.com/2015/09/11/china-workers-leisure-holidays/

I remember being personally traumatized during one of the layoffs I survived. A colleague was so distraught he committed suicide to avoid dealing with the humiliation of losing his coveted job. How could he face his family and friends with the shame he felt when the company he had dedicated his life to no longer needed him? It takes the concept of success and failure to another level when we compromise our self-worth by handing over our power to a corporation that, on the one hand, recruits us as the best talent, and on the other hand, discards us when we are no longer deemed useful according to often absurd metrics.

It is liberating when we realize that in a world of opportunities, there is no need to focus on pointless divisions and conflicts. Organizations benefit greatly when they tap into their people's talents and passions, and pursue with collective purpose the ideas that spurred the creation of their organizations in the first place. Too many people today are hanging on by leading (or following) with fear. It is easy to evoke fear; the fear of losing our jobs, our homes, our families, our friends, our health, and even our country can be evoked by a few images and words. That fear can be paralyzing, and we often look to someone else for protection. Fear and competition can force us to retreat into our perceived safety and live in anger and hurt.

Of course, fear is also important. We are wise to fear jumping out of an airplane without a parachute, or punching a tiger in the nose, but I am talking about illusory fears, which we are inundated with and which are very harmful. What if we choose to listen to our intuition and reason instead of what others tell us is important? What if we decide to become lifeaholics instead of workaholics?[23] We will still work, but it

---

[23] Lifeaholics see life as one big adventure, where work is just part of it. They do not separate life from work. According to Psychology Today, "Workaholism is a family disease often passed down from parent to child. Workaholics use work to cope with emotional discomfort and feelings of inadequacy. They get adrenaline highs from work binges and then crash from exhaustion, resulting in periods of irritability, low self-esteem, anxiety and depression. To cope with these feelings, workaholics then begin another cycle of excessive devotion to work. Workaholics are so immersed in work they have little time to invest in family life and child-rearing. In the time they do spend with their children they pass down their unrealistic and unattainable

will not define our very existence. As artists and architects, we have the choice to free ourselves from the residual industrial paradigms and chart a new journey for business and humanity.

Just Imagine

Purpose is a cornerstone of the 21st century adventure. And yet, not everyone is being guided by a pure and beautiful purpose. There are people in the world who are on a journey of destruction with hearts filled with hatred and fear. They are stuck in this mindset, and we need to be aware of how their intentions can impact our own journey. There are also many non-profit organizations with noble professed purposes who feel that because, for example, they are reducing the spread of HIV/AIDS, they can treat their employees poorly. The deeper underlying question here is whether in pursuing purpose, are we doing harm to ourselves and others?

Imagine a world where our purpose is aligned with our higher goals. Our opportunities become so much bigger, brighter, and more beautiful when we let go of these old beliefs. If we could spend as much time and effort caring about the wellbeing of people at work as we do the security of our systems and data, we would experience more positive outcomes. This era is about breaking free from our own unnecessary constraints and waking up to what is possible.

What happens when we face our biggest fears head on, so that we can do the work we are meant to do? We no longer need to live within someone else's paradigm of success. Change is happening every day despite what the mainstream media may want us to believe. Take a look at some of the shifts that are quietly (or not so quietly) taking place in our world today:

---

perfectionistic standards:" https://www.psychologytoday.com/blog/mind-over-money/201307/are-you-workaholic

Our natural environment:

- An increasing number of people around the world are recognizing the urgency of addressing climate change and taking action in small and big ways. [24]
- Renewable energy solutions are growing exponentially. [25]
- Although there is still a long road ahead of us to reconnect with nature, each climate catastrophe brings us together in greater numbers as we collectively search for new ways to live better.[26]

Our global society:

- For the first time ever, in 2015 the global child mortality rate (defined as child deaths under the age of five) dropped below the six million mark. In the last 25 years, roughly one third of the world's countries reduced under-five mortality by two thirds, while another 74 reduced rates by at least half. Since 2000, the lives of 48 million children have been spared.[27]
- The number of people living in extreme poverty fell below 10% of the world's population for the first time in 2015, according to the World Bank, who project that 702 million people (or 9.6% of the world's population) will be living in extreme poverty in 2015, down from 902 million people (or 12.8% of the global population) in 2012. Extreme poverty has long been defined as living on or below $1.25 a day, but the World Bank's adjustment now sets the poverty line at $1.90 a day.[28]
- Homelessness declined by 11 percent in the United States from 2010 to 2015.[29]

---

[24] ttp://www.pewresearch.org/fact-tank/2016/04/18/what-the-world-thinks-about-climate-change-in-7-charts/

[25] https://www.theguardian.com/vital-signs/2015/apr/20/renewable-energy-global-trends-solar-power

[26] http://www.worldpoliticsreview.com/articles/19261/new-ways-of-defining-success-in-post-disaster-recovery

[27] http://www.who.int/mediacentre/factsheets/fs178/en/

[28] http://www.worldbank.org/en/topic/poverty/overview

[29] https://news.upenn.edu/news/hud-report-penn-research-finds-us-homeless-numbers-continue-decline

- There have been increases in food supply, education, literacy, and economic growth around the globe. 9 out of 10 children worldwide are learning to read and write. The World Bank says we're only one generation away from a world where every single person is literate.[30]

Our connectivity:

- More people are connected to the Internet than ever before. Globally, we have 3.2 billion people online, and two billion of them are from developing countries, compared to the year 2000, when those numbers were 300 million and 100 million respectively.[31]
- Connectivity on the African continent has grown by 51 percent over the past five years.[32]
- Globally, mobile subscriptions number more than seven billion, and 95 percent of the world's population is now within reach of a mobile network signal. The next billion people coming online will do so from mobile phones.[33]
- For every 10 people who gain Internet access, about one person is lifted out of poverty and about one new job is created.[34]

Our health:

- Medicine and health continue to advance due to technology, and people are also getting far more involved in becoming their own experts and sharing information about health with others.[35]

---

[30] http://www.uis.unesco.org/literacy/Documents/UIS-literacy-statistics-1990-2015-en.pdf

[31] http://www.bbc.com/news/technology-32884867

[32] https://www.telegeography.com/press/press-releases/2015/08/26/african-internet-capacity-growth-continues-to-lead-world/index.html

[33]http://www.gsmamobileeconomy.com/GSMA_Global_Mobile_Economy_Report_2015.pdf

[34] http://www.independent.co.uk/news/world/politics/11-ways-the-world-got-better-in-2015-a6787371.html

[35] https://hbr.org/2013/10/the-strategy-that-will-fix-health-care

- The US Department of Agriculture (USDA) awarded more than $14.5 million in grants to support research into plant health, production, and resilience in 2016.[36]
- Non-profit group MAPS received a $2.2 million grant from State of Colorado for the first clinical trial of whole plant marijuana for PTSD treatment in veterans in 2016.[37] And the US Drug Enforcement Administration (DEA) approved the first clinical trial using MDMA along with psychotherapy to treat anxiety among people with life-threatening illnesses.[38]
- Globally, the number of malaria deaths fell from an estimated 839,000 in 2000 to 438,000 in 2015—an estimated 6.2 million people were saved from malaria in the last 15 years.[39]
- The number of people without access to improved drinking water fell below 700 million in 2015 for the first time in history. More than 6.6 billion people (or 91 percent of the global population) now uses an improved drinking water source, up from 76 percent in 1990.[40]

Adopting a 21st Century Mindset

It's time to remember our humanity and bring back sanity to business and our lives. Fellow traveler Nirit Cohen, who writes about the future of work and careers, shares with us that in the 21st century, business is personal. Nirit reminds us of what management consultant and business author Peter Drucker wrote in his 1967 book, The Effective Executive: "Any organization also needs a commitment to values and their constant reaffirmation, as a human body needs vitamins and minerals." Without something to stand for, the organization and its people are likely to end up lost. Our 21st century question is one of why are we in business. It helps us explore the deeper

---

[36] http://www.usda.gov/wps/portal/usda/usdahome?contentid=2016/06/0135.xml

[37] http://www.maps.org/news/media/6141-press-release-dea-approves-first-ever-trial-of-medical-marijuana-for-ptsd-in-veterans

[38] http://www.maps.org/index.php?option=com_content&view=category&id=381

[39] http://www.cdc.gov/features/worldmalariaday/

[40] http://www.who.int/water_sanitation_health/monitoring/jmp-2015-key-facts/en/

meaning of our purpose. It is going to be increasingly important for each organization not only to be clear on their purpose, but also to live it through how they treat the people who work with them, buy from them, and partner with them. Human-to-human communication will be key to ensuring open information exchanges.

It is no longer just the responsibility of corporations to make the change we want to see in the world. Each of us is responsible for finding our purpose and then coming together around a shared purpose that speaks to our hearts. We need to connect with those we resonate with and realize that the opportunities we seek may no longer be part of the mainstream.

Leaders with a 21st century mindset bring people together to create something meaningful in the world. One of the most important skills that 21st century leaders have is the ability to listen and have empathy for others. They are able to take on the current challenges with a mindset of opportunity and don't see their work as just a job or a title. What opportunities would emerge if we tapped into our compassion and empathy, and started truly creating shared purpose around every part of our work?

In the 21st century, business is about people. There is another way to tell the story of 21st century business and that canvass is fresh and ready for new artists. Let's celebrate the leaders who want business to be the impetus for human and planetary balance and sustainability. The expeditions in this book are filled with questions for the explorer and the adventurer, and I hope that it will help guide you to customize your own journey through the 21st century world of possibilities toward our collective sanity.

Exercises for Expedition 1

<table>
<tr><td rowspan="9">1

Un-Conditioning Part I</td><td>Our world has conditioned us to be aware of our problems, both personally and collectively. Imagine a world where we focused on opportunities instead. By imagining what is possible, we can tap into our imagination and navigate with our intuition, as well as our reason. Ask yourself:</td></tr>
<tr><td>What do I want to experience during my lifetime?</td></tr>
<tr><td></td></tr>
<tr><td>What are the questions that are important to me?</td></tr>
<tr><td></td></tr>
<tr><td>What are my two biggest opportunities right now?</td></tr>
<tr><td></td></tr>
<tr><td>What are 1-2 shifts that I need to make to un-condition myself from my limiting beliefs so I can focus on the opportunities in front of me?</td></tr>
<tr><td></td></tr>
</table>

2 **Trusting Ourselves**	
	Do I trust that I know my purpose in the world, and do I trust myself to follow that path? Why or why not?
	What would truly trusting myself look like?
	Who do I trust and why?
	Do I know who trusts me and why?
	What would others need to do to earn my trust?
	Can I imagine an organization run with a high degree of trust? What do I imagine it looking like?

3 **Shifting to a 21st Century Mindset**	Many individuals and organizations are still stuck in the old world of scarcity, competition, and fear, while we live in a world of opportunities and possibilities. Challenge your beliefs:
	What do I feel is scarce in my world?
	Am I working from a scarcity mindset where I am waiting to be chosen, or am I building a place for myself by choosing myself?
	What is abundant in my world—relationships, technology, partnerships, etc.?
	How do I move into the human-to-human purpose and experience driven era to capture the biggest opportunities available to me?

4 **Self-Exploration**	Welcome to the 21st century, where we explore what's in our hearts. Ask yourself as you go from one expedition to another in this book:
	What role can I play in re-imagining and reinventing business in the 21st century?

5 **Choosing Yourself**	
	Am I waiting for someone else to choose me to do what I want to do with my life? Why or why not?
	In what areas of my life and business have I let myself wait to be chosen?
	Where in my life and business can I start to choose myself?
	What is a limiting belief or a memory that is still holding me back?
	Am I ready to let go of that belief of memory? Why or why not?

Take a moment to jot down any further thoughts you may have.

Expedition 2
Planting a Stake in the Ground

It is time for us to assess what is working and what is not working in our current world. We have learned to fall in love with our problems, and most of them are self-created. When I worked in market research and ran Canada's Consumer Confidence Index, I helped my client, The Conference Board of Canada, report on the fluctuations of confidence in the current economic systems. What this confirmed for me was that the world can be powerfully influenced by public opinion, and too often we don't realize that we are the ones who are directly responsible for outcomes like low consumer confidence in economic and political institutions that then have an impact on our own lives.

What if the purpose of business in this century is to provide value for society? This is a turning point where people are starting to shift their views of business, and also changing their relationship with work. The beauty of creation is that if we see life as a grand adventure, we become creators instead of simply doers following someone else's manual. In this transformation, how can business serve society? How can we work with higher purpose? Can organizations be trusted to produce ethical products and services? And can value include making a measurable positive impact beyond monetary growth and shareholder value?

The Evolution of People in Business

Our professional self has been conditioned to believe that in order to succeed, we must scurry up the corporate ladder to a sense of fulfillment and accomplishment. We have been told that we needed to win at all costs in the market and get promoted to the most coveted jobs so that we could sit in that enviable corner office with the big desk and the big view from our big windows. We have been conditioned to desire being seen as more special than others by being named on endless lists that show the world how great we are. Our goal becomes being recognized and listed as much as possible. At what point do we drop this façade, this delusion, and realize that we are whole people?

The photocopier in any local office carries a set contract and a warranty for maintenance, and is guaranteed to be a part of ongoing business. We amortize our technology, and can often consider it the most valued and important asset that a business today has. Yet, on the same spreadsheet tracking assets like computer equipment, when it comes to people, they are deemed a liability. They have no warranty or guarantee of employment. Employment is "at will" in many countries around the world. Some professors in academic institutions may have tenure and some government officials may have pensions, but in most large organizations, when it comes to the bottom line, people are merely seen as a headcount, a mere list of individuals carried on an organization's payroll.

We are increasingly proclaiming, "People are our most important assets!" Yet we still struggle to truly believe this, let alone exemplify it in our businesses. We have people who, after more than 20 years of service to the same company, find themselves living with a family they no longer know since they have been too busy working to spend time with their children or partner. Then, when that company lets them go during a massive 8,000-person layoff, the company can report back to their shareholders that the bottom line is on track. There is very limited accountability for those who created the strategy to hire those 8,000 people in the first place, because people are more dispensable than furniture in most 20th century organizational models.

Over the past 50 years, management practices have become more metrics-based, with scientific and quantitative indicators determining an organization's apparent success or failure. The increased focus on standardization and scalability has us focused on a very parochial definition of growth, with the notion that more money is always better, no matter how that money is obtained. My then-boss at Cisco shared with me in 2001 that no company in the history of the world had ever grown as fast as ours had. But a few months later, the bubble burst. When I joined the company in the late 90s, there were about 20,000 employees and by 2001, there were 46,000. Then came the big layoff that no one saw coming. CEO John Chambers broke his promise as he declared over and over that the layoff at his previous company, Wang, was so traumatic that he would never do it again. Between 1999 and 2001, we were penalized as managers if we didn't hire fast enough, and most hiring involved more than 10 interviews, in our pursuit of hiring the top ten percent talent in the world. Then, before we could even catch our breath, we were letting thousands of people go. A major trust was broken.

Managing solely by the numbers, implementing another organization's best practices, and leveraging big data are our so-called new world management practices. The time has come to consciously question these so-called facts and practices on which business operates. The 21st century leader brings relationship building and trust to the center stage of business life. As a result, many 20th century organizations will find themselves being rendered obsolete over the next decades.

Empathy Matters

It is important to understand our own and other people's histories, as they are a vital part of what form us into who we become and help us let go of what no longer serves us. We must rekindle the art of conversation and learn to truly listen to ourselves and others. Too often, when we are having a conversation with someone, they interrupt us mid-sentence and ask if we have read this or that latest book, or if we are using this or that latest app, and so on. Just by articulating a few words, they have connected us back to something that is familiar to them and their intent is usually one of wanting to be helpful. And while the book or the app they mention may be valuable to us, this shows that they are not actively listening. We have been conditioned to focus on being smart and knowledgeable, when the opportunity is there to be compassionate and empathetic as well. A lot happens when we start listening more fully to each other.

While many of our technological tools serve us well, at the same time, they can't be our primary focus. Most of our current social media networks continue to be built on archaic advertising and subscription models. Most are still offered for "free" in exchange for massive amounts of personal information. They have introduced old world practices, such as "likes", that can actually inhibit or discourage people from connecting at a deeper level. The so-called "influencers" and "experts" are usually more concerned with marketing strategies than making a genuine impact. We need to remember that social networks provide us with opportunities to connect more deeply in conversation.

Start with the Why: Identify Your Opportunities

What if we chose to see opportunity instead of only problems? What if we started every meeting focused on the opportunities first? What would our stories and our world look like then?

When I was at Cisco working in worldwide sales strategy, I co-created a methodology with 12 brilliant colleagues from around the world that we prototyped over a year. We received a prioritized list of the top challenges the organization was facing from the cross-functional global senior sales leadership team. We then launched cross-functional global teams to address them, using our methodology. The goal was to find solutions to help move us forward. In retrospect, it included all the key steps in today's design thinking methodology. [41]

The team was meant to get together for a full day, which was a huge investment from the company, because many of the "top performers" and "high potentials" were recruited to this task, and it sent people the message that this was important. For half a day, people were asked to define the opportunity and the problem we were addressing. This was very challenging for many, especially sales people who like to solve problems. We never assumed we had the right people on the team to define the opportunity and we continued to engage with more people by conducting research and listening exercises. At the end of six months, each team presented the opportunity, challenges, and prototype to the executives, and many were adopted and implemented.

---

[41] For more on design thinking, go to Stanford's Design School at http://dschool.stanford.edu/redesigningtheater/the-design-thinking-process/

In talking with people afterwards, we found that the two benefits to this approach were bringing people together from different functions and geographies to work on a shared purpose, and shifting their mindset to one of opportunity instead of problems. While the program was called the Collaborative Problem Resolution—because the leadership mindset was focused on our need to constantly solve problems—spending time identifying opportunities as collective teams planted the seeds to spur innovative thinking and approaches. It also got many people out of their day-to-day routines and allowed them to learn about the importance of empathy and listening before constructing solutions. It wasn't a typical leadership development program, but rather a practical way to work together and also build new trusted relationships that connected people across internal organizations. The point of the exercise was not the methodology; the methodology was a means to a higher purpose.

The famous SWOT—Strengths, Weaknesses, Opportunities, Threats—analysis is a household name within many organizations. It is part of most long-term strategic plans, and even new product launches. When I was helping Cisco's Japanese service provider team with one of their sales strategies, the SWOT analysis was in the template they were expected to submit with their sales plan that year. There I was trying to help them, and instead I was learning an important lesson from them. If you have ever worked in Japan, you may know where this story is going. After a great conversation in the Tokyo office about the company's strengths, suddenly we were in complete and utter silence when questioned about the company's weaknesses—since they told me they had no weaknesses. I was aware of the state of their sales numbers, but kept quiet. We moved on and had a delightful deep dive into their opportunities, and then, again, complete silence when I asked them about the treats facing the company. Apparently, there were no threats. This was deeply cultural, as you generally don't talk about the negatives during office hours in Japan. So we built the plan based on the strengths and opportunities and explored what was possible for them. This was a very different approach from how we did things back in headquarters in San Jose, California.

What I brought back to the senior sales executive team in San Jose was that we needed to tailor our approaches with cultural sensitivity. Sometimes we were not seeing the results we expected because we were not asking the questions that the local teams responded to. We were imposing ways of working that did not resonate in other cultures, and therefore we needed to listen more and include them in the sales planning process in different ways.

Our Voices and Corporate Sanity

As we saw earlier, too many large organizations are focused solely on maintaining—and preferably increasing—shareholder value. But individuals are shareholders too, and we need to ask new relevant, challenging questions as shareholders and also as employees, partners, and customers. For example, if we are buying products and services from an organization, we must look at the whole picture and consider the environmental impact. There is a cost to all life when we disregard the environment in which we all co-exist.

Living in an open and connected world grants us more visibility into the way the goods we consume are produced. What happens when we realize a certain product we cherish was made by a company who paid workers a tiny wage and forced them to work in horrible conditions? What happens if the person who has to deal with the media and support the company's practices, because it's their job as the corporate social responsibility liaison, refuses to defend what is wrong? Years later, the guilt and shame surface at the individual level, because this company representative feels personally responsible for the harm or loss of human life. Meanwhile, their employer has moved on to continued monetary profitability and financial success, at whatever cost that may entail.

Powered by Purpose is the New Normal for Business

Staying competitive in today's socially conscious climate means more than merely having good products and being profitable. Not only are people more likely to buy from brands that share their social values, but they are willing to spend more on their products, are nearly twice as loyal, and employees are more than 50 percent more engaged and nearly 20 percent more productive. Turns out doing good can be good for business, and there are people doing amazing work in the world to reboot what is possible for business.

Savii Group helps companies create profits for purpose through its "PinPoint. Find It. Share It.™" program, which has saved companies over $2 million in lost profits. It uses cost recovery and optimization practices to locate "found money" from wasteful corporate spending, and in turn receives a portion of its results-based compensation. The found money is then shared by donating it to that client's non-profit of choice. Gina Manis-Anderson, founder and CEO of Savii Group, has worked with industry-leading companies such as Ulta Beauty, Honda, Sony, Melaleuca, Genesis Healthcare Partners, and others to help them find wasted capital. It is a new movement that can grow fairly quickly to find money that can be used to re-invest in people and social good.

According to Gina, the benefits of PinPoint extend beyond cost savings, in that the "found money" enables companies to fund initiatives that increase profits, brand value, customer loyalty, employee satisfaction, community outreach, and sustainability. Many business leaders acknowledge the value in investing in corporate consciousness initiatives, but struggle to locate the resources to move forward. Gina is committed to help companies eliminate unnecessary spending so they can use their businesses to make a more meaningful impact in society.

Choosing Ourselves

Why do people choose to live within their comfort zones, remaining stuck behaving like everyone else, merely playing it safe and surviving, instead of living life more passionately and thriving? What happens when we start realizing that the world as we know it is changing faster than we ever imagined, and instead of seeing comfort or safety, start seeing safety itself as being potentially too risky? We often hear about the one percent as the people holding all the power and wealth in our world today. I want to introduce you to another percentage: the population who is exploring possibilities and opportunities on the edges, outside the mainstream. This population understands that the bell curve and sameness in business are no longer helpful, and see opportunities in creating a full life by connecting with people across the world or in our local communities. We no longer need to define ourselves by what we do for a living, as we realize life itself is for living.

Change happens every time our expectations are disrupted, which means every time something makes us uncomfortable, there is an opportunity for change. The change that is here and available to each of us is a mindset shift. We don't need to wait for it to come from the boss or the leader of the organization; it needs to come from us. One of the biggest shifts that is happening in our world today is that many people are starting to wake up to the fact that life is precious and that we have more meaningful choices than we have believed possible. It's happening every day, often quietly, especially with people in their 40s, 50s, and 60s who are starting to question the judgment system that society has instilled in them.

In my previous corporate life at Cisco Systems, I worked for over a decade with many successful and brilliant people. I also traveled with them around the world, and, some years, I think we saw more of each other than our families. We were committed to the success of the company and did whatever it took to make our contributions the best they could be. We didn't spend so many years getting a great education not to put it into use, and we were success-driven. But at what cost?

Some time ago during a three-day strategy session in Singapore, I noticed that one of my colleagues was really down, and not at all acting like his usual self. When I asked him what happened, he told me that when he was leaving for the airport, his youngest son had had a meltdown and told his dad that he hates his father's company and wished his dad didn't have to work there. It appears that it was a long weekend and, with the time difference, my colleague had to leave early to get to Singapore in time for the meeting. His son didn't understand what could be so important to separate a father from his children so frequently. The parting words of his son were: "Dad, I hate Cisco for taking you away from us so much." It was a wakeup call for my colleague, and I will always respect the fact that he took a demotion and became a dedicated dad to his three boys as a result. That defining moment changed the choices he made. What choices are you making?

Exercises for Expedition 2

6 **Regaining Sanity**	
	In what key areas have I lost my own "sanity"? Why?
	What are the top opportunities for me to regain my sanity?
	What are the key areas where my business has lost its sanity?
	What are the top opportunities for my business to regain its sanity?

7 **Planting a Stake in the Ground**	
	From all the information at my fingertips, do I envision a more humane world of work with people at the center, or do I still believe we are simply doomed to repeat the old stories of our ancestors? Why or why not?

Expedition 3
Adopting a 21st Century Mindset

Business in the 21st century is not separate from the people involved, from employees to executives to customers. Unfortunately, we have created many harmful divisions, where there are such start contrasts between the haves and have-nots. But more of us are realizing that we are more connected than ever and that it is time to become whole again and take away the limiting or false labels and the boxes that society often unjustly forces us into.

If you have ever spent any time talking to someone who is labeled as being poor, you will find that they usually don't want charity or to be seen as a "give back" of a large organization. In today's business world, we have segmented an entire function called "Corporate Social Responsibility" (CSR) to focus on how a large organization gives back to the community. CSR is also often referred to as corporate conscience, corporate citizenship, or responsible business, and is a form of corporate self-regulation integrated into a business model. The term and application became popular in the 1960s, when organizations believed that CSR would have a positive financial impact on their results if their actions appeared to further some social good beyond their regular business activities.

What we rarely discuss is that CSR programs are also in the best interest of the corporation, because it creates a better market share and competitive advantage for the organization. When the executive director of a CSR department in an organization reviews the portfolio of investment to its Board of Directors, it must demonstrate, for example, the return on its investments in making a social impact that furthers the mission of the organization to be profitable. The way these departments are set up are generally noble, at least in principle, and working in CSR is a highly desirable job for many. But corporate social responsibility needs to also be embedded in the fabric of how corporations do business every day.

In a company that promotes 21st century leadership, we would be far more likely to see the sales team excited by the possibility of having conversations with customers that go beyond simply selling a product, service, or solution. And by developing deeper relationships with customers and fellow workers, the organization would be more likely to increase their sales in the long term. In the 21st century, there is no need for a separate department to act as our corporate conscience. It should simply be ingrained in how we do business—unless our business is doing harm to people, nature, and the planet, in which case those companies need to stop operating or else deeply transform. If you build great products and offer incredible services, why not integrate your conscience and responsibility into your offering? Why not work directly with the people who would benefit from it and find ways to co-create with them?

Although not obviously true in all cases, if you stop to talk to a homeless person on the street of any city in the world, or stop to talk to a teenager living in a slum, you may have the opportunity to learn a great deal. You will find they often don't want your charity. I can't speak for each person, but what I have learned from the ones my friends and I have connected with is that they want opportunities and help imagining the possibilities of what they can create in the world, like everyone else on the planet, despite being financially poor.

Imagine developing a business plan that embedded corporate conscience and citizenship from the outset. Isn't it time to integrate our strategies and think about the bigger impact business could have in the world, and how we can tap into existing and new strategies that would truly change the game? Many of us would cheer seeing these usually separate functions directly integrated into business, with funding and initiatives woven into how we do business from the outset. I have seen this done successfully, and it can work brilliantly. The human spirit can be incredibly resilient. Austrian psychiatrist and Holocaust survivor Viktor Frankl is a timeless testament to the luminous tenacity of his spirit. "Everything can be taken from a man but one thing: the last of the human freedoms—to choose one's attitude in any given set of circumstances, to choose one's own way," he writes in *Man's Search for Meaning* (1963). While some people say that the 21st century is the era to search for purpose and meaning, I believe it is not so much the search but our ability to see each other and connect in purposeful ways that will bring us back together.

Key Insights for the Future of Living Work

Steve Jobs believed that we should not be slaves to focus groups, as "customers don't know what they want until we've shown them."[42] He trusted his intuition about the desires people would have related to Apple's products instead of constantly asking them what they wanted or needed. He made products that he and his friends wanted to use, like a simple device that could carry thousands of songs, which was the seed of the iPod, a device that disrupted the music industry. He relied on his gut: "The people in the Indian countryside don't use their intellect like we do; they use their intuition instead. Intuition is a very powerful thing—more powerful than intellect, in my opinion."[43] Reed Hastings, the CEO of Netflix, seems to agree with Steve Jobs: "We start with the data. But the final call is always gut. It's informed intuition."[44]

As a former market researcher and social scientist, data has played a significant role in my life. I have listened to and analyzed tens of thousands of interviews to identify trends, and have also learned a lot about human behavior by understanding, like Steve Jobs, that often people don't know what they want or need when it comes to products, even when you ask them directly. In my current capacity as a futurist, I have been analyzing new trends that are emerging, while trusting my intuition as well as the data. We are at a crossroads today, and the path we choose matters more than ever in our history. The following insights are based on a combination of data, analysis, and intuition. (See also *The Beacon of Mind: Reason and Intuition in the Ancient and*

[42] https://hbr.org/2012/04/the-real-leadership-lessons-of-steve-jobs
[43] https://hbr.org/2012/04/the-real-leadership-lessons-of-steve-jobs
[44] http://readwrite.com/2016/01/20/netflix-big-data-intuition-reed-hastings/

Modern World, for a variety of powerful and engaging perspectives on this topic.[45])

Work and jobs as we know them are forever changing. The cracks in our business systems are starting to show, and the opportunities for change are abundant. Old employment contracts are shifting. The concept of a job for life no longer exists. We are moving into a project-based world that will transform expectations and allow people to perform more project work. Organizations will need more generalists who can move between projects, organizations, and roles, and tap into their ability to build purposeful human-to-human relationships. We will no longer separate soft and hard skills so sharply, and we will need people who are excellent community builders and connectors of people and projects. This will fundamentally change how organizations attract, retain, and engage people and bring people closer together around shared purpose. As more people declutter and simplify their lives and new lifestyle options appear, we can expect some early adopters to make different decisions when it comes to traditional careers and how they approach ownership of homes and cars, and move into sharing resources. This is already happening in many countries in the world.

It is time again to reflect on Buckminster Fuller's question: "How do we make the world work for 100 percent of humanity in the shortest possible time through spontaneous cooperation without ecological damage or disadvantage to anyone?" Maybe we are all a bit slower than Bucky. He shared with us in his 1983 *Grunch of Giants*: "I do know that technologically humanity now has the opportunity, for the first time in its history, to operate our planet in such a manner as to support and accommodate all humanity at a substantially more advanced standard of living than any humans have ever experienced." There is no better time than now to embrace this wisdom.

Our younger generations have different worldviews, which will move us to collective consciousness over the next few decades. The new generations—from the age of three to 19—are seeing everything as

---

[45] Blackie and Spencer, 2015.

connected and have an increasing affinity to nature regardless of where they live. While many children today play indoors because of safety reasons, their longing for being outdoors and in nature will likely shift as they desire to experience nature directly. The Internet and the ability to connect with people around the globe has always been available to many of them. Those under 20 years of age have witnessed tough times in their short lives. Many teens today are trying to learn from the mistakes made by Millennials or Gen Y-ers (born between 1977 and 1997). Many Gen Z-ers (born after 1997) feel education needs to be active rather than passive and that unemployment is a risk for them. They are more concerned about the future, and not just for themselves.[46]

Six in ten Gen Z-ers want to change the world, compared to four in ten Millennials.[47] In the US, for example, about 76 percent of youth today strongly believe issues like climate change can be solved if action is taken now. They also think safeguarding important lands and waters should be a priority regardless of any ancillary benefits and the struggling economy.[48] In China, 62% of Gen Z believe that financial accomplishment is no longer the main signifier of success, and 94% claim that it is essential for brands to be sustainable and environmentally conscious.[49]

This will have significant implications for the future of business, as members of the upcoming generations will no longer want to be fit into a broken system of work that is built on concepts of scarcity, competition, and fear. They will not want to be labeled, separated, or studied like generations before them. An increasing number will want to work for themselves or in new collectives that come together based on shared purpose, and disband when they achieve their goals. They

---

[46] http://www.jwt.com/blog/consumer_insights/meet-generation-z-in-j-walter-thompson-companys-latest-trend-report/

[47] http://smallbiztrends.com/2016/07/millennials-vs-generation-z.html

[48] http://www.nature.org/newsfeatures/kids-in-nature/youth-and-nature-poll-results.pdf

[49] http://luxurysociety.com/articles/2016/05/chinas-new-kid-on-the-block-generation-z

will not want to see a separation in private versus public versus non-profit sectors, and will expect businesses to be responsible in how they operate. They will seek higher purpose, integration, partnership, and deeper connection.

While this may be hard to believe as we witness the increased anger and outrage demonstrated by many in the Millennial generation today,[50] change is coming. Our current way of life is not sustainable, not just from an environmental perspective but also from a human level. Parents of Millennials in the Western world wanted their children to have many of things they didn't, from educational opportunities to material possessions, and they have often been overinvolved in their children's lives as helicopter parents.[51] In other parts of the world—such as Romania, Turkey, and South Africa—Millennials have had more opportunity to create a new path for themselves by changing their circumstances. I worked with many of them at Cisco and was blown away by their drive and passion. They gave me hope for our future.

We will learn from the younger generations, as they ask questions that many before them have not had the courage to ask about why the world is the way it is. It is up to us to choose to open our hearts, minds, and eyes to what they see, and if we do, we will benefit immensely. They are co-creating the future side by side with us. We are already witnessing new ways of education on the edge that are being developed by pioneers like Michael Strong, co-founder of KoSchool, who understand that the next generations will need more experiential skills than our traditional education systems offer. To truly create our new world of business, our fundamental education system needs to adapt and to work side by side with the business world in new ways.

Life is to be experienced. In today's world, we are seeing industry lines blurring and new opportunities to create businesses based on life experiences. If we look at what defines the health and wellness industry,

---

[50] http://www.theatlantic.com/politics/archive/2016/02/the-liberal-millennial-revolution/470826/ ; http://www.telegraph.co.uk/news/2016/06/24/millenials-fury-over-baby-boomers-vote-for-brexit/

[51]http://www.slate.com/articles/double_x/doublex/2015/07/helicopter_parenting_is_increasingly_correlated_with_college_age_depression.html

for example, we will see that it is integrated with traditional large pharmaceutical companies like Pfizer, traditional technology and solutions companies like IBM, traditional retailers like Nike, traditional cosmetic and beauty companies like L'Oreal and Clinique, traditional non-profits like Doctors Without Borders, and many others who now comprise this industry. If we think about Google, we will see the same trend as they dabble in transportation, health, advertising, and so much more. What will emerge is a new focus on experiences, and it will continue to blur the traditional separation of business into distinct segments. People will want to experience entertainment and not always sit passively and wait to be entertained. This will create possibilities for new businesses to emerge.

Those who insist on clinging to 20th century business fragmentation will see a world of winners and losers. Conscious leaders like Jim Love, chief content officer and CIO at IT World and Magatte Wade, founder and CEO at Tiossan, see a path of opportunity—of taking what can be co-created in possibilities and leaving behind what no longer serves us. In a world of meaning and purpose, the power and effectiveness of people collaborating together by connecting around shared purpose means they tap into each other and their communities, rather than being guided by what organizational box they sit in.

More people will choose themselves. In our new world, we will make choices until we get to the path that sustains us, and we will not be constrained by internal systems like incentive plans that restrict our ability to experiment and choose. The innovation is in the fabric of how we work and collaborate, and will not be relegated to a separate department. Innovation should never be a department. The artist needs freedom to create, and we are all artists, makers, creators, and doers in business.

More companies will be inclusive and whole by design. We will experience 21st century conscious leadership as more organizations create thriving workplace environments with clear shared purpose and new ways of working in trusted communities. More people-centered organizations will pop up as more of us realize that we are in the business of people. Workforce culture will be designed with more flexibility, collaboration, communication, and empathy. Leaders will know how to bring in the right people at the right time to work on key initiatives driven by shared purpose. Social networks based on purpose that allow people to communicate openly and freely and collaborate will be the norm. There will also be a realization of the diversity of skills needed, and we will stop using metrics that no longer serve us. This new generation of leaders will embrace flexibility, build community, and provide the space for people to bring their whole selves to their life's work.

Women make up half of the world's population, and we will start not only feeling this power in business, but embracing what all people bring to business. According to research conducted by Anita Wooley and Thomas Malone: "It's a preliminary finding—and not a conventional one. The standard argument is that diversity is good and you should have both men and women in a group. But so far, the data show, the more women, the better."[52] According to Gallup research, business units that are gender diverse have better financial outcomes than those dominated by one gender. And when gender diverse organizations have high engagement, financial performance improves dramatically.[53]

The conversation will begin to shift from the old narrative of inequality to the inherent knowledge that gender diversity is good for business. When 21st century leaders know that something is good for business, they will start incorporating new practices into how their organization is run, with no need for quotas or employee resource groups. It will simply be how business is done, with no need for a separate diversity department to include those who the old models left behind. When diversity is inherent in how we run our organizations, we will no longer need to call it out or separate it out as a department. We will know how to build the best organizations for the world that are integrated and reflective of our collective society.

---

[52] https://hbr.org/2011/06/defend-your-research-what-makes-a-team-smarter-more-women

[53] http://www.gallup.com/businessjournal/178355/having-women-leaders-good-business.aspx

People will matter more than ever. Organizations will not only partner with other organizations, they will also start partnering with people, whether they are employees, independent contractors, small businesses, vendors, partners, or whatever other label is created. The job of conscious leaders is to recognize that people are part of the company and not capital.

The entire nature of employment will shift. Organizations will need an infrastructure to keep their machine going, but the days of attraction, retention, and engagement will be numbered. We will need to think first about the purpose of the organization and then the people, partnerships, and alliances we will need to bring our purpose to fruition.

Organizations will follow the cycle of life and death. The average lifespan of companies in the Standard & Poor's 500 has already fallen from 61 years in 1958 to 20 years in 2016. It will only fall further. We are starting to see a shift in this century from ownership to partnership and new ways of working. It's already happening, with an increasing number of people choosing to work for themselves. The fact that we have five generations in the workplace trying to work hand in hand is changing how work is done, as older generations remain employed beyond traditional retirement ages due to either choice or necessity. Many large organizations will split into smaller ones where smaller teams will deliver on key projects.

Automation represents an opportunity to shift the world. Automation is not new to us. We have seen it implemented in many industries to make work more efficient. The headlines that create the fear of massive job losses need to simply stop. We have very smart people in the world who love to create new solutions and technologies, and they will continue to amaze us with their genius in areas like virtual reality and many other technologies that have yet to be invented for the good of humanity

Oscar Wilde, in his 1891 essay *The Soul of Man Under Socialism,* ridicules the "nonsense that is written and talked today about the dignity of manual labour," and contends that "man is made for something better than distributing dirt. All work of that kind should be done by a machine." He adds: "Machinery must work for us in coal mines, and do all sanitary services, and be the stoker of steamers, and clean the streets, and run messages on wet days, and do anything that is tedious or distressing. At present, machinery competes against man. Under proper conditions machinery will serve man."[54]

With a 21st century mindset, there is no need to fear robots replacing humans. Humans can drive purpose and create a more peaceful world with less fear and competition. Is it possible that the geniuses creating the robots and human-aided intelligence of tomorrow could invent a more equitable way for us, where we could make a life instead of just a living? What if the robots would be doing most of the manual work, while we had time to explore what it means to be human?

The Path Forward is a Conscious Choice

I delivered a keynote recently to over 500 people about becoming 21st century leaders. Over the 24 hours that followed, I kept running into people who had heard me speak, and many told me that my simple sharing had helped them to think more deeply about this topic, and some even said that I had helped them shift at their core. That is why I have written this book. I want to give us hope and the courage to live fully and co-create our journeys. I ran into one woman who told me that she wished I had done what the other two speakers had done and given her the five takeaways from my keynote. I know some people will feel the same about this book, as that is how we are currently conditioned. I told her what I am telling you now: cookie cutters only work when we are baking. In my life, I got tired of people telling me how I should be and what best practices to follow.

We can look forward to the day when personal ambitions and the purpose of business are as important as financial growth and the bottom line How great will it be when we evaluate organizations by their positive impact and not only by their balance sheets and return on investment (ROI). When we are able to regain our collective

---

[54] Oscar Wilde: The Complete Collection, HarperCollins Publishers Ltd (May 5, 1994)

common sense, business and society will fuse more deeply to become a force of social good in our lives.

It's time for a new path forward that taps into our individual and collective beauty. Come meet your fellow life passengers in Leg 2, whose stories weave together to co-create our journey to corporate sanity.

Exercises for Expedition 3

8 **Un-Conditioning Part II**	People will tell you how to live your life and offer you specific steps to success, but do they really know you? If the answer to this question is yes, please skip this exercise. But if you want to explore more deeply, take as much time as you need to capture a few areas where you have been conditioned to believe what the right path for you and your business is. Ask yourself what's working and what's not working, and start to clarify what you need to un-condition to move forward.
	My conditioning says my business and work should happen like this:
	What's working well is:
	What's not working is:
	What is a limiting belief or a memory that is still holding me back?
	Areas where I can un-condition are:

9 **Integrating the Trends**	For each trend, please note any actions you want to take.
	Work and jobs as we know them are forever changing:
	Our younger generations have different worldviews:
	Life is to be experienced:
	More people will choose themselves:
	More companies will be inclusive and whole by design:
	People will matter more than ever:
	Organizations will follow the cycle of life and death:
	Automation represents an opportunity to shift the world:
	Other trends I foresee:

Second Leg of the Journey
The Seven Signposts to Thriving in the 21st Century

"You can start by changing your story. Did you know that everything in this life is a story? Every book on every shelf is someone's account, their version of what happened...go and tell your own story. It's one the world needs to hear."

Judy Stakee, author of the award-winning *The Songwriter's Survival Guide* (with a Foreword from Sheryl Crow) (The Judy Stakee Company & Param Media 2015).

Expedition 4
In Search of Conscious 21st Century Leaders

There are an increasing number of people who are feeling unhappy or dissatisfied with their current job, and especially with the person they report to in their organization. I recently met with one young woman (let's call her Sylvi) who works at a very well respected Silicon Valley company. Her boss recently told her that, unlike her peers, she is taking too much of his time to discuss her work. And yet, she had been asking him for only an hour of his time every two weeks to discuss a brand new program they were offering. In our conversation, I learned that while the organization had mission and vision statements, there was a clear lack of shared purpose. People were fighting internally with each other to get recognition, resources, and even just to be able to get their job done. Sylvi shared that after a year of working there and being recognized more externally for her contributions than internally, she was considering leaving for a place that valued what she brought to the table.

Another woman I know (let's call her Amber) shared that she is out of a job due to her workplace becoming increasingly toxic. She and her colleagues were used to openly sharing information, then suddenly found themselves in a very secretive environment with a lot of information being withheld from them by the new executive director. Many of her colleagues started to step down from their roles. Amber also felt compelled to resign, as she did not have confidence in the new leader, and also felt that the organization no longer shared her values of integrity, transparency, community, and focus on openly sharing knowledge. Amber had worked to make a difference in the lives of women throughout her career, and is therefore rethinking her relationship with work now that is she is unemployed and has time to think about what she has learned. She is also spending more time with her seven-year-old daughter; before Amber had left her job, she was largely unaware that her own stress was being transferred through to her daughter, who then expressed that she would like her mother to make different choices with her next job. To continue her work in the world, Amber plans to build a team and start a new organization that focuses on connecting women, indigenous people, and various other communities and their stories online.

A third woman (let's call her Jayne) has successfully implemented large-scale change for many global organizations. She left her thriving consulting practice when her former colleague (let's call her Divya) joined an organization in a senior level position and asked her to come work with her. It was an exciting opportunity, as they would be able to make a significant impact together. Jayne accepted the offer, and she enjoyed her work building relationships with the executive team, and was excited by the results they were achieving in bringing innovation inside the organization. However, Divya unexpectedly accepted an offer for a more senior role at another organization, but Jayne wasn't concerned. She believed that her track record with the organization and the relationships she had built with the executive team had placed her in a safe position. Four months later, however, she was introduced to her new boss, and within a few months she had blocked Jayne from having any access to the executive team. Jayne was now no longer allowed to talk to any of the executives without permission from her new boss. Jayne's workplace transformed within a matter of months to a toxic environment where fear reigned, and she and her colleagues suffered in silence. The stress was so high that after her brother died unexpectedly, she went on medical leave. While Jayne was on leave, the organization did a reduction in force and she got a call from her new boss saying that she had been impacted, which meant that her job no longer existed. After the initial shock and anger wore off, Jayne realized this was a gift.

In these three examples of talented women who want to make a significant difference in the world through their work, we witness that instead of having the opportunity to practice their art, they were forced into internal political struggles. While they may have been trained for many years to work at something they are passionate about, most of their time was being spent trying to navigate useless, petty internal drama. I have witnessed thousands of similar stories during my time in corporate America. This is a very old story in our business history, and now it is time for transformation. The cost is too high—both for the individual and the organization—to keep mindlessly following the same tired patterns.

There are many broken parts in the old business model, and trust is one of the biggest. Too often in today's business world, we lead with organizational structure instead of purpose. We are focused on transactions instead of the thinking of how these actions translate into the foundational elements of business, which often get missed, including the need to have lasting human-to-human relationships. We read more headlines about the restructuring, layoff or re-organization and who gets to stay and who is no longer with a company than the why this change was needed (beyond the financial justifications). Imagine if your organization first talked about the changes that were happening in terms of the higher purpose. My intuition tells me that we would be having less restructuring, layoffs and reorganizations when conscious 21st century leaders lead with purpose and people-centered values.

Organizations have expected employees to be loyal to them, and yet that same level of loyalty has not been always reciprocated. No methodology, framework, or formula will provide us with a surefire method to build trust. It is the essence of being a leader and knowing how to build relationships, and it is the most important currency of our time. Fame is fleeting; we can be heroes one day and zeroes the next. But if we have trusted relationships, we can connect deeply with others who share in our purpose.

Organizations may have a great strategy in a PowerPoint slide deck that can be explained in easy terms, but unless they have conscious leaders at the helm who actually live it, they will continue to have low trust and low employee engagement across the board. Why would anyone want to get up every morning and go to work for someone who does not value them and what they bring to their work? No corporate mindfulness or meditation program can change the fact that we need a new breed of leaders who care for the people in their organizations. Because when you value the lives of people and the gifts they bring to your organization, you spark their ability to partner with you to achieve the organization's purpose. It goes beyond traditional cookie cutter employee engagement programs, which generally only pay lip service to their stated goal of truly engaging people.

The statistics that we are repeatedly witnessing in most studies and journals—see Gallup's engagement index and Imperative's purpose study—show that only a third of today's workforce is engaged or comes to work with purpose. Such statistics will continue unabated in a meaningless fashion unless we start recognizing how deep our wounds are, and take the necessary steps to address them. Remember, too, that behind these statistics are real people. Go into any restaurant in a highly dense business district, and you will likely find that seven out of 10 conversations consist of people openly complaining about some roadblock they are facing at work due to a lack of competent leadership. This is not to say that every person's complaint is justified, as sometimes people create their own roadblocks even if they work for a great leadership team, but too often poor leadership does stifle or completely eliminate many great growth opportunities. If leaders could facilitate creativity, innovative thinking, and an environment where people feel genuinely valued, then productivity and the bottom line are likely to increase.

The Opportunity of 21st Century Conscious Leadership

In the 21st century, what your product or service is matters just as much as how it helps the wellbeing of people and the planet. It's about remembering why the business or organization was started in the first place and what it offers to the world. It is tapping into that adrenaline rush the founders had when they birthed the idea for the company, and their vision of the difference it could make in people's lives.

Humans have been conditioned to want to be picked by someone. Chances are, you became a business leader either by starting a company or by being promoted through the ranks. The latter would mean that you would have to work hard and wait for that promotion to fulfill your dream of being a leader, or (something that is not often discussed) you needed to know the right people who would choose you to get ahead. The question 21st century leaders asks themselves is: why do we need to stand in line and wait to be selected?

The 21st century leader believes they serve a greater purpose and that they are contributing to the greater good in business and life. They are moving away from the false belief that you are two separate people, your professional self (work), and your personal self (life). There is only one person, and one flow of life, which happens to include working. 21st century leaders are clear on the purpose their life serves, and they are able to fuse it with business. They connect with people at a core level, and understand the importance of trust and relationships in every part of their life.

The Skills of Conscious Leaders

For the 21st century leader, whatever we create in our business should have a meaningful impact and inspire others to share in our higher purpose. To truly be the leader the world needs today, we need to consider and discuss the importance of these elements as part of our journey to creating a more humane and saner world:

Becoming more conscious: A passion for building a business that achieves a greater good and living a life that matters, and contributing to the greater good of the world.

Purpose: A clear purpose that others can easily get behind because it is compelling and visionary in the impact it makes in people's lives. Other people will want to join our efforts because of a higher purpose that resonates with their own.

Communication and empathy: A keen ability to be open, listen, and share ideas. This includes practicing ongoing two-way communication, where people easily understand what they need to do to be successful in their work. People are engaged with delivering the purpose of the organization, and sharing information openly with other team members, strategic partners, and customers.

Communication flows openly when needed, and they take time to discover and listen to what's happening around them.

Opportunity makers: An ability to stay current with what is happening in the marketplace and develop a strong vision for what is possible. By transforming our vision into a powerful purpose, we bring people into our organizations who know how to integrate new ways of working and how to implement innovative solutions seamlessly, so that innovation simply becomes part of how the business is run, instead of being fragmented into a separate department.

Trust: A strong ethical backbone that requires us to know ourselves and trust ourselves deeply, and trust others to do the work they were hired to do. By fostering open communication, people can focus on the work at hand, and leaders can trust in their own hiring ability. 21st century leaders understand that their words need to match their actions, as this is foundational for building trust.

Connecting deeply: We can bring the right people in at the right time to create something bigger than ourselves when we are in trusted communities that have shared purpose and accountability. We also know how to connect deeply, so that people know how important their contributions are to the business, allowing them to bring that purpose to life.

Integrity: Our businesses provide products or services that make the lives of others on this planet better. We understand how to run 21st century organizations that thrive, where people are at the center of business. Our purpose is at the heart of our businesses, and people can easily discern what our values represent and can join us on our mission.

Storytelling: By seeing the impact businesses can have in the world, the 21st century leader shares stories about how the world looks as a result of our work. We can wake up in the morning knowing how to make others, both inside and outside the organization, care about how to bring our stories fully to life.

Fun: A passion for lightness and an understanding that there is room to play and have fun in the work we choose to be part of in the world. By bringing our whole selves to business, there is an ability to make business a fun and enjoyable part of life.

Measuring impact: The conscious leader is clear on actions and results. It is no longer sufficient simply to measure activity and call it a day. We can track the impact of our activities by addressing the results we plan to achieve, why they are important, and how our organizations will achieve them. But we can also track our impact and creativity, even more than our transactions and activities. For example, we can track the relationships we have created and their impact on our business, instead of just the number of people who "liked" the latest post or viral campaign.

What it Means to Be a Conscious Leader: Leading from Within

The Internet can be a gift for humanity, if we choose to use it to pursue our purpose, as it allows us to connect with people around the world and share knowledge instantly. It enables a curious person to have direct conversations with someone they may have never met otherwise, simply by coming across an Internet article they wrote or a tweet they sent. "Brands" can no longer rely on one-way communication and advertising, as people can now openly have conversations about an organization, with or without them. The 21st century leader uses technology, ideally, as an ally—a way to build trusted relationships and bring people together like never before. The true leaders are not chasing "likes" and wanting to be recognized as "influencers;" they are out there building relationships and unlikely partnerships by creating shared purpose, listening, and building trust.

It is no longer possible to tell people to do one thing while you as a company do something completely different. Conscious leaders understand what this new century of business is about, and they are building 21st century organizations that thrive. Because of their faith in the value of their business, and by growing their organizations, they bring in people who can provide for themselves and their communities. In the future, we will not need Corporate Social Responsibility departments, because conscious leaders will embed this type of responsibility in their business model by caring deeply about the impact of their work on the world. It will simply be how we do business, regardless of sector. We will recognize how interconnected we are and see new possibilities for taking our businesses to new heights with simplicity and grace.

In a world where more people of all ages are starting to choose themselves, "command central" organizations will slowly start eroding. Sure, there will be many who will want to stay where they are, as it seems to be working for them, and there will be others who feel they have no choice, as they need to make a living to support their current lifestyles. But there will be an increasing number of people who will want to get off the hamster wheel by changing their relationship with work, and, as a result, shift how business is done.

Being a leader means recognizing that everything you do has an impact on the people around you. The 21st century leader has high self-awareness and is in tune with their feelings, thoughts, and actions on this journey. Leaders who deal with their fears and insecurities push through to the other side with clarity and confidence to uncover the beauty of bringing people together around a higher purpose. They are guided to serve with compassion, and care about the impact they create by truly engaging and driving shared purpose. They learn to trust themselves and others on the journey as far as possible, and they recognize the need to heal the broken trust in various organizations.

21st century leaders are the light that shines on others, not to dominate or control others, but to help them ignite their own inner light and become a leader as well, so that they can find their higher purpose that drives connections, communication, and relationships. These leaders go beyond managing people and supervising work. They lead by example, through the alignment of their words with their actions. They also are aware that life requires us to experiment, and to tap into our courage and see opportunities instead of problems. They bring people together inside and outside an organization with the purpose of creating value.

Conscious leaders continuously do work to tap into understanding who they are, and also take care of themselves. They energize people, not burn them out. They understand the importance of their own wellbeing and respect the needs of others to be whole and healthy people. If you are a 21st century leader, you have a potent imagination and a desire to explore opportunities. You have a knack for seeing more than others do because you take the time to stop and listen, and you have a deep knowing that what you do impacts others. You allow yourself to be balanced, joyful, and curious. You feel that investing in human beings is good and sustainable for your business. You learn who to trust, and then get out of people's way so they can do the work that is aligned with the overall purpose of the organization.

Conscious leaders focus on continuously asking themselves these questions:

- What is my life's purpose? What does it propel me to create in the world? How will my life's work make the world a better place for me, my community, and the world?
- Why am I trusted to conduct meaningful business?
- What is working well? What do I need to focus more on?
- How can I help other people see themselves as trusted leaders themselves, so that they can make the impact on the world they are capable of?

Are You a 21st Century Leader?

21st century leaders are not perfect, but they are willing to go through the challenging process of transformation to become more whole. They are more likely to be giving, vulnerable, compassionate, and inspiring, though they will not necessarily possess all such traits. This also doesn't mean that they don't sometimes fail to live up to these ideals. They do fail, as they are only human. The difference is that they face their failures, while also holding onto their ideals.

The Community Builder

21st century leaders take a more holistic approach to their role, as they don't simply delegate their responsibilities to a mere function or separate department, such as for communication, diversity, or innovation. The 21st century leader goes out into the world and brings communities together in conversations, even when they are tough conversations to have, and they put the important issues out on the table so they can be discussed and addressed. When they don't see the opportunity in a situation, they tend to explain why they are walking away from it instead of hiding it under the table. There is a transparency they bring to their role as leaders. In their day-to-day work, they are not simply performing on a stage; they are showing up to actualize their work. They know what it means to engage with people and have deep conversations.

The 21st century is about community and open conversations and dialogue. There's no need to yell at people and broadcast one-way information to get attention, because the opportunity is there to share information through meaningful interaction. Today, we are at a point in business where so many employees are ignoring the massive amounts of information coming at them unless it impacts their job directly or is from their immediate chain of management. And yet, with predominantly one-way communication that slots in employees as an audience or stakeholder in the communications plan, the information and change programs keep coming at them at increasing speeds. It is no wonder why so many people feel overwhelmed.

Hierarchical structure still exists in many networks—and needs to exist to some degree— in our world, but we do not need to lead with a command and control nature in the 21st century business world. 21st century leaders do make decisions on behalf of the team at critical points, and at the same time, people are not scared to share their opinion openly for fear of retribution. Let me give you an example. When I first joined Cisco, I worked in an environment where we made the best decisions for the business, as we had a shared purpose in our work. After spending 24 hours at the office and presenting a new daily IT portal at our IT Senior Staff meeting in 1999, the CIO asked whether we really needed it. At that time, most of the technology was not available for what we were introducing (like Flash and personalization), and yet we made it work. One of my colleagues simply looked at the CIO with no hesitation and said something like, "If we want to meet our business goals, we need to share information more openly." We allowed each other to innovate openly and make the best decisions for the business at that time. However, once the tech bubble burst in 2001 and people were more concerned about their own success and keeping their jobs, internal politics reigned and we were spending much more time on turf wars than on the business itself.

The Opportunity-Maker

The second trend is around demystifying our obsession with change and innovation. For the past few decades, there have been a multitude of organizational change programs introduced, all featuring the same recipes for success, including traditional sponsorship plans, ambassador programs, and one-way communication plans. But if you ask many employees, they will say that these programs are not the holy grail of senior management, nor are they anything more than another flavor of the month. As soon as a new initiative is announced, these employees tend to assume that it too shall soon pass—until the next big change program is unveiled. This also raises the question of why we are managing change in the 21st century with *conventional* change management programs in the first place, as if the flow of change somehow chooses to restrict itself to our cookie-cutter templates for managing change. Wouldn't it make more sense to take advantage of the opportunity arising out of change by simply helping people to expect change to be part of our day-to-day business environment, especially when we are more firmly grounded in self-knowledge and shared purpose? Believing that we need to fear change, and therefore that we need to try to completely manage it, greatly limits the potential opportunities that can arise from transformative change.

The 21st century leader recognizes that organizational change management is an antiquated business practice that no longer serves their organization. They understand the pace of change in business will only continue to increase, instead of trying to manage it. What these leaders know is that if they build communities and ensure that people feel listened to, they will no longer need to sell them new change programs every time a new initiative is introduced. In this new century, change and innovation are simply a reflection of day-to-day life, inside and outside of work. 21st century leaders do not need to sponsor change initiatives; they realize they need to be clear on the purpose of their organization and the initiatives that support change, so that people can fulfill their positions to make an impact.

Direct communication is not only more possible because of the technological tools that are now available, but also because that is what people need. We need simplicity in our messaging that provides the information people need to deliver on their projects. There is no need for ambassadors, posters, or t-shirts announcing the change. With collaboration platforms, for example, we can now connect people from around the world in dialogue. Conscious leaders understand the value of these platforms as a way to convene teams in conversations around critical areas. It also provides an equal playing field for people to participate asynchronously. People can ask questions wherever they may be located in the world and get answers from anyone with access to the platform. During a major change, people can interact with the people leading the change through a platform, and contribute to how the change can be rolled out. They can be active participants, rather than just an audience that needs to be communicated to.

The Relationship Builder

The third trend that is emerging is a magnification of the importance of trust and relationships. These can no longer be simply a statistic or metric that is tracked over time; they have to be a way of doing business and bringing holistic solutions to organizations. Customers no longer care how an organization is structured; they care about trusting a business to do what it promises. I recently heard a senior executive from a large telecommunications corporation speak at a conference. I arrived a bit late, and after listening for a few minutes, I leaned over and asked someone what the topic of the talk was. I was told it was about being a leader. I felt like I was sitting through a sales pitch, and for two reasons: The first was a comment the speaker made that we should all become customers of her corporation. I was already her customer, and it made me think how so many corporations first focus on attracting new customers or employees, before acknowledging the ones they already have. It felt like she was merely after the transaction, rather than the relationship. The second was when she shared with us how the corporation was structured, the organizations they had acquired, and how they were performing on the stock market. She did this with a slide that showed how these were organized into silos. This was an opportunity to tell the story of the purpose of the organization; why they exist and how these acquisitions contributed to their story. It would have been so powerful to have a glimpse into how the pieces of their puzzle came together. I would have loved to share that story with you, but the speaker didn't tell us that story, because she was too caught up in the old patterns.

The 21st century leader sees connecting directly with people in two-way conversations as a huge opportunity to build trusted relationships with their employees, customers, partners, vendors, and even the local communities they serve. They are breaking away from outdated models by building communities that are based on trust.

The Generalist

People today put a lot of trust in online reviews—for example, where they eat, where they go on vacation, and what movies they watch. Most of the hands shoot up when I ask people whether they have ever eaten at a certain restaurant, slept at a certain hotel, or seen a certain movie based on an online review. We trust strangers today for intimate decisions in our lives. We don't know these people. We don't know what they like. We simply see a two-star or five-star rating and make a decision based on that one fragment of information. In some ways this can obviously be good, but the process can also be abused (such as with fake reviews), so we need to keep a critical eye. Some online providers also allow companies to influence the reviews through their purchasing power. In any case, this type of constant communication is happening every second outside the organization's walls, and yet inside the organization we wait for the annual employee survey to give and receive feedback, which usually has only a marginal impact. This is an archaic practice.

The fourth trend is about bringing vulnerability to business. 21st century leaders are aware that they do not have all the answers. They allow the space for conversations to occur and for solutions to emerge.

In fact, the generalist model is starting to emerge. In many conversations I've had with Reuven Gorscht, former Global Vice President at SAP (an enterprise software company) and now CEO at MoveSnap (a start-up re-imagining the moving experience for people who relocate), we have discussed how organizations will be looking for generalists in the future to deal with the increasing complexity at work, to help connect the dots, and to encourage new ways of doing things, while knowing how to bring people together into projects at the right time. In his *Forbes* article, he shares the following:

The new Generalist is in fact a master of their trade. They bring expertise and experience in several areas, fueled by insatiable curiosity and the ability to "hyper-learn" new concepts and ideas. They practice empathy to fully understand and break down the nature of complex problems and collaboratively engage specialists in re-framing the problem in order to arrive at potential solutions. They complement specialists, by challenging them to think differently, but never compete with them or take credit for their ideas. They approach challenges with an open mind, using a "how might we" mindset rather than come with pre-conceived ideas. As outstanding communicators, they reframe, package and present ideas, helping decision makers visualize the future. Lastly, they encourage and promote change from within by understanding and diffusing resistance to change.

21st century leaders are unlikely to start with the organizational chart, or with who sits in what reporting box. Instead, they will generally make it their priority to bring their shared purpose to the world. For example, a Chief Operating Officer (COO) who was introducing a new approach to an organization recognized that he needed seven silo departments to work together to achieve success. Instead of introducing a traditional organizational change management approach, he chose to be open and communicate. He shared why this new approach is valuable and had conversations with the people who were key to the success of the implementation. He spent time understanding why this would be perceived as valuable and communicated the benefits, as well as being realistic that it would make some people uncomfortable. He led with the solution and painted an easily understandable picture about why people should care and how it would make a difference to the business. By doing this, people were brought together to chart a new path forward.

Transformational Stories from the Frontiers of 21st Century Leaders

This expedition shares the firsthand stories of six 21st century leaders as a way to let us peek into their life's work and learn about what they are creating in the world. Each story is transcribed from interviews I conducted. I encourage you to join in, experience the journeys, take away questions, and be open to learning lessons. Each and every one of our fellow travelers is leading from the heart. Compassionate, authentic leadership is essential—a necessity for a healthy world.

Roni Zeiger

Roni Zeiger is the first traveler on our journey, and I am so inspired by his wisdom, thoughtfulness, and what he is co-creating in the world. As a father, husband, son, friend, and a 21st century leader, Roni is making our world better. He spends most of his professional time thinking about the world of health. He believes that if we strive to understand the ways each of us is an expert, we can make better science happen faster. His aspiration as a leader is to make sure that the people he works with know why their work matters and that there is a higher purpose in what they are co-creating.

I met Roni when I was an innovator-in-residence at Roche/Genentech, where Roni was an advisory board member. I loved his passion, honesty, and curiosity, and I always felt listened to and seen by him. I learned a lot about 21st century leaders through the questions Roni asked and the insights he brought.

The Journey of Roni Zeiger: Community Builder. Connector. Learner. Cofounder and CEO, Smart Patients.

What is your story?

My story starts with my belief that we need to start giving each other more respect. My kids, my wife, and I want to live in a more respectful world. My family is from Latin America, and I moved to the US from Chile at the age of three. I grew up in a bicultural environment and learned especially from my mother how to respect and treat everyone equally.

When I worked at Google, I noticed one day that no one seemed to acknowledge the person cleaning the bathroom. I wanted the cleaners to feel like they were being seen and since that day have made an effort to make eye contact and express gratitude to everyone who cleans the bathroom. I hope to build a relationship with everyone around me and show respect to every individual. That's how I was raised; to recognize people's value regardless of the position they may hold.

We need to regain common decency and respect for others in every facet of our lives. When a patient comes to a medical appointment, they are expected to take their street clothes off and put on an ugly, flimsy gown. It immediately creates a power asymmetry between the doctor and the patient. It is not easy to change the way the world already works. When it comes to medicine, we have a lot of smart and thoughtful people working in an imperfect system. Most doctors face a dilemma of wanting to live in an ethical world where there is equality and human rights for all. And at the same time, most doctors in the U.S. work in a system optimized around reimbursement. These two desires are often in conflict with each other.

I spent six years at Google as the former Chief Health Strategist, where I led efforts ranging from Google Flu Trends to Symptom Search. We spent a lot of time looking at how Google could improve search results for health related queries. It became evident that for rare and severe diseases, a category which cancer falls into, the static web pages that you can find through searches frequently were insufficient. It was challenging to get in-depth information, especially from patients' perspectives. After leaving Google, Gilles Frydman and I co-founded Smart Patients to amplify the knowledge created by networks of engaged patients in an online community, where patients and caregivers learn from each other.

Both Gilles and I believe that the next tipping point in medicine includes tapping into the knowledge created by networks of patients. We believe patients are the most underutilized resource in healthcare. We've watched patients become experts in their conditions—and we see that their knowledge improves the care they receive. With the right tools, other patients can do the same.

Building empathy through peer-to-peer communities

One of my passions is to study and improve the ways we can learn from each other and help each other have a better life. With Smart Patients, we bring together peer-to-peer communities across a wide spectrum of illnesses. This allows patients and caregivers to help each other, while the healthcare system can learn from them. It is a vehicle for patients' voices to emerge in important aspects of medicine, from the design of a clinical trial to that of the hospital discharge process.

Smart Patients' business model is a 21st century organizational model in that there is a clear purpose of building active communities and helping medical research and practice at the same time. It broke the current model of clinical trial development, even in a highly regulated environment. If anything, what Gilles and I have co-created is a relationship-based model for a connected and open world, a path forward to what is desperately needed in business today. Educating patients allows them to have strong voices in the solutions of drug development. It is fundamentally changing medicine.

In essence, Smart Patients is an example for all leaders who have a clear business need and are shifting an entire marketplace through relationship-based solutions. The doctor who is used to seeing a patient wearing a flimsy gown in a room is now having a direct conversation with the patient. Both can learn from each other and connect in partnerships and information exchanges. This technology allows people to connect anywhere and anytime; all that is needed is a device, electrical power, connectivity, literacy, and motivation to participate. A fundamental change we now need is for the doctor-patient relationship to shift from a unidirectional model, where the doctor is providing all of the information, to one where both doctor and patient are bringing different strengths and working as a team, with the understanding that the doctor serves as a guide who shares their medical knowledge with the patient. It allows for a more meaningful interaction, where questions can be asked and novel answers sought more openly.

Doing what matters

We should be able to figure out how to make a living by doing something that matters. I look to have deep, meaningful relationships with my family and friends, where we contribute to each other's lives and also challenge each other when we need to. I hope to inspire my kids to live in this way, too. I'd like everyone I work with to have clarity about why their work matters. I'd like us to focus on the underpinnings of what we are doing—otherwise, what's the point?

We need to think about community and the ways people learn and help each other within a community. When a woman was pregnant with her first child a thousand years ago, she would spend a lot of time with women in her community who had already had babies and who helped deliver them. Later, she would teach and support others so that they could continue in the work. In the last few hundred years, we have learned to defer to and depend on experts at the expense of our own experience, which can lead to us ignoring our own vital wisdom.

As a physician, I reflect on how little we know about the practice of medicine. Most of what we do in general medicine is supported by thin evidence, because the number of decisions we need to make dwarf the resources we have to rigorously study. That doesn't mean I am a fan of basing health decisions on what people are saying on Facebook. But it does mean there is a lot of knowledge and experience in the community that we are not tapping into.

In my view, community means shared learning, experience, and a sense of belonging. We have so many stories in our community. We started a new community for women and men who had lost a child late in pregnancy or after childbirth. I have no personal or professional experience in this area. The amount of learning and giving that is going on in such an intense and accepted way is beautiful. The healthcare system is not generally prepared to deal with and help parents through the trauma of losing a child, but the online discussion forum is a perfect platform for a community where people can support each other through their grief and learning. We encourage people to propose new communities and adapt as needed.

The key for us is that the communities help people learn from each other on how to deal with challenging health issues. Peer-to-peer conversations are dramatically missing in healthcare today. When I give talks to physicians, I ask how many of them have ever introduced one of their patients to another patient with a similar health issue. About one percent have made a connection; 99 percent have not. This typically is not because they've considered it and decided it isn't a good idea. Instead, it's simply something we don't consider in healthcare.

While I was working at Google on several different health initiatives, I spent a lot time on improving the quality of results for health searches on Google. In the era of the Internet, we can access billions of unaffiliated pieces of information from billions of sources, which has interesting implications about the kind of knowledge that can actually be shared. Someone with a rare disease can search for information using a search tool, but it can be more powerful to find another person who can offer significant real life insights and stories. And maybe these two people, when they do find each, other can co-author a uniquely useful overview written from a patient or caregiver perspective.

We simply need to have more two-way conversations with people whose lives are being disrupted by health issues. I am interested in building a more effective system as defined by those it is supposed to help. Many oncology experts, for example, may feel that their expertise is being threatened by having patients talking to each other about their condition or treatment. I often speak to groups of clinicians to increase their awareness of the benefits of having patients interact with each other, and I hope they will encourage their patients to find ways to connect.

We need to look at how to integrate communities into a future healthcare system so that we have a mechanism where patients can learn from each other. Medicine needs to be more of a team sport. The science and the practice of medicine are evolving so quickly that no individual can keep up with everything. Motivated patients can help each other to get better care, and can often help their doctors deliver better care. It is a slow movement, but it is also unstoppable.

Experiencing our humanity

In March 2015, we experimented by inviting cystic fibrosis patients to help us simulate a day in their lives. Each patient became the teacher and they had a student who was a physician. Students had to simulate everything the patients did in order to better understand what one day in the life of cystic fibrosis looks and feels like. As one of the students, it was a humbling experience. One of our goals with this #1day program is to get to counteract the way medical training often dehumanizes doctors.

We had a second year medical school student at Stanford, who took a day to learn from someone who had been diagnosed with cystic fibrosis. Let me share Caroline's note to Dan with you that was posted on our blog and Smart Patients platform:

> "Thanks so much for sharing with me. Until I went through yesterday with you, I never realized how much time and effort it takes to do all the various treatments. Even something as simple as holding the nebulizer in my mouth for 20 minutes was much more tiring than I predicted. From the medical caregiver side, it's frustrating when patients don't adhere to their treatment plans, but talking to you made me think about how we might make things more convenient through technology and simply talking to the patient to figure out the best day-to-day schedule. The philosophy of going from day to day, or even week to week, is one that resonated deeply with me. The courage with which you handle your diagnosis is inspiring and motivates me to work

harder in school so that one day, I can do right by patients like yourself."[55]

Following your compass on the journey

An important challenge in healthcare is understanding the full context of what our friends, neighbors, and colleagues with chronic diseases experience every day. Many illnesses are invisible. Many have emotional tolls that are hidden from most of us. That inspired the #1day empathy exercise and we've expanded it to a variety of disease areas, form colorectal cancer to Parkinson's disease. This particular program isn't the important thing. What's critical is that each of us strive to learn what we can from others so that we can collaboratively solve our most important challenges.

Today we oversimplify health, as we try to squeeze it into occasional 15 minute appointments. I have been privy to an amazing number of stories about how health issues affect people's lives. Imagine if we captured all of those experiences and emotions and helped people connect with each other to talk about what matters most, to feel less alone and more together on this journey.

[55] https://www.smartpatients.com/stories/cystic-fibrosis-1day-the-medical-student-perspective/

Bryan Welch

My friend Kristin Kim, who I originally met at a dinner in New York City, invited me to participate in a workshop for her organization, Sansori (a global model of experiential education). I reflected on whether I could afford to get away and fly to Toronto a few weeks after my return from the Amazon rainforest. But it didn't take long to make that decision, as I strongly believe in what she is creating and decided to go. After all, it was about revolutionizing education through fun, creative, and transformative learning experience for all ages. After facing some of my deepest fears in the rainforest, I was all for changing how we learn.

While waiting for her to pick me up at the Toronto International Airport, a man approached me and asked me if I was Ayelet. He could even pronounce my name correctly! I recognized him from his LinkedIn photo, and was soon in deep conversation with Bryan Welch, who was also part of the Sansori workshop. Our journeys collided with so many heart-opening conversations.

Bryan Welch is well known for his optimism, sense of humor, and commitment to empowering people to live their own best lives. He speaks widely to businesspeople and consumers to share his belief—demonstrated unequivocally in his own work—that it is possible to do well in business without destroying the Earth's natural and human resources.

Bryan founded B The Change Media, a multi-platform media company focused on business as a force for good in the world, in the spring of 2015. Since 1985, he's held numerous executive positions in the media. He ran Ogden Publications, where he transformed it from a declining publisher of two rural lifestyle magazines into a dynamic, growing multi-media company with nine magazine titles like Mother Earth News, GRIT, and the Utne Reader, and numerous websites and ancillary products. He and his wife, Carolyn, raise organic, grass-fed cattle, sheep, and goats on a small ranch near Lawrence, Kansas. He is also the author of *Beautiful and Abundant: Building the World We Want* (2010).

The Journey of Bryan Welch: Entrepreneur. Storyteller. Rancher. Founder and CEO, B The Change Media.

What is your story?

I grew up in an impoverished, rural area in southern New Mexico, and I was drawn to nature from an early age. I went to work when I was about eight years old, taking care of the neighbor's dairy goats. I watched these goats wander around the desert and eat grass, mesquite beans, and scraps of paper. Then I'd bring them back in and milk them, and bring home this frothy, extraordinary food. I thought it was magical, and I wanted to be associated with that magic. If you care for animals in a mindful way, it teaches the value of awareness and compassion on a daily basis.

If I had to guess why I ended up doing what I have done in my career, I'd say it has a lot to do with that lesson. I learned that the survival of our own species is impossible without an understanding of, and respect for, nature's systems. As a boy, I experienced the interdependent relationships among the plants, animals, and humans that called the Southern New Mexican deserts home.

I am a storyteller and I have exercised that vocation as a businessperson running media companies. We create and distribute stories. Most of my stories have been about conscientiousness, for lack of a better umbrella term. If you are going to be successful in the media business or as a storyteller in any vocation, you have to care more about the story than anything else. You have to instinctively care about gathering audiences and communicating successfully. It is important that storytellers care more deeply about the story and the act of communication than about any of the surrounding issues.

We are on the verge of a revolution in business

Consumers are becoming more aware every day of the availability of information and their own power to understand the value systems that govern businesses, and they can demand that the businesses they patronize share their values. What's about to happen is that people are going to start exercising that power on a much grander scale. Businesses are going to need to do good in the world to earn the patronage of their customers. As this occurs, business will become the most powerful force for good that human society has ever seen.

There is a growing awareness of our power as individuals. Until now, we have not been aware of the power that we have to destroy our habitat—that we have the power to prevent the possibility of our grandchildren living as well as we live. As our awareness of that power grows, we become more conscious of the value of being conscientious and mindful, and we are seeing the impact of this awareness in many areas. More than government, more than nationality, more than religion, business is the most potent social organizer in the world. When we think about what means we can use to change the world, business becomes a very obvious and powerful tool.

Humanity is being called to grow up, take on its fears, and exercise responsibility. This can be an anxiety-producing transition for individuals, and it is a powerfully anxiety-producing transition for humanity as a whole, as social responsibility becomes very personal and ties us all to the outcome of our collective actions. It's no longer something that someone else must do. We are all in it together.

What can business learn from farming?

Business has been crafted as a vehicle for the ego. We motivate businesspeople and customers through various kinds of appeals to the ego. That is the traditional route of business. There is a general feeling that it is the only way to motivate people. But, in my experience, the practice of farming continuously lowers one's estimation of one's own ego, because you are facing life and death every day.

Some life form is dying many times a day on our farm, and we are much more aware of it than if we didn't farm. The implication is the knowledge that we will die as well. The constant awareness of looming mortality makes me feel that the fruits of my labor are more important for their long-term consequence than for how much money they can generate, or whether I can get my name on a building at my alma mater.

It strikes me as very wrong to deny my own mortality or not to plan for it every day. We achieve success on our farm by encouraging health in a very holistic way, concentrating first and foremost on the health of the soil and watching every day for things that are out of balance, and then trying to bring them back into balance without exerting so much force that we throw them out of balance in the other direction. That's how I define holistic management. I always loved the old saying that the best fertilizer for any property is the footprint of its owner or steward.

I've sensed over the years that where we really succeeded on the farm is where we focused on the fundamental health of the environment. We have not exploited the land. We let the land and the animals operate, flourish, and reproduce based on their natural design. Some of our projects will take longer than a human life span. If you are going to do it in a holistic way and respect the wholeness and encourage real health, you have to be willing to operate on timeframes that are longer than a career or a human life. You just have to trust that it's the right thing to do and derive satisfaction from knowing that it is the right thing for the land. The awareness of mortality that is fostered through our experience of farming helps us think on that long-term scale of several lifetimes, because we watch hundreds of lifetimes pass here every year.

I've learned interesting lessons from looking at the differences between farming on my property and farming on a property that is a quarter of a mile east of my house, or farming on a property that is a quarter mile west of my farm. The soils are different, the topography is different, and the hydrology is different. We would have to adopt a whole new plan—different animals, different numbers, different methods—if we were sitting even one quarter-mile away from here. I find this to be a very important lesson for business. As we institutionalize business knowledge, we like to think that we can apply universal rules to what defines success in business or how you run a business, that there are best practices that you can easily apply across the board. If you run a business in a holistic and mindful way, there are countless variations. Customers, climates, and technology vary from place to place.

Demanding more from business and people

It's been very convenient for businesspeople over the last 200 years to follow uniform definitions of success that are tied to growth and efficiency. First of all, let's remind ourselves that we have only had the industrial economy for a couple of hundred years. It's new. It's way newer than religion, music, community, and family. It's not surprising that it is not particularly well adapted to human nature. We have not been doing it very long. We need to expect and demand more of business as a presence in society and as an element in individual human lives.

As consumers, we need to demand more of businesses and ask them to be great employers and to be positive forces in the world. Sometimes these appraisals are over-simplified. I am not convinced that Amazon.com is a terrible place to work; I am convinced that it is a terrible place to work for certain people. There are people who think it is an awesome place to work, and they are the ones who should work there. From a holistic perspective, I don't feel there is one enlightened way to run a company or one way to be enlightened employer.

Anyone who wants to make a difference has to overcome their fear of the unknown. When you set out to change something, by definition, you are going to change it into something that you can't yet describe. And that is inherently frightening for some people, more so for some than for others. Some people stay in a job they hate for 40 years because they are afraid of the unknown. We've created systems that prey on that fear as a function of a bunch of propaganda about loyalty. But all this is changing for the better.

Change is coming from our growing awareness that there is a limit or ceiling to growth. In the past, as long as we were growing rapidly—doubling our population every 50 years, increasing our consumption levels constantly, improving our technology—we could maintain a hope for a future utopia. Now the limit of our habitat makes it difficult to believe in a utopia of ever-expanding consumption and population.

As a result, we have to grapple with the difficult task of creating a more utopian society in some way other than through constant growth. Growth only occurs in tandem with death. If we want to maintain a long-term existence, it will have to be a sustainable existence that balances growth and contraction.

Even though we are still seeing growth, human beings are smart enough to see that it won't—and can't—go on forever. We know we need to search for sustainable solutions. At the core of that vision of sustainability is mindfulness; doing things in a way that takes into account the short-term and long-term consequences. This is a relatively new way of thinking in business.

We are way more social and collaborative than we were 40 years ago. The digital media have created vastly greater opportunities for collaborating and communicating. Many of us spend several hours a day interacting on social media with people, and there are pluses and minuses to that. We are also somewhat more tribal than we were in the recent past; people tend to group up with others who reinforce their inherent values and prejudices rather than seeking out new ideas.

Over the course of my lifetime, I have worked in different communities, from gung-ho west coast technology centers to rigidly traditional Native American communities in New Mexico. I can describe very strong positive and negative traits of both. I am a bit leery of perceiving human collaboration in any sort of evolutionary frame. Just because collaboration and mob mentality are there, we need a lot of independent thinkers, and we need a lot of people who are great collaborators and community builders. We need to balance those impulses.

The world needs business to grow up

Business is the most powerful force organizing humanity and our aspirations. It is very new to think about business in this way. It has not been utilized so far to a fraction of its potential of doing good in the world. The prospect of raising human awareness of the potential of business to do good in the world is one of the most exciting stories I can engage with as a storyteller in launching B the Change Media. It's an opportunity to share stories and show how people are asking themselves new questions about business and how it can have a positive impact.

I visited Chad Dickerson, the CEO of Etsy, a few months ago. I was chatting with a young guy who was making coffee in Etsy's break space. I asked if him they had milk and he told me they had nine different types of milk available for my coffee. I thought it was great, and so I laughed and asked, "How do I get a job here?" I realized at some point in our short exchange that the fellow I was talking to had an intellectual disability. He said to me, "It's great to work here. Do you want to see my technique?" He showed me how to make coffee and how to maintain the area—maybe ten minutes of instruction in great detail.

When I went to see Chad, I told him I had just met the guy making coffee and that we'd had a great conversation. He told me that his employee had a great story. Etsy was going through the B Corp impact assessment process, and there is a question on it that asks whether you hire people with disabilities. They realized they never had, and they wondered what someone with a disability would be able to contribute to their business. They realized how important coffee was to them, so they decided to hire someone to make their coffee and see how it would work, and it worked out great. This new employee took the task seriously; he studied it and committed himself to it. That guy got promoted and is now a systems administrator at Etsy and makes $50,000 a year. The guy I met is his replacement.

Chad told me this story because it illustrates a couple of points. If we take the time to ask ourselves: "Are we doing as much as we can do?" all of us would come up with the same answer: No, we could do more. Above and beyond that, in the effort to do the right thing for some disadvantaged group of human beings, it became very valuable for Etsy in a material way. Both Chad and I realized this holistic management is real, and that often when you do things for good business reasons, they have good consequences that we didn't necessarily anticipate.

I tell people all the time: If you publicly say that you want to run your business in a conscientious way and you put it in your mission statement, you attract conscientious people as your employees and colleagues. They work harder, want to contribute more, and are more productive than less conscientious people. Committing yourself to that goal will make your business more efficient tomorrow. In the long run, it makes for much better businesses and, in the traditional sense, they make more money and are much more productive.

Business as a force of good

This is a time of significant change in business—a turning point. One of the most important forces shaping the 21st century is the global movement of people with a passion for using business as a force for good. This movement is large and growing: tens of millions of consumers, trillions of dollars of investment, 50 percent of the world's workforce, and tens of thousands of businesses, all with a shared purpose to harness the power of markets for positive social change. This movement, however, had no centralized platform, no center of gravity, no hub for inspiring stories, practical tools, credible insights, or contextual perspectives. Until now.

On any given day, over two billion people use Unilever's products around the world. Unilever is working on becoming a B Corp. It is the fifth largest consumer-goods company in the world. In 2000, it bought Ben and Jerry's ice cream, who is also a B Corp. In 2016 Unilever announced plans to acquire Seventh Generation, another B Corporation.

Business—and more specifically, our relationship to business—is changing, fundamentally and permanently. Business—where we work, where we shop, what we buy, where we invest—has become an emblem of our identity. B the Change Media is designed to tell the compelling stories of this movement and to disseminate them widely across print, digital, video, and live event platforms.

Imagining possibilities

I love humanity's ability to imagine and then realize extraordinary, original things. I would hate to see that capacity either lost in some kind of catastrophe or squandered for the sake of some base pursuit. It is just as tragic to see humanity squander its imagination and vision as it would be to see the species disappear. In fact, if we do squander our imagination and vision, that's very likely to be the outcome. My job at B Media is to be provocative and not think from fear, but to help us avoid destroying ourselves and to create imagination and vision. That is the opportunity we have in front of us, and it's what is so exciting about this new chapter in business as a force of good.

This current challenge of creating a sustainable human presence on the planet is an evolutionary challenge. If we fail to meet that challenge, we have simply failed to adapt and our extinction is a perfectly natural event. However you feel about the stakes of this game, that's the game. It's really kind of cool to be alive now, when we are grappling with this extraordinary evolutionary challenge. That is really thrilling and, depending on your frame of mind, it can also be scary.

We need to engage the passionate human imagination, that great engine of creativity, and challenge it to go beyond the anxious contemplation of environmental disaster to envision the world we desire—vigorous, verdant, and enduring. Once the human imagination visualizes a brilliant future, the human intellect can achieve what previously seemed impossible. The human imagination and the human intellect have, together, achieved countless astonishing things in the past. I believe they can do so again and again.

We don't need a disaster to motivate change. A great, contagious idea or two can create all the motivation we need. Every major human realization was assembled from the discoveries of lots of different people, each pursuing an individual vision and building on each other's work. Our achievements are shared achievements.

Kim Jordan

Colorado's New Belgium Brewing is known for its quirky culture, its Fat Tire beer, and its distinction as a worker-owned business. New Belgium sells four percent of all US craft beer, and one percent of all the beer in America. New Belgium's distinction as a business, however, is that it is entirely owned by its workers.

I learned a lot about the beer industry from my sister Anat Baron when she was making her award winning documentary film, *Beer Wars*. I remember watching uncut footage from New Belgium Brewing and being fascinated by their business model. I was thrilled when she connected me with Kim Jordan so I could share her story of why we should be putting people first in business.

Kim Jordan, cofounder and former CEO of New Belgium Brewing, has cultivated her passion for social work, the environment, and community to create one of the most successful corporations in America. Her lifelong commitment to developing healthy communities has informed New Belgium's culture through progressive policies like employee ownership, open-book management, and philanthropic giving.

The Journey of Kim Jordan: Pioneer. Risk taker. Advocate. Cofounder and Former CEO, New Belgium Brewing Company.

What is your story?

My story is that I found myself in the lucky circumstance of being able to create a business from the ground up. It was clear to me that I was working with people who were really motivated to do interesting things. In any endeavor, you start to really think about: What do I want to have happen here? How do I want to show up for this?

I grew up in a fairly liberal family. My dad was in political administration in Sacramento, and my mom was a social worker. Then we moved to Washington, D.C., and I went to a Quaker high school, where I learned about George Fox, one of the founders of American Quakerism, who said, "Let your life speak." That greatly informed who I am today. I graduated from high school at 16 and had friends in Colorado, so I moved west in 1976.

Since my mother was a social worker, I thought that was an interesting field. I became a social worker for low-income single parents. Philosophically, I'm a fan of systems thinking and have a generalist perspective. People want to do good work, and they want to be connected to something bigger than just their task at hand.

I find it intriguing to think about how we can build a community of people who care about our purpose. For New Belgium, our purpose is to make our love and talent manifest. That means we are able to be very good at what we do, and also take care of one another. One of the things that we think is a big societal issue is the widening gap between the haves and the have-nots, and we realized that we had an opportunity to support people by allowing them to own something that increased in value. Shared equity has been an incredibly powerful engine for us.

I'm not sure if I fit into the business world. Occasionally I run into people who I quickly realize assume that our approach to business is unnecessary fluff. And yet for us, it's been very successful. We're as profitable as we need to be in order to be able to invest in renewable energy and have people who work in advocacy. We also make great beer. So whether I fit into the traditional business world or not, I have a great understanding of business.

I recognize that there are people who still operate under the belief that the primary role of business is to make sure that we're maximizing shareholder return. Profitability is important; it's the ultimate form of sustainability, because if you can't pay your bills then you are out of business. But it's only one measure. I feel like we spend a big part of our lives at this thing that we call work, and if it can't feel like people have your back, that they care about you, and that you are in a community of people, to me that seems like squandering a great opportunity.

The creation story of New Belgium is that my then-husband, Jeff Lebesch, and I started the company in the basement of our house. We took out a second mortgage on our home, we maxed out a bunch of credit cards, and we did a lot of things on the fly, all while we were also having kids. As I said, my background is in social work. Jeff's was in electrical engineering. And that combination was exemplified in what we created together. He was really good at designing mechanical and electrical systems, and I was really interested in the design of human systems. It became clear to me pretty early on that business could be a force for good, and we had a platform where we could really talk about who we are and why what we want to do matters.

Choices should be consistent with what matters

Leadership in the context of a company is simple. We didn't really undergo a big transformation from a traditional way of leading to our current model. Some of my philosophy about it may seem fairly plain and simple; we make sure that the decisions are made in the right places, and that the systems of the organization allow for good decision-making. We make sure that people understand what the ramifications of decisions are, what resources are available, and who the interested and affected parties are. It's always important for me to stress that I don't think leaderless leadership makes people feel empowered; it makes them feel nervous. We think it's important to have systems and structures that support leadership.

We initiated an ESOP—an employee stock ownership plan—which began giving stock gradually to our people. We reward them with shares they sell back to the company when they retire, a stock-based pension plan. ESOPs represent both ownership and retirement savings, which is why the US Congress made them the only pension plans allowed to borrow money for funding. Employees feel like they have a stake in what happens here and know they play a part in making this awesome place successful. We're more profitable than our industry standards. We have a three percent turnover rate. And more important to us is our feeling of engagement with our co-workers.

A key feature of New Belgium's worker engagement is open-book management—teaching every employee how to read the books. We teach everyone how to read an income statement, how to read a balance sheet, and how to understand cash flow so that workers know exactly how the company is doing financially, and how they are doing as well.

Investing in relationships

We are in a fairly regulated industry and there are mandated tiers of go-to-market strategy. We certainly see our distributors, partners, and retail (both chains and independents) as whole customer channels unto themselves in addition to the beer drinker at the end. There's a different approach in each of those cases. But I think, generally speaking, in the parts that we can really control, we approach those relationships as opportunities to create shared purpose and trust.

We're in the hospitality business, and we approach those relationships with honesty and care, and a light touch. We think it's more fun to work with people who aren't taking themselves too seriously. It's kind of the same approach that we use with one another inside the company, in terms of trying to do good by providing good information, resources, conversations, honesty, and friendship. There are so many upsides to a culture when there is a high degree of trust, and people's good ideas are implemented regularly. Knowledge is power, and so is being trusted.

A workplace owned by employees

Business can be a force for good—good for the planet, good for our communities, and good for our co-workers. When we started New Belgium Brewing, we began with the idea that we could craft world-class beer in a way that's respectful of the environment and our co-workers. From our beginnings in our house in Fort Collins to an employee owned company of over 800 co-workers, we credit our growth to our business practices—one hundred percent employee ownership, open book management, leading with trust, and encouraging each other to use our talents in service to our stakeholders.

This way of doing business—the way that's good for the whole person—is the way we've chosen. We've chosen it because we believe that if we were going to dedicate such a large portion of our lives to working, we'd rather spend that time and energy in a way that has a positive impact on each other and our communities.

I am not directly involved with the B Corp movement, mostly because I have co-workers who have been driving it. That's a part of their work, and it's good to stay out of other people's way at some level. I'm more than conversant in it, however. We were one of the rising forces for B Corp in Colorado, and I am really supportive of the notion. It's an elegant solution to our path forward in business.

Broadly shared equity, an involvement culture, expecting one's coworkers to understand the business, rewarding their performance and the building of value in a company are all very powerful. All of my coworkers know where the money goes, and they participate in co-creating our strategy, which we review every quarter. We expect them to know what the challenges and the successes of the business are. That makes them not only engaged, but smart, on point, and dedicated, because it's more fun to feel like what you're doing has a higher purpose.

There is a dynamic that all brewers are forced to confront: Do we grow or not grow? We have had that conversation hundreds of times over the years. And growing for the sake of growth isn't inspiring to me. It wasn't important that we get bigger than someone else or have a certain amount of revenue. What turned the corner for us was realizing that growing allows us to create new opportunities for our co-workers. If we don't grow, everyone sits in the same place they were last year. We want to work with people who are vibrant and intellectually curious, and growing helps us create the kind of energy that keeps people engaged and inspired.

No balance required

I often get asked about work-life balance. My answer is usually that I don't really want work-life balance; I want to race to the thing that makes my heart swell, whatever it is, and do that until I no longer feel like doing that, then go to the next thing. I feel it's a disservice to suggest you're somehow balancing two parts of yourself. It sends a message that being intense about something is misled or not desirable, and I don't feel that way about it. I want to race to the end and then say: OK, what's next?

Kat Cole

Another 21st century leader is Kat Cole, who I met through my business partner Tim McDonald when we were engaging in Google Hangouts with 21st century leaders. Kat is about making the world a better place through communication, community, and leadership, which she strives to do one person, team, and business at a time. Kat believes you never know what a powerful impact you can have on the lives of others and what great opportunities await. She sees the possible in people and situations where other people often can't.

Kat grew up in Jacksonville, Florida with her mother and two sisters, living on $10 a week for groceries. In high school, Kat worked part-time at Hooters to help her family. She was the first of her family to go to college, and started working on engineering coursework at the University of North Florida, but dropped out when Hooters sent her all over the world to open franchise locations. She rose through the corporate ranks quickly, and applied and was accepted to Georgia State's executive MBA program without ever going back to finish her bachelor's degree. She became president of Cinnabon, the sweet-indulgence franchise with 1,100 stores in 56 countries, and is now group president of FOCUS Brands. But most importantly, as a 21st century leader, Kat is a humanitarian and philanthropist focused on elevating self-sufficiency through education, technology, and access to opportunity around the world.

The Journey of Kat Cole: Purpose-Driven. Pioneering. Coach. Former President, Cinnabon / Group President, FOCUS Brands.

What is your story?

One of the bigger opportunities we have in the world today is to address what I call the deficit of belief. This collection of great positive stories is not getting out to people. We all need to hear them so that we are empowered and inspired. We need stories that show us what is possible in the world. My question is: How do you solve the deficit of belief that exists today, preventing people from seeing what is possible? One way is to share stories of people overcoming challenges, examples of those who have big desires and big dreams for themselves, for their families, their communities, or the world, and focus on how they made those dreams and visions happen.

One of the biggest lessons I learned from Billy Shore, the founder of the non-profit Share our Strength, and from doing humanitarian work in Africa, is that sometimes in order to see what is possible for yourself, you have to take a big goal and break it down into things that seem more achievable. That is the concept of Small Enough to Change, Big Enough to Matter. It can fire up others to do the same and slowly chip away at a culture that allows such atrocities to be perpetuated in the world.

That's where we have to do some soul searching. That may be in the form of a business initiative where you have to figure out what is big enough to matter in terms of finite resources, and what's really going to be the best use of your time, money, people, and energy. You have to do that as an individual too, and think about whether you're going to spend time with friends or family or on an initiative in the community, and ask yourself whether that is something that is going to actually make a difference.

Everyone has a story

I have the big privilege and responsibility of having a very visible life and platform, and so the way that I address this issue is by using that platform for good and for change. When I have opportunities to speak publicly or interact with other leaders, I also try to talk about influencing others for good, and use those platforms to talk about how businesses can influence change.

We all have different lives, circles of influence, and communities that we affect. I work with many organizations, including the Women's Foodservice Forum, the Chambers of Commerce, and the Global Hope Network International. What each of us can do—and I share this with students all the time—is remind each other that every single person on this plant has a story to tell, and there is someone around you who can learn or be inspired by how you grew up, the challenges you faced, your successes, and the dreams that you have.

It is amazing how many people say, "Wow, thank you for sharing that, I've dealt with that too" when you share your story. I have benefited from many people's counsel my whole life, but the only reason I had access to their feedback was because I was comfortable in sharing my own flaws, mistakes, and challenges. When you put yourself in that position, it is human nature, in most cases, for people to try to be helpful or at least reciprocate by sharing their story.

What you say and what you do matter

Leadership goes beyond leading a group of people. We all have the opportunity to lead through our influence, and that means being a leader of ourselves first. A deep understanding that our actions or our lack of action and our words—what we say or what we choose not to say—mean a lot, and they not only communicate our point of view and how we want to show up in the world, but also they set an example for others who are watching.

To me, leadership is about taking the responsibility and opportunity that you have to be the best version of yourself, and then helping others in turn to be the best versions of themselves. The more classic definition of leadership that I use a lot is that it is the ability to create an environment where other people motivate themselves to achieve mutually beneficial goals. That's the classic definition of team leadership, and it also applies to self-leadership. I really do think it is the broad responsibility of leaders to challenge others to be the best that they can be, so that others around them see that example, which gives you the highest likelihood of helping everyone around you rise to their fullest capability.

Imagining possibilities

If you don't have a belief in what's possible, how can you help others believe in what is possible? It has a very cut and dry impact on leadership. If you can't believe, how can you get others to believe? My story gets told and shared often because it is seen as odd and unique, as I started out in restaurants and worked my way up the corporate ladder. But the funny thing is, my story is actually not that odd, nor is it so unique. There are lots of people who start their careers at entry-level positions. Everyone has to have their first job; they have to start somewhere and work their way up. But not everyone wants to the president of a company, and we all have different measurements of success.

I was in Africa recently with a bunch of my friends, and we were sitting around with people from a village who had experienced a great deal of positive change. We had worked on these initiatives together, and we wanted to know why they had been so unbelievably successful. And when we asked, they pointed to a young man who is the person from the village employed by the NGO to coach the village and help them help themselves to prosperity. And they said, "Because he comes with us every day and he eats what we eat, and he sleeps where we sleep, and he lives how we live, and he is willing to go through that with us, that builds trust. We are more likely to follow his coaching." It has benefited not only their village, but now all the other villages around them.

This transformation comes from having great humility and understanding that if you want to create meaningful change in the world, you have to go where things are happening and be part of it. You cannot point to it from afar. I see lots of people who sit on social media and only follow the political party that they feel a part of, or only follow or interact with leaders who share the same mindset. How do you truly have a sense of what's going on in the world when all you're doing is affirming your own beliefs and actions constantly? But that is human nature; we seek commonality. We want to be with people who are like us, but as a result of that tendency and that natural human desire, we are missing all the other input that is needed to help us connect with all the different constituents in the world, and therefore, we only believe what our immediate community is perpetuating. How can we evolve as a group of leaders and as a society if we don't give people permission to learn, expand, grow, and participate in different groups?

Our culture forces us to judge and jump to conclusions quickly, because we aren't given the coaching and the counsel to seek a deeper understanding of events. We have been trained to see a world of winners and losers and to choose a side. I have talked to politicians and business leaders who have said, "Well, the general public doesn't care about that. They don't want to go that deep." But I really don't believe that. People don't go a step deeper because they either don't know how, or they are not encouraged to go beyond what they know. They stay in their center of gravity, which can be so limiting.

Walking with purpose and colliding with destiny

I heard this wonderful woman speak at the Women's Foodservice Forum, who said, "When you walk with purpose, you collide with destiny." Purpose to me is what you realize you are really good at and what feels deeply right when you're doing it. Once your purpose is clear, you are trying to fill your life with as many as opportunities as possible to transform into the best version of yourself.

I was fortunate to learn some of the things that I was passionate about and that really were my calling and my purpose at a pretty young age, because I was paying attention to the things that I love doing. I also created change that seemed to be easier for me than for others, and I learned what things are not my purpose. For example, I am not a good singer. I am not a good driver. I shouldn't be driving people anywhere and I shouldn't be lighting up the world with my vocal gift. But I can help people realize that they are capable of more than they know, and I am particularly good at that in situations of chaos.

I have done that in many different ways throughout my career. When people ask me what I will be doing in five or 10 years, my answer is always that I have no idea, but I do know that I will be living out the same purpose. I will be helping people realize their core potential for their communities, companies, and who knows, maybe countries one day. I help people realize they're capable of more than they know, whether that is through support, training, coaching, leadership perspective expertise, or decision-making. Those are the things that I can do, and so I will always do those for the rest of my life.

Sebastián Ballerini

I met Sebastián Ballerini at a dinner in Budapest, Hungary when we both worked at Cisco. Our paths crossed frequently, as I loved working with the Latin American team, and I always learned something when working with Sebastián. He is curious, straightforward, and purpose-driven. We stayed in touch via Facebook but had not spoken in years, so I was thrilled when he agreed to share his story in this book.

Sebastián is the former General Manager of Dell Argentina, and was also responsible for Dell in Uruguay and Paraguay. He has over 25 years of experience in information technology. Before joining Dell, he was an executive with Cisco in strategic roles across Latin America. More importantly, Sebastián is an amazing father and friend, and has one of the biggest hearts of anyone I know. He believes the new business world will be looking for hearts and passion to fuel it, and that business will play a new role in our life, where we enjoy being part of something bigger.

The Journey of Sebastián Ballerini: Opportunity Seeker. Coach. Living Fully. VP of Sales for Genesys - South Region Latam / Former General Manager, Dell Argentina Paraguay Uruguay.

What is your story?

My story is about starting to leave my armor behind. I began studying coaching in the middle of my journey and got my master's degree. My thesis was about the masks we wear. When you work for a corporation, you become a kind of a character that you live with during many hours of the day, and you are somehow split between your real self and that character. For example, the character you play when you become a General Manager (GM) of a certain company or the character you play when you represent a corporation. Over time, you can start to behave in your personal life like you are on a conference call. We wear armor as a way to protect ourselves from whatever danger is out there (real or imagined). We are conditioned to put on a mask when it comes to work.

My story also has to do with connecting with people, and on a personal level, it is about loss and pain. I have lost family and friends on the journey. You wear the mask to avoid the feelings. You try to behave like a bulletproof person, and you are not. At a certain point in time, I decided to take off my armor and start connecting with the burdens and hurts I had accumulated throughout my life, and review the gaps between the person I really am and the person I had become.

I realized I was acting and performing like a character, so I made a conscious decision to connect with all my broken parts. The coaching program helped me get my direction over the course of two years. It was like getting lost and having a GPS to help me find my way. I found myself going back to places and neighborhoods I used to frequent in my 20s, and seeing friends I went to university with. I was trying to remember who I was back then so I could connect with that Sebastián.

That's what made me recognize who I was when I arrived at the office every Monday morning, and my aspiration of what I really wanted to do with my life. When I took the time to think about it, I saw a huge gap between those two things.

I started coming back to what I really wanted to do with my life. It was about getting back to my aspirational personal goals and connecting again with places, friends, and family that I thought I had lost or was distanced from by not spending any time with them. Someone shared with me that we become what we spend the most time doing. I am trying to recover myself from scratch. I've had many changes in my personal and professional life after taking a peek behind my own mask. I came to understand that my life is my full-time job.

We have two different types of people in the corporate world: The people who were in the corporate world for a while and who are now picking how they want to live their sequel movie, the second chapter of their lives. Then there are many people who are expecting to be picked by some hand that puts them on their career track, jumping up the perceived ladder of success.

Bringing people together

I was at a dinner at our local university recently, and the speaker was Felipe González, the former prime minister of Spain. He talked about how we have to think about our place in countries and communities as a bigger piece of a puzzle that is the world in order to fix many of the problems that we are facing—food, energy, and how new technologies are used to improve people's quality of life. I do think we need to take a holistic approach to solve our most pressing challenges. The biggest opportunity in front of us is to bring people together and co-create in communities together around a meaningful purpose.

A company is a network of conversations between people. Whatever the situation—whether it is a board meeting, reporting financial results to the community if you are a public company, or delivering on a commitment—it's all about conversations between people. It's a network of people talking among themselves, and hopefully they are focused on a shared purpose. The structure of the company could be aligned around the agreements, the goals, and the measures, but at the end of the day, it's all about people.

When you look at many companies, they are still working in silos. You have your business unit and their metrics, and those metrics are not related to a common approach. We have to find a way to connect and stop working in isolation. The only way to connect the dots is through integrating people around key initiatives and two-way conversations. We need to break down the silo mentality, and that includes the fact that how we get measured is getting in the way of co-creating. We need new metrics that suit the 21st century world.

To understand someone else's pain, you need to have empathy and be able to walk in their shoes. That is the only way to gain insight into their needs, perspective, and challenges. You can do rotations, where you send a person from sales to collections, from customer service to engineering, from engineering to finance, trying to feel in your own body the pain and also the excitement that the other person is feeling. This helps to create the bond between people so you can form a team that is focused on a common goal for everyone. We need to also make sure the goal is visible and clear, and that you can measure and track progress towards that goal. At the end of the day, if you keep the old world focus on a few people who are your "stars," you will not be effective and you will not reach your business goals.

Organizations must have shared purpose

The company goals act as a lighthouse, and while each of the rays of light is going to a different place, you need to work as a team, and everybody needs to be doing their part of reaching the business goal. Even if you don't measure them with a sales goal, and you fall behind on the target, the people on the team will find a way to do whatever they can. It can be tougher for the older generation to have joint goals and metrics because we have been conditioned to run like crazy towards a parochial metric without seeing anything beyond it. It is critical to have a common purpose so that people know where they are going, and it needs to be clear and simple. It's all about building shared purpose today, and if you don't have that, it's very difficult to operate.

Somehow we have overcomplicated business and have lost some of our common sense. The questions we need to be asking are: "Where are we going?" "What do we stand for?" "Do we have a shared path?" And we have to invest in listening. We have the tools we need to have amazing conversations, and yet we waste so much time trying to make a point and be right, when that's not the point at all.

Co-creating our collective future

I have conversations with people about the role of education and what kind of leaders we are preparing for the future. In the past, we focused on being bold, direct, and rational, while avoiding our feelings because they were not perceived as good for business. But now it's time for our universities to play a different role. We have to create greater diversity of thinking and allow for a new form of leadership to emerge.

Leslee Thompson

One morning I received a LinkedIn invite from Leslee Thompson, who I didn't know at the time. I wrote her back and thanked her for connecting, and also shared that I was curious about how she had found me. She told me that Roni Zeiger had mentioned me and that she wanted to be connected. We jumped on a call, and when she started sharing her story, I had chills when I realized that here was another 21st century leader showing up in my life. I instantly felt like I had known Leslee for many years and was so inspired by her stories and courage, especially our shared connection to indigenous cultures.

Leslee began her career as a critical care nurse. At the time of our conversation, she was ending her term as president and CEO of Kingston General Hospital, where she led the organization through a major turnaround. She has over 25 years of healthcare experience that extends from the bedside to the boardrooms of some of Canada's largest public and private sector health care organizations.

The Journey of Leslee Thompson: Co-creator. Advocate. Integrator of Patient-Centered Health Services. Former President and CEO at Kingston General Hospital / CEO, Accreditation Canada and Accreditation Canada International.

What is your story?

I grew up in Toronto, where my dad was a doctor and my mom was a nurse. They really inspired a "we, not me" mentality, which included going volunteering with my mom as a youngster, and which I carry with me to this day. I've been with my husband for thirty years, and we—together with our two kids—have a Team Thompson approach to family matters that is profoundly and mutually supportive. I also bring "we, not me" to work with me every day. It is a part of who I am as a person, and it shapes my philosophy of leadership which, boiled down, is to co-create change with the best possible partners, and to take great joy in watching others grow.

As someone who has worked in many different parts of the health care ecosystem—as a front-line critical care nurse, in various leadership positions in private companies and public institutions, and now as CEO of a global health standards agency—I am very pleased to say that I have grown and learned vitally important lessons from patients at every stage of my journey. No matter which job I have held, I have had most of my professional "a-ha" moments—and certainly the most profound ones—while working with patients and their families.

One of those moments came when I was working with women who had ovarian cancer and met two women from the cosmetic industry, Sherrie and Sharon. I was a clinical nurse specialist at that point. They were both patients. When we started talking about how they were dealing with their treatments, they shared that they wanted to have their lipstick close by when they came out of surgery. They told me that, for them, lipstick made them feel beautiful. For me, a penny dropped.

At the time, we health care practitioners thought we knew a fair amount about the clinical side of treating cancer. But there was next to no information to help women cope with how they felt about themselves, including about their appearance, while undergoing treatments. So, Sherrie, Sharon, I and others decided to produce some materials. We created videos about beauty and cancer. We then decided to leverage their contacts in the cosmetic industry and did a presentation to industry leaders. We focused on the opportunity for the industry to help more women maintain their confidence and self-esteem. We started a not-for-profit foundation and we got well-placed people to join the board. We recently celebrated 20 years at Look Good, Feel Better. Sherrie Abbott is now 25 years cancer-free and serves as executive director of the foundation.

In all areas of health and care, people like Sherrie see things, feel things, and need things that even the best, most dedicated paid professionals may forget or overlook. That's why involving patients is the only way to work in my view, and it's why I am such a passionate advocate for quality, patient-centered integrated health services for all. "We, not me," in word and deed.

If you can see all the pieces, you can improve the care

In 1989, after five amazing years in clinical nursing, I was given the opportunity to oversee in-patient units at a very busy cancer center. It ended up being an amazing opportunity to work with some truly inspiring people to construct new models of care centered around patients' needs. We worked in an interdisciplinary approach to form integrated clinics. We tried to put ourselves in patients' shoes as opposed to segmenting ourselves by function or disease. As it turns out, if you can see all the pieces, you can improve the care. It was only many years later that the 'patient pathway' as it became known would start to be a lens applied to health systems' effectiveness metrics. And it would be many years still before I would realize what involving patients and families themselves in *all* aspects of their care really looked like.

A broken organization in need of healing

After a number of progressively senior roles at different hospitals across Canada and at a global medical technology and services company, one day I got a call from a head-hunter about a role at Kingston General Hospital (KGH). I was flattered to be considered for the hospital's top job—my first as a CEO—but there wasn't exactly a line-up of people looking to fight me for it. In fact, nobody really wanted the post, because the place was truly broken. The provincial government, which was paying the bills, had gone in a year earlier to investigate its poor quality of care, its bad infection rates, and its low staff morale. The organization was spending money it didn't have, and was barely meeting its payroll obligations. Its relations with the community were also fractured. In short, it was an organization in distress.

It was a set of circumstances that led the government to conclude its investigation and take over the day-to-day operations of the hospital for a whole year. Then came this phone call. I canvassed widely for views on the hospital's state of affairs and did my own learning. My initial diagnostic was that the place had a series of operational challenges that exist in other places, but not all at once. I quickly found that the spirit of the place and of its people had been broken also. Staff told me they were dispirited when they woke up in the morning, and coming into work only made matters worse. Some told me they were, in fact, afraid to go on to their units because the processes in place and the conditions of work were so substandard. (This fear was later echoed by members of the community: patients and their loved ones.)

It would be a tough slough, but rather than being repelled by what I was hearing, I viewed this as an opportunity to test and pilot new ways of thinking and new ways of working. I concluded that what was needed was not so much a complete turnaround as it was a connecting back to the reasons I and others at KGH were there in the first place: patients.

I had graduated from Queen's University in Kingston, so going back was a homecoming of sorts. There was no parade, however. Far from it. The community had witnessed—and too many families had suffered—several terrible incidents at a place that was supposed to make people better. There was a gaping trust deficit. If I didn't address that meaningfully and authentically, I would be sunk, and so would my efforts to lead fundamental change.

The first 100 days of leading, listening, and learning

Organizational culture is a fancy way of referring to a bunch of micro-moments taken together: a series of things people do and decisions people make when they think no one is looking. I knew tectonic shifts in culture were needed. I knew that my biggest challenge was to ignite the heart and soul of the organization and achieve results that, at the time, we all thought were impossible. So, I asked questions and I listened in a bid to co-create our strategy to get us out of the mess we were in.

I met more than 700 employees, patients, community members, and managers—people at every level of the organization, and people beyond our walls in the community we served. These discussions centered around five key questions:

- What about KGH needs to be preserved and why?
- What are the big things that need to be changed and why?
- What would be the one most hopeful change I could make?
- What are you most afraid I could do as CEO?
- What advice do you have overall?

Those 700 conversations yielded five widely shared suggestions with respect to values people wanted to see as drivers—and fast. These five suggestions were:

- Transparency
- Engagement
- Respect
- Accountability
- Value for money

We had our guiding principles. Now we needed a plan of action.

One member of the KGH staff taught me about a concept called appreciative inquiry. We had already had so much negative talk of what was wrong or broken that we had to shift to more positive framing.

Rather than do a SWOT—strengths, weaknesses, opportunities, and threats analysis—we did SOAR—strengths, opportunities, aspirations, and results. Everyone was invited to bring their experience to the table. We asked people about outstanding care, while always following the five guiding principles. We engaged 3,000 individuals and didn't use a single consultant. I was at every session listening, taking notes, and playing back what I was hearing.

The fear I had heard from some staff members was also echoed and felt by some members of the general public. People who had had loved ones come to the hospital were themselves scarred and afraid to come back. We set a goal of eliminating the hospital's preventable harms to patients. But we all knew we needed more than goals, more than words. We needed real action to rebuild the trust we had lost. That's when we made a call that was, at its core, "we, not me" kicked into its highest gear.

Every decision that had a material impact on the experience of patients made at KGH from that point forward would be made with patients' input. We knew that to make it better for patients, we had to make it meaningful—from their perspective, not only ours. We gave a newly formed patient advisory council real decision-making powers and input. Visiting hours were soon eliminated, and a series of 'presence policies' for loved ones enacted. These turned out to be the first changes among many to our practices and policies over the course of the next seven years. It also turned out to be just the beginning of a deep learning process for all involved.

How do you handle situations where the truth hurts?

Not too long after setting our goal of eliminating preventable harm at our hospital, I got word of a case that put lie to our words. The patient involved became known to us all as Brian. He was 42. He had come to the hospital for a routine surgical procedure. He died in our care.

We had to learn from this case; learning as you go makes it easier for people to evolve. And so we called an all-staff meeting to lay out in detail what had happened to Brian. We were not singling out or laying blame, but we were frank. Our hand washing rates at the time were a dismal 34%, our goal was only 50%, yet we knew that every time someone didn't wash their hands, a patient was at greater risk. Hand washing became a 'Vital Behaviour' at KGH. It was a choice not to wash one's hands. A choice to ignore the policies in place. A choice to potentially do harm to someone in our care. So anyone who refused to engaged in the Vital Behaviour each and every time they needed to would also be given the choice to leave our employ.

I asked our patient advisors what we could do to make sure this standard was sustained. They suggested we put signs at every station with hand washing instructions and requirements in each unit. They also suggested we publicly report hand washing statistics until we were at 100 percent, and when we hit that target, we would share the results and celebrate our milestone. Compliance stats went up. By bringing things out into the open, we had created a collective consciousness. KGH's hand washing rates went from 34% to 95%—where they have remained for several years.

We celebrated our success by giving patients more diverse and prominent roles.

More than engagement, we paid collective attention to the micro-moments that go into being truly great in terms of culture and every other metric we could think of. Patients now sit on hiring boards with medical and human resources experts. They are the first to meet and orient new interns and new staff, as the hospital's "lived experience experts." Every policy change, practice, meeting, and celebration involves patients, and the learning continues. The medical safety committee, for instance, has stopped talking about percentages, percentiles, and dots on graphs; they talk instead about concrete numbers of people and families affected, about the specific number of hours people waited in the ER, and so on. Each case discussed is part of the hospital's story—a measure of its responsibility, not a number or a percentile. People can make sense of this, and as we "people-ized" the numbers, we started making measurable progress on the issues we were discussing. Leaders can own this process. Everyone can learn from it.

People are the most valuable resource in organizations

All of this, I hope, goes some way toward explaining why I am an unapologetic devotee and champion of patient-inspired leadership in health care. Practitioners, policy-makers, payers, and patients all have a role to play—with the latter occupying a crucial place at the center of it all, in my view.

Without truly involving patients and their families in decision making, we risk making a series of decisions that are superficial and based on flawed assumptions. I have found that truly involving patients led to organizational insights and learning that benefited not only the patients, but healthcare workers and their entire organizations as well. In addition, decision-making became empowering and invigorating, which led to greatly improved staff morale and other metrics of success at KGH.

KGH adopted a patient-centered leadership model that challenged each of us to always see the people beyond the numbers. To give them a say. To 'people-ize.'

The KGH model also asks two crucially important questions:

Have you included a patient and their family in the decision-making process today?

What did you learn from a patient today? (Great. Share it.)

The shared learning aspect intoned in the above is a critical point. Taxonomy, too, is important. Shared learnings shift conversations and demonstrate value to both operational success and organizational culture. The language used can demonstrate openness and respect.

Stories shape culture. Language shapes culture. And micro-moments, when shared, can demonstrate real progress on both fronts. Leaders can own this, and inspire it in their own organizations. Increasingly, it is important that we do.

Patient-centered care is not a passing fad. Some 195 countries have signed onto a World Health Organization framework on patient-centered integrated health services. There is a growing body of research linking this approach to better health outcomes. Further, patients and their families have voices that they rightly expect to be heard.

My parents, it turns out, had this "we, not me" thing all figured out long before it was popular. I count myself lucky whenever I get to learn from the best.

Exercises for Expedition 4

Imagine a world of 21st century leaders. What do you see as possible?

10 **Conscious 21st Century Leadership**	
	What do you feel you need to do, in terms of mindset and actions, on your journey to 21st century leadership?
	Where am I stuck?
	What is possible?
	Where do I shift?

11 **Your Style**	Thinking about the skills and capabilities of 21st century leaders, assess yourself and the importance of each in your own environment:		
	Competency	What's working well?	What do I need to improve?
	Purpose:		
	Communication:		
	Empathy:		
	Storytelling:		
	Intuition:		
	Trust:		
	Relationships:		
	Community Building:		
	Integrity:		
	Measuring Impact:		
	Consciousness:		
	Fun:		

12 **Connecting Stories**	Thinking about each of the stories you just experienced, what do they mean for your own journey to conscious 21st century leadership?	
	Roni Zeiger	
	Bryan Welch	
	Kim Jordan	
	Kat Cole	
	Sebastián Ballerini	
	Leslee Thompson	

Expedition 5
Uncovering the Beauty of Shared Purpose

In so many situations today when we first meet someone in the Western world, the first question we ask is: What do you do? Most people usually respond by sharing the name of the organization they work for and their title or scope of responsibility. It is very rare to hear someone say, "I am a father of three kids who love to play football outdoors," or "I am a lover of nature," or "I am a leader." And it is even rarer to ask someone, "What's your purpose? What's your calling in life?"

When I left my job at Cisco, I discovered my own loss of identity, and started to get creative about how I introduced myself. A few months later, I decided to try a new introduction at a keynote I gave. I shared that "I fired myself from corporate America." To my amazement, over 300 people applauded and cheered. Afterwards, I had a line of people who came up to say they wished they could do the same. Many came up with a long list of reasons of why they felt they had lost their sense of purpose. It forced me to start thinking about why this was happening. It was one of my biggest drivers for writing this book. I don't necessarily want more people to fire themselves from their jobs, but I would like for us to architect a more humane world of work together, where lives matter and people flourish while fulfilling their higher purpose. I want us to see work as more than just the drudgery of making a living. To do this, we need to have an understanding of what work means in the 21st century, and how we can bring people in new and ancient ways to serve humanity, rather than drive for continuous blind and pointless progress. It's time to uncover the beauty of our own purpose and our collective shared purpose.

Every great business idea is born from a need or opportunity. It happens when someone wakes up to their purpose and wants to bring it to the world. That dreamer who finds purpose in wanting to start a new restaurant to delight others with their delicacies, for example, goes out into the world, finds the investment needed, builds a community of customers, hires a team of people, and finds a location where people can come and enjoy it.

"If you want to build a ship, don't drum up people to collect wood and don't assign them tasks and work but rather, teach them to long for the endless immensity of the sea," wrote Antoine de Saint-Exupéry, the French aviator and author of *The Little Prince* (1943).

As more and more people become aware of their own purpose, they will want to work for an organization that shares their values. Purpose is becoming increasingly important in business as people look to work for or with purpose-driven organizations, ones that are simple to articulate and embrace. People are openly sharing on online forums the pros and cons of working for an organization. There is more transparency about what it's like to work for a company through platforms like glassdoor.com, which provide access to millions of company reviews, CEO approval ratings, salary reports, and much more.

Before we get into the taxonomy of purpose, let's jump into a conversation very few people are engaging in today. While many are discussing the future of work, very few are focused on what work actually means in the 21st century. We no longer have a common definition of what works means today, as there are less and less boundaries around when and where we work. Many people are experiencing work environments where their boss expects then to be available 24 hours a day, seven days a week. Surveys continue to show that Americans are less likely than Brits, for example, to take vacation; more than two fifths of full-time British employees took all their vacation days last year, whereas only a third of Americans took all their vacation days. Americans are also more likely to call in to meetings when they are on vacation. In France, a new law makes it illegal for companies with 50 or more employees to send emails to employees outside of regular work hours or on the weekend. It allows people to have the right to disconnect. But disconnect from what? Is email the

21st century definition of work? When an organization expects an employee to fly over the weekend to attend a meeting in another country on Monday morning, does that constitute work?

I have listened to the stories of tens of thousands of people at all levels of organizations through assessments I have conducted during my career. Many people have shared how overwhelmed they are by the sheer volume of their workload, and how they can't find the time to do their job because of the meetings and emails they have to attend to. Many feel they no longer have time to think.

On top of all the meetings and email, there is a plethora of new collaboration platforms that are being introduced in many organizations. And when these technologies are not integrated into people's day-to-day work, most feel they have yet another place to go to online (their email in their InBox, Instant Messaging, an online collaboration platform, text messaging, etc.), and do not see the value of these tools. Sharing of information has been lost in the pursuit of having to go to all these new online places to find out what is going on in the organization. Just because a new technology has been introduced does not mean that people know how to use it to collaborate. In fact, it is not uncommon to hear that people inside organizations do not want to share information on projects they are working on with others. I recently worked with a leader at a large multinational company who wanted advice on how to get their people in New Jersey to share information with people in their Shanghai operation, and vice versa. I helped them navigate and see they had an opportunity to start a conversation on why sharing information is critical to their business, and what work means to them. Why do people find a need to compete with each other inside their own organizations?

We are still using 20th century definitions and practices in a 21st century work environment, even when the way we work has changed substantially from previous centuries. Changes in culture, technology, financial expectations, and a host of other reasons have shifted the kind of work we do, the way we do it, and where we do it. The drive to work has also shifted as our educational systems made many of us unnecessarily competitive, preparing us for a work world where our ambition is expected to be motivated by the acquisition of ever more titles and power.

Work has been known to bring order and stability into our lives by keeping us on track with societal expectations. It is the system used to exchange knowledge, skills, or labor for pay. Earning our keep means that we can live our lives and survive. It provides for our basic needs—food, shelter, education—and it expands our ability to live an even more comfortable and materialistic life with a house, car, electronics, exotic vacations, designer clothes, and everything else a person can dream and aspire to in our materialistic society. We are indoctrinated into accepting this materialistic model, where more is always assumed to be better.

We already have a semi "robotic" workforce in many Western countries, where many people go to a place of employment and simply put in their time mindlessly at a job. When Wednesday arrives, people celebrate "hump day," meaning they're over the mid-week hump and halfway to the weekend. The illusion here is that the rest of the week goes by faster until we get to the weekend, which is our ultimate goal. But before that, we have TGIF (Thank Goodness It's Friday), where we joyfully acknowledge the end of another work week and celebrate having two days off to enjoy; no work, no school, more rest, and time to catch up on work at home.

Unfortunately, there are still many jobs today that require limited creativity but demand repetitive tasks. What the low level of employee engagement tells us is that there is a limited number of people who are fully engaged in their work; many are just going through the motions. Instead of fearing how self-driving vehicles, semi-autonomous robots, or predictive analytics will replace jobs over the next 50 years, we need to address the issue of how we want to live and what work truly means to us right now.

It is ironic that today, we do much of our living at work. Work can be addictive. As someone who used to work an average of 90-120 hours a week thanks to the responsibility of my corporate job and the international travel it required, I struggled with the mythical work-life balance and the so-called 40-hour work week. On most days, trying to balance these two separate alien entities felt like a wild science fiction movie gone mad, as I felt compelled to choose my work over my life.

I was fortunate in many ways, as I held jobs that allowed me to express myself and that were also stimulating, and often I worked with brilliant people (and some interesting characters). My work was meaningful for a time, especially when I worked in new frontiers, like bringing mobile technology to the world and connecting people in community. Yet, what I learned is that work cannot provide our identity, and that it is insane to value work at the expense of our life and our personal health. Our story changes when we wake up to the cost of the monthly paycheck and the need to make a life, not just a living. That is easy to say, but it can be very difficult to do. We are deeply conditioned to identify with our work, or with an organization, or sports team, or anything other than ourselves.

So what does work mean in the 21st century? We need to realize that it can be a form of expressing who we are and what we want to do in the world. It's an ability to practice our craft—whether we are a plumber, a pilot, a nurse, a farmer, a writer, a teacher, a healer—and a way to express our higher meaning. It no longer needs to be just a paycheck, a business card, a performance review, a title, or a physical place, as many jobs now allow us to work from anywhere.

We do not need to accept this broken system of work. We need to demand more from ourselves, and make the changes we need to move from merely surviving or existing to living more fulfilling lives. Work needs to go beyond climbing the corporate ladder and measuring progress by the size of our pay grade or the progression of our titles. Work, whether paid or volunteer, is us practicing our craft and deep interests. It requires us to reexamine our antiquated academic and educational paths. The basic foundations need to be reviewed before we can produce the next generation of lawyers, doctors, social scientists, and other professionals. It's time for those focused on the future of work to create the space for a re-examination of what works means in the 21st century on a larger, global scale. We can't just keep reporting the same statistics over and over and offer bland solutions to a broken system. We can't keep reinventing the organizational structure. We need to go much deeper. The opportunity is for leaders in every organization around the world to spark the conversations about what work means and tie it into a higher purpose by genuinely respecting human life. It's time, for example, for Human Resource departments to play a new role by going beyond advocating for the organization and bringing people centered design into the fabric of work. We don't need a redesign of process; we need to lead with the "why" and build a strong foundation around it. Structure needs to follow purpose in the 21st century.

As a conscious leader, you must find your own purpose in your life and work. If your own purpose is not clear, then how can you drive your organization's purpose? If you see your work as your art and creation, then why you are doing it becomes deeply important. This is something that usually gets lost in the creation of mission and vision statements, and it doesn't get published on the company's website or framed on the walls of the office. Why are you here? What are you longing for?

Why Purpose is the Cornerstone for 21st Century Business

Organizations are no longer judged merely by what they say, but more so by what they actually do. And everyone is watching closely, as we have greater transparency in this technological age. Leaders who are successful at building long-term relationships are consistent in sharing what they believe in and transparent in the way they conduct their business. Remember that a successful organization's biggest idea is often the one on which it was built.

When people feel valued and are treated well, they will share their experiences with their communities. By creating a shared purpose, you create a clear picture of what your business stands for and why every single person's contribution is important. And when you take the time to listen and respond to ideas and questions, then you take your shared purpose from simply being a statement to being how you run your organization every day. You know how to listen and create the space for two-way conversations. You will no longer need stale employee engagement programs as you involve people in supporting wider issues that support the communities in which you operate.

Organizations that thrive in the 21st century work with their people to understand what generates purpose for them and how they align to the greater shared purpose. It's a journey that starts with high self-awareness. It is about building strong relationships and connecting human-to-human in a world of work where people can truly make an impact. The 21st century leader is a purposeful connector who brings people together in communities.

Why Slaying the Competition is Not a Shared Purpose in the 21st Century

About nine years ago, a friend of mine (let's call her Lynne) was interviewing for the VP of culture position at a large, iconic Silicon Valley tech company. I had coffee with her a few days later. She shared that the interviews went well, but when she had asked to have a better understanding of where the organization was headed, Lynne was told that the purpose of the company was to crush and acquire all their competitors so that they could be the last man standing. I kid you not; her role would consist of aligning the figurative troops for battle. She turned down the position and the organization indeed continued to swallow other companies.

As a futurist, I sense that over the next 25 years we will be more likely to reject working for organizations that are solely fear-based. Business does not need to be a fiercely competitive, repetitive routine of greed. What is the point of working in these organizations that help pay the bills, but at the same time make people unhealthy and leave them unfulfilled, often while destroying the environment in the process?

Trusting the Small Moments

When I first joined Cisco in the late 90s, I felt like I had died and gone to heaven, as we were all focused on co-creation and I worked with some of the smartest and most passionate people on Earth. There was limited politics, and a sense of bringing the company together to have technology as an enabler of how we worked, played, and learned in the world. The job, for me, was about the power of technology for good. I was responsible for helping IT become a trusted business partner. This feeling of awe lasted a few years before the bubble burst in 2001. As managers, we went from being penalized for not growing and hiring people fast enough to letting them go en masse. When we were in growth mode, hiring was not always coordinated across the company. People hired shadow IT or marketing departments, which meant that they created their own technical or marketing support group, for example, because they had the budget to hire their own "headcount" or "resources" (otherwise known as *people*) to work directly for them.

There is no motivation to collaborate with existing teams when you can bring in your own dedicated people and hide them somewhere in your organizational chart. The internal systems allow people to build fiefdoms and create duplication. And then what usually happens is that the official IT department spends an enormous amount of time trying to locate these shadow departments and bring them into the fold. This is usually not aligned with the overall shared purpose of the organization and, ultimately, when the growth comes to a halt, people become disposable in the name of redundancy.

"And do we have a plan if it goes south?" I remember asking when it was announced at Cisco that the company planned to expand into a $50 billion corporation. The executive had no response. I really wasn't trying to be negative; I was trained to do scenario planning, which helped me immensely through my entire Cisco journey. I was experiencing how we were losing common sense, like many other Silicon Valley companies. I had a front row seat and was hoping my small voice would awaken us to what really was happening in the world. We were living in a happy but deluded bubble—and everyone knows what happens to bubbles at one point or another.

What War Has to Do with Shared Purpose

On June 1st, 1967 at 11:00 am GMT, a radio broadcast by then Iraqi President Abdel Rahman Aref on Baghdad Domestic Service in Arabic, translated into English by the Foreign Broadcast Information Service, declared: “Brethren and sons, this is the day of the battle to avenge our martyred brethren who fell in 1948. It is the day to wash away the stigma. We shall, God willing, meet in Tel Aviv and Haifa.” At the same time, Egyptian President Abdel Nasser announced at a press conference: “We will not accept any…coexistence with Israel…Today the issue is not the establishment of peace between the Arab states and Israel...The war with Israel is in effect since 1948.”

The first memory of my life is one of war. I experienced people coming together around shared purpose in the most caring and loving ways despite the deep threat and uncertainty that we faced. My short life could have come to a complete stop had my side lost the war, as declared so clearly in the transcripts above. What I witnessed at that time was a profound connection between people when their survival was at risk and they had a common reason to work together.

While my grandparents lived in different cities than us, I still remember other children’s grandparents playing with us and making sure we were in good spirits. I am sure I was too young to comprehend the threat we were under, since I was only three year old. It became more of a game of lights out, everything going dark, sleeping in our robes, and making a dash for the bomb shelters when the sirens told us it was unsafe to be outside our apartment building.

War broke out in my country, Israel, a few weeks before my fourth birthday. I was playing outside at my pre-nursery, across the street from our apartment building, when the sirens went off. We were all ushered into a bomb shelter, whose location we were familiar with because we had had practice drills. We all sat in the dark, afraid. One by one my friends’ parents arrived to take them home. I waited with one of my teachers until my mother came to pick me up and take me across the street. She tried to appear calm, but I could sense that this was not how she was truly feeling. My then seven-year-old sister arrived from school and our new routine of rushing to the bomb shelter when the sirens would sound would begin. Ironically, that morning at breakfast my sister had announced to my mom that she had forgotten that she needed to bring white sheets for a school show that day and they had both scrambled to find some.

We helped our mom put dark blankets on all the windows and were on constant alert to be ready to go to the shelter where we were supposed to be safe. Sirens and radio reports from the outside world governed our lives. I remember one of our neighbors being told that her son had been killed. I can still recall the pain and the deep loss that day. That suffering and loss stuck with me—it made me the rebel I became in the world. And more importantly, it showed me how people come together during times of crisis with clear purpose and intent. I had experienced a sense of community, long before the internet or social media.

When I was seven, my father was relocated to Montreal for his job with El Al, the Israeli airline. I had a different perspective on life than my peers. I had seen horrific things at a young age that had stuck with me. The other kids were so different than me, and I was never accepted into their world or community. It was a crazy time, too. There were death threats on our lives, and my sister and I spent a few years going to school with a bodyguard, which made our friends' parents nervous, demanding that we should go to a different school as it was too risky for their kids. I broke through the culture of sameness at an early age and I was an outlier at seven. I can see clearly how I had already intuited at that young age the importance of connecting people based on purpose.

The sense of community stuck with me. When I was 14 my family moved back to Israel, where I felt I was back with my community. I felt it every Veterans Day and Holocaust Memorial Day when for one minute a siren would sound, and wherever you were you had to stand in silence for that minute and remember. At school, we wore white shirts on that day, and again I felt the community come together around the shared purpose of honoring the fallen and never forgetting. And at the same time, I was praying for no more wars, no more deaths, and no more terror. I was young and hopeful. As a teenager living in Israel, I was active for the cause of peace and was surprised when I was invited to represent Israel in a youth delegation to Germany, Austria, and Switzerland, as I was very pro-peace at the time. A small voice in a big pond.

It is amazing what happens when a community comes together. It happened in New York City and across the east coast when the events of September 11th, 2001 unfolded. Shortly after the Twin Towers fell, America and the world began to mourn, and we began to commemorate the victims. Some flew the American flag from their front porches and car antennas. Others pinned it to their lapels or wore it on t-shirts. Sports teams postponed games. Celebrities organized benefit concerts and performances. People attended impromptu candlelight vigils and participated in moments of silence. They gathered in common places, like Chicago's Daley Plaza, Honolulu's Waikiki Beach, and especially New York City's Union Square Park, to post tributes to the dead and to share their grief with others. "I don't know why I've been coming here, except that I'm confused" one young man in Union Square told a reporter from the *New York Times*. "Also a sense of unity. We all feel differently about what to do in response, but everybody seems to agree that we've got to be together no matter what happens. So you get a little bit of hope in togetherness." In a brilliant display of the human spirit working as a collective, nearly half a million civilians were evacuated by boat from Manhattan in a sea evacuation during September 11th.

My sister Anat went missing in NYC on September 11th. She was on a business trip that included a meeting at the World Trade Center. While I was praying to find her, I was responsible for leading the IT team at Cisco that was communicating to the company in crisis mode. We had employees who were missing and customers who were under attack. My boss, the new CIO, was stuck in another city and was driving back since there were no flights. While I worked, I was also searching for my sister, trying to find her and keeping in touch with our worried mom in Toronto. It was devastating to watch it all unfold. It seemed like a terrible movie, but the stories kept coming in.

One of our sales executives who was listed on one of the planes that went down never actually boarded and was found alive, while another was on one of the planes that went down. But there was hope amid the destruction of human life. I had memories of a terrorist attack in Israel when my sister was going to university in Tel Aviv and had just left our house to go back to campus. I turned the news on and heard a bulletin that terrorists had hijacked a bus on its way to Tel Aviv. Back then, there were no cell phones. On campus, there were only pay phones so we had no viable way to get in touch. We watched the news, sickened by what was happening. We found out that it was a passenger bus coming from the north and she was coming from the south, and breathed for our miracle and mourned more senseless deaths. These memories flooded me again on September 11th as I prayed for my sister and all other missing people. Late that afternoon, we found her and I took the first flight from San Jose to Toronto where we all met.

I always wondered why it took an act of violence to bring people together in this way. If you've ever experienced it, you will know that feeling of community, compassion, and caring that prevails in the aftermath of such events. At that moment, there is a deep feeling of togetherness. There is clarity of purpose. The potent emotion that you feel when you experience terror and trauma galvanizes people. 21st century leaders understand how emotion and heartfelt connection to an opportunity inspires action.

What I learned from my childhood is that when people face overwhelming odds, they can come together around a shared purpose with trust and conviction. What I also learned as I grew older is that history repeats itself in the name of purpose, with every side fighting for their cause and survival. Had the other side won the war when I was three years old, I would not be here on this path with you. They would have achieved their goal of avenging their martyred brethren. Too often, our enemies have a shared purpose that can ignite our own. This is insanity on a whole different level based on deep rooted mutual hatred and fundamentalist dogma.

We can compare our immune system to a Department of Defense. When waging a war, the Defense Department relies on its Air Force, Navy, and Army, as well as specialized intelligence units, antiterrorist teams, and other forces, to work together in a coordinated fashion to defeat the enemy. The human immune system operates like a highly efficient killing machine to fend off germs. It employs a variety of strategies and weapons based on the specific threat it faces, and uses a complex defensive process to protect us. Our bodies work hard to repel invading viruses and illnesses, and there is a legitimate need for protection.

No one can question how ingrained war is in our world and history. When we choose to turn on the news, images flood into our field of vision of a battle somewhere on the globe. We may feel outrage as we witness these insane reports of the loss of life somewhere close or far, but the cycle continues. We may say "Never again," and yet the news keeps bringing us reports of wars from all edges of the world. And with the Internet, these stories are flooding in faster and faster every day.

For some reason, we have brought the war analogy into the fabric of business. The competition is seen as the enemy and the purpose is to win the highest market share or top spot. It is easy to get people to rally the troops and aspire to get the #1 market share spot. The deeper question is this: is it necessary to have a shared purpose of bringing down the competition, when in the 21st century the opportunity is to get people to focus on a shared higher purpose and find ways to collaborate and co-create with sometimes unlikely partners? (We will explore this in more detail in Expedition 9.) It is an opportunity to rally people around what your business is doing in the world and why it makes our planet better through our work.

In too many organizations, there is increasing competition *inside* of the organization, where people and departments are battling each other for resources and ownership. So much time and energy is spent on internal competition, when the opportunity is to find ways to come together around a shared purpose of creating an incredible offering in the marketplace that will delight and serve people, like a new co-living space or virtual reality experience. There is no reason to crush anyone when we remember why we are in business. Imagine what could happen if we brought the art of co-creation and cooperation into the fabric of how business operates. What if instead of having "war rooms" in organizations, we had co-creation spaces where we brought our internal departments together for a higher purpose that helped our organizations thrive? What if our purpose was to thrive in our higher purpose instead of winning a game that destroys our own and the planet's wellbeing?

Isn't it time for us to recognize the power business has to shift humanity in a new direction for future generations, to create a new path forward with shared purpose? We would no longer need to crush the competition at all costs. We need to have more faith in our ability to build and co-create, as we have witnessed what happens when the drive for survival transforms into blind destruction and hatred. There is another way for us as business people to change the mindset of leadership, to co-create a new path to brings back the simplicity and beauty of business. Business can be a force powered by the purpose of providing exchanges between people.

Transformational Stories from the Frontiers of 21st Century Leaders

Céline Schillinger

Being a change agent in a highly regulated sector is not for the faint-hearted. Just ask Céline Schillinger, whose efforts to push the Paris-based drug maker Sanofi to embrace diversity and social engagement were not exactly met with open arms. But this one passionate woman created a new way to bring people together around shared purpose. She has over 20 years of multi-industry experience in Asia-Pacific and in Europe. A charter member of Change Agents Worldwide LLC, Céline is passionate about business transformation. She now directs Quality Innovation and Engagement—a major stake for the vaccine manufacturer.

The Journey of Céline Schillinger: Purposeful. Transformational. Pioneer. Head Quality Innovation and Engagement, Sanofi Pasteur.

What is your story?

My story is one of a person who felt she was free. I believed I could grow with no constraints when I was in my early 20s. I was driven to overcome my fear of the unknown. I felt anything was possible. When I joined the workforce, I realized there was an unexpected constraint that I had to overcome: my gender. I started to see that it was harder to progress as a woman in the corporate world than to progress as a man. This fact became increasingly evident throughout my career.

I had believed that because my mother and grandmother had fought for women's rights, it was not going to be a challenge for me in the workforce, but I found that I was wrong. My formal education did not prepare me for the realities of the modern workplace. And even though I had great parents who helped me experience freedom and independence, I was not prepared to experience that being a woman was a barrier at work in this era.

At 23, I left France and moved to Vietnam on my own to look for a job. I moved in with a Vietnamese family, learned Vietnamese, and ended up staying for four years. I was on a quest to find out who I was and what I was made of. I found myself on my first night in Vietnam with no friends, no job, and not able to speak the local language, and yet I felt a sense of elation. Lying under the mosquito netting in a flat on a street of Ho Chi Minh City, I realized that I had definitely steered off the traditional safe track to experience life.

It was 1993 and the environment was still very challenging in Vietnam, as the US embargo was still in effect and it was tough to find basic items and have the same lifestyle I had in France. I saw this move as a great personal challenge, and I chose this location specifically to see what I was capable of achieving, far from my nurturing and comfortable environment.

After my four-year adventure in Vietnam, I returned to France and started working in international business in a mostly male-dominated defense company that supplied the armies, navies, and air forces with information systems. After traveling the world for a few years with this company, they moved me to China to manage the radio business. I was faced with another challenge—a new country, and a field that was unfamiliar, with the responsibility of managing a big team with limited management experience. What continually drove me was my appetite for newness, the unknown, and challenging my limits.

Two years later, that company was making changes and I met my now husband and decided to marry and find a new position in Lyon, France, where I joined the HR department at Sanofi Pasteur. I was now, once again, in a brand new industry, and I was sought out for my international business experience. Coming from much smaller organizations, I encountered a brand new corporate language I had to learn quickly that included the complexity of process and metrics.

I resonated with their public health mission of protecting and improving human health worldwide. I stayed in HR for a few years and then moved to commercial operations. My career faced many ups and downs. Sometimes I was thrilled with the challenges in my work, and other times I felt I was just doing a job with no personal growth. I also noticed that over 10 years I was not progressing, and there were limited opportunities to evolve. I experienced seven years with no promotion and very miniscule salary increases. I realized I had reached a plateau. It was a period of extreme discomfort and self-doubt; I was terrified I had reached my maximum ability, that I had reached the peak of what I could do and be. I started questioning whether staying at this level in one company made me less valuable. I didn't want to be one of those people who felt they had no future in their job or company. I was no longer promoted or challenged, but I didn't want to accept this as my path. I knew I could accomplish so much more in my life. I was only 39 and I had many years of work ahead of me.

It was an awakening on many levels. I was watching other people around me who had also reached this plateau and reacted to the company's increased disinterest in them with deep cynicism, depression, and by emotionally disconnecting from work. I saw so many corporate leaders sitting on a gold mine of talent, which they completely disregarded. I learned that while striving for growth and productivity, many companies still afford the luxury to waste a major resource: their own talent. They managed to have those people join the company, they were paying their salaries, infrastructure, travel, and communications, and they ended up using only a fraction of their available intelligence, passion, and energy. I wondered if talent management was an oxymoron. Why do organizations spend so much on recruiting the best and the brightest and then treat them this way?

Increasingly, I realize this frustration I was feeling was not just a personal experience. It is the natural consequence of a systemic flaw. It is the way organizations work today. Those in the driver's seat don't see how they are burning people out. They have great analytical skills, they are paid to focus on productivity and efficiency, and they are doing the jobs they were hired to do that are governed by standard metrics of success. While organizations talk a lot about having a diverse workforce and respecting the differences in people, too often they simply don't know how to build the best teams that bring people together. Building diverse teams is too often seen as an impediment that slows the system down, despite the data that supports diversity

I could no longer sit back and watch what was going on around me. I started exploring opportunities. I felt I had much to contribute to this company, and I started to think about how I could make a difference. While the company was mostly comprised of scientists and researchers, I started to think of unique ways my capabilities could complement their work and add value. I knew that it was up to me to create a path and not to wait for someone else to pave it for me.

I took a risk. I had nothing to lose. What was the worst that could happen? I sat down and wrote an email to the CEO suggesting that we could do something about the gender diversity gaps we faced and integrate more women at the top of the organization. I wanted him to know why diversity is good for business. I included some ideas from a McKinsey Report that argued that companies that have diversity in their top management do better financially. And then I hit send. It was my first intrapreneurial moment.

I forwarded the email to three girlfriends in the company, as I felt I needed their support. What I never expected was what happened next. This one email went viral: my friends sent it to three other people, who then sent it to more people. I was looking at my screen late that evening in disbelief as my husband looked over my shoulder and said, "I think you've triggered something big."

The next day a number of us gathered to talk and have lunch. There were about eleven of us, including one woman who was on the executive committee reporting to the CEO. The fact that this high level executive woman chose to be there gave us strength and purpose. She had not been appointed by the CEO to show up—she had reached out directly to us and joined our group. She was a member of this team like the rest of us.

We shared what we were feeling about what was happening in the organization, and realized we had this shared purpose that brought us together. It got us talking about how we could engage people with something that came from their hearts. We wanted to do something positive to help the company grow.

We organized debates and asked people whether they were for or against quotas. In the first debate, 30 people came from across all functions. What we discovered was that people wanted to have an open forum for discussion, and they were amazed by the opportunity to genuinely give their opinion on a topic close to their hearts. There was a sense of freedom of opinion for people to share and exchange ideas. We were there to focus on what we could do to help the company. Our group also found joy around being linked via a joint purpose, which is rare in corporate world.

We were very active in bringing people into the conversation. We brought in guests from outside the company to learn from what they were doing and to engage with us on some of our ideas. Members of our core group went to sites around the world to connect with people locally. But the biggest impact we had in connecting people was setting up an online social network through Yammer, which had only been used by IT in the past. I created the first purpose-driven group, and it reached 2,500 members in over 50 countries in 18 months. I became the co-leader of what was known as Women in Sanofi Pasteur (WiSP).

After six months, the CEO asked to have lunch with us and find out more about what we were learning. He agreed to be our sponsor and asked us to host a working session for the executive committee. We brought 63 ideas that we had crowdsourced across the network to that meeting. We discussed them, and the executive committee selected a few to be launched, including a mentoring program. What we learned was that we should have come with specific recommendations, as there were other ideas that would have had a deeper impact for the organization beyond mentoring.

Our team felt that our work was being done because we had woken up the organization by creating awareness, brought ideas to life, created a network of people around the globe, and raised consciousness to the need for a more diverse workforce. But at the end of the day when we took a close look, we realized that we had created deep relationships and connected people. Yes, we had discovered and learned a lot about inclusion and diversity. We had sparked conversations and brought ideas to the leadership team. And yes, we had created a shared purpose that we drove through social networks and engagement. But did we make a difference according to the existing metrics?

The answer was: not really. Five years later, the executive committee had zero women, one less than when we had started. We hadn't reached our goal, despite our efforts and the data from the McKinsey report making the case that organizations that have diversity in their top management do better financially. At one point, we thought we were super successful, but the metrics and results were not there. Resistance was even higher than we had anticipated.

A network alone cannot move a purpose. The network needs to be supported by the hierarchy in large organizations. We didn't raise our shared purpose to the top, so they saw us as another group chasing an idea that was not linked to the overall business strategy. We created enough noise to get their attention, but not their commitment. I learned a lot from this adventure that I took into my future work. It was very eye opening and foundational for my life's work of bringing people at all levels together around a shared purpose.

The irony was that I started getting recognized and winning awards, so some would say we were successful. But for me, success went deeper than awards. We needed results. We needed a more diverse workplace. I was named France's woman of the year by business daily *La Tribune* and Sanofi won a national diversity award, presented by the French Minster of Women's Rights. I felt ignited by a deeper mission that recognized the importance of bringing people together.

The biggest impact we had was in connecting people with others and with information outside of the organization. People who would otherwise never know each other could now collaborate because they were interested in what we were doing. We worked as a community, gathering people across silos through shared purpose. My fear of jumping into the unknown vanished, just like when I had moved to Vietnam, as I now knew that for me, facing my fears had helped me to find my own voice and connect with other voices. We may have not impacted the current metrics, but we had touched people in new ways and provided a place for people to experiment and grow. It showed many of us that we can't simply sit back and be spectators at work. We need to take action to change a situation that does not serve us, even when it sometimes feels overwhelming and a bit scary.

My definition of success also shifted. I realized that you need courage to launch, a few strategically placed friends inside the company who think what you are doing is worthwhile, and you need to be able to build community. I learned that for a company to thrive, it needs to become less "command and control" in its leadership style and learn how to listen to its own employees and its customers. And I felt a need to stay at Sanofi and continue on my mission of experimenting, because despite everything, I still felt that the company needed people like me to bring in listening and convening practices.

I took these lessons to my next role at Sanofi, where I got to practice in a business role and create a business case. I moved into stakeholder engagement in a department preparing the launch of a vaccine for dengue fever, a mosquito-borne viral infection found in tropical and subtropical regions. Dengue has become a leading cause of death among children. There is currently no cure and no preventative medicine.

Instead of doing the traditional pre-marketing, I suggested that we become a leader in behavioral changes that could prevent dengue fever, and that we try to connect everyone who was interested through a social network. I advocated to co-create a social movement across different social and digital platforms with a non-profit organization. I wanted to tap into what I had learned and create a virtual meeting space where people could have conversations. I realized that we needed to do it inside and outside of the company's walls, which was scary for some people, as it meant people could be talking about us without us controlling it. I did a social network analysis using Twitter data and found there was a lot of interest and conversation, but no meeting place for people to get together and take action. I knew we needed to build a virtual meeting space and connect these isolated voices, which would help us add value to the fight against the disease by bringing the community together.

At that time, social media was still fairly new to us, and we were just figuring out the social media policy for the company. What I wanted to do with social engagement was also new, and it made some people uneasy because we would involve many groups, which meant that we would need to give up some of our traditional notions of control. I had to convince a lot of people to move away from organizational boundaries to what a connected community can achieve. Our internal team was concerned that we would open ourselves to attacks and people would say bad things about us in public. I had to point out to them that this was already happening anyway—we just weren't out there responding and connecting with people.

As a change agent, I realized that we need to help people see what is possible, and lead more by showing a new path than just talking about it. I was part of a few external communities—like Change Agents Worldwide and Rebels at Work—where we openly talked about what can be achieved with social media tools, and I felt the support of other change agents and rebels like me. And this is where I took my next risk.

I knew that by taking the traditional route of getting approval from nine different departments would take our energy away from achieving our purpose. This project was different and needed an approach that was yet to be outlined in our standard social media policy handbook. I didn't want to be shut down by guidelines that didn't take into account the boldness we needed to bring to the organization. It was about focusing on the lives of people, who would benefit from the information we would widely share about fighting this disease, rather than fighting the system.

Connections create value

This type of shared purpose was new for the company leadership, as it went beyond the traditional purpose of creating shareholder value. We needed to think about an initiative as not revolving around the product, but the issue that product was about, and do it as an alliance of partners sharing the same purpose.

Seeing the world through a purely organizational lens is outdated. Work is no longer restricted to a strict responsibility of a box on an organizational chart. We have to connect the people who share in our purpose, whether they are inside or outside the organization, and move beyond traditional boundaries. Flexibility here is so key to bringing cross-functional projects to life. The good news is that our partners were not hiding behind neutral third parties. We removed the intermediary and had direct connections. Instead of just creating awareness of the disease, we were adding value to co-create new solutions against the disease that would complement our vaccine and partners working around this shared purpose. We were able not only to imagine what was possible, but also to create opportunities for people to experience firsthand a new way of working.

People started to understand that by connecting people, value gets created, which in turn can generate new ideas and products. With traditional change management practices, we have been conditioned to simply create awareness and talk at people, and now we demonstrated that the opportunity is to truly connect people in conversations that lead to collective action.

Six months after I took this position, everything shifted thanks to the Facebook campaign. While a static page about dengue fever had 218 followers in three years, the social activism campaign that I led—waged across different social media platforms—attracted 10,000 people in the first week and 250,000 in the first six months. That got everyone's attention. It showed people that connecting people around a common purpose was possible. You need imagination and courage to go beyond a purpose that is too directly tied to marketing.

It was a very tough process. I was convinced it would yield results for the company, but I had to show so many people who wanted to kill the project that we could do it differently. I had the gatekeeper against me, although it was not personal. It is never easy to bring in new practices that people are unfamiliar with, and help people face the fear of trying a new approach. People were not used to stakeholder engagement, and that was the work we needed to do by educating them and also showing results. In the end, the project was on its way and we found a way to get resources from the company and got support for a really important vaccine for people living in areas affected by dengue. It ended up being a huge success. We created a movement and had the #1 shared voice on dengue fever on social media. We received praise from the Bill and Melinda Gates Foundation. Sanofi won a global Shorty Award for best use of social media for healthcare, and another award for the Most Impactful Emerging Pharma Initiative.

A few months later a new leader joined the company to oversee our quality of vaccines, products, and the manufacturing process. He saw what I had done with stakeholder engagement and thought it had great potential for quality improvement. Many of the decisions were being made at the top and there were a lot of bottlenecks. The goal was to create an organization that could deliver vaccines to all the people who needed them and make sure supplies were readily available. We knew we could do better and release high quality products, serve our purpose, and save money. We figured out that we needed to transform quality from an imposed constraint to a shared passion. We needed to make everyone an activist of quality. And I felt proud that despite the odds, we were able to create a movement around the shared purpose of changing the way we work to better serve those who needed our vaccines.

We are getting back a sense of agency in people. We are putting people in situations where they create their own path. It may sound small, but it is huge in our culture. I am seeing new leaders emerging from the front line and from night shift—people who were never before asked for their opinion. There is a viral grassroots movement where people are connecting. I facilitate it, but they gather to create solutions and act—not just generate ideas—to simplify and co-create. This is an example of how things can be when you work differently. When there is a shared purpose, people feel proud of their work and they become generous in working with others. It is a fantastic fuel that positively impacts lives.

I want to pursue a higher purpose with others who want to change the way we work. People should have the ability to recognize their own purpose and find others who share it, beyond their current job titles and organizational divides. I want us to tap into the potential of the human being instead of squandering it. I want to help get rid of old systems that no longer serve us, since I know we can do better. We need more people with a strong imagination to drive open conversations that move away from old world secrecy and gossip. It is much better for the organization to have people who share information and feel they have the power to make a difference—to become a strong group of people who are heading in the same direction and have the same goal, people who feel excited and strong about what they are co-creating.

Moving beyond fear

My advice is to be brave and take action. I learned that we need to free our minds before we can advocate for something. We need to match our words with our actions. Having a clear purpose brings people together around something we are passionate about and allows us to clarify a shared direction in making it happen. More people want to work for an organization that shares their purpose. For me, knowing that we were helping people fight diseases went beyond it simply being another program or idea that needed to be implemented.

What is extremely important to me is to ask myself: Am I growing? Am I evolving and not being stuck in the same place? Movement is important to me in terms of personal growth. For me, it's about more than going through traditional steps and achieving old world success. It is important to frame yourself in a situation that is much bigger than yourself. I used to be focused on my own development, and as I matured I learned that I can grow when I am fueled by something that is bigger than myself—other people, other energies.

We have an opportunity to come together and shift from a world that focuses so narrowly on transactions to a wider world that recognizes the power of connection. Organizations need to see the beauty of connecting people and introduce new ways of working that allow us to focus more on key projects and purpose, instead of being bogged down in organizational charts. I want to find the way to help the c-suite see that, and help them adopt greater purpose. There are two Vietnamese words to say no: "Không" means 'no, never'; "Chu'a" means 'no, not yet.' If your organization seems to say no to change, don't take it as a "no, never," when it might be a "not yet." Keep trying.

Jay Coen Gilbert

Speaking about the planet and purpose leads us to the story of Jay Coen Gilbert. Jay is one of three cofounders of B Lab, which is leading a global movement to redefine success in business, recognizing that business can be used as a force for good. Jay and his cofounders have proven that we can have strong and profitable companies, robust communities, and responsible planetary stewardship simultaneously.

The Journey of Jay Coen Gilbert: Entrepreneur. Activist. Integrator. Cofounder, B Lab.

What is your story?

My parents were both entrepreneurs, and both of their parents were entrepreneurs and immigrants to the United States. They were born with all that entails in terms of the energy to create and to hustle. Both my parents, in very different ways, brought intentionality to the business they created—my mom around women in the workforce and breaking glass ceilings, and my father was ahead of his time organizing his profession around issues of social responsibility.

Most recently, it has translated into the desire to work with some of my closest friends in the world to together figure out how we could support and serve a growing global movement of people who want to use business as a tool to solve social and environmental challenges. Those current activities are a manifestation of a broader trajectory of trying to use what I have been given to the greatest benefit. This is the most distinct way I can say who I am, why I'm here, and what I'm doing.

To me, business is the most powerful human-made force yet created. And in the last 50 to 100 years, business has fallen short of its potential to be an instrument that creates community wealth and health. Business to me is a tool. It happens to be a very powerful tool, one that can be used to hammer someone over the head or to build a bridge. What is inspiring to me about the B Corp Movement is that people are consciously using business as a tool to build a bridge to a more shared prosperity for everyone—not just for the few that control the shares.

By adopting a wholeness-oriented way of thinking, we have more interdependence, integration, and a more holistic approach to the role of business in society. That has reflected in the B Corp community itself. Today, there are B Corps from over 130 different industries, from over 40 countries. B Corp businesses range from small sole proprietorships to large multinationals, they are historically private but are increasingly public, and they are led by people from a variety of different places along the political spectrum. They all share a common vision: a stakeholder-centric business model as opposed to a shareholder-centric business model. A stakeholder-centric business model is one that begins with putting a focus on relationships as opposed to transactions. If one focuses on relationships, this means that those relationships are ones that have to be of mutual benefit with a common purpose.

The B Corp movement is growing fast globally. The US is pretty small when it comes to the total population of the world, and it isn't surprising that there's more happening outside the US. We are in a global economy where capital, labor, and communications are driving a global movement. It's healthy that there are B Lab partners helping to nurture and serve the movement of these types of entrepreneurs and investors in Latin America, Europe, Australia, and the UK, and hopefully soon in Asia and Africa. We are coming together to co-create, collaborate, and serve a global need.

One example of a B Corp is a Brazilian company called Natura, a large cosmetics company that has more than one and a half million consultants who work mostly throughout Brazil in a direct selling model. They also have European divisions and Australian subsidiaries to sell sustainably produced cosmetics in a way that creates economic opportunity, primarily for women in a part of the world where having women in the workforce isn't the norm. Natura is the first publicly traded company in Brazil to become a certified B Corp, including meeting the legal requirement of the certification as a publicly traded company on the Brazilian Stock Exchange. For Natura's investors, becoming a B Corp was a non-issue, as it was not a significant change from how Natura was already operating. Natura is one of our pioneers, sparking other publicly traded companies to consider a more sustainable path for business.

Another type of multinational are companies like Unilever via their subsidiary Ben and Jerry's, Danone via their subsidiary Happy Family, Campbell's Soup Company via their subsidiary Organics, or Proctor and Gamble via their subsidiary New Chapter. These four different types of Fortune 500s are starting to be exposed to the B Corp movement through these subsidiaries. Increasingly, those larger multinationals are becoming interested themselves in how they might either qualify for B Corp certification, or at the very least how they can engage not only their subsidiaries, but their divisions around the world. There are first steps being taken by Unilever, for example, a for-profit corporate entity that is considering committing to positive social and environmental goals. Chief executive Paul Polman feels it would send a powerful message that the purpose of business is not just profit, but to have a positive impact on society and the environment. While their certification would have to take into account the complexity of Unilever's operations in multiple countries, it will also be an opportunity for them to scale their operations. We need to take one step at a time to redirect the course of business. The subsidiaries often signal to the larger organizations that there are other ways to do business in the world, but not always. Others may be too ingrained in the current practices and are starting to make inquiries but have yet to commit. We are focused on helping the ones that are ready, and planting seeds with others that are starting to realize there is another way.

As a result of this increasing interest, we announced the launch of the B Lab UK, the creation of a multinational and public markets advisory council. We are bringing together folks from multinational organizations, as well as from the capital public markets, and having them work together over the next 18 to 24 months to figure out if and how we can make the standards for certification—both performance standards and the legal standards—relevant, meaningful, and usable for companies of that massive size and scope. We know it's relevant for their subsidiaries and for their supplies, which are typically small to mid-size businesses. What we are now exploring is how the certification process can be both meaningful and manageable for a company that is larger in revenue than many countries, with hundreds of thousands of employees across dozens of countries.

Got purpose?

We know that this is a whole new area for us and we want to explore to find out what are the appropriate standards and processes for certifications of companies of that size, either to measure their impact or to do it in a way that is remotely manageable. We are at the beginning of what will be a couple year process to discern that, which is exciting, and it's coming from the growing interest of these companies themselves. Many have shared with us that they are seeing a lot of amazing stuff going on in the B Corp movement, and the small to mid-size B Corp companies are increasingly inspiring them.

There is a shift going on where an increasing number of large organizations are realizing that to attract the best talent, purpose is important both at the individual and organizational levels. They can no longer rely on a bunch of empty words that hang on the wall as a mission statement. In today's world of radical transparency, you need to back those words up with verified transparent performance. That's why they are increasingly looking to the B Corp movement as a standard for how they measure their impact, how they set up the right governing structure to manage their impact in the long term, and how they communicate their impact to current and future workers, investors, partners, and, of course, customers.

The reaction we are getting is interesting, because these large organizations are calling us. In general, B Lab isn't set up to chase elephants. We don't spend a lot of our time trying to persuade large corporations to be interested in the B Corp movement. We are focused on shining a light on our leaders and creating easy and enjoyable paths for others to join. Larger companies are calling us and saying, "Hey, that is the path I want to be on and that's the company I want to be associated with."

With purpose comes play

I'm lucky enough to have found myself in a situation where my work is my play, and my work is where I am able to make a contribution. The desire is increasingly common—or maybe no more common now than it was in our generation or the generation prior, but it's now more acceptable culturally—to voice what you would like to create in the world as opposed to repressing it. I'm not 100% sure that all the data on how Millennials are different than Generation X or Boomers is even relevant in today's world. It may be our language or comfort zone that tries to separates us into these boxes. What I am seeing is this energy surfacing to the top that gives all people permission to demand more of the companies they work for and the companies they buy from or invest in.

Work is becoming increasingly and inextricably linked to meeting fulfillment and impact. Without it, it is work in the old school language of the mechanical application of force to move an object from A to B. More people are moving increasingly past that old school industrial definition of work to a definition that couples it with meaning.

We offer rigorous standards and we are looking to raise the bar for ourselves. The path that the B Corps blaze is the path more people want to travel. Certification is a way to talk about what we are doing. It's like fair trade, but for the whole business instead of one product, like a bag of coffee. There is an easy translation from the certification items to a deeper understanding of what is possible for business to aspire to in the world.

People can also think about B Corps as a community of practice, where there are now over 1,500 businesses around the world that are united in having met rigorous standards of accountability and transparency for performance, with a culture of continuous improvement. The leaders of these organizations want to help each other in not only growing their business and their bottom line, but also by growing their positive impact for the planet. Being a part of that community of practice is increasingly important, because social change is a team sport and we go further together than we do alone. And in general, people like spending time with other people who share their purpose.

When you think about the extension of the community—the individual enterprises—the community of certified B Corps become a much broader movement of people seeing business as a force for good. As a result, they are accelerating a culture shift. There are already

35,000 businesses around the world that are using the B Impact Assessment as a free management tool to help them measure and improve on their social and environmental performance. It only exists because there is a coherent set of standards that leaders are all subscribing to in order to measure what matters most: the ability of a business to not only generate returns, but also to create value for its customers, employees, community, and the environment. And we know it is imperfect and we are constantly learning. Leaders across all of these industries and geographies are saying the world needs a good standard more than it needs a perfect standard, and we will all work to improve it over time.

Whether you are the CEO of a small consulting business or the CEO of a Fortune 50 conglomerate, everybody is a small player on the global stage and in a global economy. The power we have is to collaborate with and influence others. The B Corp community is a useful certification that acts as a market signaling device for your individual enterprise, and also a powerful community of practice to help individual businesses do more together.

Today, our community is a powerful market influencer that appeals to people who want to leave a mark in the world, and who recognize that the real mark is about the culture shift and the system change that they are able to be a part of and accelerate. It's about this system change from a generation of shareholder capitalism to a generation—or hopefully generations—of stakeholder engagement, where the objective is no longer maximizing shareholder value, but about maximizing shared value and creating a shared and lasting prosperity for all of us, and you can't do that alone. That is a reason why people are becoming more and more attracted to being a part of something bigger than themselves, and the B Corp movement is one example of a place people can go, not only to be a part of a community, but also to have that community intentionally trying to create levered change.

The B Corp movement is about a performance standard, the legal pieces that companies need to change in their legal DNA so that they are now legally accountable to consider the impact of their decisions on all of society, not just their shareholders. The transparency requirement is often one of the most difficult for people to meet, particularly for larger organizations, because the bigger you are, typically the more fearful you are about sharing information.

On the performance side, companies have to achieve a minimum verified score of 80 out of 200 available points on the B Impact Assessment, which is broken up into different areas. We ask questions about a company's impact on its workers, its impact on the community in which it does business, and its impact on the environment. Around worker issues, there are questions about compensation, benefits, culture, and ownership of the collaborative workplace. On the community side is where there are things like diversity and inclusion, as well as supply chain. This would include whether your supply chains are local, having tighter local supply chains from an environmental perspective, and a local multiplier effect from an economic development standpoint. And if you are in a business where you have to have broader supply chains, we ask whether they are fair trade supply chains and whether there are workplace coded conducts in their factories.

There would also be typical charitable giving, volunteerism, and other forms of civic engagement that would come under community. The diversity inclusion metrics would not only be about the board, management, and workforce, but also about the suppliers and the banks companies work with. It's a holistic lens. On the environmental side, there are inputs—energy, water, waste, toxins, and materials—and then there are the outputs—waste, water, and carbon. It is all measured to assess whether companies are using more renewables or more locals on-site, or whether they have more closed systems. Organizations would earn more points on the environmental side whether they are doing that for their facilities or for their fleet and distribution, and managing it all the way through their value chain.

These are examples of the questions that we ask, and we do it in a way that isn't strictly prescriptive. We don't say that you must be carbon neutral, or you have to hire returning citizens, or you must pay a living wage. Those companies that do these things earn more points and then are hopefully creating a positive market feedback loop, where we are not only measuring profit but we are measuring impact. Those with the highest impact get recognized and rewarded with customers who turn into evangelists, investors who stick with them for the long term, and employees who are incredibly loyal and productive and will go the extra yard because they believe in why they are coming to work every day. They are bringing their whole selves to work every day, and not just collecting a paycheck.

At B Lab, we do what many organizations do; there is a planning process and we try to make it as inclusive as possible, and yet decisions have to be made. We recognize that knowledge management and knowledge sharing is crucial to the organization's effectiveness. New tools are being developed, rolled out, and discarded all the time. We are still a relatively small organization with about 50 people within the US, and even when you include the folks outside of the US who are working on this full-time, maybe it's 120. In the big scheme of things, it is still a relatively small organization, even if it's incredibly distributed globally.

More importantly, there are 1,500 B Corp organizations with more than 50,000 to 60,000 people who work there. The question is: How do we communicate with that wider family? That's something that wouldn't have been possible—if at all—without the technological innovations of the Internet and all the other things that come with it.

Twists and turns on the path

There are very pedestrian challenges we face, like core business model challenges. We are still less than 40 percent supported by our budget for what B Lab does. We are still supported significantly by philanthropy, and that's a hard game to play. There are a bunch of things that make it more difficult when we are not out there serving the poor directly. So for typical philanthropy, we are a bit of a harder sell.

There's the core pedestrian organizational challenges, and those extend from funding to our own management capabilities, our ability to develop a talented team, and to rate them and support them across the globe. We are not a central organization with one home; we have five offices across the US and global partners in 27 countries. There are pure operational challenges of scaling an organization and an affiliated group of organizations that are supporting an even more distributed network of companies, and these can be complicated management challenges.

One of the challenges is asking ourselves: What does success look like? Figuring out what that is, and then building an organization, the programs, and the platforms to support that vision—not necessarily a vision of all companies becoming B Corps, but all companies managing and measuring their impact with as much rigor as they measure their profit. That is the actual cultural shift that we're after, and B Corps can be signaling devices, a lighthouse brand, or a drum major for that shift.

But the real change is not going to be when B Corps go from 1,500 to 5,000, when there are 7 million businesses in the US alone and somewhere between 25 and 100 million businesses in the world. The opportunity is figuring out how we categorize, accelerate, and support a much broader movement that can scale with integrity, as opposed to just having the words enter the popular culture. That linguistic shift may be necessary, but it certainly is woefully insufficient to actually think that we have made any change just because there is 92 percent brand recognition for the term "B Corp." This is not what I hope would go on my tombstone. Those are some of the challenges we face in growing this new path for business.

The vision of the B Corp community is for society to enjoy a more shared and global prosperity for all, and we are all working towards that collective dream. That is my life's purpose, and it's also fun. It puts me in touch with a bunch of amazing people who make my life more interesting and enjoyable. When I check out, I hope I feel that I had a life well lived with service and gratitude.

Magatte Wade

Magatte Wade was born in Senegal, educated in France, and started her entrepreneurial career in the US. Her first company, Adina World Beverages, based on indigenous Senegalese beverage recipes, became one of the most widely distributed US brands started by an African entrepreneur. Her second company, Tiossan, makes skincare products based on traditional Senegalese products. Part of the purpose of the company is to save aspects of local culture that are quickly disappearing.

I love Magatte's spirit and tenacity. We met on a panel where we both spoke at an entrepreneur conference at MIT, where she spoke her mind and held her ground about what is possible in the world. Let's join her on her journey and connect to her purpose.

The Journey of Magatte Wade: Entrepreneur. Creator. Networker. CEO and Founder, Tiossan.

What is your story?

I don't have one story. I have multiple stories. One constant story about me is that I am someone who always cared about where I came from. I come from many different places, but the one place I feel needs the most attention is Africa, and I care deeply about it. And beyond Africa, what I care about is social justice. I have always had a very strong sense of social justice, and it never settled well with me that some people are haves and some people are have-nots. But I don't think the solution is to take from those who have and transfer it those who don't. It is about opportunities.

The old story doesn't work today. It's not that Ayelet has more money and if we give some of it to Magatte because she has less, we would fix everything. The more important question to ask is: How did Ayelet get to what she has? And for us to see how Magatte can have access to similar opportunities. Ayelet, for example, may have very strong self-confidence, and self-confidence helps. So how can we help Magatte build hers? How do we share access to opportunities to help people become whole through a multitude of ways? It's not just always about money. In the 21st century, I am here to help people expand their thinking into providing opportunities, from education to networks to trusted relationships.

My journey is about someone who not only cares profoundly about social justice, but who also understands that the best way to take care of social justice is to make sure people have opportunities wherever they are, and are able to choose which ones they want to go for. Not everyone wants a big house and two cars. We should not choose the outcome for other people. Too often, when I take from Ayelet to give to Magatte, I am trying to choose the outcome. It is patronizing in that approach, and when you patronize you don't really care about the person. In this century, we need to make it personal, to see people without labels and care deeply about each one. We need to stop just caring about what makes us feel good regardless of the other person.

We have a lot of fear in the world today, with people living in a scarcity and competition mindset. They are scared of losing their place in the world and choose not to speak out. I see that, for example, with professors who don't speak out because they don't want to be seen as outcasts. It may be easier to follow, but it is having a big toll on our society as a whole. We need leaders at every level of society.

Everyone is clinging on to their tribe or social club because we want to belong. It's in our very nature. And that's ok, but maybe we should be working on creating healthier tribes. To give people the choice of belonging to their tribe, but to move away from fear and make it more of a healthy community of give and take. We are not creating enough of these communities. Why? Because it is a Goliath that all of us Davids are going up against. I look at myself in my own industry; the Goliath is so big and pervasive. They are using every tool in the world to maintain the status quo, because those are the principles that they were built on. If the status quo changes, it may be too much work for them. But a lot of these organizations that are trying to hang on through force will end up disappearing if they don't change.

Tiossan is a social enterprise that is trying to accomplish very wide but integrated goals: to preserve local Senegalese culture, create a large market, and build a sustainable local economy. A few years ago, I met with an entrepreneur in the San Francisco Bay Area who had made his millions and wanted to "make a difference." When I explained how my company, Tiossan, would create jobs and finance schools in Senegal, while also creating dignity and respect by creating the first high-end African consumer brand, he looked at me as if I was an alien. "Don't we need to be digging wells and creating schools for poor children?" he asked. For him, "helping Africa" could only mean providing charity for the poor, pathetic African children he had seen in hundreds of NGO marketing campaigns. The very notion of combining "high-end" and "Africa" was inconceivable to him.

I have spoken at dozens of conferences on college campuses and other venues around the world. Whenever I speak about the dignity and respect Africans deserve to African audiences in the United States or abroad, I receive standing ovations. It's because they too feel the pain and disrespect of these stereotypes that hurt Africa's future. Conversely, when I say the same thing to Euro-American audiences, I get blank stares asking me: What about the wells? Imagine for a moment what it is like for an African. Non-Africans often see only three things when thinking of Africa: comfortably wealthy white people; needy Africans; and the "caring" white person in the midst of a group of needy black faces.

And for Tiossan, which is dear to my heart and life, I have made the ultimate sacrifice: no kids, and recently no time with friends. But real friends understand, and it doesn't matter where we leave off; we can pick it right back up. Those who don't understand who I am don't understand this part of my life. This work is what I care about. Some people say that entrepreneurialism is the greatest personal growth process. I always used to laugh when I heard it, but it has started to make sense to me. I can honestly say that I am totally living it. It doesn't matter that I had created a successful company before; it's always hard to take a new path forward.

Tiossan has been a very interesting journey, as it has always been a reflection of my own personal journey. That's why this company is not like anything else I have ever created before; because in a way, it's me giving a version of myself to the rest of the world. And then it changes with my own understanding and beliefs; it had to flow with me to forge its identity. I will write about it one day in my own book.

I am a pioneer, and it's not easy. I feel that the world has been defining and deciding who we are as Africans, and especially African women. Our society likes to stereotype us into groups. Stereotypes exist for about every group in society and overgeneralizes predefined beliefs about a group of people. What has happened is our identity as Africans became broad stereotypes—from the colors to the sounds and the words we use, to the way we are supposed to look and feel. Every part of my identity has been so overdone with stereotypes that do not apply to me. I try to showcase my identity and tell people that this does not reflect who I am as an African woman. But the stereotypes we have in place are screaming so loud that people often can't see beyond them. When you try to reclaim your own identity, you have people flat out telling you that's not what being African is about.

Everyone needs a baseline. If you say you are African and you don't have a frame of reference people can relate to, they get completely lost. What people do is look at this new offering you are giving them and try to see what else they know that it looks like. They want to label and box everything into what is familiar to them.

I learned all this about people, and what I decided to do was to blaze my own trail. The only way I can get to where I need to go is by staying my course. I started with one idea for the packaging for Tiossan, and over the years, the packaging has changed as I distilled it down to how I want us to show up in the world, dispelling the stereotypes and offering a new bold look for the African woman and any person in the world who resonates with it. I knew what my identity was, but the journey was around how to manifest it in a product line. That has not been easy. It has been interesting to have a vision and build a company around it.

In today's business world, everything is done deliberately. There is not a lot left to the imagination in terms of being authentic and spontaneous. Everyone wants you to be able to follow a rigid plan, and that's not who I am. I am building out my vision for the people who will meet me halfway in the journey. To stay true to myself, I speak my mind and stand my ground firmly, even if it means great sacrifices. There are countless opportunities to take shortcuts, but I would destroy my mission in life if I took those shortcuts.

I am in a place of clarity now, of finding my own voice and identity for Tiossan. I am branching out to meet the real needs of people in the world who are increasingly focused on self-care as a practice. We have a new line coming out, for example, which is going to be a sleep line, and it's a result of many conversations I've had with women who tell me they are not sleeping. I have come naturally to understanding that what I want to share and create in the world is a strong sense of wellbeing. We are not a beauty brand, as people have wanted to stereotype us.

Tiossan is a wellbeing brand as modeled by the African people, and especially the Senegalese people. In our country and culture, wellbeing is about having great skin. It's the skin you live in, and at the most physical level, it needs to be healthy. It's about feeling good in your own skin.

What I am really excited about is how everything about Tiossan has become so natural for me. We are on the road to making sure women are aware of how to take care of their skin and how important it is to our overall wellbeing. Apparently many women in the United States spend a large percentage of their time, money, and energy on their face and hair. But a lot of women seem not to know that the skin is the largest organ of their body. And what many people are even less aware of is that whatever product you apply on your skin goes inside your body as well. What this means for us is that you have to be able to eat what you apply on your skin. You need to know what ingredients and chemicals you are ingesting.

Our path is to help educate women, opening their eyes and showing them loving ways to take care of themselves. Just like the organic food movement opened the eyes of so many people about the chemicals they were ingesting, we are providing people with products that contribute to their overall wellbeing.

For me as an entrepreneur, the goal has always been to provide a quality and identity I believe in. It's a labor of love. Identity for me is at two levels: the first is physically what it looks like, and the second is on a spiritual level of asking what we stand for in the world. The past year has been a bridge year between testing it in the market and introducing a new line to that market.

Being community

Our ability to tap into our communities is key to our success. While there is a lot of noise with social media, what works is to partner with the people who support and believe in me and what Tiossan brings to their lives. Word of mouth is key, because it is about connecting us through trust. Most people have a strong need to connect.

Through my speaking career, I get to play a role in so many people's lives. I receive so many emails and letters from people every day telling me how I changed their lives. It keeps me going. Just today I had a woman send me a private message on Facebook asking how she could meet with me. I saw that she was somewhere in Senegal, so I told her that the next time I am there, I will let her know. She was insistent that she needed to meet me, because her life and her two children depended on it. I don't take this lightly. There are people out there everywhere who need someone to listen to them and see them.

It's not only women in the developing world who are starting to ask for connection; it is women everywhere. People everywhere are craving to be themselves. I am collaborating with people who are focused on unleashing the human spirit. I am using Tiossan as a catalyst to create experiences where people can have deep conversations and experience what touches their hearts and souls.

People want to be part of something, whether it's giving $5 or $100 to a crowdsourcing campaign or sharing the campaign with other people and encouraging them to participate. It's one thing to say we stand with someone and it's another thing to show it. Through crowdfunding, people can practice what they preach. You might not have the money to support it now, but you can forward the campaign to people in your community who can provide financial backing. People have a need for their hearts to join with their hands.

Stepping up to our role in society

There is a battle of civilization happening as more people wake up to our need to transform. We are witnessing the breakdown of many systems, and yet we are also more connected than ever. Through my travels, I continue to talk to people from all over the world, and listen to what is on their minds and in their hearts. We are at a crossroads right now and have an opportunity to write new stories to regain our humanity. We can no longer wait. It is going to take a few outliers with the ruthless courage to go out there and say, "I'll do it even if my life is on the line." Even if only a few of us succeed, we will break through. There are millions of people standing behind us waiting for the doors to open. You may not know they are there, but they are silently watching and waiting. The reason I know this is because sometimes I get into serious arguments out there in the public domain, and then afterwards there are so many people who email me, telling me they are rooting for me behind the scenes. Many are honest and say they don't have the courage to speak out. What excites me is that I feel the minute the door is open even a crack, there are people waiting to step in. It's a cycle, and eventually that is how the tides will turn.

It is a messy, messy world. And yet, there is a lot of hope. That's what keeps me going. The poor are not always poor because they choose it. Micro-financing is better than doing nothing, but many people don't have a good understanding of the holistic system. Any society that has made it from poverty to prosperity had to rely on small and medium enterprises to get there. They are the ones who create the jobs. In a new economy, there will be new types of job. But at the end of the day, people need to find ways to make money so they can provide for themselves and their basic needs. A lot of us in the West have created what I call a "thatchwork ceiling" instead of a glass ceiling. We're excited to be buying from co-ops in the developing world, but no one is pushing it further. We've got to move things vertically—where vertical markets connect businesses around their specific needs—so that people can learn better skills that have more value.

What is the world excited about when it comes to Africa? On the one hand, we are excited about microfinance and we are pouring trillions of dollars into it. To do what in the end? People are staying below the poverty line. It really hasn't done much. There is data that supports this. When you talk to the microfinance recipients in surveys, more than 85 percent say they'd rather have decent jobs if given the choice. On the one hand, you have micro-financing mobilizing so much money and energy, and on the other hand you have multinationals who have access to the bond markets and private equity funds. And we know that neither actually create jobs. In the middle, there is nothing, and there are not many job creation programs.

What if we created jobs for all these people who get microfinance and gave them stability and an opportunity for a good life? The 2014 movie *Poverty Inc.* shows that the poor are often poor because of how these regions are regulated. People in poverty need their own incomes, which come from employment. We need to create better ecosystems for job creators.

My own village is a mecca for artisan shoemakers. Right now, it's giving hundreds of people a livelihood, selling to the local community. It feeds those who work there. Imagine that that person's worst-case scenario happening: All of a sudden a TOMS Shoes truck shows up with a bunch of free shoes. It puts local artisans out of business—and every other TOMS copycat has the potential to do the same thing. Basically, they're creating companies that give jobs to people in the developed world, while we dump all of this crap in the developing world, effectively ruining their economies that they need so badly at the end of the day.

As *Poverty, Inc.* addresses, the primary reason Africa is poor is not because Africans don't have enough stuff, nor is it because Africa hasn't received enough aid or charity. As I share in interviews and my blog, the main reason many Africans are poor is because they lack the institutions of justice that would enable them to create prosperity for themselves.[56] Celebrities can't help by reaffirming ignorant stereotypes of Africa as a barren, dependable, hopeless continent. In Bob Geldof's case, he could've made a stronger positive impact by focusing on singing about property rights, rule of law, justice in courts, and entrepreneurship—making those concepts sexy and popular to those who wouldn't care otherwise. I suggest everyone watch *Poverty, Inc.* to get an accurate glimpse of how the common idea of helping Africa can actually hurt the African people.

Finding our voice

I am excited about what's coming next for Tiossan. From a business perspective, we are soon moving our production to Africa. We are

[56] https://medium.com/@magattew/stop-raising-money-for-relief-and-start-investing-in-africa-bd5c44a75557#.r0umh8ul3

spending a lot of time building our community. I can't preach unless I practice. The practice is very important to me. You will never see me out there talking about anything unless I am doing it myself. It keeps me grounded and connected to the people I want to help. When I have a woman talking to me about a health issue she is facing, I can help by relating to her one-on-one in conversation. We have been conditioned to believe that someone else has all the answers for us, and we want to hear others share their fairytale stories of princesses and princes. Through more genuine conversations, we get to share our own stories and listen to those of others.

It is so liberating to feel that you have finally found your voice. Integrating my voice into a product can sometimes become messy. It has been one of the hardest external exercises for me so far. I never appreciated how tough it is when you simply want it to be an extension of your authenticity. And then you realize that the best teacher is life. How we have been conditioned does not translate in the new way of being connected to the products we co-create. We have to shed notions that do not serve us and make room for our voices to emerge, and learn to be gentle with ourselves in the process.

Michael Strong

Michael Strong loves learning, thinking, and exploring the world of ideas. He is also passionate about developing and promoting entrepreneurial solutions to global problems. After beginning college at Harvard as an undergraduate, he decided to leave for St. John's College in Santa Fe, where he felt he could talk more openly about ideas that mattered to him. While working on his dissertation at the University of Chicago, he began leading Socratic discussions in Chicago Public Schools, and loved it. So he went to Alaska to train teachers to lead Socratic discussion and spent the next 10 years creating schools where students got to think and talk about ideas in Alaska, Texas, Florida, California, and New Mexico. Michael then met John Mackey, CEO of Whole Foods, and they co-created a non-profit, Freedom Lights Our World (FLOW), to promote entrepreneurial solutions and opportunities.

The Journey of Michael Strong: Visionary. Entrepreneur. Pioneer. Founder of FLOW / Cofounder, KoSchool and Incubator.

What is your story?

I am both an entrepreneurial intellectual and an intellectual entrepreneur. Everything that I do is driven by the world of ideas, and yet most of my time is spent on creating real world enterprises rather than simply talking about ideas.

My parents are undereducated working class people. I had the good fortune of being raised on a farm with poor television reception, so I became a voracious reader over the long Minnesota winters. I was always attracted to doing the right thing, and by the time I had entered college I had developed a deep interest in understanding what it meant to "do the right thing" socially and politically. I initially focused on exploring and discovering the best political and economic system. It appeared to me as if capitalism, based on selfishness, was simply bad.

But then I went to the University of Chicago for graduate school to discover why the Chicago economists—who pretended to be scientists—could also be in favor of capitalism, which was clearly bad in my books. I then discovered that I had been ignorant of economics. My time in Chicago convinced me beyond a doubt that capitalism brings mass prosperity, and is therefore morally valuable. But I persisted in exploring how to integrate more of a moral sensibility into capitalism. My dissertation was on *Ideas and Culture as Human Capital* under Nobel Laureate Gary Becker, and I used it as a way to explore how ideas of the good, along with morally-motivated cultures, could inform capitalism.

While working on my dissertation, I began training Chicago Public School teachers to lead Socratic seminars in their classrooms, where we teach students to think for themselves. This led to a full-time job with the Alaska Paideia Project training teachers to lead Socratic seminars. After several years, we ran out of funding for the project. Some parents who had loved our work offered to finance my colleagues and I to create a private school based on our work if we could put together a business plan. At that point, although I had studied economics and I had done sales jobs in the summers, I had never actually started an enterprise. But I put together the initial business plan and they financed the school.

This first case of "accidental entrepreneurship" led me to a 10-year career as an educational entrepreneur creating small private and charter schools. I developed a distinctive niche as a creator of intellectually advanced alternative secondary schools. I created Montessori middle schools for a multi-campus Montessori organization based in Palo Alto; a secondary school for highly gifted students in south Florida; and a Paideia charter high school in northern New Mexico that was ranked the 36th best public high school in the US in its third year of operation.

While I was still in New Mexico I met John Mackey, CEO of Whole Foods Market, through a mutual friend. John and I quickly discovered that we shared a passion for entrepreneurial solutions to world problems. He had created Whole Foods, which had transformed America's eating habits in many ways, and I had created a series of small schools, each of which integrated a warm, healthy, creative environment with high-performance academics. Within a year of meeting John, the New Mexico State Department of Education forced me out of my position, despite the fact that my school was the top-ranked school in the state, because I did not have the required administrator's license (this was a new requirement that had not been in place when I had moved there to start the school). I arranged with John to launch Freedom Lights Our World (FLOW), a non-profit to promote entrepreneurial solutions to world problems.

For the next 10 years I had the good fortune to meet hundreds of brilliant entrepreneurs globally who were making a positive impact on the world. We spun off several programs, including Peace through Commerce, Accelerating Women Entrepreneurs, Conscious Capitalism, and Radical Social Entrepreneurs. I also helped to launch the Startup Cities Institute, an initiative designed to create new, entrepreneurial jurisdictions around the world in order to accelerate the reduction in global poverty that has been taking place. Through Accelerating Women Entrepreneurs, a program to promote developing world women entrepreneurs, I had the good fortune to meet my wife, Magatte Wade, an amazing entrepreneur from Senegal.

More recently, I've moved back to Austin, where Khotso Khabele, an educational entrepreneur, and I have founded KoSchool, an entrepreneurial incubator for teens integrated with a Socratic college prep academic program. We are dedicated to developing conscious entrepreneurs through personal development, authentic leadership, and auto didacticism.

There have always been people more inclined to care about others, and there have always been those who are less inclined to care about others. The task facing those of us who care is to develop and support institutional structures that are more likely to support "the better angels of our nature."

Opportunities for profit or power can attract the psychopaths among us. In the smaller communities of the past, reputational effects limited the damage that could be done, as anyone who harmed others quickly developed a bad reputation. As society became large and anonymous, those who did harm were able to get away with those harms over longer periods of time.

One of the immense benefits of the Internet is that we are developing scalable reputation systems. It is now easier than ever to discover the reputations of companies—there are even apps that allow one to learn about the ethics of products on store shelves while shopping. Conversely, bad corporate behaviors quickly go viral. The reputation systems that held people to standards of good behavior in small towns are now being revived in the global marketplace.

Relatedly, there is an immense increase in "conscious consumers." There are estimates that one third of American consumers include ethical criteria in their shopping decisions at least occasionally. We should expect that as more people move up Maslow's hierarchy from basic survival to psychological and self-fulfillment needs, more of them will include ethical criteria in their consumption decisions. Combined with online reputation systems, the power of conscious consumers is immense.

Many entrepreneurs begin with a personal sense of mission. One of our challenges in building out the full "Conscious Capitalist" ecosystem is to help them sustain that sense of mission as they grow. In the past, the process of growth has often meant submitting to financiers who put pressure on entrepreneurs to grow their companies at all costs. A key element in the next stage of Conscious Capitalism will consist of a growing ecosystem of conscious investing (including impact investing). The combination of online reputation systems, conscious consumers, idealist entrepreneurs, and ethically aligned investors will allow for ongoing growth and sophistication in the realm of Conscious Capitalism.

Putting imagination into real practice

I have two primary projects: 1) Transforming K-12 education and 2) Creating global prosperity. These are both immense goals, but most of my smaller projects fit within these.

On a concrete level, the KoSchool is designed to be both a replicable model of innovative K-12 education and an incubator for innovative ed tech (education technology) companies. KoSchool allows us to develop and refine state-of-the-art human technologies to create a healthy, positive teen culture focused on a purpose-driven life. We are actively working with other schools and school creators to deploy these human innovations within their systems. At the same time, KoSchool is working with various software developers to develop ed tech innovations that can contribute to large-scale educational change quickly. Finally, I'm also writing and speaking on crucial educational changes including school choice, unschooling, virtual schooling, and improving meritocratic opportunity by means of reducing occupational licensing.

With respect to creating global prosperity, my wife, Magatte, and I are both writing and speaking on the bureaucratic obstacles to entrepreneurship in developing nations. Most people are unaware that poor nations are drowning in red tape—and that that is one of the main reasons why they remain poor. I'm also involved in some innovative projects like Startup Cities to create new zones in developing nations with higher quality law and governance to accelerate prosperity.

Co-creating the path forward with purpose

Everything I do involves partners. As a consequence of my 10 years of leading FLOW, I have one of the best networks of conscious entrepreneurs in the world. Much of my work involves match-making and coordinating interesting innovators from around the world.

An example is an entrepreneur in my network who runs a large call center in Guatemala. He has created a program to train some of his best call center employees to become software developers. These working class employees will have an opportunity to move up the value chain and earn more. He'll have reliable employees with a proven track record in his company. As it turns out, a key component of the training he provides is the Socratic dialogue that I've developed for classroom use. To help call center employees become effective software developers, they need to learn to become critical thinkers. Meanwhile, I'm working with the students at KoSchool to train other developing world peoples to develop their skills so that they, too, can move up the value chain, using in part the Guatemalan model. Some of these projects involve yet other partners I've met over the years.

Many of my projects involve many such intersections. It may sound as if I'm involved in a crazy number of projects, but in fact, much of the time my work consists of setting up systems of people involved in related projects and helping them get started on win-win initiatives.

My motto is: criticize by creation. Although service has a role to play, activism has a role to play, and traditional profit seeking business has a role to play, one of the most potent—yet underdeveloped—paths to improving the world is conscious entrepreneurship. It helps us build out a better world through entrepreneurial solutions to world problems.

Sarah McNally

As a theater major from the College of St. Benedict in Minnesota, Sarah emerged with a distinctive and authentic ability to connect with people. She joined forces with her father, David, and through their shared vision they have been connecting people to a sense of purpose for their work and their lives. As the mother of a five-year-old, she is often reminded that inspiration comes from many places and often close to home.

The Journey of Sarah McNally: Courageous. Curious. Purpose-Driven. President, TransForm Corporation.

What is your story?

My company is called TransForm, and that name is no accident. My dad had the name for the company for over 30 years, but he never really used it. When he and I joined forces in 2008, we decided to use that name. If someone would have told me in college that I would be working with my dad one day, I would have said, "No way." And now here we are, working together and teaching about personal branding. Often we use the word "brand" to mean a common purpose, and sometimes we just use the word "purpose." To me, purpose relates to what contribution I can make in the world, the ultimate *why* I am here.

Although I didn't realize it until years later, my journey around purpose really began when I was in college. While a junior in college I got pregnant; it was totally unplanned, and I had never thought I wanted to have kids. The short version of the story is that I chose to make an adoption plan for my daughter. That process was difficult, but also very life-changing in many ways. While initially I kept this story very private, I discovered over time that maybe I could make a difference in the lives of other young people if I shared my story. When I got comfortable from a grieving place where I felt like I could talk about it, I realized that I have a comfort level speaking in front of groups, and so I thought that maybe this is the way that I can give back and contribute. I started sharing my journey as a volunteer, with different adoption agencies and high school students.

I started to get clear about my purpose and it helped me teach people to find their own purpose. Because I have a comfort level in telling my story and a comfort level in being vulnerable, it allows other people to more easily open up and look at the life experiences that they've had, in combination with their gifts and talents, as a way to get clear about their purpose and what they have to contribute.

About eight years ago, I was working for a creative agency where I felt very devalued, and there was such a lack of clarity around the company's purpose. I learned from my dad that when someone has no purpose, there is a lack of engagement with life itself, and each day has little meaning apart from collecting a paycheck. On the other hand, when you have purpose and feel that what you contribute to the world is important, you feel inspired to learn and grow. I finally realized that I wanted to go out on my own. I had so much energy and so much to give, and I wanted to give it to someone or to an organization that would really be able to do something with it.

My mother had passed away five years prior, and after spending some time with my dad, I realized he was now at a point in his life where he really needed my support. He had built a successful consulting company on his own and as he was getting older, he realized that there was no one to take it over and run it. He was also at a crossroads of examining the long-term vision for his life. I had been working in an agency as a project manager, working on e-learning, business simulation games, and all sorts of web-based communication. I said to my dad, "You've got all this intellectual property that could be communicated in amazing ways. You're the visionary, and I'm the doer, so let's come together and make this happen."

Our work together is really meaningful. I feel my purpose through this work. The way I sum up my purpose is I help people define who they are and what they stand for. We have an epidemic of feelings of unworthiness in the world. When people feel worthy of having the life they want, it can really be a foundation for them. I get to be with people and help create an opportunity for them to connect to their worth, and that is hugely rewarding. I also get to work with my dad, which is really powerful and rewarding for me as well. He's my greatest teacher and mentor in many ways, and in hard times he's also my mirror. It's been transformative working with him. Again, it's no accident that TransForm is the name of our company.

We've been conditioned to be two separate people

What I experienced in 2008 before starting to work with my dad through TransForm was the feeling of separateness in life. There was business, and then there was how you function personally. That, to me, was representative of a breakdown in common sense. I felt like I had to show up at work as a different person than who I was in my personal life. The person I was between 5:00 p.m. and 7:30 a.m. the next morning felt like a different person from the one who showed up at work each day, and I thought, "This doesn't feel right to me. How can I be more authentic in the workplace?" I think the piece that's often missing is a sense of humanity.

When we work with our clients today, I feel like what we do is really just common sense: to feel engaged, to feel purposeful, and to be reminded of why you are doing what you do. We take people through an exercise where they get to articulate their skills, gifts, talents, and expertise, and 98% of the time, it is one of the most difficult things that they have done, just to sit with someone and talk about what they're good at. That, to me, is so fascinating.

Most people are so focused at work on executing their goals and objectives that they spend very little time reminding themselves of why they are doing what they're doing. And the "why" is more inspiring and motivating, because that's really our human essence—what inspires us. We can have that experience of inspiration at work; we don't have to wait until we clock out and get home to be inspired. That inspiration could be part of our experience all day long. How would such inspiration at work impact how we perform, how we engage with clients, how clients engage with us, and our ability to be more innovative?

People are starting to focus on their practice

One of the other key words that I would use for work is "practice." This shows up in conversations I have professionally as well as personally. I very much enjoy the idea of personal mastery, and letting go of what no longer works for me. In 2006, I began a really significant healing journey of letting go of things that no longer worked for me. I started to intentionally wake up early in the morning to meditate, write in my journal, and do various spiritual and healing practices.

There is resistance to the word "work," but the fact is that we're always working at something. Work involves discipline and practice, and that's where the idea of worthiness comes in for me. It's an internal dialogue saying, "This is what I want to experience in my life, and I'm worthy of having that experience. From a place of self-love, I'm going to adopt a new practice. I'm going to eliminate something out of my diet that no longer serves me. I'm going to wake up earlier in the morning to have time for myself. I'm going to be aware of certain behaviors that don't serve me. Now I'm going to put in place new practices that do serve me." There are little things that people can do that they may perceive to be work, but the irony is that they create so much harder work for themselves by not implementing these little things.

It is a daily experience. And it's not about perfection; it's about having the best experience that you can have, which may only be incrementally better, but those small changes add up. You still have bad days, of course, but you can start to have many more days where you think, "I can't believe how lucky I am to be alive on this planet."

Getting clear on our own "why"

At TransForm, we take people on a deep dive. One of the processes that we take people through is understanding their personal brand. It's a full-day experience, and at the end of that day they are able to articulate their unique signature, which encompasses the different roles they play in their life, their attributes, and the specific standards that they feel passionate about. They also create a purpose statement and a vision statement, as well as articulate their values and create their unique brand promise. Often, it's the first time an individual has looked at themselves or their company in such a reflective way. I think that it's so interesting how many people don't reflect. It's almost like there is a fear that if they start reflecting and dealing with their issues, they're not going to be able to come back from it. It's too scary. It's too dark.

We also provide a lot of opportunity for dialogue, tying everything back to what they are trying to accomplish and create. What we have observed is that development is often seen as separate from operational excellence, when in essence, it's all part of a unified brand. How can you deliver on promises if you don't have people ready to deliver on them? It's all connected.

When we do development, we tell clients that they have to answer the "why" of their company. If they're just going to put 100 leaders through a leadership workshop and they haven't answered the question of "why," then nothing meaningful is going to happen. But if they tie it back to their goals and ask themselves why it's important to develop their leaders and get them ready in the first place, then there is an absolute business correlation. When we are in that kind of experience with people where we bring them in as a team and they get to talk about their purpose in connection to how they operate as a team, and in connection to how they're going to execute a goal, then there is a holistic experience that happens for the individual and for the team.

We have built a high level of trust with our clients, which is very important because the development work we do can get pretty personal and requires vulnerability. For example, we're working with a large airline now with a cross-functional team in one of the airport hubs. It's made up of ticket agents all the way up to the senior leadership at that hub. Everyone is really enthusiastic about being on the team together and having these conversations. Our job is to keep connecting them back to their purpose, because as an operational group, they immediately focus on the tactical. But we are present with them to keep bringing them back to their purpose, to why they're doing what they're doing, and what they are looking to create, so that they keep that perspective and are able to prioritize.

For my dad and me, our work at TransForm is an opportunity to break down some of the old perceptions about brand, such as the perception of it being primarily a marketing function. But when you create a brand, it's not really separate from anything else in the company, and that's part of the reason my dad co-authored a book in 2003 called *Be Your Own Brand*. His contribution to that book was about purpose, vision, and values, and what drives people. He has been passionate about the idea of human potential for many, many years.

It's no accident that my dad and I are working together, and there are many different motivations for us to work together. What I have come to realize is that he has always been a teacher for me, but it's been seeing more of his shadow side through working together that's been the greatest teacher for me. Really looking at some of our family culture, our family stories, how we were raised, and having a different perspective of my dad has been transformative.

It's a father-daughter dynamic, and it's also a male-female dynamic. He can be "command and control" sometimes, but mostly our work is collaborative. When I'm in a place of fear, I can get into "command and control" mode as well, and when I feel more comfortable, then I'm collaborative. We each have different tools, and I think I tap into the more feminine side when I trust my intuition. We have very interesting conversations about that, because my dad trusts his intuition, too. We're constantly learning. As soon as you think you know something, you get the opportunity to realize that you really are just beginning to understand.

Exercises for Expedition 5

13 **Seeing Your Purpose**	We're wired to seek someone to look up to, as well as to be looked up to by others. Many people will tell you how you must live your life; they will quote different books, paraphrase professionals, and cite models and approaches. But who really has the answer for you? Ask yourself:
	Who do I listen to and who writes my story?
	Am I my job title?
	How do I introduce myself?
	What is my highest purpose?
	Is my purpose connected with that of my organization? Why or why not?

14 **Connecting Stories**	Thinking about each of the stories you just experienced, what do they mean for your own journey to conscious 21st century leadership?	
	Céline Schillinger	
	Jay Coen Gilbert	
	Magatte Wade	
	Michael Strong	
	Sarah McNally	

Expedition 6
A Mindset of Wholeness

People are starting to feel that the way we run organizations, and our lives, no longer works. We have fragmented ourselves into too many pieces and separated ourselves from the natural flow of life, individually and collectively. The stories we have been fed of the leaders of powerful multinational organizations winning the game of success and leading lives we could only dream of are beginning to crumble. Trust in leaders continues to be on the decline as our collective dream of success transforms.

We need to pick up the pieces and become whole again as individuals and as organizations. We seem to be in such a rush to conform to what is expected of us that we end up losing pieces of ourselves along the way.

As we grow up and get conditioned into society by the roles we play as adults, we forget how to play as we become more responsible. We forget to regularly make time to spend in nature, instead telling ourselves that is what vacations, retreats, and holidays are for. We forget that our bodies simply need to move as we condition ourselves to see exercise as a chore. Many of us in the Western world have to drive somewhere just to go for a walk. We forget how important it is to have time to think, and to think more deeply than we are used to. We forget that children need free time to play and not be rushed from activity to activity.

What if we had conscious leaders paired with a shared purpose? What would happen if we trusted each other and ourselves? Would we still have departments and functions inside the corporate walls fighting each other for budgets and headcount? Isn't it time to admit we have lost corporate sanity and become whole again?

Many of our institutions, systems, and ways of life are fragmented, broken, and endangering our future on Earth. An increasing number of people are reclaiming their voices, and more businesses are going to be impacted by customers, employees, and communities asking new questions about how business is done. Compassion, empathy, and human understanding will all play a more significant role in the 21st century, as whole people demand to be heard and seen.

Busting the Myth of Separation

Many of us have been told that we are two people: a professional self and a personal self, and that we need to follow the myth of balancing work and life. In the business world, we have fragmented ourselves even further into departments, employee resource groups, and internal and external stakeholders.

Letting go of restrictive systems and beliefs is a struggle, as people still feel the need to manage change and have control over the direction they are headed. But deep change, the sort that is needed today, is not easily controlled or managed. We cannot control or manage a huge wave when we are surfing on the ocean—we have to ride the wave and go with its flow. Some senior executives are realizing that the nature of command and control structures is changing, and recognizing that communities are becoming increasingly important. But most don't know how to build communities, and are too scared to let go of control.

As Bryan Welch shared with us, everything on his farm has a season and a purpose. There is a cycle of life and death that we are all part of. Death and regeneration are simply a fact of life, a fact to be embraced and not necessarily feared. In nature, we plant seeds, we water, we nurture, and finally we harvest. And then we plant again. If we don't flow with the rhythms of nature, then we are not going to be successful farmers, and we won't have food to eat. It is amazing, therefore, that we often falsely believe that big business is somehow exempt from the laws of nature, as if existing outside of the universe in its own protected sphere. But that is a delusional view; we are all a part of nature, and we cannot escape that fact.

During my time in corporate America, I was involved in so many annual strategic planning processes, and sometimes I was the one responsible for running them globally. As much as I could, I helped create spaces for conversations to happen to co-create strategies. But of course, most of these processes had very cookie cutter approaches, influenced by with the latest and so-called greatest best practices. There wasn't a lot of listening happening, because it all came down to the increased sales numbers that would guarantee quarter over quarter growth. The metric of success was the pure brute force of capturing market share. This type of unlimited growth is not in harmony with nature, and its disastrous consequences are catching up with us.

Becoming Whole in the Web of Life

For many people, taking a holistic approach is challenging because it forces us to examine long-held (and often unconscious) beliefs. For example, we are used to trying to find a single right answer and a short-term solution to address very complex problems. Becoming whole means that we seek opportunities that take into account perspectives, that show us a broader spectrum of the possibilities at our disposal.

21st century organizations adopt a holistic perspective that goes beyond their own organizational ecosystem, acknowledging that we are all connected to one another and to the planet. 21st century leaders care deeply at a local, regional, and global level, recognizing the deeper underlying unity. It's no longer ok to think that we can go into the Amazon rainforest, for example, and take its rich natural resources and assume that damaging this ecosystem will not eventually hurt each of us. In this century, being whole and connected means that if we damage any part of our life web, we end up harming every other part.

Those same people we label "consumers" are actually people who work somewhere and live in some community in the world. As more people start choosing themselves instead of waiting to be chosen, we will recognize we have more choices in who we do business with and who we work with. More than a decade ago, the organic food movement, for example, was a small voice in a big pond. As more people started caring more about the food they consumed, they began asking new questions and making different choices that have had a direct impact on how food businesses operate. Today, more and more food labels tell us whether our food was grown humanely and safely.

Transparency takes on a new form when technology helps connect our world, allowing us to see how connected we actually are. When I was at Cisco, I loved bringing people together from different parts of the world into conversations using video conferencing technology like TelePresence. We held a session with kids from Toronto, Nairobi, London, and Guatemala, with about 10-15 participants in each location, and we had them sitting around one virtual table. Once we got them engaged in conversation, they became a united group of young people sharing stories with each other. It was not about the technology itself, but what bringing people together can create.

A Holistic Mindset is Needed

Imagine if an organization was a large body, with each person representing an organ in this body. Our bodies have integrated working parts and systems; the organs that combine into systems like the digestive system or the immune system work in groups to serve the needs of the human body. There is no part of the human body that works in isolation; each part does its jobs with the support of all our organs. In a similar way, it's time to bring dignity and respect for each person's voice and bring us together in business, where organizations are seen as systems that follow the cycle of nature. With a shared purpose, people can come together, as each aspect of the business does its part with the support of all our integrated roles.

Ask yourself: What is my purpose? How much influence is coming from the outside and how much is coming from inside? What are the consequences of the choices I make in the world, as a person and as an organization? Where are the points of separation and what are the opportunities to become whole as an individual and a collective business?

Transformational Stories from the Frontiers of 21st Century Leaders

Vanessa Reid

Vanessa Reid is a pioneering leader who brings her unique brand of artistry to the field of social innovation. She was the Executive Director of Santropol Roulant, a vibrant Montreal non-profit founded by young people in which food is a catalyst for social change. Ever since, she has been immersed in creating cultures—personal, organizational, societal—that are alive and deeply aligned with all of life. This includes working with transitions, transformation, and the natural cycles of life—from the mess and excitement of creating new systems and initiatives to hospicing endings through the practice of conscious closure.

She is a co-founder of the Living Wholeness Institute, which works with emergent movements across the globe. The Institute works in places in which systems are in fundamental shift, and in collaboration with brave souls who are calling in new ways of living that sustain people and the planet. The Institute asks, "What does it mean to truly transform our systems—ourselves included—so that they are deeply sustainable, at all levels? How do we bring together our purpose with the way we live and work in the world, so that living is an art form in service to a greater whole?"

The Journey of Vanessa Reid: Social Innovator. Designer. Architect. Cofounder, The Living Wholeness Institute.

What is your story?

I grew up in Ottawa, the capital of Canada, on the border between French and English cultures and on the land and lakes of indigenous peoples. I keep finding myself on the edges of things, of big changes in the world, on the edges of old and new stories. I come from a family of artists and public servants. On one side we are painters, dancers, librarians, and writers and on the other, diplomats and institution-builders, and so there is something in me that seeks to combine these elements of structure and the more mysterious in service of the world that my generation is inheriting.

I am energized by the stories, courage, and actions of ordinary citizens who are creating the future now. I have been both witness to and a part of these stories, from my roots in Canada and, most recently, by working more globally and living in Greece and Israel-Palestine. I see the threads of a new narrative that is emerging from places where current systems are collapsing or deteriorating. These stories are filled with the precariousness of life, the unpredictability of responses, and the shaking of the old and new. It is not comfortable. And yet these stories are filled with the richness of human emotion, historical tensions, unspoken intergenerational traumas, incredible courage and creativity, and the dance of paradoxes that are hard—but not impossible—to reconcile.

Deep roots in a holistic view of community

When reflecting on what 21st century leadership means, I realize that I was given my first big experience of leadership at the dawn of the new century. I came into my adulthood trying out what a 21st century leader could be.

In 2001, I was invited to be the new executive director of Santropol Roulant, a vibrant Montreal-based not-for-profit organization founded and run by young people that was at a turning point in its young life. Santropol Roulant (which means "the rolling Santropol") uses food as a vehicle to break social and economic isolation between generations and to strengthen and nourish the local community.

Santropol Roulant was founded in 1995 at a really challenging and divisive time for Montreal and for young people in the city. It was the year of the Referendum where the province of Quebec was deciding whether it would stay in Canada or leave. There was high uncertainty about the future, big tensions between different political views, and the re-opening of old wounds between the French and the English populations. There was also very high youth unemployment, and it was a time of major downloading of health care services from the federal to the provincial government, and ultimately to the community. Two young waiters at Café Santropol, a local and very cool café, were concerned not only about the lack of employment for themselves and their peers, but about the pain between their francophone and anglophone friends. So they took the initiative to build rather than to divide, and, using their skills from the Café created a meals-on-wheels program that was run by young people.

At the time, it was quite radical. Meals-on-wheels was thought to be for church basements. But there was a need for a next generation to emerge. Santropol Roulant saw an opportunity to connect youth across these language divides, to build skills, and most importantly, to break the social isolation of older people living with a loss of independence in the community—not to mention the isolation *between* generations. Its mission in bringing people together across generations and cultures was a new take on an old model. Santropol Roulant's kitchen—and now its rooftop gardens, bike workshop, and bee collectives—have become the heartbeat of a vibrant community. Volunteers cook and deliver 100 meals a day. They are also innovating new models of sustainable urban and organizational life, and at the same time re-framing social services as a catalyst for social change and social innovation.

I was quite young when I became executive director, so finding and unfolding my leadership in a public way was a huge learning for me at so many levels. It was amazing to be part of building a collective story of what is possible when people come together around what they care about. Santropol Roulant is now just over 20 years old and it keeps evolving at its own pace. I love how the organization listens and learns and follows the cycles of seasons and of life.

Organizations can be oral storytellers. They can capture histories and keep people's stories alive—especially for those who have become invisible in society, like senior citizens who live alone in their homes. Every week, we had regular volunteer orientations and the coordinator would tell our story again and again. But the way the story was told reflected the unique perspective of the storyteller who was sharing it. And everyday there were stories told at the doorsteps of people receiving meals, so to see so many people of all ages and cultures be part of an evolving story and to know that each of our parts mattered was pretty amazing.

Organizations can also create a new story. We did a project called *Harvesting Histories* where we gathered the recipes and memories of our elder members through talking and cooking together. Another one was called *The Map of the World Project*, which was an art and storytelling project. Some of our elder members had been refugees who had no family members in Montreal, and they were able to connect with young volunteers who spoke the same mother tongues like Russian, Vietnamese, or Spanish. We saw and heard how the world was there in Montreal. We mapped their journeys as a beautiful canvas, and shared the material artifacts of their lives in a kind of gallery.

In French, the word for organization is "*organisme.*" The leadership we took together, as an *organisme*, was to become a collective storyteller and a collective entrepreneur. I think this is one of the biggest lessons I learned—how to stitch together the visible and invisible threads that make up a community, bringing forth the richness of the past and casting it forward into a new aspiration, a new future that we can create together with our own hands.

This was also a time, in the early 2000s, when the term "social innovation" was becoming kind of hip. There was a lot of attention on us, as people were trying to figure out why things were so alive at Santropol Roulant. For us, innovation was a process, not an outcome.

It came from humans interacting meaningfully with their environment and tapping into new, formerly unseen possibilities. Innovation is not just about products and what we make; it's about culture, how we talk to each other, how we relate, how we are in hard moments together, and how we work with our disturbances and hopes to create deeper relationships and understandings. That's the ground for innovation: it comes from the juice of our lives.

We can talk about innovation as things outside of ourselves, but true innovation comes from what is inside. We didn't split our professional selves and leave our personal selves at home. This is where organizations can get stuck; they are not telling the whole story and they are not living their wholeness. We hear fragments of the story—the parts that are palatable or that we think will get us funding.

For me, 21st century leadership is about the mess of life and the nuances of our stories, and making more of life out of this complexity. What can we learn from our deep feelings, our untold histories, our failures, our loves, our whole selves? What would happen if we could tell the whole story? This is a radical act of leadership, daring to share—and live—the messiness of our wholeness.

Convening the world on an olive farm

In 2007, I went for the first time to Axladitsa-Avatakia, a 24-acre olive farm in Greece stewarded by Maria Scordialos and Sarah Whiteley. I arrived there for a 10-day gathering of 50 people from 12 different countries. We were all part of a "trans-local" learning network called the Berkana Exchange, which was founded by Margaret Wheatley and Deborah Frieze. Like Santropol Roulant, Axladitsa was one of many places in the world pioneering ways of bringing together local, and often ancient, practices with contemporary issues of social change and sustainability. We were there to learn together.

When I arrived at Axladitsa and met my Berkana Exchange friends from India, Mexico, Zimbabwe, South Africa, Pakistan, the US, and beyond, I realized there was a bigger movement afoot—and I was part of it! Many of the people at this gathering were "Walk Outs"—people walking out of systems and relationships that no longer serve, and intentionally walking onwards into new relationships or forms that do.

Berkana co-founder Deborah Frieze had walked out of her career as a high-tech executive after being disillusioned by a business culture focused on short-term results and a parochial measure of growth—a world that cared more about compliance than community. She joined Margaret Wheatley, a renowned thinker and organizational consultant, along with a community of pioneering leaders who were walking out of successful traditional organizations that were failing to contribute to the common good. Walk Outs focused on building relationships and local connections which help us remember what our wealth and resources really are. This building of connections is what helps us build the foundation for a more resilient future.

Axladitsa was—and still is—a wild and untamed land and olive grove facing the Aegean Sea. Maria and Sarah, the land stewards, are also co-initiators of a global network of practitioners of participatory methodologies called The Art of Hosting. These practices were foundational to how we learned together as a really diverse network. When I think about 21st century leadership, there is something very important about the art of how we host gatherings where we are learning and unlearning, and co-creating new knowledge together.

Hosting as a practice of leadership is both really new and really old. There is something sacred in every culture about hospitality and hosting "the other." I learned this first in India when my friends told me to stop saying "thank you" for everything; they said the way they were hosting me was their duty and way of honouring the guest. In Sanskrit, there is a saying that "the guest is God." It's similar in Greece with their culture of "philoxenia"—befriending the stranger. To me, hosting gatherings with this kind of awareness is a kind of human poetry. It allows us to access the unseen, the inanimate, the mythic, and to tap deeper than what we know into what we call "the river under the river." I think 21st century leadership means convening with this quality of attention to learning and to the wisdom that already exists between us.

Axladitsa has become a place of learning, farming, retreat, sabbatical, local community, gathering, celebration, and intentional evolution. It is part of a larger story of people seeking profoundly different ways of living and working. The land itself is a participant and host to our living and learning, rich with wisdom, lessons, and creatures, as well as trees, plants, and weather systems, all of which participate fully in our learning ecology. We have convened many networks of learners, leaders, pioneers, seekers, and change agents who are asking powerful questions about their individual and our collective purpose and potential.

One way of reframing 21st century leadership is that we are not really leading—we are listening. By listening to each other, inviting in the land and its stories, and opening to the subtle intelligences in and around us, we can become more attuned to what is really needed and act from there.

The currency of relationships and learning

These different networks of people and places have been foundational to the work that I have been doing ever since. They have quite literally opened new worlds to me. In 2009, I met and fell in love with a man whom I met at Axladitsa, and I moved to Jerusalem soon after to be with him and start a new stage of life. I arrived in Jerusalem right after the 2008 financial crisis in the UK and on the cusp of the Arab Spring in 2010. Big changes were afoot.

In 2010, Maria, Sarah, and I founded the Living Wholeness Institute as a way to respond to what was emerging in the world around us. With the economic and political collapses in Greece, the UK, and across Europe and the Middle East at that time, we saw a need to bring people together in profoundly different ways and to co-create new forms of living and working that were resonant with the new scale of change occurring.

The olive farm became the home and "source place" of the Living Wholeness practice and patterns. It's where we would host gatherings of social change makers and pioneers working with emergent new structures and forms for a world that was starting to show its cracks more fully. We were also invited to bring our practices out into the world.

We work very much in the currencies of relationships and learning. When I talk about relationships as currency, I refer to two things. One is getting invited into work based on previous relationships where trust has already been built; in this sense, most of our work comes through word of mouth and existing relationships. In many cases we are working against the norm, and it takes people who are willing to experiment and who understand the value of what we bring.

The second is that we live in an open and connected world, where we don't need to restrict groups to 40 people or known experts in a field, but rather we can open source to build relationships among people who don't normally meet, to tap into diversity and build collective intelligence. These relationships, often with unlikely bedfellows, become the foundation of a new way forward, and they are a wealth and currency in themselves.

We create this currency of relationships and learning through participation: participatory leadership, participatory methodologies, and social technologies that allow people to bring in their voice and ideas in different ways and to access collective wisdom. When we are encountering the unknown, participation is a way of building trust and connection, working with what we know and discovering in our conversations what we couldn't have known on our own.

Unlikely partners are part of the journey to becoming whole

The Finance Innovation Lab–UK was a project we co-developed that is a great example of how these ideas all fit together. It was launched in 2008 in the wake of the largest financial crisis since the Great Depression. Three women in their early 30s from two very different organizations, the World Wildlife Fund (WWF) and the Institute of Chartered Accountants in England and Wales (ICAEW), came together to initiate a new project addressing the question: How can we create a financial system that sustains people and the planet?

They brought people together who were doing research and innovative policy work and they interviewed many experts on the financial system. They had an excellent analysis, but didn't quite know how to create the conditions for people to begin to experiment. They met Maria (Scordialos), who asked, "Why not open it to whomever feels called to build this new system?" Maria then invited a team of 8 of us, which we called The Collaborative, to partner with WWF and ICAEW to build the participatory practice ground for the Finance Innovation Lab to take root. That was when I got involved.

The ICAEW invited their stakeholders: accountants, financiers, and the business community. WWF invited theirs: environmental activists, civil society, and the responsible investment community. Our Collaborative brought together our design practice, participatory methodologies, our backgrounds in social innovation and developmental evaluation, our conceptual models, as well as our skills in working with emergence, uncertainty, and the unknown. We brought together people who don't normally meet to talk about things they cared deeply about. Each new Finance Lab gathering had great energy and showed us it was a conversation that wanted to continue.

The momentum built, and we hosted more assemblies and trainings, inviting participants to call out areas of innovation within the financial system that they believed could bring about small and large-scale change. They clustered around the ideas that inspired them, and then turned the best ones into projects, securing funding and resources. Some failed, some flew. The Natural Capital Coalition looks at businesses' impact on the environment, and works with stakeholders that include big accounting firms. Positive Money is a grass-roots initiative that campaigns for the power to create money to be used in the public interest in a democratic, transparent, and accountable way, rather than by the same banks that caused the financial crisis.

The Lab always took an experimental approach—trying new things and partnering with a range of people and unexpected bedfellows. Today, the Lab looks quite different; it has grown up and is now its own entity, independent from its founding organizations. It continues to work across the system with pioneers, advocates, and intrapreneurs. Entrepreneurs pioneer alternative business models, civil society leaders advocate financial reform, and intrapreneurs in mainstream finance repurpose their professions.

Systemic change as disruption and soul work

When I look back, I can see how this process generated both interest and tension among people within different institutions. Some questioned how a Finance Lab was part of the WWF's or ICAEW's mission, or they simply didn't agree with the world view of participation and experimentation. But for fundamental change to occur, there needs to be disturbance; innovation comes from the exploration of that discomfort. Disruption has become a kind of sexy word in social innovation, but it's real and it is not so easy to navigate.

The women who launched the Finance Innovation Lab were consistent in their focus: how to address a broken financial system that is deeply unsustainable and damaging to the earth and humanity. But they had to experience a lot of discomfort and even attacks from people and groups who were still invested in the system that was breaking down.

One of the most important parts of our work was supporting the core team and founders in discovering their leadership. As young women working with a new model that challenged the establishment of finance, they were taking big risks both personally and professionally. We realized how important it was for them to be truly empowered to run their project—to learn how to design, host, and make sense of the participatory assemblies and meetings, to be able to speak to power with their own power, and to stand together for what they believed in - even when "critical friends" were not supporting them.

This systemic change work is not business as ususal. It is really deep soul work and it changes you from the inside out. If the Lab team was going to host real systemic change in the financial system, they would be inviting people to shift their paradigms, perspectives, and behaviours. As leaders, they needed to know what that felt like first hand.

So we invited them to Axladitsa to learn with other change makers who were also pioneering new projects in their own countries, to connect to the deeper patterns of life from other cultures, and connect to the olive trees and the land. These gatherings at Axladitsa nurtured their courage and a sense of being connected to a much larger global movement in which people are willing to stand up for what they want to create in the world.

Digging deep into our roots and traditions

I recently met James George, a very distinguished 94-year-old man, who it turns out was mentored by my grandfather in his early years as a young diplomat. James George served as Canadian High Commissioner of Canada to Sri Lanka (Ceylon) and to India, and was Ambassador to Nepal, and to Iran and the Gulf States. When I asked him why he thought he ended up serving in these places, he told me that they are places that have living lineages and unbroken lines to their traditions. He learned to enter these cultures as a diplomat through their living traditions.

"What you're really relating to is what it is to be a human being," he told me over tea at his place in Toronto. He went on to say that underneath the clash of civilizations, there is a tremendous need everywhere to honour diversities and find common threads. There is a need to relate at a much deeper level of being, beyond economic interests, to understand deeply where a culture is coming from.

During the last century, we have had so many disturbed and broken lineages through wars, conflicts, and economic interests, perpetuated by fear and scarcity. I have been in the extraordinary position to be living in parts of the world as things cracked open – like in Greece. I remember the first time we brought people together in Athens, in 2010, when the economic crisis was just becoming visible. There was a kind of shame and shock everywhere. It was hard for people to talk. So we slowly began to offer three and four day trainings that we called The Art of Participatory Leadership to open up the conversation.

Why these gatherings? Because in crisis, people need to know they are not alone. *Krisis*, in Greek, actually means "to take a stand" and so seeing who else is out there and what they stand for is really important—but also to find together a resilience that lies underneath the crisis. Or, like what James George said about relating not only to the crisis but what it means to be human together in that crisis. Out of necessity, many Greeks were coming up with creative ideas and innovations like alternative currencies and community kitchens. They certainly weren't calling it social innovation—they were calling it survival. Our gatherings brought these people together to share their stories, learn together, collaborate, and also gain courage together to keep going.

In the spring of 2015, for the first time in the five years we have been working on the ground with citizens in Greece, I heard some Greeks saying that they were grateful for the collapse of their systems. Not in a lighthearted way—they were not saying, "This is all good." Rather, they were looking through the pain and despair of feeling the life they knew fall away and seeing something opening on the other side of that despair.

We heard participants speak with anger and shame of encountering bureaucrats not taking pride in being civil servants, but instead relying on old responses that have nothing to do with supporting those who are wanting to change things. We heard the potency of loss—loss of identity, material life, money, hope—and the necessity of re-inventing oneself. We heard gratitude for seeing new perspectives and worldviews that offer connection with each other and with a future that has a different blueprint than consumerism. We heard statements like this: If there had been no crisis, we would not have met this way, and we could not have known this quality of conversation was possible.

Greece and the Art of Participatory Leadership have taught me some important things about leadership in moments of crisis. Coming together to be in conversation about what matters most to us is a seriously political act—one that can often be a great risk to one's personal safety, or can open the risk of being excommunicated from one's "tribe." Listening in to what we don't yet know or see is an act of faith and also a skill, and this quality of listening is the most important skill to cultivate in oneself individually and collectively. Witnessing each other in the honesty of our expression—whatever that expression may be—can be profoundly healing. And navigating chaos together by doing these simple yet very difficult things is itself the work.

Participation changes things from the inside

The 21st century is about full participation. And it's about being open to the new forms of organizing that we discover when we actually participate. One of the challenges for large organizations is facing their fear of actual participation. They hire talented people and then feel anxious about people bringing in their voice, challenging the status quo, or steering the organization into new territory. They want the system to come together and have coherence, yet they design structures with inherent fragmentation and separation. The fear of losing control keeps them stuck in that fear. They may talk about teamwork and collaboration, but there is fear of genuine participation.

We see this in bureaucracies like the European Commission and institutions that don't have a culture of participation, but desperately need it to make sense of what is happening in their internal and external contexts. They have highly rigid, hierarchical, mechanistic approaches. Siloed organizations don't often respond well to increasing complexity where new ideas and relationships need to be cultivated. It is heartbreaking to see people who signed up for public service but are suffering in their jobs because they have lost sight of the purpose of their work; they are simply making protocol. The level of burnout is astounding.

But, within the EC and other organizations, there are some wonderful institutional intrapreneurs—people who are working with purpose as opposed to protocol, and bringing in participatory methodology to develop strategy. They lead by convening and creating the opportunities for many voices to come in to shape the future. They realize they need to change their systems from within and start looking at questions like: How do projects respond to the real needs of citizens, rather than the needs of the institutions? How do we find new forms and expressions for our voices within an institution? What is possible as public servants at a time of massive change and disruption in Europe?

In our work with institutions, we have found that young people and the intrapreneurs are generally not as scared as their organizations. They are more willing to bring in fresh ideas and build architectures that allow people just enough structure to participate in a meaningful way. The 21st century leader convenes the many voices rather than rigidly controls. The conveners recognize the need for people to come together around meaningful questions in order to discover the new forms and relationships needed to navigate this wild world.

Stewardship as leadership

In December 2007, I was hired as executive publisher of a really beautiful and award winning publication called *ascent magazine.* At a time of many changes in the publishing world—and the global economy—the board was asking one question: What does it mean to be sustainable? It was not a question of: How do we keep going? or: What is our next growth strategy? but: What does it mean to really listen to what the work is asking of us?

We discerned the answers to those questions collectively over the course of a year. We saw that we had completed an important cycle of our life as a pioneering magazine of yoga, art, and engaged spirituality. Bringing the magazine to a close also ended my role as an executive publisher; it ended all of our jobs. It required the whole team to re-frame our work as a question of: What are we in service to? What is the work that needs to be done?

For me, personally, I had to re-frame the idea I had of my leadership, and understand that it included the chance to learn something important about closings and endings. This was totally different from my expectations going in, and I had to grapple with my own fear that maybe I had failed, that maybe I hadn't seen where the "growth" was. But in fact, what I learned was that a new quality of leadership was being asked of me, and that "growth" isn't just a question of keeping going or getting more visible. Growth goes down deep; it's a maturation process. And getting to know dying and endings is a big part of maturing.

Some of the fallacies of the modern world are that we always need to keep going, and that we do not need to rest, slow down or properly take care of ourselves. Pressing on like this is not humanly possible without taking breaks and having rest and respite. We see this also in how we treat the earth—we just keep taking, pushing and extracting. Many of us have separated ourselves from the natural flow of the seasons and our bodies' need to rest. We need to respect the value of each season – the growing seasons and the fallow ones. The life cycle of an idea, of a person, or of the collective entity of an organization necessitates different timings and seasons, and different leadership is needed at different stages. The leadership needed to enable creative endings—the deep transformation of letting go—is stewardship.

A big skill for the 21st century leader is to make conscious the need to foresee and steward endings in organizations. Endings are the compost for new beginnings, visions, and paradigms—and certainly the compost for new life. We cannot pour more water into an already full cup, so clearing the space to bring in the new is essential. Artists, musicians, and comedians know about the importance of this kind of timing—it is an art form.

A sustainable system has an inherent ability to shed what is not needed and transform from one form to another in order to continue to evolve. Forests, animals, and even our own families do this seasonally and with each proceeding generation. This natural process is very difficult for organizations. Yet the skillfulness in discerning when it is time to let go—and the collective practice of doing so—is one of the most crucial learning opportunities for the social sector's vibrancy and evolution, as well as our own.

Too often endings mean foreclosure; they are done quickly, aggressively, and without the celebration and acknowledgement of the work of the people who have contributed. However, when we look at endings as essential to beginnings, or dying as a natural phase of ongoing life—indeed, as the transformative element for renewal—then we have many choices (and responsibilities) in how we move through such transitions and change.

Jim Love

Jim Love has done it all. He has been in IT and business for over 30 years. He has worked his way up literally from the mailroom, doing every job from mail clerk to CEO. Today he is CIO and chief content officer of IT World Canada—Canada's leader in Information and Communication Technology (ICT) publishing and digital marketing. He's a writer and a musician, a father and a husband. He's a great guy to have around in a crisis. A former street kid, Jim is quick to point out that none of these professional descriptors really define him.

Jim believes that what we do and how we do it really matters. For him, the meaning of life comes from living it. More than that, he knows it's the intent behind what we do that defines us, and that's how he lives his life.

The Journey of Jim Love: Achiever. Purpose-Driver. Community Builder. CIO and Chief Content Officer, IT World Canada.

What is your story?

My story evolves. My story is always one that I preface with: Don't give me "Oh, poor you", because it's not really like that. I was born very bright and very poor, which is a bad combination. We lived in tough towns and I was smart. My family dissolved before I was 10 years old, and I became what would now be the modern equivalent of a street kid. I was fortunate enough to be adopted by a couple of incredible people and given another shot in life.

I look at my life mostly as a story of good luck. I've caught a lot of breaks. Yet still, I've been this mixture of optimism and pessimism. I still have the little voice in me that says: Don't enjoy this too much—it'll all be taken away from you. Then there's the voice that says, : "Bullshit—life is good.. The nice part is that as I get older, the "life is good" voice gets louder. So I don't need to fear losing it all. A small benefit? I don't have to accumulate stuff anymore. This new voice of mine says: I really don't need so much stuff. What really counts can't be taken away.

I used to be so goal oriented. It's as if another voice would say, "Come on. It's getting there that counts." That mindset occupied probably the first two thirds of my life. I got to a lot of places - I achieved a lot. But every time I got somewhere, I knew there were a lot of other places I would want to get to next. Somewhere in this all, the balanced tipped and I started living in the moment. I was able to rewrite my own story. Today my story is not the little kid who almost ended up living on the street and was full of fear. It's about a man who knows how to full enjoy and give thanks for not where he is, but who he is today.

Have we lost the plot in the world of work?

A lot of people today who don't do what they enjoy. They follow the rules, they follow the structure. The they complain a lot. We've lost our business common sense. We're working ourselves to death. There are a lot of people not fully living their lives, and I think it's because they're afraid. People live lives, if not of "quiet desperation" then out of fear, and trying to drown out that fear in intensified experiences. They watch movies. They watch endless hours of television. They are trying to drown out the noise of their fear and numb themselves.

It boggles my mind how people have bought into the idea that they have no voice. The economy and the world are so screwed up. So why don't people don't stand up collectively and say, "We're not taking it anymore." They won't do this when the world is at stake. But if you put them in line at a theater and somebody butts into the line ahead of them, then they'll speak out. We're so afraid of the power structure that we kiss up to that structure to get those little crumbs that fall from it. Yet we'll take out our frustration on those around us. That's sad.

Still, I try to find compassion in the world, because in the greater scheme of things. I think, maybe we're part of a progression to somewhere else, somewhere better.

That doesn't mean I'm going to give up, hoping "the next generation" will get it right. I'm certainly not one of those people that thinks the Millennials are going to solve the problems we created. People forget history. My generation was the sixties generation—we were supposed to change the world from selfish consumerism t be all about peace, love, and harmony.

What happened to us and our vision for the world? We got mortgages, we had to pay the bills like everybody else, but worst of all our desires kept increasing—we needed a bigger house, a nicer car, and then a better paying job to support our habits. I've always said that I wasn't surprised that we "sold out" – I am surprised at how cheap the price was.

We bought into the modern economic system requires that if I have more, somebody else will have less. That is one place where maybe the millennials will do better. Maybe that's where I find my hope.

To my daughter, exploiting someone else's ideas is a foreign concept. She thinks the way we do business today is terrible. Some of the younger generation has a fundamentally different mindset. In the 1960s, my generation was wild and anarchistic but we were also very self-centered. That is the difference with the Millennials; the center's not within them, but in their collective consciousness. That gives me hope for the future of co-creation.

The other hope I have is that as people begin to realize that when the economy takes its inevitable toll with the total automation of jobs—which I think will happen in 20 years—our whole world may shift in terms of what work means to us. I'm not talking only about automation or industrial robotics. I'm talking about an end to work as we know it—even the most highly skilled knowledge workers. I give us 10 more years before artificial intelligence will outperform doctors. And if AI can replace your doctor, what else is possible? When all of our work becomes automated, our only industry will be entertainment. When you think about the shifts that are taking place in work, we have to start thinking differently about business. In 20 years, the ones who are going to survive are those who can understand and fulfil the changing needs. Disruption and co-creation are essential to the people who get where we are headed and are finding opportunity in a new era of disruption. In today's terms, Uber is a co-creation, a co-creation between somebody who's got a great idea with a computer program, and me, a customer who hates taking cabs.

A successful business is a co-creation with its customers. You have to get them enthused and build strong relationships. With all the social media noise, word of mouth is even more critical in today's world than ever before. You can advertise all you want, but if you need to get information out, word of mouth is still the best communication between the company and customers. That intimacy, that sharing is what drives co-creation -- one of the most important forces for the next 20 years of business.

There is no need to be overwhelmed by technology

I was recently at a Gartner conference, an American research and advisory firm providing information technology, and I saw all the CIOs who were there spending the whole time looking at their cell phones. It struck me that spending time with our mobile devices is the modern equivalent of smoking. When you would smoke in the past at a party, it kept you busy and you had something to occupy your hands. You had a purpose to be there. Could it be that many CIOs are socially uncomfortable, and even though they are in positions of power, it is much easier for them to engage with their device than with people?

Could we be mistaking social awkwardness with the "isolation caused by technology"? Maybe we're not really becoming more isolated by technology. Maybe we've been isolating ourselves for decades. We've isolated ourselves with music since the invention of the Walkman. Before that, it was the transistor radio. Isolation and loneliness have both been out there for a long time. Maybe we've always felt alone and every type of technology has simply masked or fed that.

But today technology is accelerating that trend. We are not innovating with technology. It is innovating us, crushing us, and filling our internal emptiness with a need to feed the machine. We are obsessed with the novelty of things; the new phone, and the next best shiny object.

If you want proof that we serve the technology and not the other way around just look at media and content. When you think about all the information that's available at your fingertips every day, there is no way you can possibly process it all. When you have the volume we are facing, it just becomes increasingly intense. We are all trying to get people's attention by screaming louder and pushing the boundaries even harder. But for what purpose?

I saw a session recently on computers and software that can write very effectively. It made me realize that we're going to need to invent an algorithm that can actually read all the content that will be created, because right now, we're not short on writers, we're short on readers.

But ultimately the problem is not technology—it is us. Technology itself is neutral; it's about how we use it and integrate it into what is valuable for us. Being able to do video conferencing—to see each other's faces and body language across thousands of miles—is amazing. I hear so many people complaining about technology and texting. When I text with my wife, Linda, we have better conversations sometimes than if I came to her in the middle of the day to talk to her for five minutes. We have purposeful exchanges, when we need them. Technology enhances our lives and we need to stop using it as an excuse for our isolation. I personally don't feel isolated by it; I feel connected to people who are important in my life and work.

Our inner emptiness, our lack of openness to others is the problem. McLuhan was wrong, the medium is not the message. The message is within us. And if that message is that we have nothing within us, and if we feel compelled to fill an emptiness with activity, we will never be satisfied and we will have a need to constantly keep up. It ranges from thinking, "I must answer my Blackberry," to "I must answer my email on my smart phone because otherwise people will discover that they can't do without me," to "I have to stay ahead, I have to keep up." People are filling their increasing emptiness with stuff, entertainment, and consumption.

We need to reclaim our inner selves – our sense of purpose, nobility and compassion for others. We need to banish our fear and regain our power and not give that power away when it comes to work. We say we have free will, but employees are not standing up and pushing back on this crazy, unnecessary, 24/7 on-demand world of work in which people are increasingly expected to answer emails at 10 pm and take calls during their vacation or on Sunday morning. We've become docile feeders at the technology trough.

Yet there is hope. Not only in the next generation, but within my generation. I have a dream, as a bright soul once said to us. That dream is that maybe the sixties generation, now that we are closer to our own mortality, will start realizing, "Holy shit, we were robbed. We spent our whole lives at this thing called work at the expense of our life." We are whores of the karmic wheel having traded our hours for a lifestyle that enslaved us in a vicious cycle of consumption and want. A hope that we might realize that this consumption drives us to avoid the confrontation of the fact that we will ultimately die.

When the heart is ready, love arrives

There's a Buddhist teaching that says, "When the pupil is ready, a teacher will arrive." I've altered that slightly. If I could give a wish to the world, it would be a song. A song that would ring in our hearts. A sound that would harmonize with the song in the hearts of people across the world. Not the same song, but harmony. We could harmonize with the world. We could co-create a future together. And when the heart is ready? Love arrives.

Shamini Dhana

Shamini Dhana brings to the fashion world over 20 years of experience in international strategy, global operations, venture capital, business development, management, and executive leadership in corporate America. As a consultant, government foreign direct investment specialist, and banker, Shamini gained extensive experience leading global business missions. She is passionate about the outdoors, and has represented Singapore in badminton, played collegiate tennis, cycled over 300 miles three times down the California Coast, climbed the Himalayas, was an associate producer of the True Cost movie, and is a philantropist and Climate Ride Ambassador. These experiences stood her in good stead when she decided to express her passion and purpose by starting her own company, Dhana, Inc. She travels the world, spreading the Dhana™ spirit, and empowering youth to connect to people and the planet through the medium of clothing.

The Journey of Shamini Dhana: Entrepreneur. Connector. Climate Ride Ambassador. Founder, Dhana, Inc.

What is your story?

I grew up in Southeast Asia and I currently live in Northern California. I have now spent half of my life in the US and the other half in Asia. I've had the best of both worlds in terms of experiences, with my family spread over six continents, which helped me grow up with a very global mindset. Today, I consider myself a global citizen.

Growing up in Singapore, there was only one natural resource, which we call "human capital." Literally everything we had was imported, from the food we ate and the shoes we wore to the toys we played with, the music we danced to, and the water we drank. As a child, I figured out very quickly that we are one big global community, dependent on each other for the very essence of life. My ability to engage with the globe became very personal, a relevant and integral part of my being.

People talk about travel as physically going to a place. I like to travel through people's connections and their ability to share experiences and bring together their anecdotes. Travel, for me, is not about visiting seven countries in three days. I love to spend time and immerse myself in a culture and understand the different facets of what inspires and drives people, and how they feel they are connected to the earth, the physical beauty around them, and the natural environment.

Connecting with people on various levels and experiencing and seeing life through their eyes is what I do best. My personality is such that I am very curious about human nature and the human spirit. I have realized through my own personal experience that we are all part of the greater food chain. Each one of us has a unique gift to share during our existence on this earth. By paying attention and reserving judgement, each one of us has an opportunity to connect to each other, through our experiences, through our common dependence on what sustains us, as well as the material goods that we depend on.

I connect people with the planet in different ways. My mission can be summed up as "uniting humanity through fashion," with the goal of inspiring people to realize that every day we wear a piece of clothing that has the ability to connect us with other people and with planet earth. We may not think about this very often, but every piece of clothing we wear has hands and hearts behind it. The natural resources of our planet are also in this piece of clothing. My hope is that the consciousness of humanity will get to a point where we realize that a piece of clothing can make a difference in this world, and that it can serve as a connection to humanity. Perhaps it's time to revisit this journey, to step back and consider how aligned each piece of clothing is to our own values and how in turn we reflect ourselves in them. Fashion has the potential to connect us in deeper and more profound ways, to each other and to the world. The Dhana tagline "We're Wearin' the World" reflects just this sentiment and this reminder to humanity.

One in six people on our planet work in the garment industry. The fact that we have the ability to impact the second most polluting industry in the world by voting with our dollars is phenomenal. Each of us can make conscious decisions with the products we wear and consume. What excites me is that this level of curiosity and consciousness can be instilled from a very young age.

Wear what you stand for: wear your values

The business I run is a sustainable and ethical fashion brand for the youth and global leaders of tomorrow. Change happens through transformation and evolution over time, and what better way to do that than through our young people? Dhana symbolizes a way to rethink our connection with people and the planet through the medium of clothing. At Dhana, we strive to unite the beauty of nature, the choice of natural, organic elements, the celebration of world cultures, the creative genius of global artists, the passion of entrepreneurs, and the voices of children through the universal medium of fashion.

When we look at how our youth operate and function in the world, we realize they tend to be empathetic toward the natural world and to the life inhabiting it. Our youth have a propensity to care deeply, and the goodness of their hearts can extend way beyond themselves from a very young age. I often talk with and listen to the younger generation, either in classroom or community settings. Their curiosity is phenomenal, in terms of how much they grasp what is possible if we can change our behavior. They often have no desire to inflict any kind of pain or injustice on people, or to poison or pollute our environment. Many of them know that to honor the earth is to honor ourselves. When you see that very essence in a child, you realize it should be protected and preserved, like the earth itself.

We all know we are not the only species of life on this planet. If we were to step back, we would realize that we collectively rely on the same resources: the air we breathe, the water we consume, the natural heat we need to continue with life, and the minerals and plants we feed on that nourish us. We exist in a symbiotic relationship with all of the other species on earth. Once we realize and embrace this truth, the idea of living in harmony starts to become vital to our core existence.

People still feel the name of the game is to cater to the masses, but the notion of profiting at the expense of others is starting to shift. The philosophy of people doing business for the sheer goal of making money is starting to change, and the shift is taking place slowly but surely towards a more expanded consciousness. We are living in a transformative time with unprecedented amounts of content, information, and exposure to experiences via the internet, which brings with it the ability to connect with people who resonate with our message, product, or service directly. The conversation happening before the point of sale—the many people involved in the making of the goods we consume and the services we use, and the fact that they matter, too and should be honored and celebrated—have become relevant to our our survival as a human species. These are new ideas that we will see more of in the future of business as customers, workers, and communities demand more of it. These are the stories that will dominate our conversations and psyches, thereby causing us to revisit our contributions and impact at work, in society, and in life. By connecting to our purpose, we will ultimately feel connected to what we do every day and feel the reward and satisfaction of sharing our gifts.

At the end of the day, we are indeed all connected. When you are aware of where the food you eat and the clothes you wear com from, you can contribute to the triggering of massive changes in how business is done. The biggest change today is that the unheard worker, the silent consumer, and the curious customer are all reclaiming their voices and speaking up for what they want to see in the world. We are seeing new conversations emerging as people start asking new questions about the companies they do business with.

Dhana™ was founded in 2008, and we spent the last eight years building partnerships. One of the things that I have always believed is that partnerships and people don't happen overnight. For any new venture, idea, or paradigm shift to take place, we must create those paths of collaboration. You have to find avenues and platforms that share similar visions where the values are aligned. Just like anything else, it's personal. It is the propensity to share a vision of what's possible.

One of the partnerships we are proud to be part of is the B Corp movement. B Corps harness the power of business to solve social and environmental problems. Unlike conventional corporations, whose highest priority is financial gain, B Corps recognize that true profitability only comes when companies also contribute to the greater wellbeing of people and the planet. B Corps are legally required to consider the impact of their decisions not only on their shareholders, but also on their stakeholders (e.g., workers, suppliers, community, customers, and the environment). At Dhana™, we take the B Corp goals to heart. We've written environmental protection and social fairness right into our vision and our mission. We use our ethical and sustainable fashion lines to raise world consciousness about these important issues.

Apart from the B Corp community, Dhana™ is built on a strong foundation, having relationships with organizations like Green America, the Ethical Fashion Forum, Climate Ride, Fairtrade

International, Ellevate Network, and local schools and communities. Each of these organizations share similar values and help us to build awareness of our connection to people and the planet through our clothes.

We are connecting with thousands of people who belong to these platforms and communities who want a brand that understands the very essence of their human spirit. People are looking to identify and connect with brands that reflect and align with a value system that resonates with the core beliefs of humanity. Dhana™ asks a basic fundamental question: "How do you wear the world?" I want our youth—and everyone else—to start asking questions like: How do I wear the world in fashion? Where was my clothing made? Who made it? How was it made?

The gifts children bring to our world

There is a very strong bond that can exist between a mother and her child. My 11 year old daughter, Sasha, and I have a very special, priceless, and symbiotic relationship. We learn from each other. It's an opportunity for the adult, mother, parent, and friend in me to walk the journey with my child, to share her experiences and rethink moments in time with her when she questions why things are the way they are in the world. It is an opportunity to revisit beliefs and ideas with her. To witness the world through my daughter's eyes again and again is a true blessing in my life.

My biggest gift to her is to share her curiosity and passion with the world, and to help her to feel empowered to take her gifts and share them with the world. Sasha has an opportunity to share with the world how she thinks and connects through different mediums, be it poetry, dance, music, or art, and to be able to say she is drawing from different cultures, music, plants, and animals of the world.

Sometimes you don't realize how you perceive the world until you are asked. A conversation has to occur for you to realize that you may have biases or misconceived ideas. We need to have more opportunities for people to have conversations with an open mind so that we can each interact with the world and find our place. It's so important for us to ask new questions and truly listen to each other.

The Internet is a critical tool today for bringing people together all over the world so they can share their stories, receive feedback, guidance, mentorship, and help, and realize they are not alone. We are in a moment of history when our connectedness truly is far reaching and more impactful than ever. We should be ready for a world of change to unveil itself in the next few years and decades, so that we can move in a direction of harmony with our planet.

What is super exciting to me is the notion of the "I" being replaced by the collective "We." This is when we can truly embrace the connected life we live in. Until you can break away and know it's not all about the "I," you will have the mentality of being the victim and not part of the collective. Solutions come as long as one is open to life and its possibilities.

We truly have the opportunity today to bring a new awareness to our global community about our interconnectedness. By embracing the idea that we are "Wearin' the World" through our experiences with others, how we interact with the material world, and our shared dependence on our planet's gifts, we will truly be connected to the human spirit.

Martina Buchal

Martina Buchal is an internationally recognized speaker, facilitative leader, keen observer, deep-digging discoverer, and dot connector with an eye for opportunities for growth and collaboration—even in places where they seem hard to find.

Martina takes great joy in creating people-centric, empowering solutions to complex problems, and believes that to solve the most difficult challenges, we must meet people where they are, dig deep, and work together to co-create solutions for long-term success. Her favorite part of her work is building and connecting her growing global network and mentoring youth to realize their full potential in service of the greater good.

The Journey of Martina Buchal: Healer. Empowerer. Facilitator. Former Global Ambassador, Your Big Year Champion, World Merit.

What is your story?

Life is never a linear path. I'll start my story where I am right now. I am in the Czech Republic. I am grounding and centering to figure out my next steps forward after a pretty exciting and intense eight years of my life. And in particular, a pretty exciting and intense two years of my life where I traveled around the world to over 27 countries as a global ambassador and storyteller.

My background is in law and politics. I studied law and worked in politics in Canada and found out that was not the world for me, as I am not a political creature. I worked in the senate and for the courts and I trained in conflict resolution. What I wanted to do, when I stepped out of politics and decided my heart wanted to go elsewhere, was focus on how I could help move toward a future that a lot of people want to see but not many people feel empowered to work towards.

Some of my friends and I were seeing not a lack of leaders, but rather a lack of leaders with a leadership style that could lead us to where we ultimately wanted to go. There are a lot of people talking about the Sustainable Development Goals (SDG) as a global community, and it's great to talk about these important issues. Politicians are fantastic at talking about things; however, it's going to take a very different leadership style to get us to *implement* the things we are talking about. We need to get rid of past mindsets and communicate with each other through open conversations between political leaders and their constituents and citizens.

During my transition, I applied for an International Leadership competition called Your Big Year, organized by World Merit. There were over 60,000 people who applied and one person would be deemed the global ambassador. And that was me. It was an absolutely incredible two years of travel, working on the ground with young people and also being a voice for youth on an international stage. I volunteered extensively in communities, worked on social and environmental action projects alongside World Merit members, and delivered workshops and speeches on the importance of international collaboration and leadership, particularly where it concerns young people. I worked with thousands of young people, gearing them toward the need of future leaders to have more collaborative styles.

I was part of an international community of young people. There were over 100,000 young changemakers and people who were passionate and positive in their communities, but who maybe didn't have the means or the knowhow to make changes happen on their own. We created an online platform that allowed them to learn from one another, work together, and also qualify them for opportunities that they would not have access to otherwise. As the global ambassador, I worked with our community on the ground and focused on leadership development work, which I love.

What was most incredible was hearing the stories of the young people around the world and what they were doing with their lives on a small or big scale. They were significantly driving change and transforming mindsets, creating a new way together as a community.

The work was not always easy. It's one thing to be in a very receptive community and another thing to be in a community where 98 percent of its members—and sometimes more than that—is against whatever you are driving. I learned a great deal about believing in what I am doing and, at the same time, listening to the different voices out there in a new way.

I made a conscious decision while I was traveling to dig deeper and find out who I am and what skill set I wanted to bring to the world. My own personal journey blended with what I was doing in the world, and I wanted to work on my identity and bring it naturally to the surface. I also made the conscious decision that when my role as Global Ambassador came to an end, I would sit for a while and stop moving. I wanted to make sure I was fully aware of the immense gift that I was given of connecting and working with so many young people who shared so much of themselves with me. I can't explain the immense privilege that I felt being a young person from an immigrant family from the Czech Republic. If you asked me when I was 11 if I would ever imagine myself traveling around the world speaking on behalf of young people and leadership, my answer would have been no, I couldn't see that happening. I couldn't even see myself getting a university degree at that age.

Our culture has us jumping from one activity to the next, and what I learned from my journey is that we need to stop. We are better off feeling and understanding our movements rather than following this superficial need to jump into the next thing just because everyone else is doing it. And that is an important lesson the world needs to pay attention to that is coming from our young people. The youth I worked with were not as rushed into the traditional career path; their sense of urgency was around making a profound impact in our community and the world. I worked with people who understood that meaningful change in the 21st century is about redefining traditional notions of success and charting a more humane path for all life on the planet.

What I saw as a global ambassador was that it's not just about young people. Our solutions in the world have to be intergenerational no matter what goals we are striving for. We can't be siloed or separate. This is what I mean about the leadership for the future. If we continue in this separateness—whether it is dealing with poverty by only talking to economists instead of talking to women's rights activists or people working in the environment, for example, or whether it's dealing with youth issues and not inviting youth to the conferences—that's just not an effective way to get anything done in our world today. It is not sustainable or healthy, and it doesn't make anyone feel whole or appreciated.

When I was invited by the office of the Vice President of Panama to speak at the Young Americas Forum as part of the Summit of the Americas, I knew this was a rare opportunity to get the youth voice to the eardrums of world leaders. I was penciled in to speak on the Intergenerational Dialogue Panel, the purpose of which was to have young leaders from the Americas address global leaders from the United Nations Development Programme (UNDP), the United

Nations Population Fund (UNFPA), and the World Bank, as well as the UN Envoy on Youth, telling them what young people need in order to further their development globally.

But, of course, I wouldn't be much of a representative if I just went up there and told the world what I thought without actually consulting the people that matter: the youth. So, I did what any Millennial would do when faced with a big question in need of input: I took to social media to see what young people would do if they were the ones taking to the stage. I asked: "If you had a chance to tell your leaders what young people need from their governments, how they could be better involved in advancing the Post 2015 Agenda, and how youth could drive that agenda better, what would YOU tell them?"

My Facebook feed was flooded with responses. I chose several of these to read aloud on stage that day to demonstrate that young people have strong opinions and ideas about the world around them, and are willing to create solutions to some of the world's most pressing issues.

"It's really quite simple," I told the honored guests, "Nothing about us, without us. Youth must be included in every step of the process. So, what might that look like?

1) Firstly, consider us. We count on you, our leaders, to create the safe space for young people to exist, learn, and thrive. Without the basics, there isn't soil in which the seeds can grow. Consider our wellbeing in all your policy decisions. Protect our interests so we can thrive.

2) Consult us. We need inclusive and ongoing dialogue. Young people's opinions must be valued and cherished. Of course, the Young Americas Forum is exactly the perfect start. We need more of this sort of engagement at the local, national, and international level. Create these forums for our voices to be heard.

3) Work with us. Next on the to-do list is empowering action. Don't just consult. Bring us in to the process. Let us be part of the solution. We want to get our hands dirty. Let us."

I recited these suggestions to bring home the point that we must do this together. There is no better way. Young people have so much to offer; we have energy, creativity, and innovativeness, while our experienced leaders have know-how and a compass for navigating the world as it is. If we combine those strengths, surely we can reach greater heights together much faster.

If you're a young person, I urge you to go out there and take action. Share your voice. Be part of the solution by taking responsibility for being part of it. If you're a seasoned leader in any field, please open your minds and doors to young people's ideas around you. We can learn so much from each other—and accomplish even more together.

In the world we live in, we understand everything to be quite disconnected a lot of time, in particular in the West where we are very independent and competitive. That is one area where we should connect back to ancient wisdom. I feel that if somehow we could see the world in that way again, the systems we have in place might not even be systems anymore. We may develop very different things that we can't even imagine right now. Ultimately, if we genuinely come from a place of wanting to make changes, it starts with how we see ourselves and the world.

I am building a base and getting these messages out in the world. I'd love to connect with people who want to learn more and start new conversations. I dream of a world of agency and accountability. This is a world of choices made. We need to recognize the weight that these choices carry for each of us and for generations to come. It's a world of open eyes and open hearts, not afraid to see and feel deeply, and act in accordance with these clear perceptions. It's a world of hope for the future, knowing the best of it is well within our empowered control, based on individual presence and collective.

Romanus Berg

Romanus Berg strives to connect pattern-changing solutions, people, and resources. He is a curious learner, strategist, communicator, and team builder who values empathy-based ethics and the language of action. I met Romanus when I was a Cisco Leadership Fellow and he was CIO at Ashoka. We immediately started collaborating and sharing our passion around building trusted communities. He is a leader who constantly challenges himself and his story is one of continued transformation and personal growth.

Romanus began his career developing online communication systems because he was attracted to the Internet's "peer to peer," "Net-neutral" potential for individual and shared growth. Romanus served as a member of Ashoka's Leadership Group in the role of CIO/COO/CFO. He has also served on Oceana's leadership team, which established and rapidly grew a small start-up into the largest international organization focused solely on ocean conservation. Romanus currently serves on NetHope's board, which works to share social solutions across citizen, government, and private sectors.

The Journey of Romanus Berg: Thought Leader. Purpose-Driver. Entrepreneur. Former CIO, Ashoka / Board Member, Nethope / VP, Strategy, Stand Together.

What is your story?

As I look at my journey so far and consider what makes me uniquely “me,” my story is a part of the environment that I’m in, as well as my character. That is to say, I believe we're born with a certain kind of personality and for better or worse we shape our character along the way.

I was born in Guatemala to German parents. My father left East Berlin before the Wall went up and he paid to have my mother smuggled out afterwards. On occasion, she tells the story of how she left everything behind to meet a truck driver at a rest stop in the middle of nowhere. She had to pay the taxi driver extra not to miss the train, and then waited six hours in the bushes in the freezing cold for a truck driver whose code name was Whiskey. He told her she had to hide under the truck, and when they finally stopped after a long drive, he got her out from the cramped compartment and said, "There was too much activity at the border. I had to turn back." When she started crying, he slapped her on the back and said, "I'm just kidding. You're in the West, now get out of here."

My parents then immediately immigrated to Guatemala, which is where I was born, and it must have been quite a transition for them. Much of my first memories are about living in a big divide; there were people who had access to power, education, and money, and then there were those who did not and were in essence disempowered.

My parents moved to Washington, DC to work for the World Bank and I attended the German School there. It was a small school with about 500 students representing 30 to 40 nationalities, pre-Kindergarten all the way through thirteenth grade. I was in classes with kids whose parents came from “elsewhere” and were, for example, with the military, embassies, and the World Bank, and who would typically come from Germany for three to five years. I wish more people could have the powerful gift of growing up seeing the world through at least two cultural lenses every day. It has allowed me to be more aware of how people interpret the exact same things in so very different ways depending upon their perspectives.

I was also fortunate to have gone on to study in Paris through a partnership with the Sorbonne, and then in Germany before coming back to the United States to get my bachelor's degree in computer, mathematical, and physical science. I wanted to learn how the world works in the context of systems first and then to study journalism. I felt a journalist's role in society to be a valuable one because they help to make sense of what is happening and how to navigate this world.

The first apprenticeship

I clearly remember the moment I first sat down in front of a browser. It was called Mosaic, one of the first Internet browsers. I was struck by the peer-to-peer network aspect of it, and that it offered an exponential growth path for both individuals and communities alike. Value creation and not hierarchy were at the heart of it, and it was open to anyone with access to a terminal. You could just see where this thing was going to go!

After that, graduate school lost its appeal because no one was teaching this stuff, and so a week after graduation I went to a temp agency and said, "Please just get me any job, as long as it has something to do with communications." And so they got me a job answering the phones at the United States Enrichment Corporation, to which I said, "What the heck is an enrichment corporation?" Had I known the place was enriching uranium, I probably wouldn't have taken the gig. But I am glad that I showed up in my new cheap suit, fresh with my undergraduate degree to answer the phones, hoping it would lead somewhere.

I was simply terrible at it, I recall constantly forgetting who I had holding on which line, but I was very fortunate to be riding up in the elevator with the CEO within my first couple of weeks. And because he had seen me at the front desk a lot, he said, "Oh, you're the new temp.

How's it going?" I said, "To tell you the truth, I'm lousy at answering the phones. But I find it interesting that we get a lot of inquiries coming in through the front door that we're not answering consistently, and even worse, a lot of times folks are asking for the wrong people to answer their queries." I told him I thought I could probably help with that. And he said, "Well, you know what? I'll have HR introduce you to someone in Corporate Communications and we'll see."

I had a conversation with the folks on that team and they offered me a project that had languished for years because nobody had wanted to do it. It involved getting together all the historical news clips about the organization from the past decade, which were all in hard copy newspapers stacked up in a stuffy library. I eagerly agreed and went to town on them. For quite some time I came home each day with the residue of white correction fluid all over my hands and clothes; this was a literal cut and paste job. It had nothing to do with technology.

I knocked it out in a few months and because they had struggled with this project for years, they offered me a full time job. Within the four years that I was there, I learned how to develop their online presence, which meant learning how to spool up servers, starting with the PC under my desk because nobody else seemed to care or know about the technology infrastructure component of communications.

During those four years, we went from being a military operation to a publicly held organization, and I went from physically cutting and pasting to attaining technical certifications and developing their first ever online communications systems. That was enough for me at the time to say to myself: We're doing something useful here. It ended up being the largest privatization of any government entity, culminating in a $1.8 billion sale. In the process, I learned how to help an organization of 5,000 people working out of different locations to see where each team was on the playing field. I gave the organization and the individuals a view of the playing field from the skybox, so that people and projects weren't missing each other (or worse, running into each other) as often. Externally, we were for the first time able to understand why people were coming to us, give them what they were looking for, and learn from our competitors how they were positioning themselves in the marketplace.

I was there during the early dot com years, and because things were moving so quickly I gained a lot of responsibility in a short amount of time. In retrospect, my first apprenticeship was learning not only the corporate communications practice and how to develop and maintain the necessary technical infrastructure, but more importantly, the communication systems. This included asking: What is the trinity of people, processes, and technology that changes the way people perceive themselves as individuals and breaks down barriers to work as a team of teams?

On the path to the second apprenticeship

After a few years, I felt I had learned everything I was going to learn from that first job. I left and began working with startups. One day I found myself, after getting rave performance reviews, at a startup that had to shut down because we had quietly run out of money. I was dumbfounded, because I felt that I had done everything right. At the time, I was in victim mode and felt that it was the worst possible thing that could have ever happened to me. I had a mortgage to pay and real financial obligations. How did I ever find myself in this position? What could I learn from this? I felt guilty, that I had somehow failed. People around me were saying, "You got a couple of months off. Isn't that great?" And I felt that it was like water, water everywhere but not a drop to drink. I had all this time but felt I couldn't enjoy any of it. I felt I could not allow myself to take the time to think and figure out what I wanted to do next in my career. My mental model, at that time, was that my job was to find a path to fulfill my obligations to pay the bills, that fulfilling work was secondary to serving something outside of myself.

In retrospect, it turned out to be one of the best possible things that ever could have happened. I was forced to reevaluate why I was doing what I was doing, and what value I was exchanging by taking the next rung on that job ladder to some undetermined place. I knew I was being challenged by my work, but it became clearer and clearer that I was not being fulfilled by it. I did a good deal of soul searching, reading, and talking to friends and family. The truth is that I didn't realize something wasn't working for me until something external happened to throw me out of that trance of being in the rat race.

It brought me to the realization and decision that for me to be truly fulfilled at work, I needed to contribute something that would hold up to the seven-generation principle, where the contributions we make today have a shot at benefitting our descendants seven generations into the future. I don't know how life works sometimes, but as I came to this realization, a blueprint for an organization called Poseidon came my way. Its premise was that, even though roughly three quarters of our planet is covered by water, people nonetheless see fit to put whatever they want into our oceans and take whatever they want out of it. It seemed very few people were paying attention. We had these monster fishing fleets that were fishing areas literally to death so that there would be nothing left for thousands of years in some cases. I had also lost my father in a diving accident, and so on a personal level, working to protect the oceans felt like an act of healing.

I happily joined this organization that only existed at the time on paper, which we quickly renamed Oceana. I was one of the first six to join and just two and a half years later, I had the opportunity to help open 12 offices around the world. At first, I was responsible for IT, but you couldn't place the IT equipment if there wasn't a space or if there was no furniture, if there was no server room, if there wasn't a network drop, or if we didn't have a legal entity. I had a lot of fun learning so many of the aspects needed to get it all done.

At my second apprenticeship, I learned three things. One was how to launch a startup. The second was how to get that startup to become a system of people working together on a particular set of shared initiatives in a more clear and integrated way, and how to transition a startup to a more mature organization. And then I got my third lesson, which was how to transform an idea into an organization with pioneers like me who wanted to create greater awareness of what we were doing to our planet through Oceana. I thought I had a little bit of it figured out from my past work, but I did not anticipate the cultural differences, particularly in working with Latin America.

I learned that if you don't pay attention and work together on people's vocational future and growth, especially if they're strong individuals (which is the type of people we hired), they would end up feeling that they were sacrificing their own path to something that they no longer agreed with. It's one of the first times that I really shed tears over a job, because what I realized was that we had all gotten together to save the world's oceans, and yet we were fighting with each other over personal, individual needs. And that was painful. When this mismatch in organizational goals and individual aspirations resulted in people leaving abruptly, it really opened my eyes to the need for humility when working in different regions.

Looking back, given my level of experience, it's understandable that I didn't have all the answers at the time. But as a result, I would today walk into anyone's office and put my job on the line to say, "We have to fix this." The lesson is to trust your inner voice and take the time to ask yourself: What's next here? Why am I doing this? Am I doing this because it's what's expected of me, or am I doing this because this is authentic for me and my colleagues?

The third apprenticeship

My third stop was Ashoka, where I learned how ecosystems of change are co-created. Ashoka is the largest network of social entrepreneurs worldwide. I was fortunate to witness the cumulative work of the 3,000 fellows that Ashoka elected in 70 countries. These are the one in 10 million people who have given themselves permission to put their system changing ideas into practice on a global scale. Every one of them has this in common: they create ecosystems of change where the individuals in those ecosystems have a higher purpose for what they want to achieve in their work, and they voluntarily cooperate in a way that allows them to self-define their own authentic path in life.

I learned from them that we do have an inner voice, and that to listen to it allows us to become more our true selves, to be happier, more productive, and that it is ultimately transformative. In a world where the rate of change is increasing, our ability to adapt is vital. It means welcoming change, relishing change, and being able to surrender to those waters in a humble way that allows us to thrive, as opposed to drowning in them. Because if you try to swim those waters with the old pattern of wanting to manage or control it, you're lost.

That was the third apprenticeship, where I learned how ecosystems are built. Bill Drayton, CEO of Ashoka, believes the first step to an "Everyone a Changemaker" world is believing that you can make lasting change by identifying a problem in your community and giving yourself permission to overcome it. The Changemaker model is focused on the people who are making a difference and creating tipping points in society.

Awakening from a life threatening crisis

One day, I suddenly found myself confronted by a major health scare where literally, from one day to the next, I didn't know if I was going to be around in six months' time. When you have your mortality reinforced like that, there is nothing like putting yourself back into a place of asking: What am I going to do with every day of this wonderful life?

While I wouldn't have wished it upon anyone else, going through a mortal health scare woke me up, and that can be most unpleasant. It has helped me re-prioritize my life and slowly, sometimes in fits and starts, to appreciate the wonders all around me with new eyes. Water, for example, is such a wondrous thing. It is guided by both adhesive and cohesive physical inter-molecular forces. It wants to both keep to itself and also attach to other things. They are two sides of the same coin that create a natural tension while being part of the whole. This is how I see life. What makes us different, sometimes seemingly polar opposite, can also be sides of the same coin. The tragedy is that we often forget that we all share parts of the same thing. We're made of the same materials. What is equally amazing is when I look up at the night sky and realize how long that light has traveled to meet my eyes, and how short and fleeting we are as guests in our physical bodies, and yet how blessed we are to be able to live our lives every single day. If we could instill that little hint of wonder in all of us each day, I often wonder what a different world it would be.

In retrospect, I feel I followed a vocational path that was not truly of my own making. I believed that success meant things like buying a house, having kids, giving them an education, pursuing a successful career, and leaving a legacy for the family. If I did that, then I would have won by doing everything I was supposed to do. In the old days, if you reached that point by age 40 or so, you were pretty much done and could be happy you had "arrived." Today, though, many of us are living twice as many years, which means we have both the blessing and the curse of realizing that we have a whole other lifetime to ask ourselves: Is this really my life? Is this really who I am?

Part of the story is not knowing exactly how things will go. Coming from a guy who always wants to know exactly how the train is going to run and how things work, this is scary business. That's been a very humbling part of my journey. I don't want to be defined by my health scare; however, when it hit, I clearly recall having three thoughts. First: I'm grateful for the life that I've had. I'm not angry. I can't complain. Second: now that I'm on the path to full recovery, there's a lot more I want to do if I get the chance, and I would like that chance. I'm not rolling over and happy that it's over. And third: I've got to stop the suffering. That third part was probably the most interesting, because up until then, I hadn't even really realized the price of not questioning the status quo. There is a proverb that says, "Pain is inevitable. Suffering and growth are optional." I thought of what a loved one had told me once: I'd rather have an authentic mess than a perfect facade. Boy, do I wish I could have taught my younger self that one.

All this helped me to ask, "If I had a day, or a week, or 10 years, what would I do with that time?" I can tell you it's not going to the supermarket to pick out which kind of deodorants I want to use. It is to focus more on trusting and following my heart, and not to make life dependent on anyone else's happiness.

With every one of these lessons, I have moved closer to really knowing something versus merely believing it. This brings me full circle. Before, the story I told was about a sense of urgency to contribute to something and change the course of where we're headed in a constructive way that follows the "seven generation rule." Today, I find myself following my path with less urgency and more of a sense of purpose, which does not include needing affirmation from others as much as before.

I've often come back to an old proverb: Tell me, and I'll forget. Teach me, and I might remember. Involve me, and I'll understand. The involvement in community that comes from being able to voluntarily cooperate and do something together involves a very different language of action than the language that I had learned, which is to live within the mental models we have accepted without a continual reevaluation of how the world is supposed to be.

I believe we are in a historical moment, and sometimes it may feel like a very bleak one. But I do think that the system is correcting itself in many ways. We all share the same sun and the same earth, and I have hope for things like the rapidly decreasing cost of solar power being big drivers in the change we will see in the world. I do have hope for communications technology allowing us to talk to each other in ways that we haven't been able to before. We had the spoken word, then the written word, the printing press, broadcast media, and the Internet. Today, we have far more opportunity to connect more deeply to ourselves and each other, to tap into deeper shared value creation. Coming together around issues that impact our lives and the lives of those who come after us is the only way to affect dynamic and lasting positive change.

Purpose makes a comeback

For me, if I want a good vocation, I will look at how to help everyone, including myself, as well as how to understand and affect positive change. In terms of business, we all want and fundamentally deserve the chance to pursue meaningful work, and not out of fear because we feel we need to survive, but in order to truly live. It includes a sense of love for purpose and accomplishment. If I give myself permission to be vulnerable in recognizing when I am wrong, if I am open to that act of surrendering, then I will understand the key difference between merely surviving by running the same patterns and truly living.

I deeply wish for all of us to not merely survive but to fully live. I keep reflecting on how the way we behave impacts what we learn every day. What portion of any given day do I spend being in flow? By "in flow," I mean a state of forgetting time, because we are doing something we love; being in the zone, lining up thoughts, words, and deeds authentically with who we are and what we're doing. If I get anything out of this journey, it will be about the ability to question: Does this work? Today I often ask myself: Is ignorance a choice? Am I willing and able to see my ignorance, especially when it really matters?

This story is, of course, a story in the making. I count myself as fortunate to have people around me who are also learning and growing along with me. As Howard Thurman says, "Don't ask yourself what the world needs. Ask yourself what makes you come alive, and go do that, because what the world needs is people who have come alive."

Exercises for Expedition 6

15 **On Becoming Whole**		
	What is fragmented and separated in my life?	How can I make these things whole?
	What is fragmented and separated in my business?	How can I make these things whole?

16 **On the Road to Wholeness**	How happy or unhappy are you with the choices you are making for each of the following? How do you integrate these activities to make you whole?	
	The food I consume:	
	The products I use on my body:	
	The companies whose products and services I purchase: Do I know the source? Are people, animals or the environment being harmed in the process of their production? Do I know the conditions the people who produced them are working in? What do I know about the company, and can I trust their practices?	
	The time I spend by myself:	
	The time I spend with friends and family:	
	The time I spend with people at work:	
	Any other part of my life that I feel needs to be reflected on:	

17 **Connecting Stories**	Thinking about each of the stories you just experienced, what do they mean for your own journey to conscious 21st century leadership?	
	Vanessa Reid	
	Martina Buchal	
	Shamini Dhana	
	Jim Love	
	Romanus Berg	

Expedition 7
Integration: It's Time to Bring Ourselves and the Team Back Together

There are no walking paths in the Amazon rainforest, and, given the many dangers, it is wise to have people from the local tribe guide you. The tools they bring are their bodies and a machete to clear the brush, while you will need to wear much protective gear. When you take a step that sinks you deep into the muddy earth, they come and sweep you out as you continue your journey. Your boots fill with water, but you carry on with the group. This is not simply going on a hike or a walk. You keep your hands in your pockets and do not lean on anything, as you never know what you may encounter on a tree. Your focus is on being part of this environment and feeling a deep appreciation for the natural beauty around you serving as the lungs of the world.

One morning during Amazonian journey, you wake up thinking you are going to spend the day visiting the tribe's local garden and meet some of the women to hear their stories, but plans change when one of the local women is bitten by a snake. The focus shifts to her wellbeing. Immediately, you come together as one caring community. One of the greatest dangers in the rainforest is to be bitten by a venomous snake and not have any anti-venom. There is no electricity, so there is no refrigeration to store medicine. In a matter of hours, the team comes together around saving her life. There is no manual or project plan, just the simplicity of the circle of life and death staring you in the face. It is amazing to see how people can self-organize. Leaders emerge and make decisions. There is sadness and a lot of hope expressed in a matter of minutes. Together, under the leadership of Lynne Twist, co-founder of the Pachamama Alliance who is leading our group of Jungle Mamas, decisions are made quickly to charter a plane. At that point, what mattered most to each of us was coming together as one caring community to save a young life.

You end up getting a tour of the local garden after all. As you walk back to your eco-lodge, you are deep in thought, reflecting on the events of the day. You look down to see a vast colony of ants building and creating, toiling in the rain by moving leaves to their destination. You think about how intent they are and are amazed that they can accomplish so much without any organizational chart showing the structure, ranks, or positions. Given their highly complex system with so many members, that would be a big organizational chart, you muse, as a single acre of Amazon rainforest may house 3.5 million ants. You are mesmerized by them, until you notice humans approaching. They don't see the ants and step on them. You expect some sort of chaos, but what ensues is unceremoniously simple: the ants that are not crushed simply keep going. They manage to stay on their path. They adapt themselves to the change as an integrated whole.

Why Integration is Our Anchor

To integrate is to combine, form, or blend into a functioning, unified, rational whole. We integrate when we make a person or a group part of a larger group or organization. Integration happens when we end separation and bring people into membership of an organization or society. The word integration originates from the mid-17th century Latin *integrat-* 'made whole.' The antonym of integration is separation or segregation.

Once we understand why it's important for us to become whole as individuals and organizations on our journey (Expedition 4), and why it is key for business, we can then focus on integration as the linchpin of building thriving organizations. Integration is at the heart of 21st century leadership.

21st century leaders know when and how to bring people together to co-create projects and initiatives. Our conversations focus not only on differences—which we need to understand in order increase our potential for unity—but especially on what we are creating together. During an Experience I recently ran, we had the opportunity to integrate a team who had been working in the same department for years. While the leader shared with me a few days prior to the workshop that they definitely had a shared purpose, after the first 90 minutes of our session, I saw her lightly smack her head and cry out, "Wow, we need a shared purpose. We don't have one." Through conversations and interactive exercises, we were able to start on the journey and put issues on the table that were rarely discussed openly. It allowed people to start seeing themselves and each other with greater clarity of what they could co-create around their key opportunities.

When we focus on integration, we can achieve a more harmonious existence of bringing the pieces of our bigger puzzle together. It helps us put less focus on concepts and initiatives around inclusion and diversity, for example, as we integrate ourselves and our teams around the higher purpose of our organizations. By not calling for diversity, we are able to integrate our differences and bring people together. When I worked in Emerging Markets at Cisco, I worked with people across Africa, Latin America, Central Eastern Europe, Russia and the Confederate of Independent States, the Middle East, and Asia. We did not need to talk about diversity like they did in our headquarters in California. We had to recognize and respect cultural (and other) differences in this group, which paved the way to unity around a shared purpose. Our goal was to understand and respect local cultures and bring people together around what we were creating as a whole. You could not find a more diverse group of people across these geographic and cultural regions. And yet, the focus was on the vast opportunities to integrate and work together around key initiatives.

I learned that while in the west our programs pursued diversity and inclusion—which to me seemed to separate us even more—our opportunity was to drive integration around the business challenges and opportunities. At that time, we were building the foundation of a brand new region for the company, and I learned a lot from being part of that pioneering group on how to bring people together in an integrated way. The key was to create forums for conversations and let people get to know each other.

Our First Road Trip: Integrating Ourselves

In school, we learn the importance society places on being popular, where we experience the divides between the groups that are the "in crowd" and the outliers who may be bullied or seen as outcasts. We learn from a young age that there are circles of people who are more accepted or popular than others, which means that there is an invisible bar that separates people beyond demographic divides. We experience further divisions within ourselves, which renowned spiritual teacher Jiddu Krishnamurti explores in relation to intelligence:

> Now, how can education help us to be intelligent? What is intelligence? Is it a matter of passing examinations, or being clever? You may read many books, meet prominent people, have a lot of capacity, but does all that make you intelligent? Or is intelligence something which comes into being only as you become integrated? We are made up of many parts; sometimes we are resentful, jealous, violent, at other times we are humble, thoughtful, calm. At different moments we are deferent beings; we are never whole, never totally integrated, are we? When a human being has many wants, he is inwardly broken up into many beings.[57]

Divisions are inherent, built into our current systems, and accepted as the societal norm. We are constantly studying and tracking separate groups, creating more and more divides, and then calling for greater inclusion with little or no idea about how to include all the differences. And yet, our very systems are starting to crack from the overwhelming weight of their insanity.

We have an incredible opportunity to see our business from a more holistic perspective. Imagine what would happen if we each had clarity on how we could help our organization succeed and, as a result, stop grappling with our own career path and need for a personal brand. It is an opportunity to integrate our life and no longer view our career as outside of ourselves.

[57] Life Ahead: On Learning and the Search for Meaning, Jiddu Krishnamurti, New World Library (2005), pp 219-220

There is a lot of healing that needs to take place on our planet, and it starts with each of us. What I am learning is that we cannot really help others integrate unless we start with our own healing and integration. We don't learn at school how to take a journey inside of ourselves and bring our fragmented pieces back together. And yet, it is the most meaningful journey of our life. We can finally start to listen, and listening often means being aware of the people showing up in our lives and how they can help us in our integration. We don't have to face our internal battles completely on our own. In fact, being in the right kind of relationship with others not only helps to push us further, but also helps us integrate more profoundly. There is an opportunity to integrate and build our communities in new ways, as you will experience in the stories in Expeditions 8, 9, and 10.

When you tap into certain alternative news sources and pioneering books, you will discover a movement on a global scale, where people from all walks of life are starting to build new systems that focus on integration. They are not the ones constantly criticizing and yelling in outrage about how screwed up the world is; they are the ones remembering their voice and recognizing that they can make a small or a big positive impact in their lives and the lives of future generations. They are the 21st century pioneers who are passionate about a saner journey, and they expect twists and turns on the road, as there is no agreed upon map to follow.

Many have started to grow their own food so they can be assured of the purity of what they consume. Others are buying organic food and sustainable fashion. There are parents who are increasingly home schooling children so they know what their kids are learning, and they are creating new social environments for their children to integrate with others. We are seeing an increase in awareness of the need to protect nature and our environment with, for example, increased interest in alternative fuel sources. There is a new fire spreading in the hearts of many people to build a world that takes into account future generations and looks beyond a single human life span.

On the road to integrating ourselves, we start the journey of getting in touch with our own internal pieces. As more of us become whole, we can step into the greater world as integrators, conveners, and community builders, where we bring the pieces together. We no longer need to retreat from our lives. Our opportunity is to flow as we become increasingly aware of who we truly are beyond our traditional career path. We can see business as a way to build relationships, and the effect we have on others is the most powerful currency we have in integrating our higher purpose.

Our Second Road Trip: Integrating Teams

The old business models, which are currently still dominant but fast fading, are built on organizational charts, reporting structures, and power relationships. Decisions take forever to make in many large organizations. Due to a growing lack of trust, we have adults managing other adults instead of growing our opportunities. We are in love with planning, control, efficiency, and structure, which are stuck in the 200-year-old industrialized model of business that too often does not take into account purpose and people.

We are told the key to success is making people happy at work, and so much energy is wasted on tired engagement programs that do not address the fundamental core opportunities of organizations. Many organizations still establish governance protocols, communication channels that provide one-way communication, which only opens up to feedback once a year, when it's time to run the annual employee survey or performance review cycle. These processes often predetermine roles and functions with little or no relationship or accountability to other roles and functions within a closed organizational system.

There are times when organizations face challenges in the course of their operations that require them to reorganize. Cisco had a brilliant idea during its 2001 layoffs. They partnered with non-profit organizations and offered some people who they wanted to keep close an opportunity to go work for a non-profit instead of being laid off. When the economy improved, many people either came back to Cisco, joined the non-profit, or chose a different path. What the leadership learned is how much knowledge about different ways of working those who chose to come back brought to the company. As a result, a new program called the Cisco Leadership Fellowship was offered on a regular basis to Cisco executives who qualified, who would step out of their full time jobs to spend six to 18 months with a non-profit. This program helped Cisco learn and integrate what non-profits needed, as well as have stronger relationships in local communities around the world. As a Cisco Leadership Fellow, I experienced how we could join forces around a shared purpose.

One of my colleagues, Si White, for example, was the director of finance for Cisco's Global Tax and Customs Group. His fellowship was with the Grameen Foundation, and he assumed the role of CFO when their previous executive left. We worked pretty autonomously back then, and had a group of other Fellows to integrate with when we needed to compare notes and bring back to the company what we were learning. However, the challenge was that when our Fellowship was over, the company did not have an easy way to integrate us, despite all the benefits this program provided. No one kept our precious "headcount" in their department, so we had to go find our next gig on our own. I was baffled that with the richness that we brought back to the company, it became a concern during the last few months of our fellowship to find a good job back in the company. The organizational box structure was not built around integration.

Imagine a world where we trusted people on our teams and in our organizations to do what they were brought in to do. Imagine for a moment that your organization not only trusted you, but you also understood your role in delivering the shared purpose. Integrating starts with choosing the right players from the time you open for business. It's important to find people who already share the values and beliefs you want to live by in your organization, and who have the hearts, brains, and courage to deliver on them. Integration also helps in adapting to change. The best plans and strategies cannot always anticipate the unexpected twists and turns that happen along an organization's journey.

When I was 17, I worked part-time in the only donut store in Richmond, British Columbia, Nuffy's Donuts. If you know anything about Canadians, you know that we stereotypically love our donuts. As a high school student, I didn't know much about business, or so I thought. When the owners opened the store, the demand was huge. We had people standing in line outside waiting patiently to pick out their dozen donuts. We could never satisfy the demand in those early days. The owners also had a second store in another location, but it did not do as well. I overheard them talking one day, and after a chat with our bakers at the back, I suggested to the owners that we track the best-selling donuts and have them fulfilled in the other location and brought over, making sure we guaranteed freshness. Our lines got more manageable after that. We were all much happier. We were no longer overwhelmed by the lines and lines of people. And I was in a situation, at a young age, where management listened to me, because after talking to customers, employees, and our bakers, I had suggested an innovative approach that made business sense.

What could happen in organizations today if we asked more questions and actually listened? What if we trusted that people outside the executive suite could also make some great decisions about areas that impact the organization? What if we realized that we have so much of what we need in our organization—far more than we usually realize—including access to people who can connect us to others who can help us with our projects? What if we stopped focusing on attaining happy and engaged workplaces, which is generally rooted in more shallow desires, and started building people-centered structures that support our higher purpose?

Leading in this century means far less micromanaging, and instead letting people deliver on the purpose of the organization by listening and talking on a regular basis. Imagine what could happen if more people felt they could make a difference rather than fearing retribution for expressing their opinions openly, or being scared they will get a poor performance rating or lose their job. People would know other people outside of their function and could connect directly with others across the organization. They would be encouraged to build their communities and bring true collaboration to their work where information is shared openly. We need to question our current metrics and take into account the behaviors they encourage. The tools are available to us; we need to adapt them.

It is as easy as deciding to tap into our company's online collaboration platform by truly engaging through conversation and letting people find each other organically through the network. Imagine what could happen if we stopped simply "liking" social media posts and started genuinely having conversations on issues that matter to us. We may be surprised at the people we cross paths with in conversations, who may turn into new relationships. Just because the people who offer these platforms built them more on an advertising model doesn't mean that is the way we must consume them. To tap into social media platforms in a 21st century way, we need to see them as an opportunity to have two-way conversations and build relationships. It is all about integration and value.

Integration is Key to 21st Century Leadership

Let's start by asking some questions:

- Why is that we call the most important people to our business, our clients or customers, external stakeholders? Why do we see the people who are the lifeline to the services and products we create as external to us? What would happen if more leaders would provide ongoing information to people who work with them? What would be the impact of sharing information with the people who would benefit from it?
- Isn't it time to stop calling people we engage with an "audience"? Isn't it time to stop performing our scripts and start listening intently and trusting more?
- Why do we ignore our ability to engage with others in two-way conversations? What role does dialogue versus meetings need to play in our work?
- Why do we have a separate function responsible for external communication? And why is it mostly separated from the internal communication function?

- Why are we still running annual employee surveys and annual performance reviews instead of talking and listening to people on a regular basis?
- How are organizational divisions helping our business thrive?
- Where are the points of integration and wholeness?

There are so many more questions we could explore on this topic. The opportunity for business is not to own and control people, but to unleash our desire to do great work, individually and collectively.

It's time to unleash our stories in a way that resonates with people and drives engagement, conversations, and relationships. Imagine your business in the midst of a human-to-human purpose and experience driven era; how would you tap into those opportunities to integrate teams around key projects that drive the business? How can customers become a more integrated part of the equation and more actively participate in your business?

Imagine, as Sebastián Ballerini shares in his story, a world where everyone is trusted to do their job. Let's imagine the following possibilities:

What if work was organized around small, autonomous teams that could come together as needed? What if you were connected with the best talent in the world that you could bring in as though you were making a movie? Not everyone needs to work for you full-time. It's often better to bring in some advisors from other industries to challenge and broaden your thinking. More of us are seeing our working lives as structured around short-term, project-based teams, rather than long-term, open-ended jobs.

What if everyone had a shared purpose and commitment? What if you knew how to play your position and come together with your team as needed, instead of just trying to please your boss or being obsessed with reporting structures? What if you were focused on why you were there in the first place?

It's Time to Build Bridges

Despite the growing recognition of the importance of integration, the fact is that in day-to-day operations we focus on transactions. We jump from one event to another, without making sure that we involve the best people in key projects. Our reporting structures and metrics dictate how work gets done, and how people are measured for their bonuses and promotions often drives their behavior regardless of the strategic plan. Work is still labeled in functions instead of integration based on purpose in the key initiatives and projects for the organization. It is very rare to operate collectively. In today's business environment, some organizations are experiencing more internal competition with increased in-fighting and stress.

We need to connect with the people in the world who would be the best ones to forge our path forward on a project, regardless of where they are geographically. Integrating ourselves with others around shared purpose is one of the most vital building blocks of how we can work in community around the specific needs of the business. This is what Sheila Babnis created at Roche by building bridges through her connected network and trusted communities, as you will discover in Expedition 9.

It's about allowing people to show up, connect, and build relationships. When we take away the fear of unjust repercussions or judgments, we can focus on delivering significant outcomes for us and for our organizations, as well as for the local community and the planet. What teams do you want to integrate with? What do you want to explore and with whom?

It's Time to Bring the Team Back Together

Last year, when I started writing this book, I had a vision that was formed in these words: "It's time to bring the team back together". And I realized months later that part of my work in the world is to share this with the team members who are just as passionate as me to bring our team back together to create a saner world, especially, in my case, when it comes to business.

When I set out on my adventure to the Amazon rainforest, I was writing a different book that was geared more toward the individual than business. After leaving many of my fears, doubts, and worries behind in the Amazon, I emerged to write this book to help guide us through the seven signposts for building thriving businesses. Integration is our anchor to our collective journey in the world. It is time for us to find each other and come together around a higher purpose. We need to live in a world where our work is more than a job that dictates our standard of living. It's time for us to bring our teams back together with purpose and wholeness in mind.

When people care deeply about their purpose and feel appreciated for their contributions, they are able to tap into their intuition and creativity. One may believe that the most exciting and innovative ideas come from places like Silicon Valley, but that is another myth, as ideas can happen anywhere and everywhere. It's about our ability to tap into our creativity and leap into uncertainty with passion and curiosity. It is about the quality of listening, empathy, conversations, and relationships we build by integrating our hopes and dreams with those of others.

Transformational Stories from the Frontiers of 21st Century Leaders

Nirit Cohen

Nirit Cohen's wisdom guides us to see how work should be transformed and helps us set a new direction for the future of work. She encourages leaders to understand that building the future requires us to revisit many aspects of the organization that got us this far, and shift from holding power over people to enabling people to tap into their own power. Nirit provides us with hope, and demonstrates courage in how she brings the team together inside and outside corporate walls.

For the past decade, Nirit has been researching, blogging, and speaking about the future of work and careers. Her story is about her courage and wisdom to help the rest of us set a path forward to see what is possible in the different parts that make up the world of work.

The Journey of Nirit Cohen: Creator. Futurist. Connector. Globes Columnist on the Future of Work.

What is your story?

A co-worker recently summarized the story of my career very well when she said that I've made a career of doing things that nobody asked me to do. I ignore the irrelevant boundaries, many of which include organizational charts and job descriptions. I ignore the way things are "supposed" to be and instead focus on the way things ideally could be. I have always been on a mission to push the boundaries of what is possible, to find new pathways for where we need to be going. Working in this way has kept me engaged, productive, fed my curiosity, and enabled me to do interesting work and make a meaningful impact, whether it's within a company or in the wider world.

I've had wonderful managers and mentors over the years, people who have encouraged me not to look back over my shoulder and to focus instead on whatever horizon I was facing. I felt they had my back in enabling me to go wherever I needed to go, especially when I was breaking new ground, going outside the boundaries that were in the way. They supported me when I was proposing things that nobody had asked for. These wonderful managers taught me a valuable lesson about the power of leadership to engage through shared values and alignment on direction.

An example of a non-traditional path we took was when we started talking about telecommuting 20 years ago. At the time, it was unheard of to think about being able to work remotely. 20 years ago our computers and our phones were connected with cables to the walls, the office was a desk, and work was a place you went to. Most people believed work should be done in the office and that anyone working remotely would not be productive. Not only were the belief systems not in place to support working remotely, but the legal and human resources systems were also not even close to understanding the needs of remote workers and the necessary flexibility.

The same thing happened with what we now call work-life programs. Back then, I took it as my mission to help the company prepare for a workplace trend I saw emerging and making it about the business results, not only about a social benefit. At the time, one of the more ground-breaking programs at the company I was working for was a gradual return from maternity leave program. It came about as we examined turnover rates of women returning from maternity leave, and as a result we created a program that allowed our employees to come back in a way that was tailored specifically to them, to their personal and family needs. These programs were hugely successful.

Telecommuting and other flexibility programs may seem obvious today, but we started this work as pioneers, understanding that different trends would change what was possible in the world of work. We are still doing it today for whatever the future brings next.

People have answers, but you need to ask them

Recently, I introduced crowd conversations to an organization as a way to solve big problems. We had a situation where we noticed that a certain group of people was facing a high degree of stress, and there were increasing indicators that we needed to do something. Everyone kept looking upwards to their managers to find a solution. No one had any idea how to solve it, and it kept getting escalated to the next level of managers until it hit senior management.

Since I believe people have the answers when you ask them the right questions, I proposed we try crowd conversation methodologies, a many-to-many conversation taken from ideation tools. We would acknowledge the issue and ask the people involved what they thought the key problems were and how we could address them. I brought in a tool where everyone could contribute to the solution. We started by asking a very broad question: "If you could have whatever you needed to fix whatever problem you are facing, what would it be?" I shared with the group that any answer was good, because we were looking to better understand the problem and tailor customized solutions. All we needed was for them to tell us what they needed. It was that simple.

This was a huge risk. We were opening everything up. When you ask questions, you also have to be committed to fully listen and do something about what comes up. It requires receiving commitment from the management team for listening and responding, which is not to say you have to do everything that is proposed, but you do have to listen, acknowledge, and respond. The initiative was highly successful, and not just in terms of implementing a new mindset via crowd conversations, but also because we were able to uncover some fundamental issues that needed closer attention. It made us reflect and dig deeper to uncover what was really going on and what we could do about it.

We identified certain cultural elements that were causing some of the work overload, and we figured out how to deal with them. When you use crowd tools, it allows you to gain insights into how people are feeling, especially when you look beyond the details and explore more deeply the root causes that are affecting people's abilities to do their work. We already know that knowledge is no longer proprietary to those at the top. Moreover, we recognize the huge power that lies in the knowledge of the crowd, and certainly the crowd within the organization. In today's hierarchical structures, that knowledge finds it hard to rise up to the top; it gets filtered and diluted on the way up. Our purpose was to find ways to make sure senior managers understood what was going on "in the corridors," and that they valued that knowledge enough to realize that they needed to implement a conversation that kept those communication lines open.

This is another example of where we created new pathways by introducing a different course of action, one that is still not very common in organizations today. By taking a new approach, we got more people engaged in co-creating the solution. As social media tools evolve and become a central part in organizations, they will seek to involve employees in effective conversations and in decision-making processes. They will reflect the more networked nature of work, rather than an unnecessarily hierarchical one.

For decades now, I have been pushing the boundaries of what is possible in the workplace and in careers. I try to experience the changes that are happening firsthand. Work used to be a place you went to; now it is what you do. We see the workplace breaking up into the parts. It is no longer just a building with employees and projects. It can be done by people not on your payroll, and it can be co-created by people in different organizations, locations, and time zones.

Companies in the future are not going to look exactly the same as they do today. They will no longer simply be about having big buildings with company logos at the top. We already see signs of the coming change. We see what we call the freelance economy, an increase in the number of people working for themselves, and the Uber model, an app that provides on-demand service to users. Even beyond that, there is the idea that you can access talent through a very wide range of possibilities, ones that are completely different from hiring full-time employees every time you need something done. And that's not only true for accessing talent externally—it's also true internally. Are people working on projects that are the best use of their time, passion, capability, and skills? Are you trying to manage from the top down?

In today's hierarchical organization, you are part of an organizational chart, where your manager "owns" you. They own your time, and they own the decision of whether or not you're allowed to work on something else. They have access to the big picture, and their job is to find ways for you to do your part of it. What we're really doing here is managing people into their boxes on the organizational chart according to their jobs, their roles, and their titles. But people no longer want to be managed into boxes, and there is a new model emerging, though we only see it today as experiments being conducted by brave organizations who understand that they have reached the limits of the hierarchical workplace. These experiments challenge decision making processes, how information is transmitted in the organization, how resources are allocated, and how teams are formed and dispersed. In some cases, people can literally roll their physical or virtual desk into whatever project they feel they can contribute to most, enabling a self-organizing mechanism to get the right talent to the right place at the right time. There is a big shift happening, and I love being part of it.

I am really passionate about transforming the workplace, and it is very hard for me to watch organizations use the models of the past to try to solve the problems of the future. I wish they would realize that what got them here will not get them where they want to go now, that they have to open up a broader page of possibilities. That is what my work is about—to get leaders and employees to see what I think some of us can already see, to transform the workplace, and to co-create a new world of work.

The challenge is that change is happening so quickly. Ideas can be obsolete in 18 months or even less, and the processes we've taken so long to establish in the workplace no longer reflect or support how we really work. But change is hard, especially the kind that forces people out of comfortable control and into uncertainty. This kind of change requires managing people and work through shared values and purpose rather than through structures and rules.

We have to understand which levers need to stay in place and which need to be changed, and more importantly, we need to have a clear understanding of what we are trying to accomplish. Only then can we create an organization or structure that will get us where we want to go.

The dreamers of tomorrow

We don't know exactly what work will look like in 2040, but we can make some educated guesses based on our growing awareness in the present. One thing I know for certain is that part of our role today is to raise children to be able to ask new questions, think unconventionally, and explore alternatives. The current education system needs to shift quite drastically. Almost anything can be found online these days. We no longer need to remember phone numbers, for example, as much of our information gets stored for us. But we do need to make sure kids are grounded in their history and feel connected to exploring their purpose.

We need to move away from a "cut and paste" world and move back into having an ability to have conversations that drive the imagination and inquiry of young minds. It's a big challenge. The new generations in the workplace are defining work as going beyond merely making a living; they look for meaning, values, and purpose, they want to make a difference, and they want to know that what they do and how they spend their time matters in more ways than one. There are already quite a few organizations around the world whose only role is to help people find meaningful work.

There is a new leader emerging focused on integration

We wear masks to work today. We know what is expected of us and we know which parts of us are okay to bring to work and which parts are not allowed. If you are worried about how you are being perceived, you wear your armor, and that ultimately hurts the organization because you are not tapping into your whole self. If you keep going to the same people and you keep asking the same questions of these same people, you will continue to get the same answers, while the outside world continues to change. In today's workplace, leaders must create an environment where there is the necessary vulnerability to ask new questions and allow people to show up fully.

If you look at the available data—like Gallup's surveys—you will see that employee engagement is very low today, and it is just as low at the management level. For a few years now employee engagement has held steady at three out of 10 people. Think about it: seven out of 10 people are coming into work for the paycheck. They are not fully present, not fully contributing. Think of what work would look like if all 10 people were fully present, innovative, and contributing. Clearly whatever we've been doing is not working. The tools we are using in the workplace are not moving the dial. We need new tools to emotionally engage people, so that they don't opt out of caring about the bigger picture, and simply clock in and clock out.

We are already seeing shifts in performance management and compensation systems to align with how people are motivated, and with what businesses need to be accomplishing. We're seeing less carrot-and-stick models and more values-based real time conversations. But we can't move forward as long as there is still fear, as long as there is a lack of trust and a strong command and control culture. We need to bridge the gap between the slogans on the

PowerPoint slides or posters hanging on the walls and how people actually experience their workplace day-to-day.

In the past, when we talked about organizational change management, we referred to moving from one stable situation to another stable situation through a period of change. But that is no longer how change happens. The world around us moves so quickly that change is a constant and seeking to get back to stability is not an option. Change is the new normal, and the pace isn't slowing down—in fact, it's probably going to accelerate. It's not about managing change, but rather focusing on trends and future casting, and looking at possible scenarios that get us thinking into the future. It's about understanding that even though you may have chosen a direction, you have to consistently re-evaluate where you are headed. That also means the organization needs to shift from setting stable processes to enabling flexibility and change. And that requires steering through shared purpose and values, a shared understanding of the direction, and then letting go and trusting people to do the right thing.

There is a lot of knowledge available about what's coming. It's not a secret; you just need to be curious and look in the right places. We know there are big technological changes coming that will affect how we live and how we work. We need to ask ourselves what we need to do to get there. That's what I did when I was responsible for the 2020 strategies of my company, and often during my keynotes I share some of the predictions I made that I can now validate. I have a slide that shows trends about the implications of the cloud on work. A few years ago, it was a very small concept and it was fun to be part of the team that predicted its explosion. The trend was there; it was just a matter of how quickly it developed and when it would expand to new areas, services, and capabilities. When you look forward, you need to realize that the space for opportunity just shifts. What used to be seen as a problem is no longer a problem, because something or someone solved it — for them it became an opportunity. And so we ask, what is not possible today that will be possible tomorrow?

You don't have to look far: we are all connected

You have to be curious in life. Ayelet and I met by reading each other's content online, and we recognized that there was a reason for us to have a conversation. And so we did. This idea of reaching out to someone you don't know just because you connected with what they have written is still unheard of to some people. And yes, you can reach out to someone on the other side of the world just because you resonated with their article! Not because you want something from them, but because there is shared interest there. And that will lead to a conversation, which might lead to co-creating. Look where it got us...

I enjoy serendipitous browsing. What's wonderful about the Internet is that you can start somewhere and end up somewhere completely different. And when you realize there are human beings you can just reach out and communicate with, you will find how generous most people are. It feeds my curiosity, and it also helps me with my work to connect with people from around the world who care about the same things I do, and who challenge my own thinking. I now have wonderful people in my network who think of me and send me a link to an article or a video they think I may find interesting, and often I discover a whole new world through them.

If you really stop to think about it, many of us live in the modern-day equivalent of a medieval village. Many of us arrive at the office every morning and meet the same dozen or so people we are used to engaging with. Maybe if you are in sales or are a service provider, you meet many more customers, but it would probably be fair to say you don't really "meet" them. If this is true for you, then ask yourself how far you are from that village mindset. How will you find new knowledge, an unexpected lead, or something that opens up your world to a different view? Who visits your village and opens up your world to stories of faraway lands?

There are many ways today to connect with people without looking too hard. Exploring the Internet could be one of them. But for that to happen serendipitously, it needs to be done by surfing, not narrowly searching. Serendipity, for me, is finding and resonating with people and content, and recognizing when exciting new opportunities and connections can emerge from it.

Integrating our lives

If you are passionate about what you are doing in the world and feel it's feeding your soul, and if you are making an impact in the world, then you don't need to seek out balance between life and work. I often get asked where I get the time to do what I do, beyond my day job. To me, it's all about doing what is valuable to me and what fills me with energy. Many of us know, if we raise families, that we have time we spend with our kids and time we spend taking care of household needs, and we decide what we spend time on. At certain points in our lives, some of these needs change and we may no longer spend as much time as we did with our children as they get older. When you do have your own time, you can choose to watch TV or read, for example, or you can choose to start building your second or third career. You don't even need to call it a career, but rather what you want to do with your life.

When I looked at my own career and life when my kids were leaving home, I started to think that I probably had just as much career in front of me as I had behind me, and there was really no reason to assume that the time ahead was going to look the same. The future of work fascinates me because I get to help people understand it, and at the same time, I am living it.

The next time you read an article about jobs being replaced by robots or software, ask yourself if your skills, job, or profession are at risk. Then ask yourself if you know your capabilities, what value you can bring to anyone who wants to hire you, or who may work with you or for you. Ask yourself every day if you are up to date on the relevant knowledge and skills you need, and how you can innovate and grow in your area of work. Take responsibility to do whatever it takes to grow, develop, evolve, and dare to change. Whatever is required to move you forward on the path to your most important role is yours and not owned by an organization. Who you are is what you take with you wherever you go, and not the roles you performed in the organizations you've worked for. And who you are can evolve to be whatever is right for you today and tomorrow.

I hope that organizations will start having a stronger sense of purpose, and realize that it is no longer all about the organizational pyramid, but also about knowing how to ask questions and find the solutions together. Work is a significant driver for social change. I hope that if we treat people at work with respect and dignity, then we will move to a better place in the world. I am glad to see the signs of that change already emerging, and even happier to be part of this workplace transformation.

Lisa A. (Zurn) Cafferata, PhD

Lisa A. (Zurn) Cafferata seeks to impact the world by bringing people together and leveraging the strength of communities. Driven by a desire to empower people to realize their greatest potential, she builds connection, collaboration, and ownership within teams and groups that ultimately lead to growth and progress. She helps others capitalize on opportunities and succeed. As you will experience through her story, Lisa is motivated to push boundaries to deliver meaningful results.

The Journey of Lisa A. (Zurn) Cafferata, PhD: Imaginer. Collaborator. Innovator. Executive Director, Learning Design and Content, Young President's Organization (YPO).

What is your story?

My love of learning emerged during my undergraduate years when I was studying abroad in Stockholm. When you are living abroad at an early age, you have a transformational opportunity to see the world through a new lens. With that lens comes an appreciation for the diversity of our world and learning from different perspectives.

I was in Stockholm during their election cycle and also the time they voted to join the European Union. It was a very unique experience for me to be able to view the Swedish political system. I witnessed a different way to govern a nation. My time abroad opened my eyes to the possibility that there was not just one way of doing things. There was a true appreciation for the "greater good," in particular, coming from Scandinavia, their emphasis on community and consensus, not individual ego-driven processes

This had a very profound effect on me as I developed, learned, and grew into my own skin, especially when I started stepping into leadership roles. It helped me understand that what is truly better for humanity can oftentimes—and not just in a political or governmental sense—roll over into project work, business, and the way we lead teams.

After finishing graduate school, I didn't know what I wanted to do, but I found myself heading into teaching, following the academic route. But I very quickly learned that I didn't want to be hidden behind a desk, doing the "publish-or-perish" scene. I didn't feel that I had enough of an impact when I was there. I was looking for an opportunity where I could be in education yet be in the field—in the real world, not the ivory tower.

I happened upon an opportunity at the Young President's Organization (YPO) that exposed me to their global membership of presidents and CEOs. It was a very daunting opportunity, as I was just coming out of graduate school in my early 20s, to be faced with clients who were all CEOs and presidents of companies, while I was a newly-minted PhD with pretty much no experience in the business world.

I was very intimidated by who I'd be working with. All these powerful CEOs were around me, and it took me a few months before a mentor took me aside and told me, "We hired you for a reason. We hired you because you are intelligent and you have an opinion and ideas. You need to start stepping into that space and expressing them, because that's what they are looking for you to do."

Leading with vulnerability

Early in my career with YPO I went on a father-daughter weekend retreat with some of our members and their 9-11 year old daughters. We were in a forest doing a ropes course as part of a team building event. Each of the 24 sets of fathers and daughters were pairing up, climbing a tree, and going across the course. One father kept letting all the other fathers go in front of them, saying, "Go right ahead, go right ahead, go right ahead." When the last pair finally passed by, his daughter climbed up the tree and he remained firmly planted on the ground.

I could tell that he wasn't feeling well, so I walked over to find out what was going on. And when I did, he said to me, "I am afraid of heights and can't get myself off the ground. I don't want to disappoint my daughter because I know how much she wants to do this activity, but I physically can't get myself off the ground. Would you mind doing the course with her and I'll meet you on the other side?"

I said, "Absolutely, of course," and I did the activity with his daughter and came down the other side, then started walking back to the campsite. Afterwards, the father took me aside and told me how much he appreciated my stepping in so that his daughter did not feel left out. It meant a lot to him, and not only because she wanted to do the activity; this was also the first time his daughter had ever seen her father in a state other than as "super dad." She could now see that he was human and had frailty, that he could be scared. And secondly, he also had three boys and this was the first time he had spent a weekend alone with his daughter. He'd had no idea how much guts she had and how strong she was.

Later that evening, there was a candlelight ceremony where the fathers passed down to their daughters a family heirloom, and each man told a story about the artifact. By the end of the night, there were 24 emotional grown men and their daughters reflecting on their connections with their family ancestry. At the end of that retreat, I realized that these leaders I was working with were also human, they had frailties, and in that way, they were just the same as you and me. I started off by having a very intimidated view of who I'd be working with, and in that moment I realized that it was okay to be human as a leader and to show some vulnerability, to appreciate people and ask for help.

I learned so much in that one weekend about the many faces of leadership. I still share that story to this day with new colleagues as a pivotal moment in my personal leadership journey. As I grew into higher leadership roles and greater responsibilities within the organization, I learned to be honest with myself, to be honest with my team, to trust them, and to ask for help when I needed it. I really want to support people in their strengths and identify areas where they find purpose and passion.

Integrating a team as a leader

I recently transitioned to a new role within the organization, in a new portfolio. I had a meeting with my new team, and I shared with them, "If you ever feel that we are not drawing from your strengths or we are out of focus with your purpose, please tell me. We may need to redirect your activity or take some of the tasks off your plate and give them to someone else who may have the strength and passion to take it on. Let's see if we can keep this team working together efficiently and joyfully. When we are working at our optimal level, we make the most impact on the organization by producing the greatest products and services for our members."

The team shared with me that they appreciated me saying this, because they had never had a leader offer them the ability to provide feedback and tailor their experiences to the team. One team member shared that in the past, he would tend to be annoyed when something wouldn't go right for him, and that I had helped him realize that it is his responsibility as a member of the team to keep me, the team leader, informed of where he could be most effective.

It has been quite a journey having the exposure to so many different types of leaders over the past 14 years that I have been with YPO. There is such a diversity of ways people can lead. While some people need to have an official title, there are so many other leaders among us who care about being of service without taking on a title. It amazes me to no end when they are brought to the foreground and all of a sudden people realize that this person was really leading from behind and they didn't want the attention—they just wanted to support and make the people around them successful. That is the essence I hope to make shine in my own style as a leader—that people not feel "led," but rather that they feel supported, and given opportunities to grow and make an impact.

The power of community

We must leverage the community of the learners around us. That is what differentiates traditional education from learning ("sage on the stage versus guide on the side"). In the world of online learning, there are very few platforms that stand out as unique. Those that are really in a class of their own are those that leverage the community within them. The students engage and support each other, and they get academic credit for it.

I recently learned about HBX, a digital learning initiative powered by Harvard Business School. They are the virtual arm and have developed their own learning management system with three aspects: social, case-based, and active learning. They use a unique cohort model and create accountability for engagement and support amongst the community of learners. That is how they differentiate themselves: they recognize students who contribute to the community of learning.

What makes YPO so unique is not just the access to incredible speakers and resources—which is the traditional pedagogy of gaining information from an expert—but also how we provide opportunities for our members to leverage expertise among the community for learning. That is where active and experiential learning need to happen: when you are sitting around a table in a workshop and someone shares an insight, and you walk through that insight and play in the space with each other. And then you come out and realize that you can go in a different direction because of what was learned from the person sitting next to you, and not just from the person speaking in front of the room.

How we can create social learning more fluidly?

What we need to facilitate in social learning is a structure that allows for alliances in the form of integrating project teams. I am hoping we will see more flexible structures emerge, especially those that allow for greater collaboration and integration around key opportunities that bring people together on projects with shared purpose.

If you look at those organizations that have the most engaged workers, they are open and inclusive, not the traditional command and control structures. If you look at lean, agile, and successful companies and the CEOs who have the most engaged workforces, they are tapping into a variety of people to help on projects or to move initiatives forward. They are looking to leverage people's passions, purpose, and strengths towards a common goal rather than keeping projects exclusively to a traditional siloed department.

Communication, transparency, and connectivity are the traits of the new leaders. I am hopeful that we will enter a new era where decisions will no longer be made in a closed room where no one else outside the room knows what the decision was until three months later, when half the workforce is laid off. 21st century leaders are open to creative conversations and problem solving, including a variety of people in their decision-making. They will find a much happier workforce and end up with outcomes they could not have previously predicted. Maybe instead of layoffs, they will be able to reallocate certain pieces of hardware and sell off certain assets. If they asked people on the line if they were really using this piece of equipment and the people said no, the company could save $250,000 versus firing five people. The leaders of the future are the ones who do not just sit in the high office and make decisions in a vacuum; they reach across and are transparent in their leadership style.

Age and generation does not necessarily denote leadership style, as I have met experienced leaders who are adaptable and excited to lead in the fresh leadership style. They have stepped into the second or third iteration of their own journey, because they simply feel more comfortable now with this new style of leadership than what they were traditionally taught. I do see some of our older members coming back around to become entrepreneurs again in their 50s and 60s, and even early 70s. They are sparked by this new energy to lead differently and embrace new opportunities. Those are the people I really enjoy working with. They not only have a more collaborative way of leading, but they have the experience of knowing what worked well for them and where they needed to grow. They can tell stories, and leverage their connections and experiences. They have been there, done that, turned the corner, and come back around with a brand new style of leadership.

Life as a journey of learning

My parents are both in their 70s and are working on books and are visiting scholars at a local university. They had a very different perspective on my working with such high powered people when I first started with YPO. As they hear the stories of humanity and the challenges the people I work with face, they are touched and very supportive. They have also seen the ripple effect that I can have by fostering a learning environment and producing opportunities for someone to become a better leader, which then impacts that person's organization, community, and family.

When I was meeting with my new team, we created a word cloud for our new department, where everyone offered words to describe the department, and then each person circled their top three words with a different color marker on the whiteboard. We crossed off the ones that didn't make it to the top of the list. We were all part of the process to create our vision and shared purpose. It is a whole different dynamic to set up the team, seeing each person as a contributing member and making us whole. We are each a piece of the puzzle, rather than being a traditional hierarchy and chain of command with trickling down leadership. Each member of the team is empowered—and expected—to step in and contribute.

I could have come in and said, "My name is Lisa and you report to me now. This is our mission statement. This is our vision. These are the tasks and you are going to work on for this project. See you in six months when we have our review." But that doesn't empower my team members to feel they are part of the process; you just create people who become resentful and disassociated from the tasks.

I strive to be a new 21st century leader. I seek to impact the world by bringing people together and leveraging the strength of communities. I am driven by a desire to empower people to realize their greatest potential, build connection, collaboration, and ownership that ultimately leads to growth and progress. I want to help others capitalize on opportunities and succeed. One small piece of this realization happens during our weekly check-ins where we give updates, I ask how I can be of service to the team, and how the team can be of support to one another, connecting the dots and weaving the work of the team together. If we are getting significant contributions, if the team is working together and producing the highest quality, then we are realizing our vision. The key is to strive for our common purpose.

By bringing people together around shared purpose, everyone becomes part of a contributing team. A collaborative style allows you to be more agile. When we involve each other, there is more focus on the work, as everyone is aware of what our collaboration goals are. You get to the finish line with a much more effective product. As a leader, you are part of the team, where you have a responsibility and accountability for communication. You should be constantly iterating. Collaboration and co-creation are our path to making our vision happen.

Alan Schaefer

Alan Schaefer is the founder and CEO of Banding People Together, a supergroup of behaviorists, strategists and rock stars with a passion and expertise for all things collaboration. He has been described as a maestro of human capital excellence and brings his unique perspective as an entrepreneur, recording artist, songwriter, and consultant to his current work. He founded the band Five Star Iris and realized that the valuable lessons he learned from playing in bands could be applied to leadership, teams, and organizations in a number of different environments, including the business world.

Drawing from his experience with successful record producers, Alan believes in creating an environment that people truly want to be in, and works with organizations across many different industries to show them how to achieve collaborative culture or what many in the music world would call "vibe."

The Journey of Alan Schaefer: Collaborator. Integrator. Rock Star. Founder, Banding People Together.

What is your story?

My left brain and right brain have been fighting each other for most of my life. I am very much an analytic problem solver, but I am also an artist. There are not a whole lot of places where those two sides can co-exist together in our world.

I was an early dot-comer and took a $30,000 equity loan from my parents' home. I started tourdates.com with my twin brother in 1993 to level the playing field for independent bands like ours. At the time, there were websites that showed where the big acts were touring, but we were promoting the smaller bands that really needed help with promotion and connecting with their fans. We were fighting the good fight and got acquired six years later by Launch Media, who was later acquired by Yahoo.

I was now a vice president overseeing the integration of the acquisition of our company. I got an email from a vice president of the company that had acquired us, pretty much telling us they were shutting us down and no longer needed us. What took six years to build, they had dismantled in six months.

I quickly decided that I wanted to get as good as I could at writing songs, so I started hanging out in Nashville, where I was taken under the wing of some hit songwriters. I then started the band Five Star Iris and was fortunate enough to tour the world playing music. We were famous in some places and couldn't get arrested in other places if we had tried.

After some time, I started having problems with my band. In an unforgettable LA moment, I was having lunch with a friend of mine, Briggs Ferguson, who happened to be the CEO of City Search. He suggested I read a book called *Five Dysfunctions of a Team* by Patrick Lencioni. This book helped put me on the path to understanding that collaboration takes a lot of work. I had a moment of realization that we were in trouble, and I thought it was the entire fault of the other band members; they were not trying as hard as me, they didn't want it as bad as me, and they were waiting for me to do everything. I realized over time that it was partially them, but it was also me as a leader who was failing all of us.

We ran our band like a business—or so we thought. It turns out that just because you can sell your company for eight figures, it doesn't really mean that you know how to run a business. People had responsibilities, but I was the leader. I was constantly working on building the business, while everyone else had other jobs, whether it was the person in charge of our online presence or the person who made sure the band worked well together when we were on the road. I was the quarterback. I was a tyrant with a smile. Looking back, it was my way or the highway. I wasn't a complete jerk about it, but I would wear people down under the guise of debate.

Not everyone was given a voice. I wasn't able to let go of control. Everybody had a lot to bring to the table, and I was forcing people into things I perceived we needed. For example, I would build a story in my mind around why each person needed to do what I thought we needed them to do. "You like t-shirts, so you should do our merchandising." But I didn't ask them how they could make a difference. I would then be surprised and bewildered when we didn't get the results I was hoping for.

I was the one in the band who was going to Nashville to meet with the music producers and record labels. I was under the impression that I knew what was best for us. There were certain elements of how we worked that were collaborative and others that, looking back, were more like a solo project in band's clothing.

Here we were, some of the most talented people in the world, and yet there was a limit to our success and I was a big part of that limit. If I had a dime for every time someone told us that we would be the next big band like U2, I'd be on my own private island somewhere. But talent is not enough. In the music business, I learned early on that talent does not guarantee success, and lack of talent does not guarantee failure. I was so focused on how much effort I was putting into the band that I believed I knew what was best for all of us. It is these lessons that helped me want to bring collaboration to the world of business today.

The business we have now with Banding People Together is, on some dramatic level, me righting my wrongs by helping other leaders understand how to create the conditions that optimize teams in a way where the process feels as good as the result. We've taken the wisdom and lessons learned from arguably one of the most volatile collaborative environments on the planet (a band) and combined that with validated behavioral science to build a framework and methodology called True Collaboration℠. It comes from a deep understanding and knowing what it feels like to be a solo project in band's clothing. This happens every single day in today's business world, and now I get to do work I love to bring the band back together to sing in harmony. My passion is around helping leaders in organizations of all sizes collaborate by looking at how they can get the right people, give them a voice, and let them rock and do what they do with some guidance and structure, so that they can show up authentically and contribute to the overall sound. That's how you get to the greatness.

I was at a networking event in Nashville for my band Five Star Iris with some music supervisors, the people who pick music for scenes in television programs or movies. It was a kick-off event in a studio called Ocean Way in an old church in Nashville, and they put us in groups of six to eight people and had us write songs together. They took musicians and the music supervisors, split us into groups, and told us that we had two hours to write a song. It was incredible. I had just learned about this thing called team building, and I thought to myself that this could be another flavor of team building in corporate America, where we can get people together in new ways. I then found an instructional designer to help build out a curriculum, and Banding People Together was up and running.

People ask me all the time how on earth I came up with such a crazy idea of bringing music into companies in this way. It was a journey of figuring out how the insights we had from collaborating (or not) as a band could be transferred to the corporate world and create great teams. What started off as an idea around team building has evolved into collaboration training and strategy. Our core beliefs are founded on creating a workplace that people want to be in by teaching the behavioral and tactical how of collaboration. By helping establish the collaborative rules of the road, we are able to minimize what we call "collaborative insanity"—that's the notion that people will work better together by simply telling them to do so. We bring collaboration strategies and approaches to leaders who are ready to move into the 21st century, and simply use music to express the inexpressible.

At some of our larger events, it feels like a rock concert. People come into the room and see a stage and a bunch of musical instruments and go, "Oh gosh, what's going on?" Then we take the stage and rock out. When possible, we strive to create a visceral concert-like experience to help participants open up in a way that connects their heads and hearts, burrowing into their limbic brain where emotion and long term memories live. It helps our methodology stick in a freakishly profound way.

We then tell them that we are there to redefine collaboration as they know it by bringing them into our world, and showing them what it means for them. One of the ways we do it is to bring everyone into the world of music creation. We tell them that they will all be writing original songs, and that's when some people start freaking out. It used to make me uncomfortable as I saw people fidgeting in discomfort when they got the big reveal of why we were all there. I could read lips from playing so many shows, and I would see curse words being muttered and people looking at their watches. But I also knew that the more uncomfortable the person was at the beginning, the more powerful their transformation would then become.

Understanding our own sound and harmony

Our Collaborative Harmony Index (Find Your Groove℠) is the behavioral engine/instrument that drives our True Collaboration℠ framework and methodology. It has all the underpinnings of validated behavioral science, but is served up in a common sense way of everyday behaviors people exhibit. which makes it easy for people to adopt. It is communicated in a music-infused way, as everyone relates to music.

Behaviorally speaking, we show people how they show up to the collaborative process and how they naturally can make the most collaborative impact. It's about self awareness; how can you be in the groove if you don't understand your own sound and what you bring to the table? We brought in a PhD to help us create the diagnostic with the goal of measuring collaboration on an individual, team, and organizational level. We help leaders understand the collaborative competencies they need to stop the insanity of how complex collaboration has become in most organizations. What's collaborative to one person isn't always seen as collaborative to someone else. Our True Collaboration℠ methodology provides the governance and structure—the rules of the road—to get everyone playing from the same sheet of music when it comes to working together to achieve results.

In our behavioral model, we are concerned about how your personality shows up to the collaborative process, what your relevant tendencies are, and how you approach a collaborative dynamic, so we developed this index to help people not only better understand themselves when it comes to collaboration, but also to see how they come together as a team. We teach our clients about collaborative behavioral styles with a behavior model that is based on famous recording artists as a metaphor. It really helps the learning stick.

As artists, our whole job is trying to connect; we are moving energy. It's the ego part of us that says, "I can't," or, "They are going to think I am not smart if I say this," versus, "This is the totality of what I bring. I make no excuses for who I am." For me, as an artist, I never understood what being "ready" was. When I was on the quest for rock stardom and someone in the industry early in my career would say, "Alan, you are not there yet," I never knew what "there" meant.

"There" is when you are comfortable in your own skin. Rock stars, of course, want people to buy their records and love their music. However, they are not worried about whether everyone loves what they do. If I do what I do and the right people connect with it, then it's gold.

Rock stars by default create really amazing experiences for other people. They thrive on it. They are not so encumbered, beaten down, and trapped in the ego of what someone is going to think about them. They are following their hearts, and if someone feels connected to your heart, that's the real currency.

To get people to open up as a rock star on stage is no different from what we do now, and we have the behavioral science to back it up as they look in the collaborative mirror. At the end of the day, people need to learn to let go of behaviors that no longer serve them. We see people transform every day in the craziest places, and they are usually the ones who think they don't have a creative bone in their body—as if writers, musician, authors, poets, or sculptors had cornered the market on creativity.

We once did a session for a client who brought their executive team in to see how they could improve their overall performance. At the beginning of the session, we gave the big reveal and told them they would be writing songs together. Someone asked whether they would also be performing it. Of course that is part of it, but I told them that it sounded like a great idea, let's do it.

I saw a woman sitting at the front who was visibly uncomfortable. She was shaking her head with her arms folded, and she looked at me and said, "There is no way in hell you are ever getting me up there."

I looked at her and said, "What if I told you that by the time this day is over, wild horses couldn't keep you away from getting up on this stage and singing your song with your band mates?"

"Well, we'll see," she answered.

At the end of the day when the whole team came back together to share their co-creation, she came up to me and her entire body language had changed. The black clouds were gone and there was only sunshine and laughter. She grabbed my arm and said, "I can't wait to get up there with my band mates." I gave her a high five and a hug.

Our work brings out people's vulnerability and makes some people so uncomfortable, but there is something about the music-centricity that helps people go into themselves and discover what is already there. It's like remembering an old story or song that played an important role in our lives that we had simply forgotten. Music is connectedness. Everyone has some heart-centered feelings about music. When we talk about trust in our sessions, we talk about vulnerability, and we have people share stories about what music means to them.

What have I heard people share in our sessions in corporate America? Things like, "Whenever I hear Van Halen, it reminds me of the first time I smoked pot." Can you imagine saying that in corporate America today? Well, they do.

"I don't like to hear piano because when I was a kid, my teacher beat my hand with a ruler when I hit the wrong note."

"This is the song that was playing when I heard the news that my brother wasn't coming home from Iraq, and every time I hear it, it makes me think of him."

People are sharing in ways that humanize us at work, and all of a sudden it's not John from accounting anymore—that's John who had his first kiss to "Any Way You Want It" in eighth grade.

We start seeing each other as human beings. Music connects people by tearing away the boundaries and allowing us to get people to a place where they can learn and think differently. It's about applying their work through a more human lens.

And it's fun—people learn about music, and it is incredibly intentional by design. We integrate the business challenges so they can see the opportunity in how to co-create. It doesn't matter what age people are, or where they come from. Music and love are languages that hum at their own levels, and we can all tap into that. It allows people to pause, come together, and process in a way that's different than they are used to. It shifts them to be able to see themselves and others, and bring them together with a shared purpose.

Our business is to help align people around delivering on the organization's strategy. We unlock people's hearts and minds and show them how to truly collaborate and create harmony. Together, they can write songs for the business and collaborate in delivering them in a more holistic way. It helps them recognize that everyone plays a part, and that new behaviors will provide breakthroughs to the overall performance of the company.

Why does the team need to get back together?

We are in the business of integrating people and process. It's about productivity, efficiency, and outcomes. It's not about making anyone a better worker; it's about helping every person discover what's great about him or her and where they can grow and improve. They are looking through a different lens that transcends business, so when they go home and talk to their kids or their neighbors, they are communicating about how their work integrates with a higher purpose. Ironically, my aspirational goal was to change the world through music in the flavor of Bono and U2. I fundamentally believe we are doing that now, just in a different way that still profoundly touches people. It also breaks the myth that we are two people: a personal self and a professional self. Bringing music in not only helps bring us back to being whole people, it allows us an avenue to bring the whole team back together, to focus on how we will deliver our best selves to the work we do, and to learn how to co-create beyond organizational walls.

Senior executives want their people to work together better, but most often, they look at it in a very limiting way. They think it will increase overall productivity and bottom line results. Often, that's all that matters to them. But there are even greater benefits of creating a truly collaborative environment—a place where everyone has a voice and is allowed to contribute—as collaboration helps us to tap into our purpose.

Most companies don't know they have a challenge when it comes to collaboration. Most believe they are great at collaborating and that they even have it down to an art form. They believe that just because they have the technology to allow people in Hong Kong to work with people in New York City that they have collaboration. But how do you get people working together and truly leveraging diversity of thought? How do you create an environment where people care deeply, not only about their work, but about connecting with other people around shared purpose? What motivates us in the first place? Most people want to make an impact. Why not let them?

It takes such an investment of time and development. Many companies say they want it, but they don't really have the stones to do the real work. The tendency is to create training sessions with seminars and workshops, but they don't create real life experiences for people to understand how to truly collaborate and integrate as part of their day-to-day experiences.

Mixing sound in music, like human behavior, is dynamic. The sound at the concert hall at 8:00 pm when people are just arriving versus at 10:00 pm when it is a full house is different. No matter how much you stick to process, the sound is changing and never static. Most organizations don't understand the real value of this type of work in terms of sustainability and growth. They think that because they hire people, publish a strategy, and sprinkle in training that collaboration will be organic, that it will just magically happen all by itself. But it doesn't work that way. When everyone in the band (or team) knows how to play their parts and are also recognized for their contributions individually and collectively, that's where the music (or collaboration) happens.

The 21st century leaders we work with see us as a bit of disruption, in a good way. Our work is highly collaborative. It's like going out on tour. There is a continuous development journey we have built through the following steps:

- Step 1 is where we shift the conversation after one of our collaborative experiences. People go back to daily work and apply and live it.
- Step 2 is is the heart of our methodology. It helps each person and each team develop new muscles of head and heart through the application of our Collaborative Harmony Index (Find Your Groove℠) . It allows them to gain a deeper understanding of their behavioral styles, skills, operationalizing collaborations, development plans, coaching, and team deployment. At this time, the transition is to get the team or organization speaking the same language around people and process as it relates to the human collaboration dynamic. If you don't do it, what you end up with is like putting four musicians in a room and having them each play whatever they want—you'll never get a unified sound. We work on changing the

conversation and developing new muscle memory. This is head and heart; the organizations that will truly succeed understand that we need both in the 21st century.

- Step 3 is where we help leaders and individual contributors prepare and share their new music in a simple way. It becomes a big talent management piece. Like a producer in the studio, we create an ideal environment and make sure the team has the right people doing the right stuff—what they are great at.
- Step 4 is where we assess what's going on using tools, and also by observing what is happening at the organization by paying attention to the atmosphere. You can tell a lot by walking through the halls of organizations, and also by sitting in on meetings. The human side of business is not hard to read if we are awake to what we are trying to achieve in bringing our people together.

Everyone is latching on to employee engagement scores, but when you look at the methodologies in place to capture those scores, you can see that they are antiquated. We are not having the right conversations, and are just throwing more engagement ambassadors at the issue does not bring the team back together to rock.

It's simple: true 21st century leaders create a place where people want to be, a place of opportunity and gratitude. I went to the final Grateful Dead show in Chicago, and there was an overwhelming feeling of gratitude coming from both sides—the band and the audience. There was a feeling of pure harmony and joy. That type of energy is undeniable.

Where is the gratitude from senior leaders today? Leaders who are stuck in the last century are enclosed in their ivory towers dictating what needs to happen. It may be good for them (at least in the short term), but not for everyone else. They may say the right words, but they are not living it. So many organizations talk about teams and collaboration, and yet their systems continue to only recognize certain individuals. The days of showing appreciation only through a bonus are over. The 21st century leader knows there are simple ways to show appreciation and set up systems that align with individuals and teams.

The organizations that will make it will have both head and heart in the equation. More than ever, people want to feel like they belong to something bigger than themselves. If we are not creating the vibe in organizations for people to be connected, then, to paraphrase Einstein's definition of insanity, we will only have more of the same.

Exercises for Expedition 7

18 **Internalizing Integration**		
	What does integration mean to me?	
	Am I focused on transactions or integration?	
	What would integration look like in my life?	
	What is my dream of integration in the world and in business?	
	What gets in the way of integration for me? What can I do about it?	
	What is working well for me in terms of integration? How can I take it further?	
	What systems do I feel are breaking down that I see as opportunities for me to make a difference?	

19 **Bringing the Team Back Together**		
	What does the word "team" mean to me? Who is part of my team?	
	Are there other people I need to reach out to and dialogue with about how we can bring our team back together? Who are they? What can I do to reach out to them?	
	Is my team integrated or fragmented? Why?	
	What would "bringing the team back together" look like for me and my team?	

20 **Making Connections**		
	I appreciate (name one person):	
	I also appreciate (name another person):	
	Do they know I appreciate them? Why or why not?	
	How can I let them know I appreciate them?	
	Someone who may need my help is:	
	Another person who may need my help is:	
	How can I reach out to them?	
	Someone who may be able to help me is:	
	Another person who may be able to help me is:	
	How can I ask them for help?	

21 **Connecting Stories**	Thinking about each of the stories you just experienced, what do they mean for your own journey to conscious 21st century leadership?	
	Nirit Cohen	
	Lisa A. (Zurn) Cafferata, PhD	
	Alan Schaefer	

Expedition 8
New Ways of Being

Under the old business mindset, this Expedition would be called New Ways of *Working*, but our world is evolving, and for many people, working as a way of life is just not enough anymore. This change is happening as more of us wake up and realize we want to live an integrated life rather than being reduced to a job we don't enjoy just to make a living.

Business and society are starting to fuse, and, despite what the news tells us, this is an amazing time to be alive and be a pioneer in a growing movement of people who are ready for a new way of being. At some point, many more leaders in large organizations will need to get their heads out of the sand if they want to write a new story that resonates with people and helps their organizations thrive. Command and control is hanging on by a thread and is an illusion fueled by 20th century fear, scarcity, and competition.

Technology has made it possible to reach out and connect more people than ever before, which has led to more of a focus on being able to customize and personalize our experiences. We can now jump on a video call with someone across the world and build relationships and partnerships like never before. Our familiar frameworks are in a state of flux in our increasingly connected world. Ironically, the old world powers would like us to continue to believe that our voice does not count. But many of us, who can now connect with people and get news instantly from all over the world, can no longer stay silent.

Today, news travels fast through our networks and in our communities. And we need to recognize that it is not simply *the news*; these are real events happening to real people. How should we react? When a friend posts on their Facebook page that their relative has died of cancer, do we simply "like" it or send a sad emoji, or do we reach out to them directly? We need to go beyond being a spectator to becoming an active participant in every aspect of our lives. It's an open invitation available to all who choose to accept it.

Society and business are fusing as we move into a world where technology is not considered to be evil (although it can, of course, still be used for evil purposes by people). We should be more focused on understanding the value technology brings to our lives and business, while also spending more time being silent and appreciating the beauty of the world we live in and connecting with others. We too often blame technology for our poor choices in how we spend our time. As a child, I loved to read, but my father would not allow us to read during dinnertime, even though he shared our love of books. He wanted us to share our time together, focused on each other. We can do the same with our mobile devices by setting them aside when spending quality time with those close to us, and then using them wisely to connect with people and open new opportunities.

We are hiding behind a fairly recent belief that we need to detox from technology. While it is true that some people believe they need to be responsive 24/7 to any message that comes through their device, it is rarely an issue of technology. Did we blame the telephone or the lightbulb for bringing new connectivity into our lives? While it can be so invigorating and healthy to spend time in nature or simply go for a walk, it doesn't mean that we necessarily need to detox ourselves from our technology. What if we looked at our underlying addictive patterns instead? Thinking that we need to answer emails or texts in the middle of the night is a whole different conversation that brings us again to the deeper issue of what work really means for us today. We can't blame technology for our own misguided behavioral patterns.

We need more integrated gatherings focused on what we are creating together in our business, rather than simply attending technology detox camps. When used in a common sense way, technology can take us to new heights. Juan Francisco Tellez, a co-founder of Param Media, reminds us that technology is part of nature. He clarifies further by stating that "instead of using the phrase 'artificial intelligence,' what we essentially mean is 'human-aided intelligence.' In other words, human-synthesized technology in one way or another is capable of capturing or expressing different degrees of intelligence."

How a Connected World Saved a Life

Technology is key to our integration into new ways of being, where technology is a part of us and part of nature in general. There is no better way to explain new ways of being in harmony with technology than to share the story of Theo Menswar, as originally written by Sheila Babnis.

—

Theo was your average 13-year old boy. He was busy going to school, playing soccer and spending time with his friends and family—loving life. Then he was diagnosed with a blood cancer called Myelodysplastic Syndrome in May 2012. His cure required a bone marrow transplant. After receiving the transplant, Theo developed another deadly disease, Stage 4 Graft vs. Host disease (GVHD). Treatment for GVHD includes suppressing the immune system to extreme levels. Dr. Yasser Khaled, Theo's bone marrow physician, followed the prescribed protocol and suppressed his immune system. Unfortunately, while this was being done, Theo contracted a deadly fungal infection called Mucormycosis (caused by the fungus Mucor). The proper treatment for Mucormycosis is to boost the immune system so that the body can attack the fungus. These two issues created a "zero sum game" for Theo's health.

On March 23, 2013, the doctors pulled his family into a room and explained that no matter which issue they treated, the other would take Theo's life. The doctors suggested the family say their goodbyes, as they believed Theo wouldn't make it through the night.

Theo's father, Brant, shared this devastating news with the extended family. Brant's younger brother, Todd, who lives in New Hampshire, was devastated. Unbeknownst to Brant and his wife, Todd took five minutes and filmed a video of him holding poster boards pleading for help from anyone who could help save Theo's life, and uploaded the video to YouTube. In his heart, he believed there were other experts beyond their hospital system who might be able to help save Theo.

Within 48 hours, the video had over 500,000 views. Brant and his wife started to receive calls from people all over the world who believed they could help. Early the next morning, Brant Menswar received a call from Dr. Dimitrios Kontoyiannis at MD Anderson in Houston. He said, "I saw your video and I believe I can help save your son. Mucormycosis is my specialty." Dr. Dimitrios Kontoyiannis was joined by close friend Dr. Tom Walsh, who was a leading researcher on the Mucor fungus at Cornell University.

Brant also received a call later that morning from Dr. Tim Johnson of *Good Morning America*. Dr. Johnson asked Brant to speak with Dr. Khaled, their personal physician and the bone marrow specialist, to make a list of any doctors he wanted to speak with in the country. Dr. Johnson said he would personally make it happen within 24 hours. True to his word, Dr. Johnson connected them with Dr. Joseph Antin at Dana Farber Cancer Institute in Boston. Dr. Antin was the foremost expert on GVHD. Dr. Khaled put aside his own ego and embraced the ideas he was hearing from the other experts. With their guidance, Dr. Khaled had one of the best teams fighting for Theo's life. The local and extended team integrated and came together to save Theo. It took the wisdom of the collective community to make it happen.

Although the four physicians were not co-located, they were able to get on the phone and video conference to work together to discuss the pros and cons of the options for Theo's care. Together with Dr. Khaled, the four physicians came up with a plan to treat Theo. Each placed their egos aside to listen, learn, and consider the very best alternatives for Theo, which ended up being alternatively boosting and suppressing his immunity. After several weeks of care and minor changes in therapy, Theo grew stronger day by day and was eventually able to thrive.

—

Imagine a world in which we had more 21st century leaders helping each other on a larger scale. In her story, Sheila Babnis sends a strong call to action to the medical community to join an online collaboration community like Doximity or Sermo, allowing them to stay connected to others so that more help can be offered to save lives. She also asks physicians to take at least 30 minutes once a week to offer advice and help to a family or another physician who needs someone with specific knowledge. A strong collaborative community strategy, including using social media tools with purpose, is the new way of being. Social media is not just for the younger generations—it's for all of us.

A strong collaborative community strategy is one new way of being in community. The technology that connects us also binds us together in new ways. Today, a few people can affect so many others regardless of where they are located geographically. It's our responsibility to understand the power we have, and recognize that the world is changing and operating in new ways. For those who want to hold onto their titles and old ways of thinking, this is very threatening and will generate more fear-based responses. What if you were in Theo's position—would you prefer to have medical specialists stuck in their egos refusing to co-create a solution to save your life, or would you want them to embrace the new collaborative model?

What Does This Mean for Business?

The shifts that are taking place have been moving us from an industrial economy (where we hired laborers), to a knowledge economy (where we hired specialists and experts), to today's emerging human-to-human purpose and experience driven era (where we engage to create purposeful experiences). And more organizations today are seeking to offer an added value beyond their traditional offerings. In the 21st century, business is personal. The opportunity is to shape a new face of leadership and business in this new human economy. Consider the following 7 points.

1. The whole notion of having jobs is shifting with new mindsets. While we hear mostly in the media about what is happening with large organizations, only five percent of jobs have come from companies classified as "large" in recent US job creation reports. Europe is facing an aging population and the EU's workforce is shrinking as a result of demographic changes, which has to support a growing number of dependent people. There are different trends in Africa, Latin America, and Asia Pacific, but they all share the need for small and midsize organizations to create jobs.

Many people in the large organizations that are stuck in 20th century practices will share with you why they can't work in new ways. It's either the command and control structure, or their bosses won't let them. When you talk to people in smaller businesses, they are more likely to share with you the experiments they are doing to test the waters to develop opportunities. It's a mindset that leads to creation.

2. Whatever you want to call it, more people are choosing the independent lifestyle, becoming free agents, and discovering new ways of living. According to the 5th Annual MBO Partners State of Independence workforce study in 2016, conducted by Emergent Research, the number of independent workers aged 21 and over held firm at 29.3 million in the US. Freelancers are becoming a vital economic force, and over the past year, independent workers generated more than $1.1 trillion of revenue. That sum, just over six percent of US GDP, was 26 percent higher than the 2011 total. Close to 81 percent reported that they were happier working on their own, and a solid majority—60 percent—indicated that working on their own was better for their health.

As this shift continues, people are increasingly tuning in to the fact that independence allows them to spread employment risk across multiple sources and streams of income. As they mature into the workforce, Millennials are pursuing independent career paths like no other group before. For example, there was a 79 percent growth in America's telecommuting workforce between 2005 and 2012. And Millennials are driving the phenomenon, with nearly half of global freelancers between the ages of 26 and 35. Millennials do enter the workforce to gain skills and experience, but many have dreams of starting their own business or working with others to make a difference in the world.

Organizations are going to need to offer more opportunities for independent workers who will come work with them but will not want to be on the payroll as full-time employees. Their interest is in project-based work. Skills around partnering are going to become increasingly important in how to bring people together and integrate teams. There will be a need to change the antiquated back-end processes of procurement and legal departments as well.

3. We need to excel at integrating the best people to work on key projects. 21st century leaders recognize that the need to deliver on our shared purpose is to bring in the best people in their markets, regardless of age, gender, geography, sexual orientation, and other dividing elements otherwise known as demographics. That initial divide of labor from the industrial era and the notion of the "bread winner" is shifting, and the divisions that were constructed in the past are no longer serving us. We will need to adapt to changing needs as we create more people-centered organizations that take into account various viewpoints from a wider range of people, which will help create the best structure based on the higher purpose of the organization.

4. For many of us, the notion of retirement has also drastically changed. Some people will choose to retire at 65, but an increasing number of people around the world will either not be able to afford to retire, or will decide to pursue some different type of work later in life. People will choose what they want to do and find ways to apply their passions as we live longer.

The world population of those 65 years of age and older is predicted to rise from 600 million in 2015 to more than 1 billion by 2030. 17 percent of Europe's population is now over 65, 10 percent in North America, and 7 percent in Asia. As the global population ages, especially across Europe, governments are struggling to pay out pensions and afford increasing healthcare costs. It will also be more challenging for people to stretch out their retirement savings as the average life expectancy rises. Governments will start helping people transition from staying home to staying in the workforce. For example, the Japanese government invests in helping the over 60s find work through the Silver Human Center.

But if people don't have traditional jobs, then what would they by retiring from? We will no longer need to design a life where we need to retire at a certain age. These are big considerations, but the directions we take will demand a much better business mindset.

5. We are on a journey to a higher purpose and we need all generations to reflect on what is possible. With Gen Z (those born after 1997) entering the workforce, they join Millennials (born 1977-1997), Gen Xers (born 1965-1976), Boomers (born 1946-1964), and Traditionalists (born 1900-1945), making up five generations working side by side. This is the first time in the history of work that we have five generations together, and this represents a huge opportunity for business to integrate their skills and capabilities around key projects.

6. We are recognizing our addiction to and obsession with busyness, to-do lists, and limited definitions of success. We are so busy doing, achieving, tweeting, following, emailing, texting, connecting, keeping up, and just working. And yes, we live in a 24/7 world. We are always on the job. We may laugh about having predefined working hours, and some people drive for hours every day to sit in a cubicle from 9 to 5, but work can reach us anywhere and anytime. We are mired in increasing complexity and because we don't see a way out, we feel overwhelmed and overworked.

The rising cost of healthcare due to stress-related ailments make us realize that we need to go beyond digital detox, and re-evaluate how we invest our precious time during our life. We need to remember that we are part of nature, and we need to invest in ourselves by learning how to integrate and regain healthy lifestyles. We need to ask new questions that go beyond simply trying to work remotely, and instead reflect further on how our work can fit our lifestyle in general. For example, some jobs require access to a lab in order to do our work, but we can still start making different choices that speak more to our hearts than merely to making a wage. It is only when we ourselves make a shift through our own actions that the systems will then shift in response. In the 21st century, change will come from each of us individually, as well as collectively, as we introduce new ways of living based on our needs.

7. Spirituality and business are also fusing at a societal level. It is still mostly taboo to talk about spirituality in business, as there is a continued notion of separation between the two, where business has rigid boundaries. But businesses have been crushing the human spirit, and now we are beginning to awaken with a strong voice. The idea that there is an impenetrable barrier between spirit and business is no longer valid.

More people are recognizing the need to be mindful in our lives. Many are questioning the separation between work and life and are wondering if they were able to live their purpose, wouldn't their work, and their lives, be more enjoyable? With the increased rate of burnout associated with work pressures, an increasing number of corporations from Apple to Nike offer mindfulness and meditation at work, as their employees become increasingly overworked and stressed out. Employees see the free organic food, yurts, and yoga classes their employers are offering, but these things don't mesh with the overly demanding work culture they experience daily. Instead of looking at the root cause of why burnout is increasing, mindfulness has become the program of the day, and it is growing, perhaps even adding to the stress. People are asking themselves: Do I have time to attend my work-sponsored meditation class? Are my coworkers more mindful than me? When we are still stuck in the same mindset, holding to the same implicit or underlying assumptions that got us into such a mess in the first place, then no amount of mindfulness training or workplace yoga will bring transformation at the root.

While mindfulness is undoubtedly good for business, corporate practices have become trendy and not really a solution to the deeper underlying problems. The same companies that have been creating the stress with long hours, demanding jobs, and workplace volatility are now offering safe spaces for people to retreat and reflect. While there are definite benefits to be gleaned from practices like meditation and yoga, the primary focus should be on why it is needed in the workplace in the first place. If it is for health reasons, then let's examine the underlying causes of stress.

Obviously, work life is better when more people make mindful decisions. Leaders who practice mindfulness can potentially engage at deeper levels and create new ways of being in business. But before we jump on the mindfulness bandwagon, let's focus on creating a more humane workplace and stop stressing and burning people out in the first place.

We have to build better systems that reward responsible behavior at all levels, do less harm, and enable us to do more good. The human spirit will thrive at work in the 21st century if we are able to integrate new ways of being when it comes to life and work.

Transformational Stories from the Frontiers of 21st Century Leaders

Joseph Bowers

Always ahead of his time, Joseph Bowers builds systems and communities designed to convene like-minded people possessing the spirit, desire, and ability to collectively make the world a better place. He recently left a successful leadership role building networks designed to connect 24,000 CEOs at Young Presidents' Organization (YPO), where he made a profound impact in building the foundation for networks and communities. He is now President of a startup that will rock our world. Joseph is an inspiring leader, innovative architect, and deeply passionate about connecting people and ideas in new ways.

The Journey of Joseph Bowers: Global Connector. Convener. Musician. President and COO, Geniecast.

What is your story?

At an early age, I was really tuned into the fact that I was an "E" (extroverted) personality type. I have always received my energy, or recharge, from being around people. To a large degree, I've always been a connector. I am incredibly fulfilled when I can introduce two people and a spark occurs. It took me a while, as I got through my youth and through college and even into the work world, to really understand and identify that my passion could be translated into a career. It was then that I started working on purpose, with purpose to figure out how to make that passion a reality.

The first step I identified was embodied in my second job out of college. It didn't find me—I went after it. There was a lot of satisfaction in successfully putting a goal out there and achieving it. I was tasked with connecting retailers and manufacturers to do business together. I spent several years understanding the mechanics of the role and realized that there had to be a better way, by integrating technology into the mix.

The Internet began to enter our household lexicon in the mid-90s, and I ended up attending seminars at Georgia Tech to understand how the Internet and technology could help me in my work. Ultimately, we found a way to build a technology platform that would connect retailers and wholesalers locally, as well as connecting east coast retailers with west coast retailers to better understand what was selling, because the west coast traditionally moves faster than any other part of the US with respect to fashion. What if we could go beyond that and connect retailers in the Americas with Milan or other fashion capitals? That's where the whole idea of connectivity began to click for me. We started building buy/sell communities and launched the first wholesale trade mart model at AmericasMart in 1996, where we were literally connecting retailers and wholesalers, and then retailers with retailers, around the world.

I ended up moving on after 10 years with that company into a relationship management job with a technology company. Again, it was all about the relationships and the connectivity. I continued to hone my skills as technology continued to improve and become more and more ubiquitous. I also became increasingly clear about what it was I wanted to do, which was the same thing I felt I wanted to do as a young man—convening and bringing people together.

Fast forward a few years, and I was running my own branding agency in Atlanta with two partners. I received a call from a company referring to itself by an acronym: YPO, the Young Presidents' Organization. They told me they had a global community—at the time around 18,000 CEOs managing large businesses around the world—and they were looking for someone who could come in and help connect these men and women, more as a self-support system than anything else. It was about taking this community to the next level by providing them with peer-to-peer support and advice in their work and personal lives.

These CEOs live a very different life than many, and most get so busy running their companies that they inadvertently become isolated. This was an exciting opportunity to experiment with connectivity structures and methodologies aimed at convening the communities in conversation and support. I came in to figure this puzzle out. I love a good puzzle, and I'm much better at planting a seed than watering a tree. It was something big for me to build, and I was very drawn to the opportunity as well as the caliber of people on the larger, global management team. It was in the networking/convening space, and it just made all the sense in the world to me. It was almost as if everything I had worked on up until that point in my life was coming together—an incredible opportunity with a global, decentralized organization that had an mission-critical opportunity to grow and innovate.

I left my branding agency for this opportunity in 2008. Along with a great team, we built out a platform for CEOs to convene around areas of passion and interest, such as cricket, soccer, the Helping

Disadvantaged Kids Network, the Western Diplomacy and Peace Action Network, or the Sustainable Businesses Network. What immediately occurred to me was the thought that I had been given the runway to build a platform to connect these individuals in positions of power and influence, people who have the ability and resources to change the world and ultimately make it a better place. That closed the deal for me straight away.

I didn't have to think about it very long, because once I understood the potential impact I could have if I could connect what are now 24,000 CEOs around the world—52 percent outside the United States - I could play a small part in helping them make a wider positive impact. That's exactly what we did, and YPO networks ecosystem continues to grow today. Out of an organization of 24,000 CEOs, we obtained 70+ percent engagement across the entire global community of leaders, with cumulatively millions of interactions occurring inside the networks. YPO hosts over 50 official member networks inside of the organization, and another 1,000-plus groups with varying levels of engagement. These communities have a three-year strategy, they have a budget, they have a calendar of events, and the people who participate in these networks and groups value relationships. They have the resources to create opportunities for the right people to connect and meet; such as the Peace Action network convening to support peace initiatives with Israel and the Gaza Strip.

It was clear to me that YPO also understood the value inherent in funding an opportunity for leaders to get together in-person and shake hands, or share a cup of coffee. The entire lifecycle of a relationship is more than just transactional. It allows leaders to meet online around issues that interest them, and then they can strengthen that relationship by sitting across the table from each other—a round table, a forum, focused on peace action initiatives, or whatever the case may be.

All of this influenced my decision to join the YPO management team, and ultimately to take on my role as Chief Networking Officer. I recognized my impact could be immense when I was able to connect YPO members around key issues and initiatives through these online communities and networks.

Communities allow us to listen and co-create

A community is a collection of individuals with similar interests. I always encouraged my management team at YPO to present ideas to the members in our networks. If we start conversations by tossing a relevant topic or "ball on the field," we're already 50 percent of the way down the line, instead of sitting in the room and saying, "So, what do you want to talk about?" The power of communities powered through new technology is absolutely changing the world. Many times, people gain their voice from being in these communities—sharing ideas, bouncing them against others, and then going forth into the world and making it a better place.

I learned in my ninth grade civics class that in order to evoke change, one must first convene a group of like-minded individuals; you have to pull together your group before you march. That's always been the rule, and that hasn't changed. What has changed is the availability of technology convene people more effectively and broadly. The concept of community has been around since the age of the caveman. The power to convene so much more effectively and efficiently has only come upon us in the past 10-15 years. It started in the military, then in the universities, and now it's available to everyone. Anyone with a device and connectivity can open an account on Facebook and start a group for free, or build their own communities with a multitude of available platforms.

One of the key reasons I was passionate about rapidly growing the management team staff at YPO on the network side was because my experience pointed to the fact that communities need facilitation. They need someone to ensure the care and feeding of the community. They need someone to ensure that everyone is being heard, including those less likely to speak up. They need to be there to ensure that if a member asks a question and no one answers it, then perhaps the member could use some coaching on how to ask or position the question differently.

As fantastic as it would be to say that this whole co-creation thing happens organically, I believe it seldom does. Facilitation or co-facilitation is key to ensure healthy and efficient co-creation. The facilitation piece has been mandatory only because, left to their own devices, communities with no facilitation, no leadership, or no community management rarely succeed. It has to be an engaged and fully enlisted member of the community leading the vision or leading the charge because, left to themselves, communities won't naturally flourish.

In 2010, we invited a notable guest speaker to a Global Leadership Conference (GLC). Two unfortunate events landed him under house arrest at the time he was supposed to be appearing on our Denver stage. Partnering with our production company, we did some last minute scrambling to position a satellite truck in front of the speaker's house in London. We produced a live, two-way video/audio session with he and 3,000 CEOs sitting in the Denver Convention Center. It was one of the highest rated events of the three-day conference, and he wasn't even in the physical room.

Several years later, at a similar conference in Singapore, we hosted Aung San Suu Kyi from Myanmar, who was hiding in exile at the time. Through the YPO network, we were able to locate her. As our production lights switched to green, an associate steadied a satellite dish over Aung San Suu Kyi's remote housing for the signal while we once again delivered a live two-way interactive experience. She spoke and then took questions from an audience of 3,000 CEOs sitting in Singapore. There wasn't a dry eye in the audience. She wasn't physically there in the room with us, and yet she was present with us.

Convening people around opportunities

My life has always been about convening people, whether it was through social platforms back in 1996 before Facebook existed, or at YPO where world leaders are convened to collaborate, improve themselves and their businesses, and make the world a better place.

Following the success of our virtual Global Leadership events, the opportunity was too obvious to ignore. After brainstorming concepts with a YPO member and a great network of support, we decided to co-create our new company called Geniecast. I joined as President and we launched in early 2016. Geniecast is transforming the way the world connects people, ideas, and inspiration as the largest online marketplace of authors, experts, speakers, consultants, athletes, and celebrities via live, two-way, interactive video.

At Geniecast, we set out to recruit a great team to change the world. It's all about finding a new way to make inspiration accessible, whether by way of the descendants of Martin Luther King or Nelson Mandela to Richard Branson himself—all accessible to audiences who've never had access to them before. We're making ideas and inspiration more accessible. It's people like Inc. Magazine's top 50 most creative Chief Marketing Officers of 2015. We're signing them up because they have a story and a message to share. We're giving them a voice through a channel that's never existed before.

Suddenly, an opportunity had arisen to create something new in the world. Born of events which transpired at a Global Leadership meetings with the power of video, an idea emerged: if this worked for top leaders across the world, what would happen if the platform was accessible to others around the world as well? What if you read this book by Ayelet Baron and it's a game changer for you, and you want your entire executive team in New York City to benefit from her ideas and unique world view? What if you ordered Ayelet's book and then booked an hour of her time to cast her into your executive boardroom for your senior team meeting for live, interactive Q & A?— Ayelet gets paid, Geniecast gets paid, the client gets Ayelet, her ideas, and her inspiration for a hell of a lot less than flying her in, and Ayelet gets to stay at home and do three or four of these sessions a day, instead of spending four days in total to fly to the east coast, coming into a senior team meeting, hanging out, and trying to make some more meetings while she's there. It all goes away with the new platform. It's really about the democratization of content, talent, and making the niche content of these talks much more accessible to everyone, rather than just the elite. Also, as we mitigate the use of trains, planes, and automobiles, we thought: why not issue carbon credits in exchange for the use of our system?

As far as getting the team together and becoming whole, Geniecast allows companies and individuals to meet and convene around topics of interest on a much more frequent basis. Consider the benefits of offering a learning series for your team at a fraction of the cost of in-person meetings, with no travel expenses for anyone, yet all of the interactivity remaining intact. The opportunity is to convene as needed, and we see video as the most amazing business enabler of the 21st century. So much happens when we can see each other on video. I can see the person on the screen nodding their head, and I can read their body language just as well as they can read mine. From a wholeness perspective, people no longer need to feel left out of conversations because they are not in central locations. Many continue to grapple with how to integrate video into their business or how to effectively use it. We need more leaders who understand the intrinsic business value that video technology brings, and to make it an operationalized element of how an organization conducts business on a daily basis. Video is the next best thing to physically being there.

We need to remember how to practice our art

Our existence and the very nature of our being is about rhythm. The earth has a rhythm. We are at our best when we are in tune with our natural rhythms. Music is based on rhythms. There is nothing better than making people dance, making people move, getting people to interact, and finding a rhythm that comes along with being a musician. As I mentioned earlier, the recurring theme in my life has been convening, and I have so much fun getting together with four or five others to play music in the DejaBlue Grass Band. And it is completely different to get together and convene 5,000 people to listen to our music, to play on stage, and see people dancing and smiling. There is truly nothing like it.

Occasionally, my wife will say, "Do you have a gig or anything coming up anytime soon?" It's really shorthand for, "You seem a bit stressed out. Maybe you should go play some music." Music brings that balance for me. It is in line with the rhythms I recognize. Rhythms connect me to other people, the environment, and the planet. I never want to be all about work.

Rhythm is important for me, because it brings great balance. I tend to work a lot and I work hard. I do it because I love it, not because I feel like I have to. I enjoy my work, and life's too short to not be doing what you dig. Any person who's ever been a part of one of my teams knows that I am all about doing what you dig. If you're not doing what you dig, let's find something else. Life is far too short.

There's something about the gig economy

It's amazing how easily we can connect with other people today to get stuff done. I often visit Fiverr, 99Designs, and other crowdsourcing sites for creative talent and to survey what the designers are doing. It's really quite amazing. One highly-rated designer on Fiverr created 700 logo designs over the past two years, and he's part of the gig economy in a part of the world where most people live on two dollars a day. He gets to pick and select the work he takes on, and he can make as much or as little as he chooses.

When I look at Millennials and the generation to follow, they're all about the gig. They're not about the job. They're not about the nine-to-five grind. Those I work with sometimes come in at noon and leave at midnight. From a leadership perspective, I believe in the mantra that I have always embraced that doing what you really enjoy is key, and being able to connect that to something bigger than yourself is nirvana. It's important to know your people well; to meet them where they are and to ensure they are in roles where they're doing what they enjoy. With that in place, everything else pretty much takes care of itself. Team members will engage on an emotional level far beyond those who simply in it for the money. The result is better work, happier people, and they have a better quality of life. You get much better collaboration and work product when your team members are in roles where they are doing what they dig.

We have to rethink our paradigms because whether we like it or not, the world is shifting. It's shifting because technology has enabled those who have never had a voice to convene in the present and create a collective voice to be seen and heard. These are the shifts that are influencing the workplace and every other element of our lives, from the music scene, to business card design, to social and political movements. We can choose to be a dinosaur and slide into extinction, or we can choose to update our outlook and our perspectives, to shift our paradigms—to know our people and what they dig. Only then can we help them align to make an impact in areas that interest them while connecting their work to the bigger picture. From there, we can step back and watch them bloom.

The answers to everything that's wrong with our planet right now exist within us. It's left to the power of the community to make it happen. We're a global community—we're more connected than we've ever been before. The world is at crossroads right now. It's up to the power of the community to get people facilitating the right conversations to move us to where we want to be. I have kids and they're going to have kids, and I would love for them to have similar, and even better, experiences than I've had in my life on this planet.

I've traveled the world extensively and it's a wondrous place. I love this planet we call earth, and some say it's a bit sick right now, but I believe we have the opportunity and means to improve it. We've been able to convene some really bright minds around how to make it a better place, but I do believe that ultimately it's in the hands of the community. We have to ensure that the right people are at the table to have those conversations, those who will affect the policy and decisions being made around how we can preserve this place and allow future generations to thrive.

Carol Read

Carol Read is a transformation fellow at Horizons National Health Services England (NHSE) and was listed by the *Health Service Journal* (HSJ) as one of the top 50 innovators in Health in 2014. Carol launched an award winning skincare range for the NHS where all profits go back into patient care. She has edited and curated *The Edge* (*@theedgenhs*), a knowledge hub and platform for change, which is now at 44,000 subscribers in 140 countries.

I met Carol Read on Twitter, and I feel I have known her my entire life. Carol has an amazing story that reflects her passionate belief that positive radicals are needed to challenge the status quo. We live in extraordinary times of groundbreaking technology and social media connections, yet compassionate care and being part of a supportive network are still what matters. Carol definitely rocks the boat when it needs rocking. She brings positive change to the world, and believes in the power of building strong partnerships by being open to connecting people who can help each other.

The Journey of Carol Read: Innovator. Visionary. Photographer. Transformation Fellow, National Health Service UK.

What is your story?

I'm an innovator. I develop products and connect with people, where we do a bit of co-creation and co-production, whether that be on blogs or other projects. My background is in health, but what I find with being online is that you can connect across a whole range of industries, and it gives you access to people who you would never have met in your day-to-day life.

My current story started two and a half years ago. I've been online, and especially on Twitter, and that's really where I've been able to collaborate with people all over the world and work out loud. Working out loud means that we openly share what we are working on in a way that brings other people to understand how they can also contribute. When you work out loud, you build and strengthen relationships. It's brought me great richness to see how we can make connections with people anywhere in the world.

Ayelet introduced the idea of LIFEworking (where work is merely a part of life), and I suppose that's how I feel about my own life. With my Twitter account, that is work, but it's also part of me; it's the richness of the work I do in the world. When you step back and realize that you have just discovered a fantastic piece of work, you can be amazed by how easy it was to access information that otherwise would never cross your path—it's true serendipity.

I work on *The Edge*, which is a knowledge hub that makes connections between people, ideas, and knowledge for transformational change in healthcare. *The Edge* brings together ideas and the very latest sources of knowledge so people can inspire and inform each other to be positive disruptive innovators. The knowledge we share comes from many diverse disciplines, schools of thought, industries, and sectors from across the world.

Our premise is that by sharing and making sense of leading edge knowledge about change in a generic sense and applying it to our own contexts, we can dramatically improve our prospects for transforming healthcare. *The Edge* is aimed at all who are committed to bold thinking and swift action for change, from patient leaders and front line change activists to improvement specialists, educationalists, researchers, and senior leaders.

The Edge, in essence, is a platform where today over 44,000 people around the world are collaborating and adding their own commentary. It was set up and run by the Horizons Group of NHS England, which is led by Helen Bevan, our chief transformation officer. We realized that there was so much information out in the world today and there is a need to filter it somehow. I am the chief content curator for *The Edge.* We filter content from a whole range of different industries to bring good stuff to people who want to engage with us on transformational change in healthcare and beyond.

Transformation means different things to different people all over the world. In the United Kingdom, we are facing a very difficult time at the moment. We talk about scarcity and abundance, and some people would say that we're in a great period of scarcity. In fact, there is a constant tension between having enough resources to fund the National Health Service (NHS), and trying to provide for more and more people.

But then we have to look at the flip side of this picture: there is hope. The 21st century is a time of richness of connection that was never there before technology. We can now pull together a social movement to drive a particular change in our community and/or in the world. Regardless of the particular change, we can impact healthcare by finding different ways that meet people's needs. What's really interesting at the moment with *The Edge* is that part of it is about co-production; we're pulling together patient leaders, frontline staff carers and patients' relatives, and we're all working together to see how they can improve health services. We are starting new conversations and listening to the voices that are emerging.

Finding the edge in unchartered waters

This adventure all started for me two years ago when I took part in the School for Health Care Radicals (SHCR). I did it in stealth mode; I managed to do it while I was an innovation leader in a small district hospital. And the way I got to it was through Twitter; I clicked on a link that took me to the SHCR website, which immediately grabbed my attention. It said: "Anyone who wants to bring about change has to be ready to break the rules. But in health and social care, that can be really difficult. The art of rocking the boat while staying in it is something it seems no-one is ready to help you learn." I thought, "Wow! This is exciting! I can do this and don't need to ask for anyone's permission. I can just sit in my office, log on when I take breaks, and be part of a bigger community."

I loved the community aspect of people from all over the world connecting by listening to a particular course, and even though it was a Massive Open Online Course (MOOC), the people made it a very special experience. I had just launched a skincare product and was asked to present via WebEx video conferencing on the SHCR program. Then the Finance Department at the hospital wanted me to make a presentation about the skincare range and my other innovation work. I included some of the content I had presented at the SHCR. I also gave them some background on the school and told them that by being involved in this course, it would get the hospital major external exposure through Twitter and other networks. People looked at me like I came from another planet, since most of the people I worked with thought Twitter was where people shared photos of what they were eating and other mundane things. In fact, I was in my office doing a course that not only connected me with people from all over the world, but also led me to do things I would never have dreamt of doing. This was a transformational time for me that started the ball rolling.

The other life changing part was that at the same time, I was developing a product. I'd never developed a skin care product before in my life, so I had to ask myself, "How will I do this?" Knowing there is a community out in the world, I simply searched online to see who could help us.

We launched a product that we made on a very small scale in our hospital. We started selling it in tiny pots. It became popular, so we needed to scale it up and make it outside the organisation. My manager was supportive and encouraged me to step outside my comfort zone. I found myself on the production line doing things like telling people to run the product again because the color on the tubes we were printing was off. This was all new to me, and there were so many great people generously helping me along the way.

We then started exploring the development of another product. I found myself pitching my idea for face oil and body butter products to a group for funding. They didn't even know what face and body oils were, and body butter was a foreign concept to them, but they did provide support, and the face and body butter became two of our most successful products and won national beauty awards. We came in second to Dove in major beauty industry awards. To me, that was quite an achievement—to not know anything about the cosmetic industry at all and yet be able to bring something healthy and powerful to the world was amazing. I also tapped into my connected networks; I connected with people at conferences and I started talking to people in the cosmetic industry who were very kind and generous, who were fascinated by the fact that a hospital was making a skincare range.

Two months after the skin care range launch, we were invited on to a national TV show called the BBC One Show, which is a popular program in the UK. This was a big deal for us. They asked us, "Why is a hospital making a beauty product? How does that fit with everything?" And we shared that it was because the money went back into support patient care. We were challenged on the One Show about our venture being outside of traditional boundaries. We replied that this was actually a good thing, because it was bringing money back into patient care. The British public and even people from America emailed us and said, "How fantastic. How different is this, to do something with purpose." We knew that we had the public on our side and we knew that we were doing the right thing.

It was incredible to truly be an innovator, and we sold the skin care brand, My Trusty®, through our website, Amazon, other hospitals, GP practices, pharmacies, and retailers. The values of the brand fit with our ethos, as all profits go back to patient care, and formulations are carefully designed to reflect the research undertaken on current trends, such as natural products. Some people said it could not be done, but it's a full on team effort, with support from NHS leaders, staff, customers, and retailers who believed in us and made it happen.

Working Out Loud (WOL) counts

I didn't know there was such a thing as a movement called Working Out Loud—I just did it. For me, social media is a way to connect with other people and build community. What I would do would be to post something like: "I'm putting this together and if anyone would like to collaborate with me, that would be great." What I try to do is diversify my network, so I don't particularly want my network to be all the people who know me and who I know, because then you don't get any diversity.

I came to realize that there was a group of people on Twitter tweeting under the hashtag "working out loud." That connected me to people like John Stepper from Deutsche Bank and Simon Terry, who is helping organizations work out loud and collaborate in Sydney, Australia. They have been really helpful with my work. When John Stepper came over to Horizons, we met and felt like we'd known each other for years because we'd been tweeting and developing new ideas together. I used ideas from his 2015 book, *Working Out Loud*, in what I was trying to do to connect with other people.

Sometimes working out loud isn't so great when you get people who attack you online. It can be quite difficult, and it does put you off. But you've got to be true to yourself. What I've learned is that when people attack you and try to take you down, the best response is to recommend that they focus on their own stuff; you don't need them to drag you down.

I joined an online conversation about improving healthcare last year, and it grew to include many voices. There were lots of people coming from either a patient background, a clinician background, or an administration background. What we didn't know was that one of the people was working on setting up a big conference in Manchester called The NHS Innovation Expo, which invited speakers to talk about how we can bring innovation to health. To my surprise, I was invited to do a joint presentation with someone who I had only talked with on Twitter. We had never met each other before and didn't even live in the same part of the country.

We eventually met two weeks before the event, when I was in Leeds for a business meeting. We worked out what we were going to say in our presentation, and decided to base it around how we can:

- Bring people together to do co-creation projects, such as connecting people via Twitter or on other social media platforms;
- Pull people together in a community to develop some form of work stream or something that actually gives people joy; and
- Introduce that process and make it work.

We presented all of this at the Expo, and we had people who got very fired up by the possibility of co-creation who wanted to actually jump in and do it. Many people were intrigued by the fact that my presentation partner and I had never met face to face until two weeks before the event, and that we also came from very different areas in health. John Walsh is a practice manager of a doctor surgery, where people with no residency can go and get medical care. I'm a nurse by background, an innovation leader, and a curator of *The Edge*. We wrote a blog together which sums up our work. It's incredible what happens when we can connect so seamlessly with each other around shared purpose in community.

Trust is key

Most hospitals in England don't have Wi-Fi. I am very proud to say that they are going to give patients Wi-Fi access now, because they realized how important it is to be connected. That's quite an achievement, because they wouldn't have been in that space two years ago, or even a year ago for a number of reasons.

What I have learned from all of this is that we can't wait for someone else to give us permission. We can't wait for them to ask us to do it. We have to take responsibility for figuring it out and have an endless curiosity to explore what's possible in today's world.

To work in the 21st century way, trust is key. You have to trust yourself to let go and explore. I try to be authentic online and show up as much as I can. I share work-related information and a bit of who I am in my life. For example, I love photography and surfing and I also have a VW Beetle and Camper Van, so sometimes I find myself in conversations about VW Camper Vans or surfing. It's always fun to get into conversations with people from America, where I have to explain that we actually do extreme surfing in England.

Like many people I know, I do what I care about. I worked for 12 years in a bank at a fairly straight forward job. That type of work may be great for some people, but for me, it was a bit soul-destroying. I became ill with a long-term condition called endometriosis, and eventually I moved into nursing because of this illness. I wanted to make a difference. I worked in a whole range of roles like intensive care, neonatal intensive care, and surgery, and then in an innovation role.

If your work is what you enjoy and what you're passionate about, and if you can be your authentic self at work, that makes a big difference. A lot of people go through life and are never their authentic selves, and they say, "I wish I could do that." Sometimes when I tell people about my job they say things like, "God, I'd love to do that." And all I can say is, "Well, work your way towards doing it."

Imagined fear versus an open heart

There are so many people today who are scared. They would rather stick with what they know, which could be toxic, than go toward the unknown, which scares them to the core. I have left toxic work environments, while I have seen other people choose to stay in them because of fear. I would run into former colleagues and they would say, "It's still awful, two years later." And I say, "Well, why don't you leave?" Then they reply, "Well, you know…" And so I say, "No, I don't know. What is it? If it makes you so miserable, are you prepared to stay miserable like that?" Obviously, if you have no choice, I understand.

But most people can take more control of their lives. I am living proof of believing in myself and navigating the currents.

When I went into my first innovation job, it was scary because I had never done anything like this before, and I was being asked to innovate with other people. When I look back, I've probably been an innovator all of my life and just didn't realize it. I've always been a curious person and connected the dots in my head and thought, "That would be brilliant if we could do that." Obviously, it helped that I was a natural connector. I can talk to anybody on a clinical level. It was still scary for me because I didn't know how to develop products, but you just have to find your own way, because there are no particular formulas to follow. Even if you took a course, it doesn't really prepare you to pull people's ideas together.

As a child, I used to play in the fields with other children. The adults told us to be careful, and yet we walked for miles, built dens, climbed hills, and swam across the dangerous river. These days, because people are overly protective, we have lost our natural ability to sense what is truly dangerous and what is more of an imagined fear, such as a fear of what would happen if we changed jobs and moved away from the safety of our current job and company.

It would be great if people could tap into their creativity and use it to build their community. We need to tap into our intuition and creativity. We need to open our eyes and see what we can actually do. Chance favors the open heart.

Peter Vander Auwera

Peter Vander Auwera's ambition is to inspire other people to dream. He loves connecting with musicians and artists of all kinds to bring out the very best in them, working together to show personal intent and integrity. He can get pretty excited about design and real disruptive transformation through multidisciplinary teams. He is less excited about technology for technology's sake, and is more interested in technology's application and societal impact.

The Journey of Peter Vander Auwera: Artist. Innovator. Experimentalist. Former Cofounder, Innotribe, SWIFT.

What is your story?

As I'm getting older, I'm questioning my own story. The story that I usually tell is that while I was studying architecture, I decided to drop out of the program. My father was not very happy with my decision. He basically told me, "Go and find yourself an apartment and a job, and the only thing you get from home is the kitchen table, one chair, and your bed."

And so I did. I started my career working at a retailer in Brussels and I had to manually count the discount vouchers that came in from all the shops. So every day, 35 years ago, my job was emptying a bag of discount vouchers, counting and recording them. I am grateful to this company that provided me with professional and personal development on many levels.

After seven years, I left that company and joined an organization today known as GS1, which originally started barcode standards and then moved into electronic data interchange. I continued working in what I knew: retail. My day job was very easy and I still had energy left, so I combined that with being a manager of a nightclub for two years. I went from the guy collecting the empty glasses at the club to being asked to manage it. The club opened at 11:00 pm and closed at 9:00 am every Friday, Saturday, and Sunday night. On Monday morning after taking a shower, I went to my day job. Before working at that nightclub, I had been a DJ for 18 years, and I started one of the first pirate radio stations in Brussels.

My career progressed and I moved from retail to insurance and reinsurance, where I was responsible for making Electronic Data Interchange (EDI) standards for exchanging information electronically from scratch. After six or seven years there, I thought I was big enough to start my own company. I learned the hard way that there is a difference between getting interest from a client and getting a purchase order signed. It started as a very niche activity in pre-production EDI testing for large hubs. All my customers were international, from the US to Hong Kong and everything in between.

Sometimes things fall out of the clear blue sky, and on a Monday I got a call from someone working for Hewlett Packard (HP) in Switzerland who heard I was freelancing. He told me they might have a project for me, but it was in Hong Kong and I would need to be there in two weeks. When I asked him for information about the project, he said, "I don't know yet, but are you available?" I suggested quite a good rate and they agreed. They paid for my business class ticket to Hong Kong, and I got a contract for six months.

I'll never forget the first day I entered the HP office in Hong Kong. I was supposed to connect with a guy—I don't remember his name, so let's say it's Eric. So I asked for Eric, and after an hour or so Eric came down. "Hey, are you Peter? Come with me. I don't know what you are supposed to do, but here are two binders of information. Please take a look at them and let me know by noon what we are doing." I cracked open the binders and basically saw they were transitioning from doing EDI over value-added networks to doing it online, and it was a nice opportunity for my business.

I was hungry to grow fast, and I consciously agreed to bring in four additional partners to my company. All of them left their corporate jobs to jump into the start-up boom in the year 2000. I thought I was smarter than my legal adviser, who basically advised me against making this deal. I didn't listen. Three years later they kicked me out of my own company. It was an unpleasant experience. I didn't lose money, but I didn't make money out of this deal. It could have been much worse.

I wanted to take a six-month sabbatical in 2001 to rethink what I wanted to do with my life and work. Before I made that choice, somebody contacted me about a possible role at Microsoft Belgium. I was hired for BizTalk, an application integration software enterprise product.

The project of a lifetime

I have stepped out of the blueprints of every job I have held. Companies like Microsoft are very sales driven, and incentives are all based on product and customer segments. One of the partner managers approached me with an opportunity to work on an electronic identity card, and Belgium was one of the first countries rolling out this type of card. While it was not in my objectives as a solution sales person, I approached my country manager who took it to his committee to find out if I could work on this project.

During the annual sales convention that year, there was a meeting where the country managers met with Bill Gates and Steve Ballmer. The Belgian country manager told me that he had shown the mockup of that identity card to Bill Gates, who thought it was interesting for Windows and our relationship with the government, which was going open source. When he asked who was managing the project, he was told it was me and said, "Well, tell Peter as from now I am his executive sponsor."

Suddenly all the doors were opened. I still had to fight for the budgets, but when I put the business case forward and highlighted the benefits, the project got funded. I got quite a large budget, and it created all sorts of jealousy. The innovator usually gets sabotaged in some way. I didn't get any support locally because the marketing people were measured on what was in their objectives, and the sales people were measured on sales. In the end, I went full steam ahead with this project, which resulted in it becoming a standard that was built into the OS support for electronic identity cards worldwide.

I was awarded the Chairman's Award at Microsoft. When you win this award, you get special treatment at the sales convention. Every day there is a nice present in your room, you get upgraded to an executive suite, you get a limo picking you up at the hotel, and you go onstage with Bill Gates and Steve Ballmer. Half an hour before I was to go onstage to receive the award, the head of the region came to see me and said, "I just want you to know that we have changed the priorities for the next fiscal year, and we will not continue your project." My job was no more.

When I had started the project, my country manager was obviously aware of the whole EMEA (Europe, the Middle East, and Africa) organizational structure, but I was still in the solutions sales headcount for BizTalk. They had expected this role to produce revenue, and they didn't care that I was doing a project with Bill Gates as the executive sponsor. It didn't reflect on what they cared about and what they got measured on: the sales numbers.

I got this prestigious award from Bill Gates, and at the same time, I lost my job because of a headcount issue on an organization chart. But they did find something else for me. My country manager did his very best and arranged for me to get what is called a "bubble head," which is a temporary hat for a year. But I was so pissed off, and at that moment somebody from SWIFT, a global member-owned cooperative and the world's leading provider of secure financial messaging services, called me about joining them. My wife was eight months pregnant and the SWIFT headquarters was two miles from my home. I got a nice package. I got an international job. I left Microsoft.

Stuck in an old paradigm

I was hired as head of interfaces—a group product manager for the software products that our clients use to connect to the payments network. It's a $100-million business, and it's probably the biggest mismatch in my career for all sorts of reasons. I was presented the job as something where I could start from scratch, and really blow away everything that was there. But I discovered, after two months, that the whole development pipeline was filled for the next five years and there was not much to create.

There were some other corporate challenges I encountered. Two days after joining the company, I got an email from the CEO with two words: "Honeymoon over." I thought to myself, "What is this?" Two months later my manager says, " Can you present next week to the executive team your vision for the evolution of this portfolio?"

I was on the agenda at the very end of their meeting. I didn't know they'd had a very difficult day. Everything that could have gone wrong had already gone wrong. I had half an hour to present. They had 10 minutes left in the meeting, and the CEO said, "Can you do this in five minutes?" I said, "I'll try." I should have said no, but I did not have enough guts.

I started with my first slide and the CEO said, "You can stop here. What I want to see is, what is the problem you're trying to solve, and then later on you can talk about vision, so come back in two weeks."

We had a terrible relationship with IT. I got a call from a support guy about a customer problem. I asked to meet the person responsible for the delivery and I invited someone (let's call him Joe) from Support to come with me. There were three of us in the room. The IT guy looked at me and said, "Who is that?" I said, "That's Joe." He said, "I know that's Joe, but what is he doing here?" "He got the support call," I replied, "so he's probably the best person to explain what the problem is. I'm new here." The IT guy says, "He is not on the list of invited people to this meeting, so he needs to leave."

We got a new CEO in 2007 who brought an innovation focus. He identified a need for SWIFT Lite, a new product for low-volume customers. Our big customers, bump through one million messages per day, while a low-volume customer bumps through five per week, but we basically forced all the customers to go through the same process. I got a slide deck from one of the executives, and the solution that was being proposed was an antiquated e-mail with attachments.

The following week I was at our software booth in St. Petersburg and ran into the executive running the project. I questioned his approach, and when he asked me if I had a better solution, I told him I did. I suggested we should do a prototype, instead of customer requirement specs and PowerPoints. To my surprise he agreed. We decided to do two prototypes and go head to head in front of the executive team in a 15- minute demo. I got some budget to build a prototype with my ex-Microsoft colleagues, he would make a prototype with our own internal developers. I got two weeks. I accepted. What I didn't know at the time was that he was already four months into development. We worked day and night, and I will never forget this. The executive meeting was on a Friday, and he wanted to have a dry run on Thursday at 2 pm. The Microsoft people came in with their latest build at 10 am, one of the developers decided to make a small tweak, and the whole thing crashed. We got it back up and running at 1:30 pm and the prototype was accepted.

I then joined the newly formed innovation team that the new CEO had created. We launched SWIFT Lite one year later. The most important lesson I learned was that the only thing that works in innovation is power. Everything else about open innovation—pipelines, prototypes, and voting mechanisms—is all bullshit. The only thing that works is power. Why? Because in our current business world, it takes power and an executive on a mission to make innovation happen in a large organization. People will give you a million reasons why something can't happen, but it's still your job to innovate.

We get all sorts of antibodies working in a company. Even when the project was launched and even when we had 600 customers, it didn't measure up to the business case. We didn't make the revenues that we were anticipating. There was always something that somebody wanted to criticize, but for me, the most important thing as an innovator in a corporation—or in our case, a cooperative—is our role to ignite or to create new waves of thinking.

We shipped the product in 2008 on Sibos Monday, SWIFT's annual conference in Vienna. Thinking about it now, I realize that big things have happened in my life at the moment of big catastrophes. On this Sibos Monday, Lehman Brothers declared bankruptcy. It was the start of the financial crisis. Our product was to be test-launched on Wednesday of that week, but nobody was interested in the launch of a product for a low value customer. Everybody was just hoping that their companies would survive.

A few years later, we spent a lot of money on a very advanced, almost production-ready prototype. This was a very forward-looking project. If I describe it, you might immediately say that it's Blockchain, and indeed it was basically about a peer-to-peer network of nodes in grids that could share data in a real-time way. There was a new CEO who came on board in 2012 who – like any new CEO should do - wanted an inventory of all the projects, and his mission was to kill 50 percent of the projects and to liberate the resources to the projects that were left and in line with the board approved strategy. The two criteria were: 1) is it in support of the strategy, and 2) does it have a revenue potential within the next 12 months? By definition, all innovation projects get killed.

I was super disappointed, but there were three main lessons learned. First, the brand of the project needed to be positioned in the context of a customer problem. We failed because we called the project *Digital Asset Grid.* Imagine that you have a conference room, and in room number one you can learn about the Digital Asset Grids, and in room number two you can learn about Mobile Banking. Where do you think the bankers will go? The name and brand of the project need to resonate with your target audience.

The second lesson is about narrative. We created a review committee with ten people from the business, our top customers, and people from outside our company like John Hagel, Co-Chairman, Center for the Edge, Deloitte & Touche and JP Rangaswami, at that time Chief Scientist at Salesforce and now Chief Data Officer at Deutsche Bank—people who could listen to a pitch of a baby idea and translate it into a language that resonated with an executive mindset. After a number of reviews, we presented it to the executives who told us they didn't understand it fully, but that they trusted that we knew what we were talking about and gave us the green light. They wanted a review in 18 months. We had milestone operational review meetings. We failed to share the narrative to the whole hierarchy from the CEO to the executive team. After 18 months we were talking a language that was so different from their normal day-to-day language that they didn't understand it, and we didn't get it into their brain as an important project. If you don't have this narrative mindshare with the people who are looking at that spreadsheet of the 50% project to be killed, you are dead.

The third lesson was that I failed to tell the story of how this project could be relevant for existing customer problems. For the executives, it was just a technology project, which it obviously was not.

Nevertheless, we presented the project with a lot of fanfare at Sibos in Osaka, Japan. I will never forget it. It was the big show in the big conference room, with flashing lights, smoke, and the whole shebang, and two weeks later the company decided to kill the project.

After killing the project, another re-organization followed, to steer the ship back closer to what they perceived to be the core. Innovation budgets got cut back, new managers appointed, more processes introduced. The team got completely demotivated and the whole innovation team disintegrated. A lot of people left the company or were forced to leave the company. While all the others were writing their resignation letters, I wrote my staying letter and I attached to it a 40-page white paper on what the next five years of innovation at SWIFT should look like. The white paper got some attention, but was basically ignored and ditched. On top of that, out of the blue, a new manager was appointed out of the blue who told me he was taking over.

Taking a much needed break

I asked to take a six-month sabbatical. I was exhausted from seven years of being in the innovation trenches. I wanted to find that spark of creativity, which the pursuit of success had buried in drudgery and sucked out of me.

My intention was to study philosophy, learn to play music, and go back to art school. I felt a need to fill my life with creative endeavors. But my timing was off and I missed the art school deadlines, so I started fiddling on my own. I installed a small studio at home with a MIDI keyboard attached to my Mac running Garageband and Ableton Software. It got me thinking about how I could bring art to work and transform my presentations to include illustrations and music. I wanted to include my own sound in the landscapes, and for the words to become my own poetry.

Good work—not only the end result, but also the journey of creating it—is work that allows you to stretch your lines of development and to become an integral human being. The essence of work goes beyond fulfilling your needs and includes inspiring yourself and others to produce work that has passion and purpose.

I didn't want to scale business anymore; I wanted to do things that were super unique, really tailored to the individual customer, and not replicable at all. There is room for people who don't want to scale at all.

Introducing curated events and experiences in business

Six months before the Sibos conference in 2009, someone asked whether we should include two to three speakers on innovation. I suggested we have 70 speakers over a full week. I was told I was crazy. But with our awesome team, we made it happen. It was a huge success. It was the real start of the Innotribe journey.

I became the architect and content curator for Innotribe at Sibos, and event within an event connecting people, networks, and ideas, bringing together global innovators and investors, strategists, and influential decision-makers from leading financial institutions across the globe. We reinvented the complete format of the conference by creating highly facilitated creation space. Our purpose was to create awareness about what's cooking on the edges of our ecosystem, and what we think has the potential to become more mainstream in three to four years' time.

I always say I am NOT in the events business. I am in the business of creating high quality feedback loops to enable immersive learning experiences, and long ago stepped away from speakers delivering talks using PowerPoint presentations to a passive audience. One way we like to facilitate a session and get the speaker's point across is to break up what the speaker is saying into bite size chunks, and to give an assignment between these chunks to the audience to allow them to internalize what they have heard and then build up a story from there. Sometimes we work with sound or with lights, and it becomes an exciting production which feels as if everything is happening live, resembling a late night television show but then for four days. Being able to launch an event that showcased so many voices of people creating new paths was incredible, and it's where I am today.

My story right now completes a circle with my start in retail. My former employer organized a cooking academy at this cool new place, and my nine-year-old daughter was invited to attend. I had a conference call while she was at the class, and I asked if I could make my call in one of their meeting rooms and use their Wi-Fi, and they said sure. After my call, I started chatting with someone from the academy and commented on how great their space was. From the design, you could feel there was a strong culture. When I shared my passion for running innovation events, he wanted to introduce me to their chief learning officer, because they were in the process of rethinking how they brought their executive team together for off-sites, which are simply locations outside their office space.

When we met a few weeks later, he asked me to come and advise them on how to design their next executive off-site, because they were fed up with the traditional facilitated post-it note sessions. They wanted to resonate at the non-cognitive level. As a retailer, they have several brands and were starting to think about the brand as a family of products. They wanted to position their products in a range of shops from baby stores to toy stores. They wanted to create a life cycle of the customer, and so it's not about pitting the brands against each other, but about how they can bring a customer from one environment to another and still have them as an overall umbrella customer. That's the family thinking around brands. It's really interesting.

It's a big company now with 35,000 people, and they had held off-sites for their top 10, 20, and 100 people. Now they wanted to bring together their top 500 and wanted my insights. I did a lot of listening and we started to think about bringing them together around a huge family table. This idea came from fashion designer Dries Van Noten. He had a show that started at a huge table with 300 guests who were being served personally, with everything beautifully orchestrated like a symphony, and it was a magical experience. Suddenly the chandeliers above the table started rising and the table became the catwalk for his new show and exquisite designs. His goal was to create an unforgettable experience for people to connect with each other and his fashion. He wanted to make people feel deeply about an experience he had created and hoped they would share his story with their communities.

Like life, the story continues and evolves

I would like to create a content festival like a rock festival, for 400 to 500 people. A week-long festival with high-quality content injected with art and performances at a quality level of Cirque du Soleil. And on the other side of the bar, I want to create very intimate invitation-only events with ten people and take them to a nice location, whether that's in Flanders or the Scottish Highlands. It doesn't have to be spectacular from a luxury point of view, but it has to be spectacular in the overall setting, and disconnected from the day-to-day world. The whole idea of an event like that would not be to try to solve a problem in one week; it would be a week where you don't have to solve a problem, because that's what you already do the whole year.

I want to resonate with my guests way beyond the pure cognitive level, by using non-cognitive tools like art, sound, culture, and poetry. I want to pair people up and say, "This morning, you're assigned this: go for a walk and come back by noon, and then you do not have to report back."

I had a manager who told me, "Peter, you should start thinking about your work as a job. Just don't bother about it so much. It's just the way to get your paycheck." I said to him, "I deeply disagree. Never, never, never am I going to work when I have to consider my work as a job." I write my blog posts on work to put something out into the world that inspires people not to look at their work as a job, but as something to realize their potential.

I carve out some quality time for myself on Fridays, when I experiment with art, sound, and poetry. I started thinking about what it would take to evolve my presentations into some sort of performance, where I only use my own artwork, my own self-composed sound landscapes, and my poetry. And I would do it live, standing in full vulnerability. I created a trailer and showed it to some friends, and I was surprised how much a little thing like this can create emotional reactions.

We need to introduce new design elements that are not just about rapid prototyping, or fast iteration tracks to find a solution for a problem. We have to get out of problem solving mode, which does not bring us to examining opportunities. We already do that the whole year long. We are hungry for a higher quality of presence. Maybe I am onto something that may lead to another level of awareness and articulation of corporate narratives beyond the hollow mission statements, entering a new age of enchantment in search for something bigger and more valuable than all that can be measured; the beauty of things that don't scale.

That's why on November 1, 2016 I left the company for a long term sabbatical to launch Petervan Productions, to realize my dream to tap into people's imagination, and combining smartness with beauty, and to move from mastery to mystery.

Beth Laking

When I think about social business and community, I think of Beth Laking, who describes herself as not only the VP of Customer Success at Social Edge, but also someone who loves mixing dark humor with integrity. Beth's purpose in life is to provide people with the ability to be heard and to connect in meaningful ways. She has built a brilliant career working in many well-known organizations and has made a deep impact not only on their bottom lines, but in connecting people together with purpose. Her journey is one of passionately imagining possibilities and making them happen for herself and the people around her.

The Journey of Beth Laking: Digital Connector. Community Builder. Pathfinder. VP Customer Success, Social Edge Consulting, LLC.

What is your story?

My story is that my career has taken many different paths. In my work, my role is to get the boots-on-the-ground perspective for the c-suite executives and find out what people need and want. I am the translator. I give people a voice. It's a very personal passion of mine. I didn't have much of a voice growing up, and that's part of my inspiration. I'm a huge advocate, no matter what I'm doing or where I'm working, of bringing forward the greater good. It's about connecting with people, listening to what they need, and then helping them find their way in the world. Relationships are really important to me, and I seek deep connections with people.

When I was in college, I was pursuing a degree in international relations with a focus on Africa and third world development. I did a semester in Brussels where I interned for a non-profit which trained people to support village-based projects around the world. The people who volunteered paid for the training and travel to that village. Once they arrived and over the course of the next 10 months, they had to gain the trust of the villagers to prove this was not just an aspiration of coming in to "save the world." Then the village would assume care for the volunteer, creating a vested trust between them. A two-way commitment was essential to these partnerships. I was in awe of the people of all ages who were showing up to be of service, and impressed with the design of the program that created a level playing field.

Seeing this program gave me the "aha" moment of the need for us to be fully committed with our actions, not just our desires. My grandmother was a very powerful force in my life since my mother had passed away when I was 15, and I wanted to spend time with her in her 80's. I realized I really needed to invest where I was locally, and be connected with her and my own community. As much as I thought that I was going to head to Africa and spend years there, I determined that was not the right fit for me; it wasn't going to be my connection or place in the world. I wanted to make a difference, I wanted to give of myself, but I needed to do it in my own community so that I could stay connected with my own network.

Being in Brussels and experiencing these new models firsthand shifted the game for me and made me appreciate the next few fabulous years with my grandmother. After finishing university, I started working in a consulting firm, and around that time my father passed. A year later, I moved my job to another office and went part time when my grandmother was diagnosed with brain cancer. I moved in and took care of her for nine months until she passed. At 24, with that much life perspective and level of loss, I had the realization that I had to focus on what was important, and not be driven by the materialistic culture around me.

Finding your voice

I have worked mostly for corporations, but I have always had my hands in non-profits. I've worked locally with groups that help people from falling through the cracks, inlcuding homeless people, drug addicts, and children seeking connection. I love working with youth groups, and have an affinity for teenagers in trying to help them find their voice and let them know that they can be authentically themselves with self-confidence.

From a business point of view, I'm an advocate for everyone's voice being heard. I've worked for most of my career leading boutique consulting to support reorganzing corporations. I worked at CSC (Computer Science Corporation) where I ran social business, getting the connections going across the global company. Today, I'm working in the digital transformation and digital workplace space. It's been a theme that's run through my career.

People finding their voice is a resonating point for me and a strong piece of who I am to the core. It took me a number of years to realize why I was doing this work, why it was so important to me, and why it was such a huge draw. I realized I dedicate my life to this work because I grew up in an abusive household where I did not have a voice, and have continued to drive myself from that starting point. Recently, I was diagnosed with Post Traumatic Stress Disorder (PTSD) as a ramification of 20-plus years of abuse, which has helped me see so many connections to my decisions and aspirations in life.

For a long time I was in conflict, thinking I should leave the corporate setting because I thought I would do "more good" in a non-profit organization. But what I realized is that both the private companies and the non-profits need to do good in the world. I began to recognize I was suited for a corporate setting where I could help people across businesses to communicate with each other in open and honest dialogue. Business can fundamentally be a force of good.

One important fact that has taken me years to admit is that it is challenging for me to work in organizations that operate with command and control models. I was an independent contractor for the majority of my career, but it did not keep me out of that line of fire. In those situations, I was repeatedly told what exactly I could share, and at times was not privy to the whole story. I was told, "You do not need to know the bigger picture to do your job." I believed I could help, if only information would be shared with me. I could never understand why leaders did not want their employees to have access to the understanding they needed, and why they weren't giving feedback on how each employee could play a role in the bigger picture of the company's story.

I am seeing a shift starting to happen, at the business level as well as the personal level. As parents, my husband and I have always been advocates for our two daughters having a voice. On the business level, we need to listen deeply and pay attention to what people have to share. We also need a greater level of discernment as more people start expressing their opinions openly. We need to not only create a platform for people to express themselves, but also understand what comes with unleashing the variety of views that have been expressed. I now work for a company that is self managed and transparent with their financials and decisions, which helps facilitate this kind of open communication.

Command and control environments trigger my PTSD, even if that command-control isn't aimed at me; it's how the organization operates and communicates. Even when I am deemed to be accomplishing goals in that kind of environment, I find myself going into survival mode by overworking to stay off the radar. I find it impossible for me not to be impacted by what is happening to my teammates.

Large organizations often talk about the importance of digital transformation, but the agility to work in this way is not there. I personally don't think large organizations, with 100,000-plus employees, will survive in the long term. It is not viable. People need to have voices, and organizations need to be agile and responsive.

We have a wide variety of channels for connecting people in the 21st century, and we can connect with people where and when we want. Being the mother of teenage girls, I know I need to connect with them on Instagram or Snapchat. With other family members, I'm on Facebook. From a business point of view, we are using collaborative online platforms.

From fear to open connection

There's a lot of fear right now in business, and much of that fear stems from downsizing and quarterly stock market reports. The fear stems from people wondering what will be in their annual review and how it will impact whether they can feed their family. People are making business decisions because their bonus is based on specific metrics, but too often it's not the best business decision for the project or the company. The system is out of whack. We have people working really hard to ensure they get their bonus instead of focusing on company goals, and it frustrates everyone because at the end of the day, people want to do work that matters. Micro-measuring employees' performance has turned all kinds of work into factory work, and that is not acceptable in today's world.

I really want to break that dynamic apart going forward, and see how we can integrate all the fragments in the business into a holistic focus of what work means for us today. If you're going to really have open communication, you have to have alignment and allow people to express where they're coming from, because shutting down from your personal ego or through fear is really damaging, both personally and professionally.

When one of my previous companies converted their collaboration platform into an intranet, it was very interesting to see the new transparency that c-suite executives embraced in their communication. Even if people weren't affiliated with a particular leader, employees were tracking the ones who openly shared what they knew and did not know online through their posts, because is was the best and most honest information about the company. It forced the entire c-suite to start connecting, understanding the power of collaboration, and recognizing that they needed to shift their workflow; they needed to realize that it wasn't a question of saying, "I don't have time for that," but rather, "I absolutely have to make time for that."

You could see these different examples where a business leader would post something like, "We're considering changing this policy based on this. What do you think?" And it blew up to 6,000 people commenting over the course of a few days, sharing how they felt about the proposed change. This kind of communication can be really powerful. People were feeling very anxious, and they were expressing that, but they were also expressing their opinions. This feedback provided the leadership with impressive insight that they never would have had access to before. Before that point, they were pretty much making decisions in a vacuum.

We not only created the new intranet, but we created the business unit opportunity around communications to connect people around the globe. We created a cross-platform of communities of practice. The communities of practice already existed across program managers or solution architects; they had been doing this for probably five or 10 years, by getting groups together or having conference calls. This gave them a whole other avenue in which they could have open conversations and exchanges in an online forum. It allowed a program manager to set expectations or provide information to everyone and get feedback. It also broke the organization silos, as it was focused on a shared project that brought people in from across the organization. People also started a monthly WebEx video chat to talk about personal experiences and share stories. They are also creating a mentoring relationship through that collaboration platform.

Did everyone understand it? Absolutely not. There were people who were staying in their own workflows because they didn't see the value in it. But there were also people who were completely engaged in it. Out of 90,000 people internally, we had 80 percent who were engaged. As far as adoption, we achieved 100 percent, but adoption to me is when you're functionally using the platform or have access to it. Engagement is consciously using it, and being able to get value out of the information and the connections with other people.

I stood on the shoulders of Claire Flanagan when she was leading knowledge management and social business collaboration at CSC. I built on what she had created. One of the very simple things we built on was creating a widget called "Ask Your Colleagues" for information or help. Across this enormous organization, this could be anything from saying, "Hey, I'm working on this solution. Has anyone ever done this before?" to "I'm working with this client. Does anyone have experience working on projects like these?"

There was so much information out there and people had not been sharing it openly, because there was no way to communicate across the organization. This one widget was adopted quickly and people would jump in to help others and share openly. They also started finding and connecting with experts in the company who they hadn't known were there previously. All of a sudden, these connections were being made across this international company to address pressing business needs.

We also had a dedicated community manager who had the responsibility of trying to solve these issues and connecting people when it wasn't happening naturally. That was one of the more powerful tools we introduced to the organization, because people opened themselves to saying, "I don't know this; can someone please help me?" And the beauty of it was that they were able to meet people who they never would have connected with before and exchange stories and ideas.

The community manager is the connector

A community manager wears many hats. At the root, a community manager is a connector. You really have to understand how or why people need to be connected, and get them involved in the questions that need to be raised in order to drive those connections and sharing. It's about bringing people together and understanding how to do it, which means they also need to have a good understanding of the business. You can't just hand it over to an intern who doesn't know your business.

When someone has a question on your collaborative platform, the community manager has the big picture of everyone who's out there and says, "You know who you should talk to, who you probably never connected with? Mary in this area or Rajesh over here." Being able to facilitate these connections is a big role. It can be a microcosm of a particular project, or a business unit, or it can be enterprise-wide. But in the end, community managers are facilitators.

Community managers need to know every aspect of the business, and they need to understand the people they are connecting—what motivates them, what they need, and how they can connect them to ideas, information, and people. By serving the community, they need to be able to ask a lot of questions to make sure they understand why people need the information they are asking for. They need to ask questions like, "Why is this important? Where does this fall in your workflow? What is your ultimate goal? How is this going to impact the client if you get the answer? Where have you been trying to find this information already? What resources have you already used?"

Community managers have specific skills. They need a combination of a deep understanding of the business and the knowledge of how to build strong, trusted relationships so they can find the right people at the right time.

We need long term vision

What's really tough is the 90-day shot clock used in publicly owned organizations. There are so many major decisions that are being made based on the quarterly reports and revenue in a company. There's a fear factor that comes through, because they have to answer every 12 weeks to questions like, "Why did you make that decision? Do you know what it did to the bottom line?"

Instead of making good long-term decisions, they're making incremental transactional decisions that will not serve them in the long run. The work is simply focused on the immediate results that can be published in the 12-week report, quarterly opportunity, or the press release. And they're losing people because of it. They automatically lose the human component of what it looks like to work for a company.

What matters in this system are the numbers that show the level of profitability, productivity, and operational efficiency of the corporation. The people are mostly important in their role in facilitating the creation of those numbers and metrics. No one ever talks about the growth threshold of a company that is over performing quarter over quarter as their main focus continues to be shareholder value. People most often don't even get to celebrate how far they've come as the next quarterly reporting period is right around the corner.

With the recent recession, there was a huge workforce reduction, and all of a sudden businesses started realizing they could survive with fewer people—who are then insanely overworked. Even as they start to become more profitable, they're not necessarily going to aim to increase their workforce or give employees some breathing space, because in their view, they are still making their numbers and so they are burning their people out.

Shifts are taking place

There's a personal side of working 10-12 hours a day, and often it's related to health issues. Stress starts having an impact on your body. When people are on the road a big part of their day, it's hard for them to stay connected, especially with family. Sadly, it can take a life altering health issue for some people to make a shift.

By decreasing the workforce through downsizing and layoffs, many corporations are forcing people into more contractual arrangements. In the United States, it's a way for them not to have to pay the increasing costs of healthcare. At the same time, more people are seeing a greater freedom in taking on a few gigs instead of fulltime work. They like the flexibility of having work that lets them live their life.

We have more options today when it comes to work than previous generations, and our relationship with work continues to evolve. My grandmother was born in 1909, and the perspective of her generation was that you had one job in your lifetime, maybe two. It really freaked her out to see her grandchildren hold one job, and then a couple of years later have a new job. She saw it as too risky. Today, people not only have the opportunity of changing jobs every few years, but they can also choose to have a few gigs with different companies. That's the piece that business needs to connect with; they need to start valuing people and treating them so much better, if they want to stay in business in the future.

Exercises for Expedition 8

22 **New Ways of Being**	How do each of the following translate into your world of work? Are there any shifts you need to make to adopt them?	
	Experimenting with new ways of working:	
	Implications of the gig economy and contingent workers:	
	Being part of smaller teams focused on key initiatives and opportunities:	
	Non-traditional career paths and working beyond retirement:	
	Being part of the multi-generational workforce:	
	Focusing on personal health and mindfulness:	
	Fusing business and spirituality/Integrating the whole person and business:	

23 **Connecting Stories**	Thinking about each of the stories you just experienced, what do they mean for your own journey to conscious 21st century leadership?	
	Carol Read	
	Peter Vander Auwera	
	Beth Laking	

Expedition 9
Co-Creating Opportunities: Connected Networks, Trusted Communities, and Unlikely Partnerships

Are you ready for the best-kept secret of the 21st century? The key to the future of work and a healthy life is available to each of us in different and unique ways. One of the most important 21st century skills we need to develop and maintain is our ability to build strong partnerships and connect deeply with ourselves and others. We can all teach and learn from each other in different and sometimes surprising ways.

We are more interconnected to each other than we could ever imagine. And in today's open and connected world, if we are awake to co-creating, we will discover ways to build communities and unlikely partnerships as we start to move beyond the boundaries of traditional frameworks and systems that no longer serve us. While many of us are playing the game by following the rules of how we are supposed to pursue our careers and have a full life, there are pioneers who are changing the game. And while many believe this is mostly true of the younger generation, people of all ages are starting to question what is possible when it comes to looking at life through a lens of co-creation. We are starting to decide what we personally want to create and how it impacts the legacy we leave for future generations and the planet.

What does co-creation really mean in the 21st century? It is a mindset of partnership that we can bring to life by connecting with others around a shared purpose. We may have a great business idea, but whether we are in a small organization or a large one, we need to be clear within ourselves about what we believe and what we want to create. Who do we create and design with and what brings us together to become whole? What will help us expand our thinking and bring unlikely partners into our designs and projects? We can also create greater harmony and unity as we find new ways to co-create with our customers, rather than viewing them merely as a stakeholder or a target audience. Co-creation sparks the need to master the art of conversation and shifts us to new ways of working and being. By having trusted relationships, co-creation provides us with the space to share thoughts and ideas openly with the understanding that we are in it together.

In the 21st century, we no longer need to go it alone. We can connect with other people to co-create something beautiful in the world. For many organizations, there is a huge untapped potential for rethinking how we can co-create in connected networks, trusted communities, and unlikely partnerships. Here are the key principles and questions to ask with respect to co-creation:

- Focus more on the shared purpose than the means or the tools. *Who can you co-design with?*
- Everyone is an active participant. *How can you co-create around new insights? How can you network and connect people together and leverage their individual capabilities to help each other?*
- Tap into the value of bringing people together around an opportunity and allow for open collaboration. *How can you provide experiences to generate new insights, platforms, products, or services?*
- Focus on integrating learning and increasing capabilities. *How can you merge capabilities to create value?*

We Are at a Crossroads

There are over 7.4 billion people on the planet. Many are simply surviving and keeping their lives together. It is a daily struggle of making ends meets for many—finding a job, going to work, getting some rest, and starting over in the morning.

On the edges, there are new conversations emerging where more interconnected people, who care deeply about future generations, are asking new questions about their lives and the world around them. The seductions of wealth, fame, and social elevation are not as appealing to some people as finding deeper meaning and truth. There is a desire to uncover the simplicity of life in its abundance of opportunity on this planet, along with the ability to connect deeply with others. It is an opportunity to redefine our current system of work.

The world of work is at a crossroads right now as so many employment contracts have been broken. The younger generations have witnessed a world of work where their parents, who worked endless hours and missed their football matches or parent-teacher meetings, ended up heartbroken at home when the organization no longer needed them and they were out of a job. Careers spanning 30-plus year careers are few and far between, and trust is at an all-time global low.

One of the biggest shifts that is happening (which gets very little press) is that people in their 40s, 50s, and 60s are also asking new questions—it's not just the younger generations. It's as though a veil has been lifted and more people can see the opportunities that surround us when we look at life in its simplicity and beauty. What happens when we start understanding that we don't necessarily need to be the best and the most popular? What if we could be happy with living our purpose and having enough to create a fulfilling life? What if we started asking questions like how are we treating life, instead of how is life treating us?

What if we understood that the path inherently has highs and lows, which means we don't have to naively (and even deceptively) pretend that we must always aspire to create the happy and optimistic workplace as our goal? When we innovate, for example, we often fail, which brings different emotions to the surface, like disappointment and frustration. If we constantly aim to be happy as the goal, how can we bring new ideas to the world that encompass the entire range of human emotion? What if instead, we chose to focus on creating healthy and humane organizations that can celebrate a wider range of human emotion and experience?

The workplace itself will not change until people rethink what work means to us. We need to think about the cost to our health and wellbeing of making a living and how we want to live our lives. While new practices are available, as shared in the last Expedition, we need to recognize that most employers will continue their current practice of getting their labor cheaper in all kinds of ways without worrying about the consequences. For example, there are more organizations today that are bringing people on as contingent workers so that they don't need to pay any benefits. There are other organizations who are laying people off and bringing them back as contractors as a way to benefit their bottom line. As long as shareholder value and growth continue to be the driving forces of business success, people will continue to be marginalized in how organizations act. They will still talk about employee engagement and loyalty in a system where it is most often a one-way transaction.

What if all this is showing us that we are now living in an era of change, where each of us can create and co-create in new ways when we see opportunities and possibilities around us? As a steward and 21st century leader, it is up to each of us to consciously try to co-create the kind of world we want to live in, so far as we are able. Our world does not need more segmentation or more Chief Relationship Officers who own the relationships within corporations; we need more people who can trust each other with purpose and build strong relationships and communities. We can no longer wait for someone else to do what we know needs to be done. It is up to each of us to write the next chapter, and we can do it together. This is the time where we can choose our direction and connect with others on our path.

We are moving into a world where we will connect and interact with people to share and co-create together, not just consume and provide status updates. This is not a new idea; we had these types of thriving communities in the late 1980s and 1990s with online community platforms like The Well (Whole Earth 'Lectronic Link) and Compuserve, which got swallowed up by more commercial companies. While they no longer exist in the same light, many of us early adopters have experienced global communities and open networks that connect us through deep purpose and meaningful conversations.

Open networks are self-organizing structures that allow us to organize in very different forms. The Internet provides new forums for networks to grow and for communities to connect around ideas. While there are platforms available to us to find likeminded people, it's not always easy and straightforward to find people outside the reach of our networks, beyond following someone on Twitter and hoping they will follow us back. The 21st century leader is a community builder who knows how to navigate the existing structures and find innovative ways to connect people around a shared purpose or interest. For example, leaders like John Kellden—creator of the Conversation Community FaceBook[58], a global community of over 3,000 engaging in conversations about networks and the role of business in society—are already experimenting with the power of conversations to connect people on different online platforms. John deeply believes that as we become increasingly interconnected, we are tasked with building a sustainable global village, and the need to design relevant bridges and artifacts, sustainable practices, and convivial models has never been as urgently called for as it is now.

The Edges Matter

The organizations that are re-inventing themselves are the ones that are moving to the edges with purpose. They know how to create streamlined and integrated two-way communication internally and externally. They value dialogue, and understand that people are at the center of everything. The currency is trust, which leads to strong partnerships. Conscious 21st century leaders facilitate conversations where ideas flow openly, without worrying about internal or external silos. People are simply connecting and having conversations to drive shared purpose, using whatever platforms best connect people in meaningful ways. We've experienced too many organizations introducing technology platforms while totally ignoring the people who would benefit from connecting with each other. We need to focus on the people and integrate technology into how people work and live, rather than leading with the technology.

---

[58] https://www.facebook.com/groups/conversationsthatmindandmatter/

That is what is so exciting about the 21st century: our ability to find the right people at the right time to partner with us in new ways. To truly understand the power of connections and communities, you need to start with what you want to create in your organization—your purpose—and only then find the technology or platform that will connect people around that shared purpose. The technology won't teach you how to create two-way conversations; you need to start with the human element of building communities, asking what is the value of connecting person to person with purpose.

Tapping Connected Networks

A connected network is a foundational tool for the 21st century leader, as it enables people internally and externally to connect around purpose and common needs and interests. It surpasses stagnated organizational hierarchies to connect people to each other and to ideas. In the 21st century, leaders are moving from seeing a world of scarcity where they need to compete to seeing one of great opportunities where they can create new markets.

In most large organizations, few people have vast networks that span across the entire organization. Smaller companies can innovate faster, because they are nimble in terms of size, and also because they don't have to reach consensus and fill out a massive amount of templates to get work done. They can have conversations with the right people at the right time. But like large organizations, they don't always focus on how to streamline their work through robust internal and external connections.

There are three elements to building a thriving and purposeful connected network:

1) Connections: People who are connectors know how to look inside their network and connect the right people at the right time. They often get out of the middle and let these connections build and continue to grow on their own. Ask yourself: How can you leverage connections in existing networks to grow your business? How do you build a trusted network and then grow it with people who can help you meet your goals?

2) Conversations: When the right people can connect over specific needs, they engage in two-way conversations. 21st century meetings are no longer about reviewing PowerPoint slides and having a group of people on a one-hour conference call listening to one-way presentations with no dialogue. Imagine being surrounded by engaging conversations that contribute to the project you are working on. In a connected network, people know who to bring into the conversation at the right time to drive it further. In a business, organizational silos no longer dictate who is invited into the conversation, and the shift is to making sure the business issue is being addressed by the right connections. For example, it's no longer the "marketing" meeting, but the meeting to discuss how we introduce a new product to the market with all the people who need to be engaged in this conversation as part of their work.

3) Co-creation: When the connected network brings together the right people to have conversations to innovate and create opportunities, co-creation takes place. This is why partnership becomes a critical edge for 21st century organizations, as they recognize that through their connected network, they are able to drive business results. For example, ask yourself: Who are my unlikely partners, and how do I get connected to them to drive my go-to-market strategy?

The walls are coming down between departments, and all the divisions that have been created by antiquated management practices are eroding. In the 20th century, we not only fragmented companies to fight against each other, but we also fragmented functions within the organization. The antiquated systems in so many of today's organizations restrict our ability to connect with people who can help us be more effective in our work and meet the organization's needs. We may have had a successful team-building event or offsite, but we still have unnecessary divides within the organization.

There is a big difference between a connected network and a trusted community. A connected network includes people you are connected to, but with whom you may not have deep relationships. A trusted community includes people you trust and who trust you, and usually has a common purpose. Once you understand who is in your connected network and how it serves your purpose, you can then build stronger relationships with specific people and connect them in trusted communities. Sometimes all it takes is to connect people in new ways and encourage conversations around similarities to better understand differences and address them.

The Path to Co-Creating Possibilities in Communities

#1 — Be Clear on Your Purpose for Co-Creating. Once conscious leaders have a clear understanding of their shared purpose, they can integrate a team by co-creating possibilities and focusing on key opportunities. Two important guiding questions for gaining clarity on your purpose are:

- Why do I need a connected network to achieve my purpose?
- Why are trusted communities important to me?

Being clear on why having a connected network of people with whom you are constantly nurturing and building relationships becomes integral to how we work in the 21st century.

When I took over as chief strategy and innovation officer at Cisco Canada, I had over 100 face-to-face conversations with employees across the country using video and in-person meetings. By listening to what people felt were our biggest opportunities and challenges, it became clear to me that communication was a major opportunity. In a matter of a few months, we launched a manager's meeting, using video, to connect all the managers across the country in conversation. It not only connected people more closely, but allowed us to share with customers how we ran our meetings using our own technology and the outcomes it produced. The purpose of building this community was to create more connections between people so that they could talk directly with each other, share information openly, and meet our overall shared purpose.

#2 — Know Who You Trust and Who Trusts You. My friend Marilyn recently told me that she had cancelled a reservation for a local moving company based on online reviews she had read, where people shared their horror stories of how the organization treated them versus how they had marketed and positioned their "brand." Her decision was informed by trusting strangers who warned her against using this company. People increasingly trust strangers' online recommendations and opinions much more than paid advertising—and even their friends in some cases. Think about what this means for your business, when people can so easily provide feedback on your product or service.

Co-creation means finding people who you trust to do work in the world—work that makes a difference around a shared purpose. There are three guiding principles when it comes to trust:

- Who do you trust?
- Who trusts you?
- What fosters trust?

Trust is the key currency for us in the human-to-human purpose and experience driven era. Trust allows us to collaborate, co-create, and build empathy. Trust requires openness and honesty with yourself and the other person. It is trusting ourselves and trusting each other that bonds us around having a common purpose. But there is no formula for trust, as it is a deeply inherent feeling that comes from our gut and intuition. We either trust someone or we don't. Someone either trusts us or they don't.

#3 — Build Empathy and Listen Deeply. The 21st century leader is a connector and community builder who brings the best people to work on opportunities, whether they are employees, contractors, consultants, customers, or partners. When co-creating, empathy and the ability to truly listen to people matters deeply. It is simply how we need to do business in the 21st century.

For a business model that values empathy, there has to be recognition that feelings have a place at work, as do people. Empathy takes effort. It requires us to be open and receptive to another's feelings and experiences. Empathy can make people uncomfortable, because it requires us to expose ourselves to the risk of hearing something we may not like. At the same time, it also opens us up to seeing a different point of view that can be valuable to us. It may be easier to not want to know or listen, but it is usually worth it to walk in someone else's shoes and try to empathize with their experience.

When deciding to co-create in your connected networks, trusted communities, and even unlikely partnerships, empathy matters. Can you imagine what the other person needs? If you want to know why someone does what they do, start with finding out what they know, what they believe, and why they believe what they do. And listen deeply—that's how we connect. Truly listen for opportunities and identify what sparks people to co-create. Be curious about other people.

#4 — Partnerships Matter. Partnerships don't just happen; they take curiosity, imagination, and an investment of energy to explore possibilities. Take a few minutes to think about the partnerships in your life. What are the deepest relationships in the various areas of your life? What are some of the reasons some partnerships have thrived, some are stressful, and others have fizzled? In a human-to-human purpose and experience driven era, partnerships and relationships become increasingly important in business. Leaders who understand the value of relationships and connecting deeply will thrive in a new world of possibilities.

Amazing relationships and partnerships have a bond called shared purpose that connects at least two people. At the core of this are many characteristics, but the three key ones are confidence, trust, and communication. To have fulfilling partnerships, you also need to have self-awareness and empathy. How can you have a partnership and bond with someone else when you are not clear with yourself and your intentions?

There are times when you meet people who become part of your connected network, and then there are times when you become part of someone else's trusted community. It takes an investment to understand the importance of having a community of people that trusts you. It comes with responsibility. In some ways it's about growing up and taking our place in the world. It stems from a basic human desire to be connected to each other and to something worthwhile. Over the next five to 10 years, we will see more co-creation taking place as more people join the freelance or gig economy. People will be seeking out others with complementary skills to offer their services. They will each run their own business and come together around shared projects. It is already happening faster outside corporate walls with new "super groups" and "collectives" banding together to find ways of co-creating, and sometimes disbanding as they realize they do not share a common purpose. The experimentation is taking hold, and large organizations need to learn more about how people are coming together with shared purpose. At the end of the day, life and work are all about relationships. The ones that turn into true partnerships glitter with possibilities.

We tend to think about partnerships in a linear way, but when we start with purpose, we can partner with people and organizations in new ways. All we have to do is find the people who care about what we are creating in the world and figure out unlikely and unusual partnerships.

#5 — Meaningful Conversations. Our ability to listen to each other is key to our survival. We have become so addicted to being busy and being right that we don't always see what is right in front of us. In so many organizations, we hire the best and the brightest and too often, don't ask for their opinion and tap into their wisdom.

The coming years will be about going back to business basics when it comes to people, and rethinking businesses to include clearly communicating their visions and connecting with others. It will be a world in which employees and contingent workers will know their roles in implementing the organization's purpose without endless meetings and turf wars. It will be about executing a shared purpose.

Roger Aines is an inspirational scientist focused on the carbon management program at Lawrence Livermore National Laboratory. He shared a story that illustrates why we should freely share our ideas in conversations. Once upon an out-of-town meeting, a conversation about new types of environmental and energy technology turned brisk. After a clipped discussion of a carbon capture demonstration going on in North Carolina, Roger turned to the dapper older gentleman next to him and introduced himself. The gentleman returned the pleasantry and said he was from a major Southern university, adding that he had spent several decades at a flagship industrial firm. He was at the meeting to try to get a sense of whether the Department of Energy (DOE) might be interested in his new technology. At this point he had

Roger's interest, and he anticipated a lively and informative discussion, perhaps even a new friend. But when he asked for more detailed information, the gentleman replied, "I'm sorry, I can't tell you. We are here to talk to the DOE folks and we haven't received all the patents yet."

Roger often hears about new technologies, but he was surprised at the secrecy he experienced from an experienced and seemingly worldly academic. When he pressed on and asked, "What products do you make?" he was also rebuffed. The man wouldn't even tell him what the process *did*, let alone what it *was*.

Roger was frustrated by people thinking that secrecy had any place in environmental and energy technology. In this case, his academic lunch partner missed several valuable opportunities. He missed the chance to try out his story. (The more you share your story on people, the better it gets.) Seven other lunch partners with experience in his field would have been able to provide valuable reactions. Second, he didn't recognize that the pitch you make directly to a funding agency—as he was intending to do by buttonholing a DOE person—is never as powerful as the pitch someone else makes on your behalf. When Roger hears about interesting new approaches, he is delighted to mention them to the program managers—his friends who value his input. Of course, this gentleman had no idea Roger could play that kind of direct role, but that misses the point.

The idea that cloaking your brilliant idea in secrecy is the best path forward is strongly associated with the snake oils and overhyped tech failures of the last decade. When finally exposed to the light of full evaluation after extensive hype and major investment, flaws in supposedly perfect technology can be fatal. Fixing those flaws early, and having an open conversation with your peers about them, can get you valuable help and even more valuable supporters. And in today's connected world of billions of educated people, the odds that no one else has had your idea are possibly zero. If it is a good idea, someone else has probably had it, too.

Anonymity is hard to monetize. If no one knows about your idea, no one can support it. If you are working alone, you don't have the connections and breadth to bring an idea to market, no matter how smart you are. Secrecy is rarely as valuable as collaborators and supporters. Share your story to people who will listen, and pay attention to their feedback. Become a better champion, and bring your game-changing idea to fruition. People who will fall in love with your idea will spread it. And sometimes you will touch people with your story, people who you may never even meet.

#6 — Working Out Loud Could Lead to Living Out Loud. As mentioned Carol Read's story in Expedition 8, working out loud is about sharing what you are working on in a way that brings other people to understand how they can contribute. When you work out loud, you don't need endless one-way presentations and conversations. You put your work out in the world and find unexpected and unlikely partners. Working out loud is about more than just sharing information; it is key to building and strengthening relationships, helping to identify the right connections, and having the right conversations that open the door to co-creation. The key benefits include:

- Less time in mind-numbing meetings, which means more conversations about what matters most, as you can share information openly in online forums and communities;
- More access to information and people that leads to increased effectiveness, because we are working in an open environment;
- An opportunity to build trusted relationships and communities with people across geographies, focused around a shared purpose;
- Improved ability to have meaningful connections and relationships in our day-to-day lives and work.

I ran a workshop for an IT leadership team on working out loud. In the beginning, the participants simply wanted the mythical "seven steps to success" (what I call the mechanics). When I sat down with each of them weeks before the workshop and had one-on-one empathy sessions, I learned that they had not tapped into the possibilities inherent in their ability to work together every day. As I talked to people and listened deeply, I realized that this team first needed to adopt the values of working out loud in their daily work. There was no way they would be successful in moving to working out loud when they wanted to compete with each other or couldn't trust each other. I could run a great workshop showing them the mechanics of running the program, but to be effective I first had to help them deal with the dynamics of building trust around shared purpose. Each person had to write down and share their biggest opportunity, and we then had an open conversation about each opportunity and how the team could support each other around them. We modeled the required behavior in an all-day meeting where all we did was build trust and share openly. All of a sudden there was a realization of the duplication in efforts, inefficiency, frustration, and mistrust that we could now address.

It was not about moving to the technology as the answer to all their woes; rather, we uncovered their ability to trust each other and become whole with purpose. If we want people to feel valued, co-create, and trust each other, then we must first make sure the workplace values people above all else. Trust will work wonders, and working out loud is not a gimmick. It works when people show up and are vulnerable and courageous.

Look at the introduction of the collaborative Enterprise 2.0 social platforms, and consider why they have not been an overwhelming success. If we lead with technology, we will fail. If we see technology as a place to go, rather than focusing on people, we fail miserably. Too often, internal communication and IT were given responsibility for these platforms, and they used 20th century thinking in implementing them. Too many internal communication functions still practice one-way communication, when these platforms could be used to have meaningful conversations and encourage co-creating. If you are simply using these platforms for one-way communication (such as executive announcements and memorandums), you are missing their true value. But that's what I have seen so many organizations continue to do over and over. We use relevant technologies because they help connect us with people, but it is up to us to use the technologies most effectively.

#7 — Co-creation of Opportunities. There are multiple ways people can co-create, from creating shared experiences to partnering with unusual partners inside and/or outside the organization. Many companies don't understand the power of co-creation, as they are still stuck in 20th century team-building, with most teams built in isolation without an overall shared purpose. The real opportunity is to tap into the skills and passions of people to co-create products, services, and offerings. There are people sitting in open spaces, cubicles, home offices, and backrooms looking for opportunities to contribute, grow, and co-create, but the old mindset doesn't give them a voice, and so many potential lucrative opportunities are being missed.

When I was introduced to Phlilip Bouchard through my connected network, I thought I was going to learn about a new platform that connects experts to projects. We talked about how TrustedPeer is a way for executives to connect with world-class experts on-demand through a digital platform that schedules micro-sessions online. But what I found was a passion that Phillip and I share around co-creation and integrating social responsibility into the fabric of how business is done. He shared a story about how TrustedPeer was partnering with the Global Business School Network (GBSN) to build management education capacity for the developing world. What I took away from this conversation was that their platform helps member business schools on six continents to create the management talent needed for the developing world to generate prosperity.

Phillip also started the Next Experts Program, which enables students to have access to the expertise they need to become the next business leaders. Watching a video with two young future leaders, I was inspired by his vision to connect undergraduate students at the Orfalea Business School at California Polytechnic State University with the TrustedPeer network so they could learn from each other. By experimenting together, everyone found value:

- The students received invaluable preparation for the next stage of their lives, along with access to an exceptional professional network;
- The administration gained knowledge on how to better prepare and educate their students for moving on to professional careers, and

- The TrustedPeer experts gained a better understanding of how a technology-raised generation of new professionals will shape the business world of the future.

How did this happen? A 21st century leader with passion and purpose went out into the world and formed unusual partnerships that are touching the lives of many people. Conscious leaders are creating a new path for business as a force of good for our planet.

Transformational Stories from the Frontiers of 21st Century Leaders

Arlene Samen

In 1997, the Dalai Lama asked Arlene Samen to go to Tibet to help women and children who were dying during childbirth. This one request opened her eyes to the alarming mortality rate of Tibetan mothers and infants. She moved to Tibet and started One Heart World-Wide. In 2009, One Heart World-Wide took its life-saving model to remote villages in Nepal and in the Copper Canyon of Mexico. It is no surprise that Arlene has received several awards, such as the Unsung Hero of Compassion from CNN.

I met Arlene on our Jungle Mamas journey with the Achuar Nation of Ecuador to improve the health and wellbeing of mothers and newborns through women's and local community empowerment. Arlene was one of the chief architects of the program introducing the Network of Safety model, a program that works with a connected network of families, communities, and local and national governments in the active engagement of reducing maternal and newborn death. I immediately knew I had found a new friend and co-creator for life.

The Journey of Arlene Samen: Courageous. Visionary. Community Builder. President and Founder, One Heart World-Wide.

What is your story?

This journey of mine is really about connection and being human. I've been a nurse practitioner for 35 years. I was minding my own business at the University of Utah, working in high-risk obstetrics, when one day I had the opportunity to go to India. I went with a number of plastic surgeons who were going to operate on several Tibetan children with cleft lip and palate. While we were there, we were asked if we would like to have an audience with his holiness, the Dalai Lama. And of course, we said yes.

Never in my wildest imagination did I ever think that the Dalai Lama would ask anything of me, but at the end of our hour-long conversation, he looked at me and said, "You're a nurse, right?" And I said, "Yes." He said, "You work in maternal health?" I replied, "Yes." He said, "My mother had 16 children and 7 of them died. You must go to Tibet and help the women and children who are dying there." I thought, "Wow. Okay. He must not really mean that."

I went back to my life and put the conversation with the Dalai Lama behind me. A few months later, I received a letter from the Ministry of Health asking me to please return to India, which I did. They told me, "His Holiness meant what he said. You need to go to Tibet and help the women and children." At that time, Tibet was closed to the outside world. And I said, "Well, how can I do that? How will I even be able to get a permit to enter Tibet?" And then I remembered what His Holiness had said to me: "On the path of service, all doors will open."

I had no idea what those words really meant, or the challenges that I would face along this journey. And indeed, the Dalai Lama was right. I found a doctor in Lhasa who got a permit for me and some other doctors to enter Tibet. Once I entered the country, I started hearing story after story about women dying in childbirth. Although I worked at the University of Utah and that was what I did every day, I had no idea that globally, every 90 seconds somewhere around the world, a woman is dying in childbirth. Another 45 million women each year deliver without the assistance of a skilled birth attendant. It was astonishing to me that in modern society, women were delivering alone and that there was no one there to help them.

I convinced some of the doctors from the University of Utah to join my trip in 1998 to this unknown mystery land of Tibet, with no guarantee of what the outcome was going to be or what we would even be able to do while we were there. While in Tibet, it was revealed to us firsthand that every day, one out of 100 women would die in childbirth. And even more shocking was that one out of 10 babies died. We were outraged and wanted to find out how this could be happening.

When we dug deeper, we discovered that they were dying of causes that were preventable in the US and in most countries around the world: hemorrhage, hypertensive disorders, serious infections, or obstructed labor. But all these conditions were treatable and not expensive to address. There was no doubt in our minds that we could make a difference.

We started asking questions and spending time with the women. We found that over 95 percent of the women were delivering their babies alone, either outdoors or in a cowshed. There are a multitude of cultural and spiritual beliefs about childbirth that exist in every country in the world. In Tibet, the rationale for delivering the baby outdoors was the belief that blood from childbirth was polluted, and if women delivered within the home, the people in the home would then get sick and polluted by bad spirits. We spent a lot of time with the people to understand their traditions and beliefs. We knew that we were not going to expect them to adapt to our ways, so we adapted to theirs. We designed the solutions together. We proposed having a clean delivery kit with a drape that they could use to deliver the baby on inside the home. We would also provide razor blades instead of using their knives; this way there would be no risk of pollution, as these items were later buried, which was part of their tradition.

We also proposed to have the birthing kits blessed by the local Tibetan Lama. They told us it would work for them. It was that one innovation that made the difference, that one thought process of reaching out to understand their culture and what worked for them, instead of asking them to adopt our culture. The birthing kit is now used all over Tibet, and women are no longer delivering outdoors. They deliver in the home with the clean birthing kits and a skilled provider.

We soon realized there was no tradition of midwives and women delivered alone or with an unskilled family member. We started the first Skilled Birth Attendant training program and started training the Women's Federation to be the first line of health workers to recognize danger signs and enroll women in prenatal care. They came to be known as our foot soldiers.

People often ask us how we did it. It's simple: we went to the people, we lived with them, and we loved them. And we helped them to come up with ways to address their problems, because there's no one in the world who wants their mother, daughter, or sister to die in childbirth. When we were asked how we made it sustainable, I'd share that not losing a community or family member was a pretty highly motivating factor.

Being forced to leave

On the morning of March 14th, 2008, I woke up to find I had been nominated as a CNN Hero, and by the afternoon, I found myself embroiled in a political uprising. I will never forget that day as long as I live. I told my staff that we must not give up, that they must continue this work. It became difficult and unsafe for us to remain in Lhasa, so we turned the project over to our Tibetan staff who are to this day carrying on the legacy of safe motherhood passages. We learned in Tibet that with simple messages and a very simple birth kit that cost only a few dollars, skilled birth attendants, and a clean delivery room, we could turn back the tide on birth related deaths. While we were in Tibet, we were able to reduce maternal mortality to zero. There were no maternal deaths in 2008, and newborn deaths dropped from 10 percent to three percent.

After we were forced to leave Tibet, we set up our work in Mexico, and then transitioned out of there when a local foundation wanted to take over the work and run it locally. One Heart World-Wide is now in Nepal. In a four-year period of time in a much larger population, we have seen the same results. We have reduced maternal mortality by 86 percent and newborn deaths by 60 percent. Before the earthquake in Nepal, there were no maternal deaths in two of the most challenging districts of Nepal.

A network of safety

Every 90 seconds, a woman dies due to complications of pregnancy and childbirth. Every 10 seconds, a newborn dies during delivery, or within the first 28 days of birth. Most of these deaths occur in low-resource settings without a skilled birth attendant, and could have been prevented with simple interventions. Studies show that the greatest burden of maternal and perinatal mortality is clustered around the time of birth, with the majority of deaths occurring within the first 24 hours after delivery.

Based on over 10 years of experience in Tibet, One Heart World-Wide developed an internationally recognized model—the Network of Safety—which is a simple yet effective healthcare model that has been shown to reliably reduce preventable maternal and newborn deaths in remote, rural areas of the world. We implemented our model in remote areas of Tibet, the Copper Canyon of Mexico, the Amazon Jungle in Ecuador, and now scaling across Nepal.

The Network of Safety's long-term success is based on partnerships with local governments and local partners. We integrate local resources and collaborate with local stakeholders, key leaders, local community members, and maternal healthcare providers. Core to our values, and integral to our ability to partner with communities to reduce newborn and maternal mortality, is a deep respect for women, their families, and local cultures and practices.

Centered around expectant mothers and their babies, the Network of Safety model is made up of six essential elements. While these elements are simple, they are not easy to implement. The overall plan of action includes a six month program setting the foundation of the model (phase one), three years of full program implementation (phase two), followed by two years of support and transition to the local government (phase three). During these five and a half years, we create a self-sustaining Network of Safety for women and newborns along a continuum of healthcare, from the community to the referral hospital, and from pregnancy to the post-natal period. In collaboration with the local health departments and stakeholders, we build local capacity, expand the outreach of existing healthcare infrastructure, and improve government-supported health services. We provide health education to local communities and local healthcare providers, foster community empowerment, and integrate information technology into medical service provision. After the programs are fully implemented, they are transitioned to the local government. These coordinated efforts continue to save lives. To date, we have significantly lowered maternal and infant mortality rates in every country we have served.

At the center of our model are the expectant mother and her baby. They are why we are so passionately committed to the work we do. We are dedicated to:

Family: We teach families how to support healthy pregnancies, prepare for birth, recognize danger signs when they arise, and respond appropriately to potential problems with the pregnancy.

Community: We work with locals to create community systems that support women, from healthy pregnancies to emergency care, and medical evacuation when necessary.

Outreach providers: Along with our partners, we train female community health volunteers to reach out directly to women and their families, including enrolling women in prenatal care, recognizing and responding to danger signs, and referring expectant mothers to skilled birth attendants.

Skilled birth attendants: We provide funds and equipment for local nurses to receive advanced training to provide birthing care, ranging from safe and healthy deliveries to emergency situations.

Healthcare facilities: We upgrade health centers and hospitals so they have the equipment, facilities, and training necessary to provide appropriate obstetrical services.

Government: We work with local governments to build capacity within local healthcare systems, ensuring that our work complements—and does not parallel—local life-protecting and health-enhancing services.

Our road ahead

There are currently 35 under-served districts in Nepal that need help in the area of maternal and neonatal health. This represents a combined population of 7.5 million people, and 200,000 pregnancies per year. In these 35 districts, the maternal and neonatal mortality rates are anywhere between two and five times the national average (171 out of 100,000 in maternal deaths and 33 out of 1,000 in neonatal deaths). One Heart World-Wide is one of the very few international organizations partnering with the Nepali government and local NGOs to cover these areas of desperate need.

We are currently implementing our model, the Network of Safety, in 14 districts, and we are planning to take our model to scale and cover all 35 districts in need. We are also developing the concept of a Center of Excellence based in Kavre, northeast of Kathmandu, Nepal, to improve maternal and neonatal health around the world.

Our goal is to extend the success of our proven programs to other organizations operating in Nepal and in other nations around the globe, by hosting teams for objective and immersive exposure to our model and cross-cultural transfer of learning. Our focus is to create a shared facility that provides leadership, best practices, research, support, and training on maternal and neonatal healthcare in low-resource settings. With an eye toward replicating our Network of Safety, One Heart World-Wide will provide the growing network of health providers a research and development center that will allow them to implement our life-saving skills model in their target areas. We want to bring the community together so we can learn from each other.

It is sometimes complicated to drive behavior change, but it is possible. Our stories matter, and we all need to stand out and tell our stories. I'm so grateful that I've been asked to tell mine, because it's not actually about me, but it's about the women I serve. I've learned a few lessons over the years:

Relationships save lives. By working together with others we can serve so many more.

Effective solutions come from understanding the issue as a member of the community, not an outsider.

No matter what you face in life, never give up. The ripple effect knows no boundaries.

We all have the capacity to be innovators. If we start with ourselves, and the relationships we form, we have the building blocks for creating purposeful change that will touch the lives of many.

My dream is for all women worldwide to have access to a safe delivery. It is not acceptable to me that any woman has to die while giving birth. Our work is ongoing, and we are always looking for further support to help save more mothers and their babies.

Tara Kelly

Clearly born with business savvy and an entrepreneurial spirit, it's no surprise Tara Kelly went into business for herself, first opening a health-food store, then Simply Health Systems, an appointment reminder software company. In 2006, she started SPLICE Software Inc., introducing a new generation of enterprise voice applications to the international market. SPLICE gives companies the ability to listen to and communicate with their customers and employees on a large scale, 24/7, without deploying an expensive live network.

The Journey of Tara Kelly: Innovator. Thinker. Leader. President and CEO, SPLICE Software Incorporated.

What is your story?

I consider myself an accidental entrepreneur, although a lot of people who know me think I was born this way. I always try to solve big problems and follow new paths filled with opportunity to create something great in the world.

My dad was my inspiration for his love of technology. He was a programmer, and with his help I wrote my first program in COLBOL when I was nine years old. For me, technology is love and family; writing code was an act of love for us. I also learned early on that taking the road less traveled can be rewarding. I watched my father build a company as an entrepreneur with a lot of hard work, and eventually he sold it to IBM. It was an important lesson for me about the choices we get to make in life. Both my parents instilled a strong value system in me and encouraged me to make a difference in the world.

In grade school I rented out my scented markers in school for milk money, my first excursion into business. I was also involved in some small endeavors when I was in college, like running a vending machine business, which was good for cash flow but was not a serious business. Halfway through my time in college, I wrote a business plan that was submitted to one of the five biggest banks in Canada, and they were crazy enough to give me the money to make it happen. I walked away from being a full-time student to become an entrepreneur. I followed my heart in doing it, and it has led me from one company to the next.

I have been self-employed since then, and it has been about seeing an opportunity, bringing a team together, and making money to sustain it. And I'm not afraid to talk about money—money is neither good nor bad in my books, nor is it something to be chased.

Building businesses based on needs

I founded the Kelly Center of Wellness in 1997, which included a retail health food store and professional alternative health services. It was a great experience that allowed me to understand supply and demand and partnerships. I built great relationships with local health food brands and I did a lot of speaking and promotion. At that time, not everyone had email, and most people were using dial-up to go online. I was scared to death of cash flow, like any good entrepreneur, so I started renting out the empty back offices to healthcare practitioners, taking a percentage of their appointment and charging them low rent. I didn't know what the store traffic was going to be, so I wanted some security. Most of the people who work in alternative health don't work a regular week, so I could rent out the offices to multiple people. It didn't take me long to realize that if they did appointment reminders, I made way more money—about 28-30 percent more—because more appointments showed up.

When I realized that, I knew I had to create a reminder system. I didn't lie in bed dreaming this up—I just saw a need and went for it. I built a reminder system and set out to develop software with a team to personalize customer phone calls for my clients. The internal system we built evolved into my next venture, Simply Health Systems, which then licensed the software to small businesses.

I sold the Kelly Center of Wellness in chunks. I sold my client list to one person, and my product, furniture, and lease to someone else. One day I want to write a book for technology companies called *The Great Yard Sale*. People build companies full of value, and sometimes when it changes direction and they decide to abandon it, they end up making nothing in the sale. I want to help them see how much opportunity there is for them in the transition.

Listening to the voice of the customer

For me, it's about solving problems and turning them into opportunities as they come across your path. Let's fast forward to 2006, when I had a bad experience as a customer during a phone interaction with a company. Despite that company having tons of data about me, they failed to use that data properly. Although cloud computing allowed real-time interactions, my customer experience was terrible, and I knew it could be better given the data and technology available.

I set out to prove it, applying the technology to a different service model. This became SPLICE Software, my third company. I focused on our ability to change the way people feel. We use our patent-pending technology to linguistically optimize each customer experience with accurate data, tone, language, and dialect—just to name a few factors. This process ensures that our voice files create higher levels of an emotional connection and deliver superior results.

I've always believed in my heart that you can't hide under a rock. You won't accomplish much if you do. People have brilliant ideas all over the world all the time, but that's not enough. It's all about execution, and SPLICE was already executing really well. But then I took a leap of faith because I believed that as a small, lean, mean machine, I could do it at a better cost factor. Each business is only focusing on a limited number of factors. If you can help them with something else, you're going to make a meaningful contribution. We focused all of our energy on building this phenomenal audio component, because that was our key differentiator. There were big lessons to learn from this part of the business, and we knew that we could fulfill that service beyond compare.

This is a part of the story that I've never shared with anybody else. I met with a friend, Mike, who was in oil and financial services, and then there was me, who's been in health and then software industries. We didn't have anything in common. But business is business, and one of the greatest things you can do is talk to somebody completely outside of your business. Mike hit the point home when he asked me, "Tara, what's the fastest horse in your shed? Where's the fastest turnover of your dollar? When that dollar leaves your office, when does it come back the fastest and the biggest? Where does that happen?"

I started to think about what happened when each dollar left my office—where did it go and how did it come back? And it was so clear: it was in the automated reminders. We were doing appointment scheduling and we had an Application Programming Interface (API) into Microsoft Small Business Accounting, QuickBooks, and Simply Accounting. I realized that large-scale enterprise would pay more. And that is around the time that I had that horrible automated call.

When people ask me, "Why did you start SPLICE?" this is the reason. At that moment, it went back to the realization that it wasn't just about chasing a dollar through a cycle. My passion went from a few embers to a wildfire, and I was just crazy enough to say, "I have no idea how we're going to fix this at scale. I've never sold to a large enterprise, but I'm going to do it. And I'm going to do it right now." That's when I realized the world could be touched in a much bigger way by going to a large enterprise and challenging the public by asking people why they tolerate such bad customer service with automated calls. People needed to remember that as long as we accept the status quo, no one's ever going to do better. We need to challenge it. The responsibility lies on us to ask for more. I was excited and ecstatic, and so I launched SPLICE.

SPLICE purchased the assets of the splicing and digital technology from Simply Health, and Simply Health customers went on to Geek Squad, who supported all the scheduling. A lot of people talk about knowing when to pivot, when to quit, and when to start, and those are the defining moments.

A new view of competition

At the start of each day, we face choices about who gets our attention. Is it my children, my husband, my dog, or checking what email came in overnight? We are constantly making choices about how we spend our time, and competition for our time is an increased pressure when we are juggling many priorities.

What I learned is to focus on what is valuable. I focus on offering the highest value for customers. I am guided by making the right choice for them. By investing in creating experiences for our customers, I am focused more on creating value than worrying about the competition. When you find a competitor that's awesome, you have some choices. You can choose to partner with them and integrate, or you can choose to take the game to the next level and refocus. You can also find a way to monetize things that are valuable; sometimes you just have to look at it differently.

We are all connected

Your community is very much defined by who you choose to allow into it. Community is also defined by where you get your inspiration. There are organizations that don't have their customers in their community, and that's a dangerous place to be. You need to challenge yourself to be as inclusive of others as you possibly can.

My community is also the people I ride the train with on the way to work. They're part of my community as a whole, because they're part of the humanity with whom I share this planet. As I watch the way the people around me work and live, maybe I can find insight into how my app needs to work. For example, I see that people around me want to be able to write emails and listen to music while they work, which Samsung and Apple have both obviously realized.

We were recently named in Alberta's Best Places to Work Under 100 Employees. I shout this out because we only have 26 employees, and it was all because of our team. We rely on our values, and the number one core value for SPLICE is that we believe everything can be better. We give our staff time to volunteer at a place of their choice, and we also take total direct action in our community. One of the things we're known for in Chicago, Toronto, and Calgary is that we pack lunches for the homeless. It's such an easy thing to do. Our entire company spends eight hours together four times a year doing this.

It doesn't matter how small or big your company is; anyone can do this. It's so easy to make it happen. It's about doing little things, like making sure people have socks during the winter and making sure people have water during the summer. It feels so nice to know you have time in your life to care, because when you tell your heart and your mind that you have time to care, then you have time to look at the world with curiosity and opportunity. You develop a pathway where you naturally look for opportunity, and you naturally stay curious.

We don't push anything on social media as a way to get people to know about us. If we share something online, it's because we're hoping to inspire or challenge somebody else. Do you think lovely, trustworthy, great people want to work with you? Would your kids be proud of you? Would your coworkers? Would your family? These are the questions to ask. It's the same when you're writing a business deal. Ask yourself: could you explain the basic terms of this letter of intent to your five-year-old? If you can't, then it's not right for the business.

We need to ask new questions

I love to ask kids, "What do you want to change in the world? What do you want to make better? What do you want to challenge?" We are always bringing in students to SPLICE and having them do projects, because this new generation is full of genius. We've got robotic manufacturing coming in, and we've got all these young people with the best hand-eye coordination out there, and in the future they're going to be controlling these monster machines worth millions of dollars with grand precision. They are helping us make needed changes to work.

I don't think technology belongs at every stage of life, and so I'm not saying every child should play video games 12 hours a day. At the same time, we should not make our kids feel bad that they're using technology. After all, they could turn out to be the greatest brain surgeon ever using a robotic arm. All these kids are training right now for careers we have yet to imagine.

We have a lot of Millennials at SPLICE, and they are our hardest workers. They're sharing things with the team that they see at 9 o'clock at night, and even at 2 in the morning on some days. They're constantly on. As a boss and a co-worker, you don't want to overstep by demanding too much at those kinds of hours, but they want to talk about how these things relate to work, because they naturally put less separation between work and life.

Trust is also key to business today. When we want to move and change together, we need a foundation of trust, and openness fosters trust. Think about the people you trust the most: they are trustworthy because they have invested in those deep roots of honesty and openness.

Dreaming a new path for business

The human world is getting smaller, so it's important to find your community—online or offline—and get involved in something you care about. We should each be taking on some challenges that allow us to be of service. If you pursue your passion, you can connect with the whole planet. Technology allows us to get to know someone in nearly every country, and on every continent, who's working on what we are passionate about. I want to know the best leaders and connect with them. I want to build my community, regardless of geography.

The challenge is to truly get involved and not just talk about it. Make the time and raise the bar higher. Ask for more from yourself. Ask more from humanity. It can't just be lip service. We don't necessarily need to ask for more from our government or policymakers—we need to ask for more from ourselves, and then take action. The accountability starts with us, and we need to focus on what impact we can make in the world.

People need to be open. I want us to move together as a planet. Competition can be healthy, but there are so many brilliant and unique ideas out there that we need to do a much better job of sharing, so that we can create and learn from each other more deeply. Open-source is our future, as we can share our knowledge and publish openly. We need more people with attitudes like Elon Musk saying, "Here's all my information. Here's the patent. Here's the spec. Please build forward. Please make the right choices for humanity."

It's time to drop the barriers and create harmony. Let's share knowledge around the world. Let's grow together. Let's create great communities. We will get so much further together.

Sheila Babnis

Sheila Babnis leverages working out loud, virtual collaboration, connected networks, human-centered design, and other new ways of working to accelerate decision-making, build trusted communities, reduce time spent in meetings and free up time to do critical thinking and the real work needed in business. When asked about her journey, she shares that she can never go back to the old ways of working. Once you discover these new ways of being, new doors and opportunities show up in your life, and not only that—the impact you can create goes up exponentially.

Sheila is currently an innovator in residence at GLIDR/Launch Pad Central, a board member for Future State and advisor to several other innovation companies. She also works with CEOs, COOs, and their leadership teams to evolve their business models, relevance, and organizations so that they can thrive. Sheila was formerly the Global Head of Innovation Management for Roche's Product Development organization and came in through the Genentech acquisition.

The Journey of Sheila Babnis: Innovator. Coach. Trusted Advisor. Free Agent and Former Head of Global Innovation, Roche.

What is your story?

My contribution in life is to manifest potential and see the possible. I am all about helping people figure out a new way of working in the world—whether the new way is for an individual, a process, a function, a division, or even an ecosystem. The world is changing quickly, from both a technological and a connectivity perspective. If you are not evolving and adapting quickly, you will not be able to do what is required to create the impact, contribution, and value that you want to make in the world.

I work as a guide and a thought partner helping others accelerate the outcomes they want to deliver in their life, their organization, and the world. The shifts or evolutions could be done in half the time if we spent more time upfront figuring out who the people involved are, what the partnerships with them need to look like, and how we want to integrate them into what we are doing. Understanding our risk tolerance as an individual, function, or organization is essential. We also need to understand how much we are willing to shift our business model and competencies, as this is key to being relevant and sustainable in today's world.

If you look over the course of my career, you will see time and time again, in every company I have worked for and every position I have held, I have realized that the way things were being done needed to shift. Understanding patterns, trends, and connections, and knowing not just what is needed today but what is needed for tomorrow for the business are pivotal to sustainability, relevance, and longevity.

When I started my career working for Frito-Lay, my job was to redesign their quality systems so that they could make real-time quality and product decisions to produce superior quality, deliver on profit and loss goals, and keep employees engaged, motivated, and learning, all while maintaining or exceeding customer satisfaction. My experience at Frito-Lay taught me I had a love of numbers, analyzing data and information and uncover opportunities. To enhance those skills, I went back to school to gain expertise in statistics and quantified analytics. It opened a new door and industry opportunity for me: biotech and pharmaceuticals.

After completing my graduate work, I had the opportunity to work for several biotech and pharma companies as a result of mergers and acquisitions, which afforded me the opportunity to work on several complex business opportunities. One of them was to simplify, streamline, and improve the day to day working process of employees within the development organization. To do this required a shift in mindset about Standard Operating Procedures (SOP)—more specifically, the value, structure, risk assessments, and downsizing the numbers of SOP we used in our business. We ended up moving from 1,500 standard operating procedures down to 50. As an employee, it made it very easy to work, knowing you had a high degree of confidence that the quality and integrity of your process underpinned what was required to insure safe, efficacious medicine to our patients. We later added Operational Excellence Process Mapping as an easy to use tool for anyone anywhere in the process. My early career work in consumer and health continued to reinforce my desire to create and drive impact needed today in business.

Environment is a big enabler and driver of satisfaction for employees and leaders alike. Later on in my career I had the honor to work for Hal Barron, the Chief Medical Officer for Product Development at Genentech. Hal and I, along with his leadership team, worked to identify the one or two big opportunities for product development, which led us to discover that how well you select, collect, clean, and use data impacts the business in every aspect of its inner workings. Asking new questions, driving a clear focus on data, creating and institutionalizing new mindsets, changing compensation and outcomes, and driving new ways of working enabled this organization to adopt a changing business model in health for patients and the health eco-system and double employee engagement—all in less than three years.

In my new role as an entrepreneur and innovator in residence, I continue to do similar work with companies to identify the one or two areas where, if they were to truly shift, they would have massive downstream impact. Those shifts don't need to take four to seven years, like they have typically taken companies in the past. You can make those shifts in six to 24 months if you create an environment or culture that enables new ways of thinking, working, and partnering, then tell the day-to-day stories of the company, sharing and illustrating what they are creating and shifting so that the shift or evolution accelerates. People do what they are rewarded and recognized for in life and work. By expanding our ability to co-create, and by having conversations inside and outside of the organizational walls, we can and do solve problems faster and better than we ever have been able to do in the past. Here are a few examples:

Collaborative Partnering: To work in new ways, we need to understand partnership in a new way. We need to not only have a slogan, but truly internalize that we are all in it together. In the past, when we worked with the outside it was mostly with a vendor in a one-sided relationship. Today, it's about looking at how we can both win and create something together that is new and different and that the world needs.

Bringing the Outside In With Community: Another example of new ways of working is in connecting to our communities. Sharing information on Twitter and other social collaboration platforms can help us solve problems and create new opportunities. I didn't use Twitter two years ago, and never thought I would. I didn't understand it. But what I learned is that even though there are many tools available to us, we need to have the courage to find the ones that are valuable to us, because that's where the people we want to connect with are hanging out. Today, I recognize that the people I really need to connect with—the change agents who can help accelerate things and make a difference when working on a project—are all connecting in this community and supporting and working with each other. I recently found a hospital in St. Louis that works completely virtually using digital technology, and if I wasn't connecting to my Twitter world, I never would have heard about it.

Accelerating Decision Making: Another new way of working is found in shifting how leadership teams make decisions. Today, leadership teams meet once a month or once a quarter, and during that meeting time they share information and try to solve problems. Working in new ways for me is about working on a collaborative problem where you can start to share information easily with everyone in the group and ask for their support and help, so that in perhaps 24 hours you can make a decision, rather than waiting an entire month for the next big leadership team meeting.

For me, it's all about accelerating access to information and access to decision making, and also accelerating our connections to the people we need to have in our community.

Appreciating Diversity and Inclusion: My experience of moving to Switzerland was a really interesting one, as it highlighted for me the fact that in the US we tend to work on a very individual level, whereas in Europe they tend to consider what is best for the community. It reinforced the importance of the community for me. In making decisions, it is not only about what is important to me, but it's also important to consider what matters to the community or eco-system, particularly if we want to work for the good of an eco-system, not just our industry.

I also learned that when you are willing to look outside of your boundaries—for example, to look outside of Switzerland and think about what France, Germany, or Sweden can bring to the table and how and why things are important to them—you find new questions and answers to opportunities, and new ways of thinking and working. There is an opportunity for all of us to start to work and think this way to solve these bigger world problems, like the ones we are facing in health care.

Impact on Family: My husband came over to Switzerland on sabbatical and stayed with me for 14 months. When he first made the decision to come, I am not sure he knew if it was going to fit. In the end, he was really sad to leave, because he had seen a different world and a different way of being in community in the world. We found that we had a better life-work balance, because the culture wanted people to slow down and spend time together on Saturdays and Sundays. Europeans recognized that when we don't take the time to relax, slow down, and have conversations to build trust, connection, and community, we don't replenish ourselves. Replenishing ourselves is a key part of staying alive and staying vibrant.

I've come to realize that where I used to talk about work-life balance, I now just talk about LIFEworking. I love having the flexibility to choose what I want to do with my week, my month, or my day. I recognize that it doesn't have to be a nine to five routine—it can be whenever I want. I've started painting, which is something I'd always wanted to do. I have less boundaries or constraints in how I am spending my life. You have to love what you are doing for work, because work is a such a big part of your life.

The problem and the opportunity

In 2012, it was clear to Hal Barron, the CMO and Head of Product Development at Roche, that we had a problem: the cost of drug development was way too high. On average, it cost $1.6 billion to bring a drug to market. It was clear that dosing, safety, and efficacy were incredibly important data points in getting a drug approved, but it was equally as important to be able to articulate the value of the drug for the patients, physicians, and payers. For example: was the patient able to function more effectively (i.e. spend time with their kids, take a walk, go to lunch, or even go back to work) as a result of taking the drug? Were we designing trials that enabled patients to be a part of designing outcomes? Was this option more cost effective than other options available for patients? We needed to be able to demonstrate with certainty that this patient solution truly created value for the patient, the payer (such as an insurance company), and the physician.

The opportunity at hand was complex and involved many customers and interested parties who were all looking to solve this problem—or rather, this opportunity. The reality was that this issue was not going to be solved by any one group, but had to be solved in support of the healthcare ecosystem. It had to be solved by us and for us, as we are all patients in one way or another. We had to look at this opportunity in a whole new way, from a community and ecosystem perspective. I don't think we realized when we started that it was truly about creating and building a new company set up to design patient solutions with and for the health care ecosystems and the patients within it.

Our journey became integrated with how we did business

It was clear from the recent merger and acquisition of Genentech by Roche that we needed a single set of product development behaviors, so that employees understood what we were looking for in terms of a way of working, a mindset, and approach to the work. We established a set of behaviors to evoke a new way of working, thinking, and being: take smart risks, foster learning and creativity, speak up and challenge, and focus on the right work.

We focused on engaging the senior leaders, who selected three projects to work on. One was for our patients, which was known as "Trial to Patient," which focused on how patients could participate in trials anywhere, at any time. Another was for ourselves, which was named "Smarter Information." Its goal was to address how we could access the information and data we needed in more streamlined, simplified ways. The third idea selected was the "Innovation Hub," which focused on how we could create a self-sustaining environment where innovation and doing our work in new and more relevant ways could continue.

We engaged our workforce in looking for and designing options. Our first foray into engagement was an internally crowdsourced program, where every employee in Product Development had an opportunity to provide a solution to one of three questions about our business and our patients. We had over 500 solutions and over 15,000 votes on the "top ideas." We also visited small, medium, and large organizations to learn more about their environment, how they engaged both inside and outside of their organization, and how they innovated to help us determine what would work for us.

Another key factor was pushing the inside out and bringing the outside in, which was one of the most important lessons. We come from an industry of incredibly brilliant people who have always had to figure things out on their own. We learned we could not solve this problem on our own. We brought the inside out and the outside in very thoughtfully. This included the following approaches:

- Open the Door Visits: We went out to visit many companies to learn from them, asking how they approached the topic of innovation, creativity, and doing things differently.
- Innovation Advisory Board: We invited our top creatives (sales people, mavericks, and connectors from our business), along with some very interesting and provocative leaders with diverse profiles from the outside. We had this distinct board provide input into strategic projects and approaches, and had them co-create our top opportunities together.
- Design Thinking, Prototyping, and Testing: We learned we were great at thinking of ideas, but not necessarily great at executing on them. Design thinking gave us a way to engage from a more human- or patient-centered approach. We learned to prototype and refine our ideas via testing with our patients, our physicians, our payers, and ourselves. We were able to move forward projects that had value, and this enabled us to shift into new ways of working, connecting, and enabling, and also to let go of those old ways that were no longer working well for us.
- Imaginariums (Design Labs) and Storytelling: We worked directly with patients, caregivers, physicians, experts, and payers for one to two days to really understand and build what was needed to answer our opportunity and challenge. The Imaginariums were probably the most game-changing elements of our shifts. We had the opportunity to empathize, listen, and really work to understand how we could design and execute today's clinical trials—anywhere, anytime, with our

customers, by our customers, and for our customers. And the customer is us—we are all patients.

If you get clear on and share your values and the behaviors needed today and create a safe environment or container for your employees and partners to innovate and think differently, you will unleash talent both inside and outside of your organization to deliver remarkable shifts, changes, and relevant products both for today and tomorrow. Be sure to recognize and reward—and the best way to do that is to help others tell their stories. Keep the prototypes small, and easy. Use short turn around times for the testings and always use a human-centered approach in the design and execution. And finally, as more people feel connected to the shared purpose of the organization, remember to tell their stories.

The results speak for themselves

In less than three years, we:

- Reduced the cost of our Product Development drug by 15%;
- Engaged patients, physicians, and payers in the design and execution of our trials;
- Tested new solutions in more than 85%of our teams (each testing one to three innovations or new approaches on their studies); and
- Doubled our employee satisfaction and engagement scores.

Having an internal and external innovation board helped us with our strategy by:

- Telling stories of our heroic teams, not the stories of innovation; and
- Demonstrating innovation as a way of being, evolving, and sustaining our business and ourselves.

I have worked for several large pharmas over the last 20 years, and this is the first one that is truly creating new value, and doing it with their patients.

Unfortunately, businesses are often still governed by metrics that too often force us to take a short-term view of the world, when the world around us is changing exponentially. We experience it hourly through increasing news updates, whether we choose a traditional newspaper or online news sources. For those working in healthcare, we get to see firsthand the changes in our ecosystems, from disruptions in nanotechnology and health technology to how we connect with patients, as well as the increasing need to recognize the ever-diminishing healthcare budgets of countries where payers' needs are shifting dramatically.

Some call it the perfect storm. I call it the perfect opportunity. This is the time to become more attuned to the fundamental changes and take action before the cracks, which are starting to show, become too big to mend. It is the perfect opportunity to be proactive and help bring much needed change to how we run large organizations. I want to share with you an example that will hopefully inspire leaders like you to act differently.

New ways of working: the dilemma

At Roche, my group was responsible for strategic innovation in our big phase three and four studies. So how did we—and in particular, the product development organization running the studies—break this chain of strictly working in what was assumed to be an efficient and effective business model predominately focused on continuous improvement?

To address this complexity, we decided to bring the outside in. We realized that while we had some of the most brilliant minds in the business working at Roche, we needed to tap into our network to reach out to others who could help us achieve our goals. We also identified strategic partnerships as a key component of our success, and we needed to find people who could help us test our strategy and provide input on what experiments and projects made the most sense. We also asked the outside to work with us to teach us what we did not know. We needed diversity in thinking. People from other industries and, most importantly, our patients, were part of the solution.

It takes a lot of courage and humility to be in a place of asking for help, instead of always playing the expert role. And it also requires understanding that in the 21st century, we live and work in a world that is full of possibilities. By co-creating and collaborating, we are able to tap into a collective imagination of what's possible in pharma by including the entire community—patients, payers, physicians, regulators, and employees.

What we learned was that bringing the outside in required a change in our mindset—a mindset of needing to know all the answers and how to do everything on your own (either by yourself or as a company). The difficulty of this kind of change should not be underestimated, as we needed to change a way of thinking that most of us have grown up with.

What were the principles we used in working with the outside?

1 – Diversity of experience brings diversity of perspectives: Bring a diverse group of people into the circle (i.e. not all pharma—we invited people from the banking industry, from oil and gas, patients, social communities, big data leaders, etc.). Diversity of experience brings diversity of perspectives.

2 – It's all about co-creation: Allow open space and thinking together to design the future together. Be curious and ask lots of questions. The future is about co-creation, strategic partnership, and accelerating our learning so that we remain innovative and relevant.

3 – Be prepared for the unexpected and be open to unusual partnerships: We brought in an Innovator in Residence from the technology industry who challenged our thinking and showed us new ways of working that we could integrate into our work. What you start with is never what you end up with, whether in your conversations, the work you chose to do, or who you work with.

4 – Ask for help on the thing you do not know or need help learning: Our external advisors help us not only with strategy, experiments, and partnerships, but also offer to help us learn new ways of working, like tele-medicine and the use of payer databases to understand and find patients for our clinical trials.

Using these principles, we were able to start a new way of thinking and embark on a new journey together, both in terms of the business model and in what we needed to be today and in the future.

Here are a couple of interesting stories from the experiment:

One of our advisors started a new business as a result of listening and working with us. Another advisor worked closely with us to connect us to cancer patients to better understand outcomes of trial participation—anywhere, anytime. A third advisor provided us with new insights, such as where to potentially access patients, and important stratifications of patient types (from those who naturally adhere to their regime to those who do not, or who have difficulty adhering). And our patients gave us profound insights into what they really needed, beyond just the safety of dosing and the efficacy of our drugs or solutions.

We started with our Roche needs and ended up addressing many questions that could help change the healthcare ecosystem. We were not creating the changes alone in Roche or in product development. We began co-creating the future of health—and in particular, amazing solutions for patients that go way beyond just developing a drug. We have a whole new appreciation of what patients need and want today, and we are delivering dramatically different options.

My advice for anyone looking at new ways of working and co-creating:

- Don't do it alone;
- Incorporate diversity from the inside and outside into as many aspects of your business as much as you can;
- Come from a place of generosity in your co-creation;
- Know your executive team may feel uncomfortable at times, and demonstrate value with stories and by including them at every step;
- Competencies will change and shift over time, just as behaviors and mindsets will, and you need to do your best to understand them;
- Persevere and model the new path; and
- Finally, enjoy the ride—you will be amazed at what you can deliver together.

It is a whole new business world out there. Embrace the outside as part of your inside business. Once you take this new path, you will never be able to go back to the old. This is an opportunity for us to thrive.

Kare Anderson

Emmy-winning former NBC and Wall Street Journal journalist and TED presenter on Becoming an Opportunity Maker (with over 1.9 million views) Kare Anderson is a Forbes columnist who speaks and consults on becoming more deeply connected and widely quoted. She's the cofounder of the Say it Better Center and the author of several books, including *Mutuality Matters*, *Mutuality Matters More*, *Moving From Me to We* (2012), *Walk Your Talk* (1994), and *Resolving Conflict Sooner* (1999).

The Journey of Kare Anderson: Influencer. Connector. Speaker. Emmy-winning former reporter.

What is your story?

Coming from a sheltered background, I wanted to explore a wider world of adventuresome, purposeful people. In this increasingly tech-enabled era, The Law of Unintended Consequences is increasingly becoming the norm, not the exception. Most new inventions can be used for good and bad things. Thus, our most noble calling may be our capacity to recruit apt allies to motivate more people and organizations to use technology and connective behavior for the greater good. That's why my core mission is to motivate individuals to redefine their life around a mutuality mindset, seeking the "us" opportunity in every situation, to use our best talents together around strong sweet spots of mutual interest.

Some of the ways I support that core mission are to enable others to:

1. Cultivate extremely diverse allies so they can get unexpected help, discover more sides of a situation and solutions for it, plus attract more serendipitous opportunities, adventure, and accomplishment.

2. See the value and visibility-boosting power of unexpected allies taking a public stand or co-creating a service or product for a niche market they all seek to serve better.

3. Become more quotable, so that what they say sticks in other people's minds and they want to share it with others. An example is when I worked with a hospital system to increase their blood drives, we created the Got Blood billboards in line with the "Got Milk?" campaign in the United States. It just stuck with people.

4. Practice the power of specificity in their messaging to boost self-clarity and reduce the chance they will be misunderstood—plus increase their message's credibility and memorability.

5. Recognize that the healthiest relationships involve not a quid pro quo, but an ebb and flow of support over time. Hint: If you give enough

other people what they need, you often get what you need too—sometimes even before you need it, and sometimes from people you did not know could provide it.

6. Identify ways to collectively act that are efficient and generate virtuous circles with benefits to all players.

A client of mine, the CEO of a large pharmaceutical company, spoke at an investors conference where each presenter had only 20 minutes to speak, He strolled onto the stage slightly slower than the others, stopped, and looked around at the audience. Then he rolled up his shirtsleeve and pointed to a patch on his inner elbow. "See this patch?" he said, then paused to boost interest. "When this patch goes on the market, users will feel the effects throughout their body faster than a Porshe can go from zero to 90 miles an hour." As he spoke that last sentence, he swept his arm in a arc from one side to the other, making his body a "moving billboard" to reinforce his message. He was dancing his hands from left to right. "This will be the Porsche of the body." (Porsches matched the aspirations of those in the audience at that time). The result? Even though his product announcement was not the most important news at the conference, it was the one most quoted by attendees and reporters in the audience.

Hint: Opportunity-makers are actively seeking situations with people who are different than them, and they're building relationships. Because they do that, they have trusted relationships where they can bring the right team in and recruit them to solve a problem better and faster and seize more opportunities. They're not affronted by differences—they're fascinated by them. That is a huge shift in mindset, and once you feel it, you want it to happen a lot more. This world is calling out for us to have a collective mindset, and it's especially important now. Why is it important now? Because things like drones, drugs, and data collection are being devised, and they can be devised by more people in cheaper ways for more beneficial purposes. On the other hand, as we know from the news every day, they can also be used for dangerous purposes as well.

More than traditional "leaders" the world needs apt connectors who can be the glue that can recruit and hold the right teams together to solve problems and seize opportunities faster and better than others. Such opportunity makers enable us to reimagine a world where we use our best talents together more often to accomplish greater things together than we could on our own.

New ways of working

Gore-Tex and Saddleback Church are frequently cited as examples of the connective, giving power of small, strong, interconnected teams or groups within a larger organization. That's why Gore-Tex can justify citing this core truth as their credo: "A unique, nonhierarchical culture fosters the innovative spirit of individuals and small teams." As different as Gore-Tex and Saddleback Church are, in many ways, they share the core value of being part of a purpose-driven small group that interacts with other small groups within the organization, which boosts fresh thinking as well as a feeling of belonging. Some call this "approach-networked teams" or a "team of teams."

Since more individuals are working and/or living alone in the United States, we need more mutually beneficial ways to create one-time and ongoing teams and communities. Some may exist online, others in person, and others will be hybrids of both. One of my favorite models to emulate is Quantified Self, as it spurs the desire to design a team of teams or community model, one that might be adapted to other situations in the future so that more people can benefit from it.

Opportunities to model 21st century leadership

As a reporter, I was covering Brazilian soccer star Dani Alves at a game in Barcelona. At the game, some sports fans in the stadium that day were yelling racial epithets at Alves. After a break in the game, Alves came back on the field and someone threw a banana down, landing a few feet in front of him. Without a pause, he walked forward, picked up the banana, peeled it, took one bite, and with a warm smile, nonchalantly threw it over his shoulder, then proceeded out to play. Many of the onlookers broke out in cheers and applause at his aplomb. "Dani Alves owned him," tweeted his Brazilian's teammate Neymar. "Take THAT, bunch of racists. We are all Monkeys. So What." Former

England international Gary Lineker, who played for Barcelona, also applauded Alves' quick thinking. "Utterly brilliant reaction from Alves," tweeted Lineker. The story of that incident spread far beyond sports coverage and enabled Alves to become a role model for far more people around the world.

People are increasingly living and working on their own, so they will crave community more and more. We haven't gotten good yet at creating new kinds of communities. I believe in virtuous circles—methods and mechanisms that leverage greater value for all participants.

In our increasingly complex yet connected world, the key to a meaningful life may well be our capacity to instill a sense of mutuality in more situations. Speak sooner to the strongest sweet spot of shared interest. More than smarts, money, titles, or even charisma, our capacity to connect with diverse people is vital for leading an adventuresome, satisfying life with others. Become the glue that holds groups together. Be more deeply connected and widely-quoted. Then we can accomplish something greater together than we ever could on our own.

Hital Muraj

Hital Muraj works in underserved communities to address the digital divide. Her passion is around empowering, as well as showing girls, women, and youth what is possible. I'll never forget the first time we met in a TelePresence video meeting. Hital had been told that there was a Cisco executive who was coming to do work in East Africa, and that she would need to work with her—and that executive was me. When I entered the meeting, I got the sense that I was taking her away from her real work. But after a few days together in Nairobi and Rwanda, we both realized how much our work intertwined and what an impact we could make by joining forces. I was amazed by her spirit and the deep relationships she had wherever we went—from an academy she started with former house girls and street girls, to the offices of key government officials.

At Cisco, Hital is responsible for the Social Investments in East and Central Southern Africa which include the company's education initiative called the Cisco Networking Academy Program. She successfully launched the first Cisco Networking Academy for the deaf in the world, which has enabled a traditionally forgotten group of people to get access to information communication technology (ICT), education that will empower them for the future. She has also pioneered a TeleHealth project, which connects East Africa's top pediatric hospital to rural clinics to diagnose and treat young children—a first in Africa. Hital has been recognized as the global ambassador for youth from Usher's New Look Foundation and has been nominated as Kenya's Top 40 Most Powerful Women Under 40 for two consecutive years. She is an Acumen and Rockfeller Fellow.

The Journey of Hital Muraj: Inspirational. Team Integrator. Activist. Corporate Affairs Manager, Cisco Systems, East and Central Southern Africa.

What is your story?

I am a change agent, a transformer, a mother, and a wife. I'm an Asian African. Above all, I'm very passionate about what is currently happening in Africa, and how each one of us can step in and be part of this transformation that Africa is going through. I also work for Cisco, but I'm all about changing communities through the powerful use of technology for good. When people ask me what I do, I tell them I am an ambassador of change, I am passionate about using ICT for development, and I live to make a difference. I am a voice speaking out against injustice.

In today's world, access to digital information must be a basic human right, and it is a necessity for economic viability. Unfortunately, Africa is disadvantaged compared to other continents because of its lack of a reliable broadband infrastructure. The rural poor have been left out of many stages in the development process due to their lack of information and communications. The rural poor are suffering from information poverty.

50 percent of the population living in 38 countries in Sub Saharan Africa lives without electricity, and the majority of the population have to walk many miles to overcrowded schools without desks. Few communities have libraries or resource centers, and are thus socially and economically deprived of the much-needed resources of information, including information about their own country. There is not always a sense of belonging to the wider global village.

In Kenya, 75% of our population is under 30 years of age, which we call the youth. In Africa, 60% of youth are unemployed and this is a ticking time bomb. There is a serious problem of engaging these youths in positive activities. What this actually means is poverty and crime cycling together. The youth get bound up in the cycle of poverty and have to fight every day to go and look for their daily needs. Many loose lose their self-value as a result. I am trying to shift the youth to start believing in themselves and start knowing that they can do incredible things in their communities, and that they don't need anybody else to go and change their community. I work on fixing the cup first (the person) before filling it up.

This is the movement that I'm currently running with the youth. In addition to that, I have a movement for young girls that I'm trying to mentor. These girls come from similar backgrounds where they don't have access to sanitation on a monthly basis. They are often raped by their relatives because they do not speak up and fight for themselves. What I'm trying to do there is give the girls a voice and power so that they can actually decide what they want to do and how they will be treated.

What I work on is very much about people and giving them hope and letting them know that their life can also be full of endless possibilities and those possibilities can happen. Each of us is driven by hope and dreams.

Most of the people I'm helping get stuck in the day-to-day search for their needs. Every day, when they're out on the street, they're trying to think about where they are going to get their next meal. For them to see outside that picture, I have to really try and make them see that they are human beings, that they have value, that they can also be part of the solution to changing their community. They can believe in themselves, in little things like getting them to identify what their talents and strengths are.

There is a lot of hope and positivity now in the youth that I work with. And the good thing is that they also see that it's not somebody from the outside affecting the change; they can do it themselves. They have the power to change their situation, and that doesn't necessarily require money. That's really the biggest thing, because the system we come from is extremely corrupt, and the only way to directly change that system is by giving them money. That has been the tradition, and that's something that I'm trying to fight with. I want to show that it's not all about money. Even without money, you can do small things in your community to make a change.

We have a pay-it-forward program where they are expected to identify projects that we can work on together in their community. It is really amazing to see these youth taking ownership, taking responsibility to make a change. It's very interesting to see that it's not about money. Nobody's giving them money to make that change—there is a different motivation. You can actually see that motivation now coming out of our youth.

So much is possible with a new mindset. Steve Orioki is a great example. Steve was a high school student and social entrepreneur at Kibera, and he wanted to be a matatu (minibus) driver once he finished his high of school. He came across the Cisco Academy program where we taught him ICT skills, and his career path totally changed. When he graduated from high school, Steve and a couple of his friends started repairing computers for a couple of businesses, and they collected some money from that. The next thing they did was start a small ICT center in Kibera—Steve's hometown, his slum. With two computers, Steve started reaching out to the youth in his community, and also to the youth on drugs.

Five years ago I received an award for youth leadership from Usher and Former President Bill Clinton. When I came back from the US, I felt like I wasn't doing enough, and that I needed to start a movement where I could start making a change in a bigger way. I'm just scratching the surface, and wish I could do much more than that I currently am. We often get stuck in changing the system which is very complex.

I started going around the streets and seeing youth who were idling around doing nothing, and I asked them, "What can I do to help you make a change? What can I do to assist you?" It was not about money; I wanted to know how I could assist them in whatever problems they were facing. Listening to them, I came up with a program that focuses on several different areas. One component is empowering them to make a change in their communities. The second is shifting their entire paradigm and helping them start to think about how they can all work together as a team, because they face the same challenges every day.

There have been a lot of team-building activities that have led to understanding different personalities, and working with the diversity of the communities.

The third area is helping them to use technology to actually find their voice. You can use technology to give people a voice, and they now have a platform where they can share that voice. Once they can share themselves in this way, who cares where they come from, or how poor their background is? The youth in my community now know that if you have a voice, you have a choice.

Over 90 youths have gone through our program. We've had a lot of ups and downs, because these youths are constantly facing the question of where they will find their next meal, and often their family's next meal, too. Sometimes getting them to engage becomes difficult because of the basic priorities that they have in their lives. A number of them drop out, a lot of them move on, but a lot of them have stayed and we've seen amazing things happen.

We have a youth group that started social enterprises. They started an organization in 2012 called COVIT (Connecting Voices of Inspiration for a Better Tomorrow). They've started a project making solar lamps out of water bottles and distributed about 7,000 of them. It's the youth who have come up with the projects they want to do to change their community. One has been selected to represent the entire country on a Youth Forum in Sri Lanka. These are the kinds of things that we're trying to do—help each person change their mindset and situation, one person at a time.

For the girl's movement that I started, I move school to school for a period of 3-6 months. I want to figure out how we can get them to tell their own stories and open up. These girls have undergone so much trauma in their short lives, and we need to ask how they can start sharing their stories. How do you get them to build their self-confidence? We need help from people with big hearts who can take the time to co-create local solutions.

Being community

There are about 700,000 people living in this particular area of the slum, in a 2.5 square-kilometer area, with no access to clean water or sanitation. The irony is that there are thousands of non-governmental organizations (NGOs) that come in to do work here, but don't leave much for the community and there is no real impact seen in those communities. They come in quickly with their big ideas, fill someone's pocket with cash, and then the people who need the help remain poor. They continue to be exploited in many ways including slum tourism, where a number of foreigners pay to see how people live in poverty. That's what I have been working with the youth on—how do we put a stop to this cycle so we can address these issues locally? We don't want to be on display. These are human lives and it is hurtful to make a mockery out of how we live. We don't want to be portrayed in this way in photos anymore. We want people to not just travel through our lives, but find ways to do something positive.

The perception of NGOs is really bad in this part of the world. They often feel like a get-rich-quick scheme. A lot of celebrities have come into our particular area and invested millions of dollars, but really nothing has happened. The investments magically vanish as the celebrities leave.

We want to experience the impact of solutions coming from our community by co-creating locally. You don't always have to give us money; you can come and give us 10 or 20 coaching sessions, or guidance on starting a business, for example. Show us how to use some new tools in the world. It goes beyond mentoring. It is about job creation from a local perspective. I really want to see that impact, and I want to see a change in these youths.

For me, working at Cisco has been a gateway to what we can do locally in our communities. For companies, social responsibility needs to be part of our DNA. It's simply how we practice our art in the world, regardless of what business we are in. It has not always been a smooth road navigating corporate America, but I am grateful that I have the spot to do my work now. I am so integrated into my work that, because of the passion I have, everything fits in together to form one body of purposeful work.

We need more leaders in the world who are humble and who understand that we can learn from each other on this journey. It's no longer just about the title. People want to be around people they trust, not people they fear. Being able to emotionally connect with people, and being able to really define the challenges in this leadership position, are key. The new type of leader is great at listening and bringing people together with purpose.

I would love to live in a world where we can each play our role and not have it be seen as Africans needing to be saved. What we need is opportunity. The way people can help is to be the voice. I want to be the voice of my people and our youth. What I know is that when you don't have a voice, you are in an unlucky situation because you didn't choose to be there, and yet, that is exactly where you are. We are all responsible for being the voices out in the world, to tell people that there is much more behind poverty than what is being shared in the media. We have amazing people with hope and skills who simply need the chance to make a life for themselves. And they want to solve their own problem, with coaching and guidance. They need job creation and skills development. And most importantly, they need to know that they matter. How do we ignite their fire and change their environment? By helping to give them a very loud voice in the world.

It would be fantastic if we could share information more easily. For example, we would love to have access to tools, curriculum, or training ideas that we can actually put together to help the youth. I'm not a professional coach or a trainer, but I do my best. Wouldn't it be wonderful to create new programs where people from any place in the world could share their skills and information with the youth? It could be a one-hour WebEx or video call where they coach or teach new skills.

Jeff Power

From his background in global humanitarian aid, Jeff Power launched Pangeo Coffee & Tea as the socially-fanatical company that created the Adopt-a-Village model. As coffee shops, restaurants, hotels, and others pour Pangeo, Jeff and his team connect each of them with "their own" village in Africa, the Middle East, or Asia. Pangeo invests a high percentage of its profits into the transformation of those villages, while supplying monthly pictures and updates about the village's progress out of poverty.

A true coffee geek, Jeff believes we should love people well, and the rest will take care of itself. One essential tip he has for social entrepreneurs is to start with the heart and learn to listen to yourself. He also believes life is too short for bad coffee.

The Journey of Jeff Power:
Humanitarian. Opportunity Maker. Coffee Geek.
Founder and CEO, Pangeo Coffee & Tea.

What is your story?

The problem I have been trying to solve in the world is how to sustainably help the poorest villages in the world lift themselves out of poverty, with a little bit of outside help and not a ton of aid. We are talking about self-sustainability for people in villages who live on one dollar a day or less. Did you know that 25 percent of people in the world live in these conditions? That is what we are trying to solve in our own way. We can't do it from a distance. We don't have the answers for them, but we can hire local coaches who will listen and work with them side by side for five to six years.

I have traveled on many planes to visit villages in Africa, the Middle East, and Asia to listen, learn, and build relationships. I believe in reaching out to our neighbors who may live far away and investing in their development in partnership with them. Changing the world is about connection, love, relationships, and respect. What I'm doing is finding partners for villages—individuals, clubs, offices, churches, and schools—who want to adopt specific villages and build relationships, village by village.

When I was visiting a village in Kenya, we had a video call over satellite with a restaurant in Chicago that was pouring Pangeo coffee and iced tea. The people who poured the coffee talked to the people who produced the coffee. There was a human-to-human connection that was enhanced by the fact that the conversations took place over video, where everyone could experience each other face to face. It is no longer about someone who is poor or living in a different country; it is a connection between people. I often get calls from employees at coffee shops and restaurants who have made these new connections, telling me they want to visit their village with me next time I go, on their own dime.

Coffee has followed a similar story to wine. In recent years, people have realized there's truly a difference between cheap beans and good ones, and even amazing ones. So they pay a bit more for the good ones (or a lot more for the amazing ones), and the taste difference is clear. We'd like to think we're in the good-to-amazing category, and beans from the areas we serve keep winning international awards.

I want to create connections that change people's circumstances. I want to put a human face on each side. In these hot spots in the world, the villagers are not afraid of the Americans and the Americans are not afraid of them. We are all helping each other around a shared purpose.

A wise dance of development and integration

It doesn't matter if you are a parent developing children to become self-sustaining adults, if you are an employer developing new employees to be knowledgeable and self-sustaining, if you are a coach with a little league team, or you are helping a village in the Middle East. Development should always be a wise dance and represent the integration of two extremes—one extreme is abandoning the other party and doing nothing for them, and the other extreme is doing everything you can for them.

Real development means you wisely watch and observe at what point a person simply needs knowledge, at what point they need training, and at what point they need direct feedback that could help them have a greater awareness of themselves. Sometimes you need to tell people something about themselves that they might not want to hear, and you may also find that they are simply afraid and need help finding their courage. It involves wise coaches who bring the right amount of outside resources to help the village, the employee, or the team member to develop sustainably.

Our local staff (from the tribes they are helping) spends time in the village every single week and works with their committees. Together, they look at their own assets first, and they help the village learn problem-solving skills. We work with the community in five key areas, and they form committees around each: water, food, health and wellness, income, and education. Then we focus on developing these areas, hopefully with the right amount of balance.

Co-creating local solutions

When I took some American restaurant leaders to East Ethiopia, they saw that the villagers were facing starvation. The Food Agriculture Committee met with them and talked to our staff member who is coaching that village. It was decided that with a little bit of outside help, they could create irrigation systems from a dry riverbed nearby. We figured out that with a small pumping system, we could pump the water up the hill into a channel that would then carry the water down into the village. During our second visit, the difference we saw was like night and day; this village, with a few thousand dollars of outside investment to set up the pumps, had created a sustainable system to address their food shortage challenge.

When we went back to the village, the restaurant leaders were blown away. There were acres and acres of family farms and vegetables growing. What is wonderful is the community is making money from the vegetables and they are feeding every family in the village. Due to their success, the government assigned a young agriculture worker to help other villages within a 50-kilometer radius. Other villages are learning from the methods and the initiatives that this village took.

People think we are only a for-profit business, but we are trying to model something that any business can do. When we launched Pangeo Coffee, we said our reason for existing was to change lives and change the world. Of course, our own employees have to get paid, and so it is a for-profit business. But we said from the outset that at a minimum, 20 percent of all our margins on all of our coffee and iced tea sales were going to go back into the villages we support around the world.

We also want to raise awareness and make sure coffee and tea farmers around the world are truly getting competitive, living wages for the hard work they put in. We want to make sure that they are earning enough money to feed their families and clothe their children, get their kids to school, and receive health care. We want to make sure it's fair.

In the space of five to seven years, we see villages go from destitute poverty to having sustainable, clean water sources, food for their families, and an ability to sell the excess. We have also shared health and wellness tips with the committee and they have reduced infant mortality by 80-90 percent. Family incomes have gone from less than a dollar a day to four, five, or 10 dollars a day. All of the kids in the villages are enrolled in primary school. The United Nations asked us to present our work, because within five years the villages we work with went from zero to sustainability in all five areas we had set out to improve.

Leaders need empathy and an ability to listen

Leadership, in general, is getting people together and accomplishing something big that they couldn't otherwise do on their own. The best leaders have a vision and lead with their hearts.

It is tempting, when you come from material opulence like many of us do in the West, to assume that material opulence equals automatic validation. That is a terrible conclusion, because what we hide in the West is our massive suicide rate, and the increasing obesity, heart disease, and cancer that is killing us off like flies. Those are all by-products of the Western ways of thinking. As leaders, we need to be absolutely honest about this. I am starting to see an increased willingness in the West to observe, listen, and learn from other parts of the world.

In the communities we work with in Africa, people are dying from other things like hunger more than suicide. What does that tell us about our world? In a village, people generally take care of each other. They do not discard people in their community, but figure out how to live together and lead together. We in corporate America can learn a lot from these villages about leadership and building community.

Our story with Pangeo Coffee is that we are still in the early stages and building relationships. It is the kindness of people that is getting our story out into the world. When a coffee shop or organization pours our coffee or iced tea, we connect them online with the villagers who bring it to market. My team visits their operations people and ask them to pour Pangeo and then adopt a village. People can also go to their local coffee shops or restaurants and ask them to pour our coffee and connect directly with a village that produces it.

The people who get involved with us usually pick one village or a group of villages in one country. They invest there, one village at a time. There are many villages that live at the bottom end of the economic spectrum in the world, called the "bottom billion." My belief is that we play a role in connecting people with the villages, and, as a result, people's circumstances can change in a positive way. We are co-creating more than economic development.

We have a phrase that we use at Pangeo: "If it does not fly in the village, it should not fly at the corporate level." You do not treat people at the corporate level any differently than you would treat them if you had to live with them day after day in your own village.

Exercises for Expedition 9

24 **Purpose for Co-Creating**		
	Do I need a connected network to achieve my purpose? Why or why not?	Are trusted communities important to me? Why or why not?

25 **Building Trusted Relationships**		
	Who do I trust?	Why?
	1)	
	2)	
	3)	
	Who trusts me?	Why?
	1)	
	2)	
	3)	
	What fosters trust?	Why?

26 **Building Empathy and Listening Deeply**		
	When was the last time I had a two-way conversation with no specific agenda, apart from trusting that I would learn something or connect with someone?	When is the next time I am likely to have this type of conversation?
	What does having a two-way conversation mean to me? What does it look like?	What, if any, changes would I like to make in the way I hold conversations?
	Do I truly listen to the other person in conversations, or am I waiting to make my point?	What, if any, changes would I like to make in my ability to listen during conversations?

27 **Partnerships**		
	What are the deepest relationships in the various areas of my life?	
	What are some of the reasons some partnerships have thrived, some have been stressful, and others have fizzled?	

28 **Co-Creation**		
	What is my definition of co-creation? What are some examples?	
	What can I improve when it comes to co-creating?	What is working well for me in co-creating?

29

My Opportunities

What are the opportunities for me to co-create in my connected networks and trusted communities, and what unlikely or unusual partnerships can I go out and create?

Connected Networks	Who do I need to reach out to?
Trusted Communities	**Who do I need to reach out to?**
Unlikely Partnerships	**Who do I need to reach out to?**
What does working out loud mean to me?	**How can I work out loud?**

30

Connecting Stories

Thinking about each of the stories you just experienced, what do they mean for your own journey to conscious 21st century leadership?

Arlene Samen	
Tara Kelly	
Sheila Babnis	
Kare Anderson	
Hital Muraj	
Jeff Power	

Expedition 10
LIFEworking Means Choosing Yourself

What could you do if you had more courage to do what's in your heart? Have you taken this journey to explore what possibilities are open to you? What nurtures you? What if before we started to save the world or help everyone else, we first focused on ourselves? What if there was only life to be lived—no balance between work and life required?

While we have been led to believe that we can separate our personal and work personas, in reality we are only one person. We don't need to have this separation and supposed balancing act in our lives. Let's become whole as people, and remember that external validation is fleeting.

The questions we should be asking in the 21st century are: How do we want to show up in the world as human beings? What do we want to create in the world? What's our purpose? Who do we want to co-create with around this purpose? We need to know that the people we work with care enough about what they are creating that they will do great work with pride.

We need to value technology for how it enables us to connect more deeply with each other. For example, when we turn on our video cameras for a virtual meeting, we sometimes can have more effective conversations than when we are sitting in the same room. I have experienced this firsthand, having more engaged conversation on video calls than in conference rooms. I gave up my physical office at Cisco in 2003 and worked remotely with people from around the world—my managers, employees, peers, and customers. Today, I prefer talking with people on camera so that we can experience our conversation "face to face". I am always baffled at why there are still so many people who refuse to turn on their cameras during calls; the only reason I can think of is that they are not fully engaged in the conversation (or perhaps they are camera shy). But it really doesn't matter why in this case; what matters is that today we can have a conversation with someone in a different location with the same level of engagement as if we were sharing the same physical space. And then when you do finally meet that person or people in physical space, you will feel like you already know them.

Why am I telling you this? Because a year ago, my friend Renee connected me with "management guru" Professor Jamie Anderson. We jumped on a Skype call and 20 minutes into the conversation Jamie said, "I love what you are doing with LIFEworking; do you want to co-author an article?" The next day he sent me his 5,000 words and we started co-creating. To this day, I have yet to meet Jamie in physical space as he lives across the pond, but I know that when we do, I will give him a big hug in appreciation of the contribution he has made in my life.

My friend and co-creator Jamie Anderson and I co-authored a groundbreaking article on LIFEworking for *The London Business School Review*.[59] In fact, our brainstorming and drafts have become part of this expedition.

Paving a New Path

Since the turn of the century, the higher education systems in much of the Western world have worked towards the standardization of learning according to the functional division of labor. By the age of 15 or 16—and even earlier in some countries—individuals are put on an educational track that leads them into increasingly specialized learning paths. The undergraduate, graduate, and doctoral degrees originally awarded by European universities have been adopted in the most diverse societies throughout the world, and while generalist degrees do exist, degrees in fields such as accountancy and finance, commerce, engineering, information systems, law, and medicine have become increasingly prominent. As a student progresses further and further up

---

[59] https://www.london.edu/faculty-and-research/lbsr/achieving-lifeworks#.V8l8eZMrJp8

the educational hierarchy, the more functionally specialized their learning tends to become.

This linear educational path then often sets an individual onto a more or less linear career path: law students become lawyers, engineering students become engineers, and accounting students become accountants. And once in an organization, career paths often unfold in an equally linear way: first as an individual contributor within a functional department, then as a team leader, and on to middle and sometimes senior management in the same function. Of course, this is not to say that a humanities major cannot become a chief financial officer, and some organizations do actively encourage cross-functional experience as part of an overall talent development framework. But in most large organizations, this kind of zigzag career path is the exception rather than the rule.

Something else starts to happen on this linear educational and professional track; as we progress, we are ranked and compared to others, typically according to a narrow range of performance criteria. First are academic grades, and then organizational performance indicators such as productivity or sales results. Indeed, achievement of these metrics often provides the basis for the next stage of progression. As we progress, we start to accrue artifacts of recognition: degree certificates and job titles, for example. So it is not surprising that many career professionals start to define their success—and sometimes their identity—through the accrual of these artifacts by their late 20s and early 30s.

For some people, these artifacts become important indicators of social status and position, and encourage a kind of career snobbery whereby one determines the value of another according to the academic and career achievements they have attained. At the cocktail parties hosted by corporations and prestigious academic institutions, social interactions with new acquaintances are often short lived if the other party realizes that you are not within their own bandwidth of high-level career achievement. In these situations, it seems that your worth is interpreted through little more than a title on a business card.

High achievers bring energy and focus to their roles, and this is often rewarded with recognition and promotion. Many organizations even single out these people for special development, and they are shepherded towards "future leaders" or "high potentials" career tracks. This can be a very exciting experience for a young and ambitious professional, as doors start opening towards more responsibility and accountability and, in an increasingly global business world, coveted international assignments.

As one starts to progress further and further up the career ladder, there is little encouragement to stop and consider wider life goals. Business mentors are more than ready to set out the exciting path ahead, but this is typically defined in the narrow context of your relationship with the organization. Rarely does this future take into account wider life goals, such as fulfilling private relationships and parenting, or the pursuit of personal passions such as art, music, health, and wellbeing. But of course, in the back of their minds, many people still hold the underlying belief that if one achieves career success, then these other things will follow.

All too often, the result is that the quest to "be the best" becomes narrowly defined around career achievement. What often starts as a belief in the need to temporarily subjugate other life goals, to be able to invest in achieving a high level of professional achievement, eventually becomes habitual and permanent. At the same time that the individual can be experiencing meteoric career success, receiving recognition and financial rewards for their commitment to the organization, their personal relationships, parenting commitments, health, and private passions start to suffer.

This stress is particularly acute for career professionals who have children—juggling job, family, friends, and self becomes almost impossible. And the result is far from happiness for most people, as they desperately try to deal with the conflicting pressures that they are experiencing. The first to be abandoned is often the self—pursuing one's own interests and passions, and of course, taking care of the body. The result is often stress and various physical ailments.

As many people start to experience these conflicts, they decide they want to make some changes, but too often they don't know where to start. They try to compartmentalize their lives and to squeeze in other life goals, like going to the gym or spending time with their family, around the demands of the 50- or 60-hour work week in the pursuit of the coveted "work-life" balance, blending, or integration.

Guilt is also a feeling that many high achievers start to experience as they try to reconcile loyalty and commitment to the organization with commitment and loyalty towards their partners and children. While recognized as "being the best" at work, these individuals frequently feel conflicted, inadequate, and unappreciated at home. All too often the result is relationship breakdown and even estrangement from partners and children.

The Fallacy of Work-Life Balance

Today we can be productive almost anywhere at any time, whether we are working on our own or in teams, and yet most organizations still adhere to regimented start and end times to the workday. It is interesting that organizations define our leisure time as being constrained to evenings, weekends, and a regimented number of vacation days per year. Imagine if organization took a different approach and followed a seasonal calendar, where people could work when they were most productive. This is how many free agents already work today.

The reason that organizations have been slow to truly rethink the concept of work-life balance is due more to cultural inertia than any other factor. The industrial age assumptions about technology, organization, and processes have become deeply ingrained within society, and have been reinforced through general and business education and the media. In most organizations, these deeply entrenched assumptions have become orthodoxy, and this is why the question of work-life balance remains. Some enlightened organizations have made progress in some areas, especially with regard to virtual working and flexible working time, but in most cases these initiatives only patch the much deeper underlying problems.

The continued adherence to the industrial age mindset makes it impossible for those who recognize that this is the human era to end the separation and come to work as who they are. And more people of all ages want to show up at work as one person with purpose. Here are a few suggestions to help all of us engage in our LIFEwork:

Re-negotiate the terms of engagement with the existing organization to better integrate your life goals. This requires a track record of high performance (for example, an ability to demonstrate one's value to the organization), trusted relationships with senior management and peers, and a willingness for the organization to be output rather than input focused. The organization and the individual need to rethink performance targets and rewards, and in some cases to accept that promotion to wider levels of responsibility is not an objective—at least for the time being. The shift might also require you to develop stronger skills in collaboration, as the transition to LIFEworking within an established organization typically involves greater task sharing with others.

Create or join an organization (often small) that rejects industrial age work orthodoxy. Such organizations are often less locked into the kind of industrial age organizational orthodoxy. They reject a philosophy of scarcity in favor of embracing opportunities and are comfortable to provide individuals with a greater degree of autonomy over how they achieve performance goals.

Become a free agent, and offer knowledge as a consultant, advisor, or interim manager. This approach delivery is a key element of LIFEworking—autonomy. It requires self-belief, resilience, and a commitment to lifelong learning. It might also require the individual to learn how to configure Outlook email on a smartphone, network a printer, set-up multi-party videoconferences on Skype, or find the best flight deals.

Whatever choice you make—and sometimes people choose more than one option—you are the one driving the shift towards LIFEworking. You are not waiting for your organization to create the necessary environment. There are two fundamental barriers that prevent individuals from doing so: defining purpose and addressing fear.

Defining Purpose

After many years of climbing the corporate ladder to what I thought was success, I was invited to an airline event at the Asian Art Museum in San Francisco to celebrate the top 100 flyers in the San Francisco Bay area. I was surprised to find myself in this club, but perhaps not so surprised to see that I was one of the few women in the group. As I looked around at the exhausted and (what I perceived to be) unhappy faces in the room, I found myself deeply disturbed. I realized that I had certainly broken the glass ceiling in terms of career progression, but at what cost? In the months before the event I had gotten divorced, and the endless stress and travel was also having a damaging impact upon my health.

At that moment I realized that my quest to "be the best" had become narrowly defined, and I stepped back to reflect. This began a process whereby I started to question the meaning of success, and to create purposeful goals that went beyond promotion and generating value for the organization. I loved many of the people I worked with and felt they needed me, especially as an advocate for the younger generation and women at work. But I realized that I had lost a sense of purpose. I made the dramatic decision to step away from the corporate environment to take time to define what "success" really meant for me.

My definition of success did not come quickly. I experienced a period where I lacked direction, but that was to be expected after more than 20 years on a linear career path. On my trip to the Amazon rainforest, I had the time to reflect and face my fears, doubts, and worries. Ironically, I realized that my real passion was for supporting individuals and organizations to be more creative about the journey towards LIFEworking—the very journey I found myself on.

Jamie was also pursuing a similar path at this time, but his exploration of the meaning of success was a team effort. To develop the concept of their LIFEworking project, Jamie and his wife Anne-Mie spent many hours talking together, and these discussions culminated in a drawing exercise. In late 2009, the two sat together with a large sheet of paper and co-created a hand drawn picture of what success really meant to them. The pencil and ink sketches they created revealed a much wider definition of success; they aspired to have a loving relationship and to live in a semi-urban environment in which their three children could play and be free. They desired more family leisure time, and the opportunity to actively participate in their children's social, artistic, and sporting activities. Both Jamie and Anne-Mie wanted to work, but to engage in professional activities that they enjoyed and which (for Jamie) still provided the opportunity for occasional international travel. Jamie also dreamed of returning to elite-level competitive cycling—quite an ambition, after almost 20 years had passed since he had last raced a bicycle.

Facing Our Own Fears

When Jamie and I embarked on our respective journeys towards LIFEworking, we both recognized the need to confront a number of deep-rooted fears. The first set of fears were personal, and for Jamie these related primarily to financial security. He had grown up with six siblings, and as a child money was scarce. Financial stability meant a lot to him, and the fear of economic uncertainty for his family weighed heavily on his mind. So a critical element of his LIFEworking project was to calculate how much money his family really needed to live a fulfilling life—and the result was much less than he expected. He also needed to step back and realize that he still had at least 20 years of productive working years ahead of him, and that many earning opportunities lay ahead.

The second set of fears related to the respective social and professional environments in which we found ourselves. I come from a family where both parents valued education and career success. My mother had a dream of becoming a nurse, but her parents did not feel that was a good profession for a woman at the time. Both my parents pursued undergraduate and graduate degrees while I was in elementary school. When I dropped out of my PhD program in my 20s, my father was so disappointed that in a moment of anger he told me that I would never amount to much. To my parents, who started with nothing, success meant having a great education and career, and to move in the "right" social circles. I was no different than most kids around me, in that I grew up with what I call a "cookie cutter" formula for life.

Fear of the possible reactions of bosses, peers, and colleagues also weighed heavily on us. Jamie and I had been mentored through our careers by leaders who had chosen to follow linear career paths, and now we were telling those mentors that we wanted a different path. We often encountered shock and disbelief, and in some cases anger and a sense of betrayal. One of us was called to a meeting with senior management and offered a significant increase in salary to realign to the organizational career track. Both of us were exposed to hurtful gossip, as some colleagues spread rumors about burnout and failure.

In the end—and as we have discovered through conversations with countless other professionals who are pursuing LIFEworking—one needs to accept that not everyone in a given social or professional circle will understand the decision of a non-linear career path choice. The people who matter the most are close friends and family, as they are the ones who will live with the consequences, and need to have their own fears addressed. We have sometimes been asked about how one should respond if they want to pursue LIFEworking when spouses or partners do not support such a choice. That is a very difficult question indeed, as it gets to the very roots of trust and empathy in our relationships. What we have seen is often when one begins to LIFEwork, it forces limiting beliefs like fear to the surface. Sometimes instead of conversations around the question of "Why we can't do it," people find themselves in deep reflection about why they can't stay in their current situations. A lot depends on the level of communication, trust, and shared purpose that people have in their relationships.

LIFEworking is an approach that meshes life and work into an integrated existence, but most importantly, it is a way of living in which the individual and not the organization defines the meaning of success. There is nothing wrong with career success; professional achievement often provides a platform for subsequent life choices. But the reality is that the responsibilities that accompany high achievement in most established organizations place an overwhelming emphasis on loyalty to the institution ahead of wider life goals. This is due to the fact that today's dominant organizational model is based upon industrial era thinking, and has not evolved in alignment with wider techno-social shifts. To achieve LIFEworking, we need to first understand what success really means to people, and then systematically address the fears that stand in the way of change. These fears typically relate to personal anxiety and the social consequences of choice.

Anyone who pursues the path of LIFEworking needs to acknowledge that certain "givens" in the world of work are no longer valid. For example, most of us expect that our income will increase year by year throughout our career, and that our reputation or status will steadily grow. Indeed, if this is not the case then most people feel insecurity and fear. But embarking on this adventure often requires an investment in time and money as one builds new skills, explores new contacts and networks, and creates their platform.

When Jamie stepped away from full-time work in academia and consultancy to pursue his LIFEworking goals of being a committed husband, father, and elite-level cyclist, his income level dropped by more than 70% in the first two years. After several months of reflection and exploration, he decided to focus his professional activities on becoming a keynote speaker, but to do so he recognized the need to first write a book, take acting lessons, study stand-up comedy, connect with speaker agencies, and create a website—and all of these things required effort. At the same time, he needed to ride his bicycle for at least 10 hours a week, participate in his kids' hobbies, and take some extended vacations.

The decline in Jamie's income meant that his family needed to adjust their living expenses—but that was easy when he realized he had been earning money to buy things he didn't really need, to impress people he didn't always like. And two years later (five years after commencing his LIFEworking journey) he was still not earning what he was when he had first embarked on the journey. But the combined income of Jamie and his wife was more than enough to sustain the life that the family desired. They let go of what they assumed they needed and made different conscious choices.

This journey usually starts with a mindset of wanting to make a life and knowing that making a living is just part of your life. Some people who are LIFEworking have two or three gigs or realize they want less material belongings. They are more attached to how they want to show up in the world than to be boxed into a career path.

Jamie let go of his academic career track, no longer conducted applied academic research, discontinued attending academic conferences, and dramatically reduced long-haul travel for business trips. But he had not stepped away from academia completely, as he still loved teaching and the intellectual stimulation of a business school environment. He worked on a free agent basis with a number of institutions, including his previous employer, with the flexibility to choose only those projects that resonated with his wider LIFEworking goals. He had also established himself as an international keynote speaker, and after the publication of his book, the *Financial Times* named him a "management guru." He races regularly in international masters cycling events, and in mid-2013 won a bronze medal in the cycling road race at the World Masters Games in Torino. A year later he achieved another life goal by founding a semi-professional cycling team, followed by a podium finish in a week-long stage race.

Redefining Success in the 21st Century

The existing organizational model, and the pressure it places on high achievers to continually succeed and exceed expectations, is fundamentally in conflict with LIFEworking. This means that the individual needs to either re-negotiate the terms of engagement, create or join organizations that have rejected industrial age thinking, or become a free agent. In all of these cases the individual is typically required to make trade-offs in terms of income, formal status, and scope of responsibility.

Most importantly, one needs the inspiration and fortitude to drive the shift towards LIFEworking, and not expect that the organization will ever create it for them. Do you have the courage to re-define success, and in doing so achieve the fulfillment you have always desired?

Transformational Stories from the Frontiers of 21st Century Leaders

Tim McDonald

Tim McDonald is passionate about connecting people with purpose. It's been said that Tim is ahead of his time, from his high school years of wanting to be a free spirit to building a community for community managers before most people had even heard of the term. This also led him to be a pioneer in establishing community management at *The Huffington Post*.

Tim experiences life on the edges, connecting deeply with people and building long-term, purposeful relationships. Working directly on the No Kid Hungry campaign, GivingTuesday fundraising increased from $56,000 to over $249,000 in 2015, which translated into 2.49 million meals for kids in the United States. Tim brings many lessons to his creations in the world that he openly speaks and writes about. By dealing with weighty issues, he has found meaning and is doing his life's work.

The Journey of Tim McDonald: Co-Creator. Purposeful Connector. Trusted Community Builder. Free Agent and Former Director of Community, Huffington Post.

What is your story?

My story is diverse—it's varied and evolving. When people ask me, "What is your story?" I simply say, "I change the world." If they want to know more, I generally start going into the work I do with No Kid Hungry to end childhood hunger in America. I want more of us to realize that we build our communities by connecting with people and purpose, and that every person has a story or can create a story that matters.

I first had to get clear on my own purpose, and that's a big part of my story. I started looking at the world differently by understanding that I had the opportunity to say, "I am changing the world" and mean it, just by my everyday actions.

A lot of this is about giving and receiving. It's like there's an invisible cycle: when we give, we also receive something back. Most of us have been conditioned to "give and take" as an exchange that needs to take place between people. Even in business, we have social corporate responsibility departments that are responsible for how the organization "gives back" to the community. But most of us have never been taught how to receive. It has always been about how to give and take something. Imagine if more of us not only gave, but also knew how to graciously receive.

I started to look at the subtle differences between receiving and taking. There is a vast difference in the approach and the response that you get from doing each one of those actions. And so the pure fact of receiving means that you don't have to match it quid pro quo. Giving cannot take place without receiving, and in our world most people don't know how to fully receive.

Some people would say that changing the world is like something that Gandhi or Rosa Parks did, or in the business world, people would look at Elon Musk or Steve Jobs. And they are right; they have changed the world. But so can you, and so can I.

Small ripples create waves

We may never know the impact that the ripples we are creating here today are going to have on so many other people, but we just need to trust it. We need to understand that we will impact some people and never hear about it, and the fact that we're taking these actions will create an impact in the world, even though we might not be able to tangibly put our finger on it, or put our eyes on it to see that it happened.

Reframing how you approach things, doing something different, and being vulnerable by doing something that you've never done before makes us feel uncomfortable. And most of us don't like these feelings. We have been conditioned to avoid these feelings, especially when it comes to business.

The first time I really did this was when I was depressed and had contemplated committing suicide. While I had shared the story privately with a few trusted friends, I had never done it in writing. For me, putting it down on paper makes it more tangible. And I finally did it—I finished writing my blog post about this story. I remember that moment so clearly. It had been a long time since I had hesitated to hit the publish button on a post. It brought back some old fears, because I was opening myself up to the world in a way that I'd never opened myself up before. But it allowed me to start seeing how important it was to share with others our vulnerability and how we have become who we are in the world. Once I published the story, I had so many people messaging me—not publicly, because they were not ready to share their own story yet with the world, but they were ready to share it with me privately and feel safe. I learned that by sharing my experience and my story, I could open up the conversation for others who may not have felt they had anyone to talk to.

Finding our humanity in life and work

We need to start being ourselves, instead of being what we think other people want us to be in life and work. The world of work is stuck in the industrial age. We've come a long way, but in a very similar way, workers have also become robotic in the 9-5 world of work, where we spend hours commuting to sit in a cubicle and send emails to each other. Corporations want to know how much everything is going to cost, how much we can produce, and what the ROI is going to be. If we can tweak that person to be 2% more efficient, we can increase our profits by 4%. That works when you're producing a commodity product, doing the same thing over and over. But in today's economy, there is an increasing opportunity for customization and personalization. There are a multitude of tools available to listen more and design solutions with the people who need them.

Living in an open and connected world means that each of us can reclaim our voice. What we are seeing is that people want to be in control of their own self. We want to customize our experiences and have our specific needs met, instead of just going to a shelf and pulling something off. We are each on a journey to discover ourselves, and our needs are massively changing. People don't just want commodities anymore, and they don't want to be commoditized.

Many of us find ourselves being part of a workforce that is killing us or numbing us. We're killing ourselves for somebody else's purpose just to keep a roof over our heads and to feed our families. We need to question the reasons we accept this way of life. I'm not a proponent of everyone simply quitting their jobs to follow their passion. We need to understand the implications of what following our passion means to our life path as part of our individual journey.

What I do believe is that you need to understand what your purpose is, and find the organization that shares it. If you're at a place that won't allow that to happen, then start creating something on your own, or look outside of your work hours for something that you can start creating, or that will allow you to create within their structure so that it benefits them and it benefits you.

When you're in a situation that only benefits one party, you are not being true to yourself. The organization might be getting a bigger ROI, but ultimately, if you burn out, your health is at risk. It's all a matter of understanding what we really need, which can allow everybody to walk away while getting something out of the situation. The days of employee-employer relationships where it's strictly based on a paycheck or performance type of model are starting to shift. We are slowly moving into a "what can we co-create together" mindset where both sides benefit from it, and we leave the world a better place as a result.

The fear that surrounds us comes from the stories we tell ourselves about why we can't do something. Facing my fears created opportunities that benefited me. I was working for a real estate developer, and he told me he didn't need me anymore so he let me go. I was out on my own. It pushed me beyond worrying about an income to also worrying about making sure I was doing something I felt good about.

When I was at The Huffington Post, I started experimenting. We launched Huffington Post Live without a budget or resources. When I let go of fear, I found there was so much that could be done. I found small-scale experiments that didn't cost anything but that reaped huge results. I would find someone who believed in my ideas and who let me experiment. All you need is another stakeholder also thinks you have a good idea. If you can pull it off with your existing resources, and if you prove that it works, all of a sudden you have success. If it fails, guess what? Nobody cares, because you didn't spend any money, and you didn't use up anybody else's resources. And if it works, people will come to you and say, "This is great. Why aren't we doing more?" Then you can say, "Well, if I had the resources and budget to do it, I would." And they become engaged, asking, "How much do you need?"

Most of us tell ourselves in our heads that if we do anything that the company doesn't dictate, then we'll get fired. And the truth of the matter is that's not always the case, because companies grow through creativity and innovation. Companies innovate when people take chances by experimenting. If you don't take a different action, you're never going to get a different reaction.

Building community by listening

The easiest way to approach community is to learn how to listen and engage with others. It's that simple. It's about listening to the people beyond the small group that may be sitting right next to you. We need to be listening to people who are in different departments internally. We need to be listening to people in different offices. We need to be listening to our customers, and not just our top consumers who are on all the advisory boards, but also the ones who might buy our product once and never buy it again. We need to be talking to the ones who are maybe not our highest volume customers, but the ones who are the most passionate about the brand. When you start looking at all these people and listening to what they're saying, that's how you start to build community. And why is that important? Because we're not living in a world where you can just run a focus group and then develop a product based on the research, because by the time you do that, it's obsolete.

We live in a world where we can let the community tell us what they want instead of us guessing what we think they want. We run into problems when we're too busy thinking we have all the answers, instead of just admitting that we don't and that we need to be listening to what people are responding to us. Then we can build on top of that together, instead of just pushing out a product. It's now a two-way communication where both sides are creating it together.

It doesn't mean you need to have the other party on your employee payroll. It doesn't mean that you need to make them an official partner. It can be about crowdsourcing your ideas from your community and joining your purpose with others. It's something that every human being yearns for—just to belong to something greater than themselves. That is the essence of community. When you can provide that sense of belonging to somebody, you're filling a need for them, and you're getting something in return because they will invest in what you're doing. And together, you will create something that's greater than either of you could have created on your own.

LIFEworking is a matter of living a life with work being part of it, not with work consuming it. We don't need to live in a world where we try and balance work and life. We don't need to place a dividing line between them. We don't even need to try and blend them. What we need to understand is that work is a subset of our entire life. There's so much else that fits into it, and work can overlap with all of that.

If you can start to look at it from the holistic standpoint—if you can look at life as a whole, with work just being a component of that—that to me is what LIFEworking is. There's a reason why work comes first in the term "work-life balance." But it's not just a matter of flipping the words; it's a matter of understanding that one is a subset of the other.

Grace Clapham

Grace Clapham is an award winning entrepreneur, coming in first in the 'Inspirational Leadership' Awards at the Talent Unleashed Awards judged by Sir Richard Branson and Steve Wozniak.

Grace has built strong communities across Southeast Asia, such as Secret {W} Business, CreativeMornings Singapore, and SheSays Singapore. In 2009, she founded her first company, Agent Grace, a boutique agency which helps companies navigate the Asia Pacific region. In 2013 she co-founded The Change School, an institute that helps individuals align their values and life choices.

Grace is passionate about connecting people to themselves and the world around them in order to catalyze change.

The Journey of Grace Clapham: Global Citizen. Changepreneur. Interculturist. Cofounder, The Change School.

What is your story?

I am half Indonesian and half Australian. I grew up mainly in Asia, so I am what I call a third culture kid—someone raised in a culture outside of their parents' culture for a significant part of their childhood.

My professional background was initially in marketing and brand management within the fashion sector. I had something like a quarter life crisis after my father passed away, and I realized what I was doing wasn't what I wanted to do in the world. At that time, I was already an entrepreneur running my own business focused on Australian businesses coming into Southeast Asia. But there was something missing. I was unfulfilled in the work I was doing.

I reached a pivotal moment and decided to take some time out. I was looking for a community or a space that would allow me to grow, and I didn't really want to pursue an MBA or go to a yoga retreat. Exploring my options led to where I am now and led me to start The Change School, which is that space that I was missing.

The Change School is a lifestyle brand and life school providing holistic learning experiences for personal and professional advancement. We design and deliver programs to develop every person's intellectual, emotional, physiological, and creative potential, encouraging individuals to self-direct their learning and development. We work with individuals and organizations to build positive transformation, connection, meaning, and transdisciplinary inquiry for life and work in the 21st century and beyond.

I'm somewhat of a multi-hyphenate and a changepreneur, working within the entrepreneurial, social innovation, and creative space. I co-founded The Change School to help individuals at key pivotal moments of their lives have clarity in order to move forward and take positive action. We help individuals and organizations align values and life/business choices in three different ways: 1. Immersive Learning

Retreats; 2. Change GYM (a Gym for Your Mind); and 3. Bespoke / Tailored Programs. We are not bound by any particular space, so we can pop up in different locations around the word. My other hats have included co-founding Secret {W} Business, a community and network of women entrepreneurs and changemakers, now located across six cities in Southeast Asia. I also co-organize SheSays Singapore and Creative Mornings Singapore. Much of my work is about providing spaces, such as programs or communities, to help individuals build greater self awareness, connection to others, and self-direct their learning, all with the vision of becoming better global citizens through better cultural intelligence and understanding.

I look at business as what Ayelet calls LIFEworking. I don't see life as separate from my purpose. Once individuals are better able to understand themselves, they are better able to create a life by design. The Change School inspires participants to do more, to be more, and to experience transformation through taking action in making the change. We mix experiences and programs to create an all-encompassing approach to aligning lives and work. People who are doing what they love to do and making a difference inspire me.

Being awarded the Inspirational Leadership Awards by Talent Unleashed—judged by Sir Richard Branson and Steve Wozniak—was a big moment for me, and it was an honor for me to be recognized by such big game changers. This is just the beginning of the journey, as it has given me a platform to do even more in the world and touch more people and organizations.

Expect change to happen

We expect change to simply be a part of life. Business now is like tectonic plates moving and shifting. There is a lot of transition taking place and we are seeing more and more people starting to create their own businesses. We are transitioning into a purpose-driven economy and experiencing a values revolution, where people are more fulfilled. There is also a complimentary movement emerging toward smaller clusters of businesses working together in creation. You can think about it as a co-op style versus a larger business model. From an Asian perspective, we are still trying to understand how to grow our economies to a more knowledge-based economy in a way that works for us vs what has worked in the Western world, as so much is changing and coming to fruition. And there are so many complexities in the Asian context, Asia being a large part of this world made of so many different countries and cultures. The shift will force businesses to set up a different way from that of the Western world. Many of the new businesses entering into Asia have very limited knowledge when they enter new markets and limited cultural intelligence, which can impact or hinder their work or ability to scale and grow.

Asia also has many more family businesses than the West. This next generation of business leaders are emerging, and they are very different than their founders and their relatives. They are questioning what's next for their family's business, and with Asia being such a large region, they are thinking more about what impact they can have in their part of world. They are also thinking about what role they will play in the future of business, and are moving away from simply being told by their parents or other relatives what is expected of them. There is still a long way to go, as there is still a lot of pressure from the family about how the business should be run.

A lot depends on where you are geographically. We are seeing increased innovation coming from the Indian and Indonesian markets and a bit more conservatism from markets in Singapore. While the government in Singapore is encouraging more innovation and entrepreneurial risk taking, it is still hard for many Singaporeans to get outside the comfort zone of their structured career path and be ok with "failure" or risk taking. Once they are able to be ok with going against what is considered the norm, then will they be able to really drive change more purposefully and build a more knowledge-based and creative-based economy. There is a move to create more impact in Indonesia, but there is also increasing concern about growing their economy and consistent changes in the laws making it challenging for new business owners, investors, and startups that are foreign. It's an interesting time across the region. I see a lot of boom in the Philippines, Myanmar, and Vietnam in the tech space. Talent development is going to be a huge area within this part of the world—in particular, in the emotional intelligence realm and what is seen as soft skills.

Western management systems are still very much in place in our region, but the future here needs to be about Asian values and Asian management systems. We need to develop them locally and make sure they work for us. We need to uplift ourselves to a level where our economies are successful in our own way and we are living our local culture, not living out something based on what has worked in the West. We need more local innovation and creative thinking that taps into our own communities and our own culture.

We run a Future Ready track at The Change School, which equips individuals and organizations with skills for the 21st century and beyond. We see the need for a lot more cultural and emotional intelligence in business today. Unfortunately, a lot of the change work is intangible, and organizations are mostly driven by Key Performance Indicators (KPIs) and Return on Investment (ROI). We really need to find ways to move away from these practices.

In Singapore, we still have a cookie cutter mentality where we opt to take an idea or practice from the West and run with it. Ultimately, we will face hurdles, as sticking to the best practices model won't work and we need to make our own models through experimenting (trial and error). We are still in a fear-based mindset that drives people to compete against each other or simply copy what has worked abroad, when the opportunity is here for something more meaningful. It's going to take a long time for people to see the possibilities, because their way of thinking has been shaped for generations.

Bringing the team together

I believe in cross-pollination and bringing people together based on purpose. At The Change School we don't focus on age specific programs, but rather on life stages. We do provide space for people to connect in conversation and through experiential or "peer 2 peer" learning. We also offer sessions for mothers who want to come back into the workforce to meet their specific needs. Our approach is one of integration where we see each person as an individual with an artist's palate. We each have unique colors and dimensions, and when we try to put people under one umbrella or sort them into neat boxes, it doesn't work. We have different parts of us that have been fragmented and that want to be integrated into a whole. What's most important to us is to not to lose shared purpose. We focus on how we can connect the dots, even in our smaller groups.

Conscious leaders need apply

A 21st century leader needs to be a cultural chameleon. Southeast Asia is the third largest global territory, and it is made up of multiple countries that are very different from each other. To do business in this part of the world, you need be able to move and adapt to the different needs of the areas and adapt culturally. You also need to be locally relevant and globally connected to keep a finger on the pulse. To do this, leaders need to have emotional and cultural intelligence and operate in a more conscious way. Competencies need to be developed for future leaders, and this is missing in schools. Future leaders need to have more empathy. They are going to need to have a better understanding of individuals, and also have a better understanding of themselves and the world around them.

We start with the individual. We take an inside-out approach to helping individuals establish their place, purpose, and potential in the world to think about how we can make a difference globally, thinking about the whole planet and not just where we live. Many people we interact with want to make a difference, do good work, and make stuff work better—but in order to change the world, we must first change ourselves and have greater self-awareness.

We had an organization approach us to help them build a diversity program, but what we discovered was that they didn't recognize that diversity was connected to the values of their organization and their company culture. If diversity is not engraved into the culture of how you operate, it is only a program. If no one lives or breathes it, and instead just talks about it, the impact it will have will be limited. We helped this organization connect these dots and see how diversity could be part of the fabric of their organization in their day-to-day business.

On the individual level, Karen, a 53-year-old woman, came to our residency program in Bali after leaving her big corporate job. Change Ventur.es is our signature 21-day program for career breakers, career shifters, or sabbatical takers—individuals who are at a crossroads and looking for clarity in their next direction. She was burned out and didn't know which direction to go in. She had lost some of her confidence because of her age, and also felt she was losing her identity. She was clear that she didn't want to go back into a corporate environment.

Our 21-day program allows you to work through key questions about yourself and where you want to move forward, in order to help you take action to make positive change in your life and work. It is broken down into three weeks. In week one, we focus on the deconstructing process—a deep dive into understanding who you are, what drives you, and why. In week two, we focus on the breakthrough and reconstructing—understanding your place and purpose in the world and uncovering the many opportunities to solve problems, create solutions, and make sense of the world and the tools available for you. In our final week, we focus on taking action and moving forward—designing a personalized action plan for reaching your milestones and hitting the ground running.

Karen was able to tap into her self-awareness and also gain new skills, like how to use social media, do business canvassing, and learn new technologies in a safe environment. Because we also had people in all age groups, there were strong peer-to-peer opportunities for people to learn from each other. The youngest person in that group was 21 and was incredibly helpful to Karen in overcoming her fear of technology. In the end, she was comfortable enough to go into the world and take action for herself. It took her eight months until she got herself on solid ground, and she has now written a book that is about to be released. Karen is now an integrative health coach in Australia.

There was also a 36-year-old man who came through our signatory program. He was extremely self-aware, but lacking in business acumen. It was quite daunting for him to integrate so much new thinking initially. Now, he is setting up amazing festivals and events in Australia.

He is starting to write more and is being interviewed through various channels about the impact that he is creating in this open-source event space. It's amazing to experience him coming into his element, taking everything he learned and putting it into practice in his own way.

We do video diaries for all of our participants so they can monitor themselves, because sometimes the changes may appear slight as they are occurring, but in the end when you look at everything they are quite significant. We are in such a paradigm shift that we just can't see the small changes that are happening. We each need expansion time for self-reflection. That is what I see as the opportunity for us to connect with ourselves and each other, in ways where we can listen and really remove ourselves from our usual environment, where thought and action can be clouded by other people's pressure or judgement.

Imagine what is possible if we can get a group of people from the same organization taking the time to deconstruct, reconstruct, and take action around shared purpose. We often perceive that we don't have the time to do this work, when really this work needs to be done or we will burn out our people. Otherwise, why did we invest so much in recruiting the best people in the first place?

Driving meaningful purpose

At The Change School, we are slowly measuring the impact of the changes that take place for the individual or the organization. Success to me is about seeing a change in an individual, even in the smallest possible way. We've had people share that, for them, The Change School is a school you never graduate from, and some people have said that our bite size classes held in the Change GYM is like an addiction—keeping them coming back for more. That yearning for learning is important, as is seeing individuals realize their potential and keep moving forward. It goes beyond the traditional monetary indicators.

I believe in building a business that is doing good in the world. Corporate Social Responsibility (CSR) should not be a separate function; it should be part and parcel of your business. We should all be creating businesses that create some good in the world. That is simply being part of the purpose-driven economy. We have immersive programs in our Bali retreats that we open to local fellows. Whenever we pop up in a different location, we always open fellowships for locals of that country. We are looking at ways we can develop our fellowship programs more, and I think it's important to be able to provide access to everyone on this path.

On our website, we have a section called Explore Life Schools where you can discover programs from life schools around the globe, or recommend one. We are one of the first ones in Asia, and we want to have our roots here. People across the entire Asia Pacific region don't need to travel to other cultures, but can gain what they need locally. It's important to build this part of the world and equip people with the skills they need.

To be visionaries of what is possible can be a lonely road at times, and that's when I need to breathe and continue to believe in what we are co-creating. I need to connect with other people who can also see a new path forward.

Too often we are stuck in our boxes, but if we are able to expand our horizons and be open to things, we can surprise ourselves with where we find inspiration. You never know where ideas will come from. They can be found in the most unusual places if we let ourselves flow. Knowing your "why" allows you to have a better direction, and your "why" can change, but I think questioning it regularly allows you to keep moving in the direction of your path. Nothing is constant and nothing should be stagnant; we just need to know what we stand for, know our values, and not stop because someone tries to knock us down.

Moving forward

I've always been a very stubborn person. My father was also very stubborn and believed in social responsibility. He set up mobile libraries and multiple different businesses in his lifetime. He was a great businessman and also incorporated caring about the world into his work. If he were alive today, he would want to make sure we had a good financial plan and would be happy to see what we are co-creating in the world. He would want me to keep moving forward and build on the foundation we created. He is always in my heart as I do my work in the world.

I always knew I wanted to do work in my community in some shape or form, but I started off in the traditional route because of societal pressure. I grew up with the conditioning that I needed to be this big powerhouse corporate person making a lot of money. I was lucky to have parents who always asked how I could become passionate in what I do, and think about other people and the community. It's just been engraved in me to follow my "why." I'm lucky that I found my LIFEwork, and hopefully it continues and sustains itself in more ways than one. I am now able to help others on this path, and have empathy for their journeys.

A lot of times people don't step back to see where they are going, and I think setting aside that time for yourself is important. If people can take the time to reflect and align their "why," it just helps everyone in general. At different stages of your life you go through pivotal moments, and when this happens you need a space that allows you to work on different parts of yourself while being surrounded by a value-led community, all while building better global citizens. The Change School intersects education, travel, wellness, and personal development. We create experiences to help people align life and work. The world would be a better place if people were more connected to themselves and to each other, building upon a shared goal of self-realization and the desire to make a positive impact on the global community.

Samuel Poh

I was invited recently by my friend Giulia Rancati to join a collective of people coming together to work with companies to design go-to-market strategies and co-execute sales enablement programs. I found myself in a meeting in Napa Valley with an amazing group of people from Portugal, India, the UK, Australia, and Singapore who make up the VMI Collective. It was at this meeting that I met Samuel Poh, and knew intuitively that he had a deeper story to share with the world.

Samuel is a senior executive with more than 22 years in the information technology industry. A transformational leader with a diverse background, he established new businesses and implemented aggressive growth for both large and small companies. He was appointed General Manager and Director of Operations, Global MidMarket Acceleration Greater China Region at Cisco, and held previous senior sales operations roles at Cisco and Dimension Data.

The Journey of Samuel Poh: Connector. Community Builder. Entrepreneur and Startup Coach. Former General Manager/Director Operations, Cisco Systems (China) / Managing Partner, VMI Collective.

What is your story?

Imagine an 18 year old kid who was very skinny and could not even do one chin-up or run two miles. I was brought up in a very pampered family. My grandmother had 13 children; it was a big Chinese family with many grandchildren. Academia was the most important thing for us, and we were expected to grow up and become a doctor or a lawyer. None of us got a chance to play football or soccer under the hot sun, because we had to be protected. When I turned 18, I received a letter saying that I was supposed to join the military. To help begin my training, my mom gave me a bag stuffed with canned food and told me to go for a run on a hot and humid afternoon in Singapore while carrying this bag. I came back panting.

I got recruited to basic military training and they shipped us out to be part of a company of over 200 recruits on a small island north-east of Singapore. I had to do my first chin-up, and I was struggling. I could hardly do 10 push-ups. Then we had to do a 2.4 kilometer run in 15 minutes. I came in at 16 minutes. I realized I had two options: I could barely graduate from the training and become a cook or a clerk for my two and a halfyear military career, or I could do something bigger and better, which meant I had to train like I had never done before in my life.

While the rest of the recruits were sleeping, I got up early every morning and started doing push-ups and chin-ups. Three months before the training was complete, I was able to do 16 chin-ups, and run the 2.4 km run in 9 minutes and 32 seconds. When I graduated from the training, I came in second out of 240 people. I was selected to go to the Officer Cadet School in Singapore, and I realized that I was going to compete with the best of the best when I saw one guy doing 33 chin-ups. I thought I was not going to survive. Not many recruits end up graduating, and those who do get commissioned often become officers of the Singapore Armed Forces. It was one of the most prestigious roles that an 18 year old boy could dream about.

It was a very rigorous training program, and I graduated to the senior term. My best running time for the 2.4 kilometer run became 7 minutes and 40 seconds. With chin-ups, I went from 16 to 22. One thing I learned from the officer cadet school was to always do the right thing, because our training emphasized our duty, honor, and country in serving the nation.

I then applied for an overseas training scholarship and was selected to go to the Tokyo Military College. When my mom heard the news, she started crying and told me that it was not for someone who comes from a pampered family like ours; she still saw me as the weak boy who had left home just 12 months before. I decided not to pursue this track, and instead I focused on exceling in the military by becoming one of the best special forces intelligence officers.

The military gave me a platform to set high standards for myself, and to push myself to achieve them, which transformed my mindset and thinking of what I call Mind-Over-Body (MOB). It prepared me to be a situational leader. Since I was young, I had the tendency to be able to take care of problems. My superiors always said, "Send Sam when there is a mission that cannot be solved." They knew that I would be out there driving the troops.

My corporate story takes me from India to China

My story is not just about a job or being in a corporate environment; it is about my life and what I have learned through my experiences. I found that once you hit the age of 40 you start thinking about what else you can do in the world. And, for me, much of it came down to having my own personal transformation when I was sent to work in China.

This story starts when I was hired by Cisco's Global Sales Operations to design and reconstruct the Inside Sales structure to better support its partner model evolvement. I was a newbie to Sales Operations at that time, and I was on a steep learning curve on how they did things at Cisco.

I left my family behind in Singapore to take my first assignment in India, which was to last for 18 months. It was a very different culture than what I was used to after living in Singapore most of my life, and I found many aspects of life there to be quite challenging. I didn't really want to stay, but what kept me going was the discipline I received from my military training, where I learned to be very systematic in driving operations and not putting up with anything that tried to push me off course. I learned that the people I worked with could talk endlessly, negotiating and discussing, but without always accomplishing what was needed. I came in with a very stringent approach using the right sales methodologies and processes, knowing I had a big job to do. As the new kid on the block, no one knew me, and I had the runway to make the changes that needed to happen.

I was the first senior manager within my group to fire a manager and a vendor. This had never been done before in this part of the world. No one had ever fired a vendor before. I realized there was a lot of work to do, and it was about making sure we had the right people and relationships in place to meet our business goals. I ended up working about 20 hours a day. On top of that, to be two hours behind Singapore and 11 hours behind the corporate office in the US was quite challenging.

One of the managers under my responsibility was running a $15 million business, and his previous managers ranked him 0 out of 10 on his reviews. No one really could tell me why his ranking was so low, or why he was kept on despite such a low ranking. I noticed that when I was in the office, he was very attentive and worked hard, but when I wasn't there, he was much less engaged. One day I decided that we had to let him go. I called him into my office and we sat down to talk about his performance, but the conversation went to an unexpected place. He opened up and shared with me that he could not survive without this job because he had a very sick daughter who had a degenerative gene disease. He broke down in front of me and started crying. But I didn't believe him. I thought he was trying to sell me a story to tug at my heartstrings, because I had experienced this before in this part of the world.

In India, coming to the office early in the morning is basically viewed as very rude. Due to the traffic, people come in late because it takes so long to get to where you are going, and I learned that the local people get upset when people come in early. So I was surprised that the next morning when I got to the office early (I was still being rude), this manager came in early carrying a girl who was about seven years old. He placed her on the floor and she collapsed. She could not sit up. She was very ill. I now knew that his story was real.

I found myself in a catch-22. I had fired a lot of people in my career, but this was different. My local boss left, and the senior management in San Francisco was telling me to do the right thing for the company and do the right thing for the individual. I took 24 hours to think it through. Being an Asian Chinese guy, I had been trained to be very ruthless, and my military training taught me to make tough decisions.

The reason I am sharing this story is because it is reflective of the need to make a corporate decision versus taking into account the humane side of life. It was a point where I realized that my role was to get the job done for the good of the company, and individuals were not a priority.

I didn't sleep for 24 hours as I thought through the entire situation. I called him into my office the next day and told him that, from a business perspective, we needed to let him go. I gave him the letter, and he broke down. While he was sitting there, I picked up the phone and called a friend of mine in another tech company. I asked him if he had a job opening in Bangalore. My friend told me he had an Account Manager role, and I got this guy a new job at another company.

Emotions aside, as a senior executive I had to make a decision that looked at the results the company measured us on. This incident taught me some very important lessons. The first one was that I need to treat everyone with equal respect. You are the one in front of the individual and you have to make a call that will impact them, their family, and their lifestyle. No one is there with you from corporate headquarters when you make the decision and give the bad news. You are the one that needs to perform at your job and also live with the consequences of your decisions.

The second lesson concerned having to balance being a senior executive who needs to make smart business decisions and seeing the impact these decisions can have on a human life. And also realizing that the employee has a family that is dependent on them, so you are having a wider societal impact when you are making these type of decisions. It gets you to think about what role, if any, compassion plays in the world of work. The third lesson was that in a corporate environment you are expected to do a job, which is why I knew firing people was simply part of what I was expected to do.

An assignment in China

The next part of my story took place when I was asked to go to China. I was told there were major challenges in that operation, and corporate headquarters wanted someone to go there to fix it.

I was very skeptical about going to China. You'd think that being Chinese, going to China would be very easy, but that is not true. Not a lot of people who go to work in China can survive what happens there, at least not when they work at senior executive positions and are expected to lead. I knew other people who were sent in from the corporate world who got blocked by the local teams, and they could not get the work done due to all the undercurrents that exist.

My management told me I was the best person to do this job, and they gave me this assignment for two years. I arrived at my new assignment and quickly realized that I had limited local support. While I was there to run a $130 million business from the ground up, I needed to learn the local rules of the game first. And the key rule of this game was: you are either with me or against me. I was told not to rock the boat by the local management. For them, everything was already working perfectly. The engine was humming and everyone was benefiting. I was caught between understanding that being with them meant following the local culture and not always following what my management wanted back in headquarters. I also realized that my corporate management would not understand the local culture, or what I had to do in order to fit in. I decided to be with them, while also ensuring that my team was compliant with the corporate rules. I met my first challenge by learning that I needed to be with them; there was no point to be seen as being against them.

In general, people in China (at least those who I worked with) want to know your personal business. They want to know whether you are single or married. They want to know whether you have a mistress or not. In China, it's good for your business reputation for the male to be seen with a pretty, young woman or what we call a Sweet Young Thing (SYT). You are expected to have a very flamboyant lifestyle, whether you play golf or go to dinner parties. None of this fit with who I was, so I had to change to fit into how business is done in China. I had to create the impression that I fit in without actually doing anything like finding a mistress.

I changed my persona to be a global tech guy who had a very interesting lifestyle that included running marathons, participating in Ironman, and being someone who loves watches and fast cars. Because of my position in the company, the media came to interview and profile me in some magazines, and this is the story I told them. When people started getting to know me, they realized I was quite different from what was being said about me in the press and the community.

I learned that in life we need to wear many masks and too often, we need to bury how we are feeling deep inside of us in our pursuit of success. There is a price to the success we have been conditioned to attain. I was trained to be the best and excel at whatever I did. I took the lessons that I received as a child and excelled at school and then when I joined the military, I followed that same belief by training my body so I could be one of the best. When I arrived in China, I studied the landscape and did my best to fit in without losing myself. I knew that I had to become a trusted insider to succeed, but what I did not take into account was the personal toll it would take on me. I was literally living two separate lives, where in one I had a wonderful family who did not live with me and who I tried to see as much as possible, and the other was the successful corporate guy who was making deals in China.

After 18 months into my time in China, I had a mental breakdown. Every night when I went to sleep, I didn't know if I was going to wake up the next morning, as I felt the level of stress I was under was overwhelming. I had no one to talk to about what I was experiencing by playing this game of illusion. Everyone around me assumed I was living the dream of being a successful company man. I was not sure if the stress would overtake me in my sleep, which simply contributed even more to my stress level. I had a cook who came to cook for me three days a week, and a cleaner who came six times a week. The only day I was left alone was Sunday. If I would have died in my bed in my house, it would only be less than 24 hours before someone would find me.

I did a lot of work on myself where I focused on MOB. I tried to pump myself up and get my energy up by running and doing various physical activities. But I was living in two different worlds. My management in San Francisco was focused on introducing new systems and processes that the local teams did not accept. The locals were just giving lip service to corporate. I also had a responsibility to take care of my team by auditing them and making sure they do not come under any scrutiny. For a while, some of them still saw me as an outsider, and I could feel their fear.

Even though I was Chinese, I felt alone in a foreign land. My family could not understand what I was facing. My boss could not understand what was happening. And my colleagues would definitely not be able to empathize with what I was feeling.

I decided to take a short break and go to Singapore to see a mental health professional, hoping they could help me through my breakdown. They told me to be very careful, as I could end up in a bipolar state because I was being asked to so radically split who I was just to survive in my job. After this meeting, I went to meet with my manager in Singapore. My boss shared with me that he was hearing that I was leading a colorful lifestyle with a mistress, drinking and partying like crazy. I was quite shocked. I felt that I had sacrificed so much to fix something that people more senior in the organization than me couldn't ever fix, and yet this was not an accurate portrayal of my lifestyle and who I was. I did help to create that false impression of myself, but I was forced to do that in order to be accepted as "one of the team" by the local team in China.

After some reflection, I realized that a job is a job, and my job was to get done what I was being asked to do. It seems like no one really pays attention to your internal trouble until you break, so I decided to keep going until I finally broke. I went back to Shanghai and decided it might be good for me to do extreme sports. I thought it would keep me alive.

I also realized that I needed more structure in my personal life. I started a social group in China focused on giving back to the community. Every quarter we brought together remote teams and adopted an organization like the Sunshine Association, a home for handicapped kids. We not only gave donations, but over 20 of us also went in to work with the kids. I wanted people to start caring about society and the bigger picture. It was to bring the team together around a bigger purpose and, more importantly at that time, it was for me. I needed this in my life, to see what possibilities existed for me to do something worthwhile outside of the confines of my work. This was also the start of my journey of giving back.

I started seeing a shift in some of the people around me. For example, several colleagues loved to eat, but they were not taking care of their health. But as we started to do this work in the community, I started seeing others around me beginning to exercise, even participating in marathons, and caring more about their health in general. It made me feel that my presence was having a positive impact.

My time in China was tough on me. In general, China is very enclosed in many ways, rejecting corporate initiatives and influence, especially from outsiders and foreigners. The Chinese team might tell the head office that they agree, but then they will do what they believe needs to be done locally without regard for outside orders. That is why I was surprised to learn that the local team wanted me to stay after my two years were done. I learned that I was now trusted. They saw that I was with them, and I had learned that what happens in China stays in China. I had learned how to navigate the undercurrents of doing business there. From being in survival mode, I had gone on to become a master of my own destiny in China.

On top of the general cultural challenges, food was also a big concern. Every day I was not sure what I would eat, because the food was often contaminated. The cooking oil was recycled—I don't know how many times. I also found unknown chemicals in my food, so I started to bring my own oil and gave it to the chef at work to cook with. I came down with numerous food poisonings. And yet, I learned how to navigate and survive.

I coached people who came to China and advised them that just because they spoke Mandarin or were corporate executives did not mean that they would make it. In fact, many of these people do not survive in China, and either end up having to return to their own country or are unable to do the job they came for. To do business in China, unfortunately, it's not so much about relationships today. Hopefully that can change. You need to understand the potholes along the path and how to approach people. You need to let people see what you are about so you can become one of them and be trusted.

After spending four years in China, seeing my family when I could, I had a lot of knowledge about how the market worked and what you could realistically get done and how. I learned that China needs another generation of people who can really connect with people internationally. Right now, business is done with a Chinese mindset and approach. But that will not be sufficient for China to really become one the major powers in the world. The opportunity is for a new generation of Chinese to connect more globally with purpose, to break through the unnecessary constraints that keep them isolated, and learn to develop more authentic relationships. If they can do this, then will be far more successful on the global stage.

It's pretty sad how materialistic China currently is. It is not uncommon for people to sell a kidney to get an iPhone 6—or to steal just to have one. Everyone has to have the latest technology, car, jewelry, and clothes. It is a rite of passage. In one of the media interviews I did, a local journalist asked me why I wanted to come to China when everyone in China wants to go to the US and elsewhere. From an early age, my dad told me that I was Chinese and you must speak Mandarin. I came to China to experience it. But what I saw was a rat race lifestyle—far beyond the rat race of the western world—where people care whether or not you are wearing an Omega watch, or, for women, whether you have a $40,000 Hermes handbag. I know some of these people are middle working class, and I don't know how they can even afford these luxury items. The restaurants and nightclubs are always packed, and purchases made there are often on the expense reports of large companies. This is where the arm twisting happens. It is a lifestyle of branded materialism and excess.

The common view about one's lifestyle ranges from how much money they earn to how many trips they will take in a year, to how much time they spend posting online to all their friends all their photos showing them driving a Ferrari or being in Iceland or Las Vegas. I don't think that this way of life is sustainable. To me, the more you post out there with all these photos and selfies, the emptier you probably feel inside.

This is all behind me now, and I feel compassion for the people who believe this way of life will bring them fulfillment. My life is much more simple. I don't need much. But many people in China continue to wear their money through the products they consume, because it is considered necessary to be seen as being financially successful. For me, life is a simple. Even my wardrobe is simple; what you will see me wearing most of the time is a plain white t-shirt, blue denim jeans, and white sneakers.

It has been quite a journey, and I am very thankful for having a good ride in China. While I pointed out some frustrating aspects of China, I also love it. There are problems everywhere, in every country, and I hope that China can address their pervasive problem of materialism. If they can focus on relationships over money, they could be so much more successful in many ways.

During my journey in China, I was also given many names from various people, including:

- Corporate calling me a **bridge,** as I mediated between corporate and the local Greater China team;
- Greater China leaders calling me an **outsider** because I was from corporate;
- Locals calling me a **foreigner**, even though I am Chinese and speak Mandarin;
- My boss calling me a **mechanic**, because I fixed so many issues and made sure that everything ran well;
- Some calling me **ruthless** because I fired 477 people, three different vendors, and 14 managers;
- Some calling me **sentimental** because I built the Giving Back Initiatives in Greater China;
- And my mates calling me a **bulldozer**, because I never gave up and trained my mind and body.

Breathing again

When I got back to Singapore, I knew I had to decide what I wanted to do next. I went on a 10-day silent meditation in a nearby country, and I had to surrender my mobile phone and cut myself off from everyone and everything when I got there. They woke us up every morning at 4:30am, and we started our breathing meditation at 5:00am. I realized that it was so powerful to communicate with myself in this way. But on the fourth day, I started to doubt whether I could stay disconnected from people for the whole 10 days. It made me think about the role of relationships in my life moving forward. I stuck it out, and found that this experience brought me a degree of inner peace with myself for the first time in years. It taught me to slow things down.

After that, I decided to train to climb Mount Everest Basecamp. When I saw the determination of the climbers, I started to think about their aspiration, and the power of mind over the body. That was a moment when I recognized how incredible the mind is.

We were doing a climb of 17,000 feet, and we each carried an oxygen canister with us because there is such little oxygen at the higher levels. We also had Diamox, a drug that you can take to equalize the pressure, but it can give you the side effect of having to pee a lot while you are climbing in the snow. My team made a bet that the first person to open an oxygen canister would have to pay US$1,000 to the others, and so it was quite the challenge. We were pushing ourselves, and we reached the 17,000 foot mark on January 1, 2015. We wanted to catch the first light, and it was beautiful. When I sat down, I realized how wonderful and peaceful life could be. It was time for me to stop living the rat race and caring about how much money I was going to make. I realized that I needed to be asking myself how I want to live the next 40 years of my life fruitfully, to be able to enjoy every single day with God's grace and my faith.

I decided that I would resign from my job. I had found my calling. I wanted to spend more time with my family and friends. I also wanted to spend more time with myself, and do God's work by being of service.

My son was having some challenges with school and growing up. He is turning 14, and I wanted to be there for him when he needed me, and to enjoy our time together. This is one of the reasons I joined the VMI Collective. I get to work with great people like my partners Pasquale Gallifuoco in Portugal, Gurmukh Singh in India, and Giulia Rancati in the UK. I've been helping entrepreneurs, and I have been connecting people around their purpose. I want people to benefit from my experience and contacts. I also want to control my own time and be selective in what I do. I have never worked this way before, and I like being my own boss and co-creating with people I respect in a collective where we each have a say in how the business is run.

Every single day I am reconnecting with people I have missed over the years. I am seeing former classmates and focusing on building my relationships. It is time to rekindle my friendships without wanting anything from anyone. I disappeared from the lives of so many people when I left Singapore, and I want to be present for them now in my life.

The turning point has been choosing my life over my job, and understanding that I get to live my life. I want to enjoy the ride. I tend to be more sensitive and observant now. Over the last few months, I have become a lot nicer to be around and less rigid, and I love spending time coaching and listening to people.

Having a job is no longer a priority for me. I want my days to be filled with my connections with others. I want to make an impact and also have more joy and laughter. I now see the simplicity and beauty in life. My goal is to be present and experience life to the fullest, where work is just one element that satisfies me. I think this new mindset is part of the future.

Hillary Brook Levy

I was so excited when Hillary Brook Levy agreed to share her story, as I knew we would all benefit from her journey. Hillary had a long career as a speech pathologist, which culminated at Stanford Hospital in Palo Alto, California, where she specialized in helping head trauma and stroke patients regain their communication abilities. Then, for the past 15 years, her work took a different direction as she practiced and studied the path of meditation and healing methods under Buddhist master Segyu Rinpoche. In 2003, together with Segyu Rinpoche, her husband Lawrence Levy, Pam Moriarty, and Christina Juskiewicz, Hillary co-founded Juniper Foundation, an organization dedicated to bringing Buddhist methods for developing the mind into contemporary culture. As you will see, from her efforts to enhance the lives of stroke and head trauma victims to co-founding a meditation tradition, Hillary is quite the entrepreneur and visionary.

The Journey of Hillary Brook Levy: Healer. Visionary. Trusted Partner. Cofounder, Juniper Foundation.

What is your story?

I have quite a traditional background. I am married and have three children. My husband Lawrence is a former Silicon Valley lawyer and executive hired by Steve Jobs in 1994 as CFO and member of the Office of the President of Pixar Animation Studios. We live in Silicon Valley, where I worked as a speech pathologist for many years at Stanford Hospital in their rehabilitation department. My main interest there was stroke patients—individuals who had lost their ability to speak, understand speech, read, or write, and usually a combination of all of these.

The highlight of my time at Stanford was working with people, both the clients I would see and my peers in the department. This was the late 1980s and early 1990s, and I enjoyed the environment and culture at Stanford at this time. Everyone was very supportive of each other. We focused on helping the patients first and foremost. I enjoyed taking someone from a moment of crisis, usually triggered by a stroke or head trauma, through re-learning their language and speech, to helping them deal with that crisis. My goal was to optimize their speech and language ability and, where full recovery was not possible, to help them accept and adjust to their new level of language capability.

When my children were young I continued to work, but eventually I went part-time. For me, work was a way to balance the time at home with my other passions. I wanted to do something that was creative and meaningful in a different way, and I found that part of my life at work. Having both together was very good.

Then the hospital setting started changing. We were under new management and people began to leave. There were also major changes happening in healthcare. For example, some patients were only allocated six to eight visits after having a stroke. That made little sense as far as rehabilitation was concerned; people needed more time. After a while I decided to leave Stanford and open up a pro bono speech pathology practice for low income individuals who needed more services than their insurance provided. I didn't need to advertise or market my services because I was getting all of my patients through relationships I had built at Stanford.

A personal search

In my mid to late 30s, I had a sense that there was something else I wanted to find or do in my life, that there was more to explore, especially in the spiritual domain, but I didn't have any idea what that was. It was almost an unconscious craving. I started reading lots of books in my spare time and going to classes, seminars, and weekend retreats to explore and find out what it was that I was looking for. This exploration was fascinating, but I wasn't yet finding what really inspired me.

At the same time my husband Lawrence was on a sabbatical from his job. Back then he was what I would call a closet philosopher. He loved religion and philosophy but outwardly he was still a lawyer and executive. We had shared a common interest in that subject matter—I remember us repeatedly listening to the famous PBS Joseph Campbell lectures on myths when we were younger—but we were now exploring these ideas in different ways.

One day I came back from one of the classes I had taken, feeling especially disappointed. Sitting in our living room was a person Lawrence had met, a well-known scholar of yoga and Indian philosophy. He was a PhD who had written numerous books, more on the spiritual aspects of yoga than the physical practice. This scholar came over to our house for dinner and I shared my search with him, that I was not finding what I was looking for, and how I was feeling like I was chasing my tail.

He asked me one question that changed my life. He said, "Have you found somebody—a good teacher that you admire—who could help you along the way?" I told him that I had not. For some reason, that question really stuck with me. I had never even thought about finding a school or a teacher. I had felt I needed to find what I was looking for on my own.

A few months later Lawrence and I met that scholar's teacher, a Tibetan Buddhist master named Segyu Rinpoche. At that time, I knew little about Segyu Rinpoche's background or what it meant to be a Tibetan Buddhist teacher and healer. I did not know the first thing about Buddhism.

Yet, this was the first time in my years of exploration that I felt someone I had met knew something really deep, something that I was missing, the kind of thing I yearned to discover even though I couldn't put any words to it. I had never felt that with any of the other places or teachers or books that I had encountered. The idea of a spiritual teacher had never even entered my consciousness, but I was very intrigued.

I needed to find out more about Segyu Rinpoche and why I found myself so interested in him. The only way I could do that was to get to know him better. And that's exactly what I started to do. I began to take some of his classes, this time with Lawrence, too, as he already knew at that point that he was very attracted to Buddhist ideas and philosophy.

At that time, Segyu Rinpoche taught in the traditional style of Tibetan Buddhist philosophies and techniques. This included a strong cultural overlay that reflected the traditional manifestations of Tibetan Buddhism, which tended to be oriented toward ritual and monasticism. Although Segyu Rinpoche was a Tibetan Buddhist monk, because he is a Brazilian born Western individual, he related extremely well to his Western students and really tried to help us see beyond the cultural elements that were hard for us to relate to. There was this tension between, on the one hand, moving toward Segyu Rinpoche and wanting more of what he was teaching, and on the other hand being repelled somewhat by the cultural elements that were so foreign to us. But we knew he had the essence of these practices and we really wanted to learn that.

My relationship with Segyu Rinpoche did not begin with lightning bolts flashing in the sky or anything like that. I wasn't consciously thinking, "This is my teacher. I need to follow him." Like any important relationship, it evolved and took time to build a deep bond and trust. I really began to have that trust when I realized that Segyu Rinpoche's only motivation was to help me overcome my inner impediments to wellbeing and to bring out my own potential. We developed a tremendous mutual respect. It wasn't a one-way relationship; he was the teacher, yes, but as a student he showed great respect for me and my life. That is when I really began to learn.

Inner and outer work

In today's world, work can be all consuming. The pressures to perform are intense, especially with the younger generation that we are pushing to succeed in a world of competition and overachieving. It is easy to lose our sense of balance and wellbeing. I feel it is important to look at life, including work, from a holistic perspective. After all, work and life are not separated; work is just another experience of life. But how do we do that—how do we integrate all the different parts of our lives, business and personal? This requires transformation in how we think and behave.

Ultimately, for this type of integration to happen, we have to start looking within ourselves. We have to become aware of the inner patterns and stories that drive our experience so we can change them for the better. This is counter to how most of us were raised, with the focus on outer achievement. But to reform our attitude towards business and work, we have to do this inner work.

These ideas are really not new. There is a long history of thought which holds that, to be most effective in the world, we first need to evolve within ourselves. We need to go beyond the inner conflicts that could be making us less content and less effective, so that we can then act in the world in much more positive and rewarding ways.

Pursuing purpose: the quest for depth without dogma

Founded in 2003, Juniper is a non-profit dedicated to bringing an authentic tradition of meditation and inner growth to modern culture in a secular form. Our work is tailored to contemporary Western culture, knowledge, and sensibilities, and its goal is to give us the inner freedom to be who we are and to discover our capacities for peace of mind, joy, harmony, and being a positive contributor in the world. The goal of all the Juniper founders is to make the essence of these practices accessible in contemporary life so we can use them for positive transformation.

The foundation of our practices at Juniper has four parts. One is the methodology itself, which is meditation. There are many different types of meditation and they each have unique benefits. Meditation to us is the idea of setting a space to turn inward and to work inside of yourself. Just a few minutes a day of this kind of work can make a big difference in our lives.

The second part of our foundational practices we call balancing emotions. Balance means understanding and gaining control over the emotional swings and extremes that cause agitation. Our emotions have an enormous effect on our experience, often impeding our inner growth. Gaining control over our emotions can create a dramatic shift in our wellbeing. We work on balancing emotions, because we find this fundamental to truly being the productive, joyful individuals that we have the capacity to be.

The third part is compassion. By compassion, we're talking about how we engage in the world—are we engaging from a perspective of "me, me, me," from our individualistic desires? Or, are we able to engage the world with more empathy, openness, sharing, concern, and care for others? Compassion calls for deepening our sensitivity and concern for others. We learn the power of thinking of others and how to enable that to infuse all we do.

Finally, the fourth aspect is what we call insight, or wisdom. That, in essence, is about going beyond the stories in our heads about who we are, how we and others should be, and how we should behave and feel about ourselves. Often it is the stories in our heads that limit us, because they seem so real to us that we cannot escape them. The insights gleaned from meditations help us deconstruct those stories and examine them, especially the ones that are causing us unnecessary hardship. Through these insights we can expand our awareness and break free from the limited perspectives, dogmas, and conventions that hold us back. This often involves a change of perspective in how we see and deal with the world.

Getting back to our humanity

Juniper's story continues to unfold. In 2009, we opened a meditation hall in Redwood City, California; in 2011 we launched an integrative care clinic in Palo Alto, California; and in 2015 we opened a beautiful meditation center in San Francisco and moved our integrative care clinic there. We also introduced our first online meditation offerings, created to enable individuals anywhere to engage in these practices.

A few years ago, the type of person who joined us at Juniper were women in their 40s or above. We also had some men and some younger people, but they were the minority. As soon as we opened the center in San Francisco, we saw a change in the demographics, which is one reason we wanted to expand there in the first place. Almost two thirds of people coming are in their 20s and 30s. It's been fascinating and wonderful. It confirmed to us how individuals of all ages are seeking to enhance themselves and to make a positive shift in their lifestyle.

For example, we had a mother who brought her daughter to a meditation class. The daughter was in her late 20s. She had gone to the best of the best schools—Harvard, Yale, and Princeton. She had come back home to visit her mom and was completely drained. The question she had for us was, "How do I find out who I am?"

We are seeing this type of inquiry over and over again. It is quite prevalent among the younger generation raised in a world of overachievement. They can jump through any hoop, and yet they aren't sure who they are or what they want. Their inner being and sense of self hasn't fully developed. This takes time. Our goal at Juniper is to provide the method and techniques to help find these answers.

We are finding that more people of all ages are beginning to think about these things. They may be at the beginning of their careers, or they may be at the end of their career and thinking, "What am I going to do now?" They often feel stressed and have challenging issues in their lives, so now they are more open to and interested in the work that we've been doing.

A final part of the equation that I believe is vital going forward is *community*. This was always valued highly in the tradition of meditation I practice. The teachers, the practices, and the community—those were the three components. This involves a recognition that, ultimately, we are social beings and feeling that we belong, that we are part of something, is important. More than that, our humanity is a reflection of our community. When our communities are fragmented and disjointed, as many are today, we will feel fragmented and disjointed within ourselves.

This is why we emphasize community at Juniper. We love it when others share the experiences they've had at Juniper with their families, co-workers, and friends. This is our biggest source of new participants. Imagine what could happen if more and more people were to engage in this type of inner work and then teach this to their children and others. We would have people coming together with shared purpose around these ideas. Through building communities that value these ideas, we will at the same time shape our humanity.

Exercises for Expedition 10

31 What Gets My Attention			
		"I am making a life—living my purpose."	*"I am making a living—supporting my needs."*
	Which of these resonates most with me? Why?		
	What's working well for me?		
	What is my biggest opportunity?		

32 **Describing My Lifestyle**			
		"I am a workaholic who is trying to balance work and life."	*"I am a lifeaholic seeing life as an adventure."*
	Which of these resonates most with me? Why?		
	What's working well for me?		
	What is my biggest opportunity?		

33 **Connecting Stories**	Thinking about each of the stories you just experienced, what do they mean for your own journey to conscious 21st century leadership?	
	Tim McDonald	
	Grace Clapham	
	Samuel Poh	
	Hillary Brook Levy	

Third Leg of the Journey
Creating the 21st Century Organization on the Edge

"A martial artist is a human being first. Just as nationalities have nothing to do with one's humanity, so they have nothing to do with martial arts. Leave your protective shell of isolation and relate directly *to what is being said. Return to your senses by ceasing all the intervening intellectual mumbo jumbo. Remember that life is a constant process of relating. Remember, too, that I seek neither your approval nor to influence you toward my way of thinking. I will be more than satisfied if, as a result of this article, you begin to investigate everything for yourself and cease to uncritically accept prescribed formulas that dictate "this is this" and "that is that.""*

Bruce Lee, "Liberate Yourself from Classical Karate," *Black Belt Magazine* (1971)

Expedition 11
Thriving in the 21st Century

In high school in Israel, I did pre-military training where they taught us how to construct tents from blankets, ropes, and rocks, how to jump off buildings safely, and how to navigate with a compass. During one exercise in the field, our teachers, who were serving in the military, gave us a map and a compass and showed us our destination on the map. They told us they would meet us there. There were no GPS devices or apps back then; they were training us how to navigate and survive in nature. My small team started on our journey. Soon we ran into a group of locals taking a hike in the wilderness. They were very friendly and helpful. When I asked them for directions, they smiled and pointed us toward our destination. We had a great time and arrived at the designated spot, only to find out that our teachers were perched above watching us, and were not amused that we had not followed their rules.

Sometimes you need to put the map down. No one has the course charted for us, no matter how much they may try to convince you that they know what you need in your life right now. Even in this book, I have introduced the seven signposts knowing full well that there are many more paths for us to take beyond what has been outlined here. Whatever your path, it is vividly and painfully clear that we have to stop the insanity of putting profits ahead of people, and evolve the world of work as a more purpose-driven experience. My hope is that by experiencing your own journey with greater self-awareness and more focused intention, you can engage in more profound conversations, ask more questions, connect more deeply with others, and co-create new stories for our planet.

There is a change happening in business, and whether we like it or not, traditional frameworks and practices are lacking what people of all ages are increasingly seeking: purpose-driven organizations that respect life and our planet. Our future belongs to organizations whose leaders navigate with higher purpose, and create opportunities, rather than simply trying to solve problems. Some people may see a huge pile of junk materials as nothing more than a problem to be solved, while others may stop and imagine how those materials could be used to create an opportunity, such as designing an affordable housing alternative.

While many people believe change only comes from the top of organizations,[60] in purpose-driven organizations this is starting to shift as more people have access to information and communities of people. Companies like Etsy, for example, offer free entrepreneurship courses for the unemployed and underemployed in cities across the US and the UK, and include an optional session on how to set up a store on Etsy's platform. These courses help artists and designers find a way to earn an income from their creative pursuits and also adds more offerings to Etsy's customers. Etsy has built a global online community of 40 million people with sales over $1 billion in 2013. They also partner with local community organizations and are generating what they call "Etsy economic opportunity" throughout the US and some international markets.[61] Their customers look for thoughtful alternatives to mass commerce retail by choosing goods with more individuality and meaning. With a 21st century mindset, any organization can make a significant difference on social issues and create economic value. In an Etsy Economy, people come first as the company can sustain their profitability and, at the same time, create programs that help people sustain themselves.

By being able to connect deeply with others, new opportunities can emerge. There are simple ways for us to break away from the complexity that surrounds us. Some days it is as easy as reaching out to someone who can listen to what is in our heart, without needing to schedule it days or weeks in advance. We have a plethora of tools that can connect us person to person, and we need to have the courage to

---

[60] http://www.strategy-business.com/article/00255?gko=9d35b

[61] https://blog.etsy.com/news/2014/notes-from-chad-creating-an-etsy-economy-together/

use them in ways that serve us. The gift of feeling deeply is not for the faint of heart, and yet, it is such a vital and intrinsic part of what being human is all about. Our opportunity is to have deep conversations and make more purposeful connections with people, rather than merely jumping from transaction to transaction. What if trust, relationships, and community are the most important currencies of the 21st century and beyond?

What no one tells us is that life is for living, and when we are grounded in reality, much can happen through our connection to ourselves and others. It's up to each of us to customize and tailor our journey as we take out our own personal compass and start navigating the intricate pathways of our lives. Some people may want to share with you the secret productivity success tips for people like Elon Musk or Richard Branson, but what worked for them is not necessarily going to work for you. And why are we celebrating productivity and efficiency as the ultimate success of a human being and an organization? What happens when we discover there is no secret formula, framework, or method that can guarantee you success?

Far too often we want the easy way handed to us, but we need to do the work ourselves. Of course, this book itself has offered many helpful hints, suggestions, and insights, as well as numerous transformative and inspiring stories, but another person's story is not our own. While there are universal principles that can guide us, those principles apply uniquely to each of us. There is an interesting tension to be found in the fact that we have to do the work for ourselves, and yet it is a collective effort. Being in a community that fosters each members' wellbeing and highest purpose is essential to help each member discover their own unique path. It is difficult to extract ourselves from society and meditate in isolation in a cave, but it is even more difficult to live an authentic life aspiring to our highest potential while being immersed in the world. We may feel compassion when sitting alone, but it is a far greater challenge to continue feeling that compassion while riding an overcrowded subway to work every day.

So long as we worship the same type of business heroes, the more likely we are to bring forth another generation of command central leaders. If we can break the culture of sameness, we might find an opportunity to truly unleash our own art and voice. That is the journey no one talks about. We are rushed from childhood to succeed and accomplish. We have been taught to win at all costs and always be the very best in school, sports, business, and so on. We have been conditioned that more is better and winning the prize is the only success.

When we listen to our own compass, we will often be surprised at what it is telling us. Many of us have been conditioned to turn the volume on our intuition down to the lowest setting. We often do not listen to that voice inside of us that tells us to do something simply because our friends and family would think we were crazy.

My friend Mei Xu lived through the chaotic Chinese Cultural Revolution, and at the age of 17 she was inducted into the People's Liberation Army, where she was assigned to spy on a visiting American professor. Her story is captured in the best-selling book, *Daughter of China: A True Story of Love and Betrayal* (1999). Mei has witnessed much in her life when it comes to conflict. She escaped to America where she had a new start as a successful tech executive and venture capitalist. During a recent lunch, she shared with me that she started taking a Tai Chi class as a form of meditative practice. At her most recent class, the teacher had her stand against her classmate and asked her to take down her opponent. At that moment, she realized that while this type of practice can help us build a certain kind of strength, she did not want to take anyone down as part of her own personal practice. She felt she had witnessed enough war in her lifetime, and that she is ready for a new renaissance of peace and healing. She decided to leave the class instead. That is what her intuition told her.

So much shifts when we start listening to ourselves and knowing how it makes us feel. Being told to take down an opponent was not aligned with Mei's own path at that moment. That doesn't mean that no one should study martial arts or learn combat practices, but it does show that she had the courage to follow her own inner voice, which was leading her to other opportunities that she needed to experience.

Adopting a Mindset of Adventure

Our current culture forces us to specialize and become an expert in a specific field. From a young age, we are asked what we want to do when we grow up and are focused on finding our way in the world through making a living. While having specialists in certain fields is clearly important and necessary, it can also be needlessly restrictive and shut us out from the expansiveness of the world. It is remaining curious and having the mindset of an adventurer that allows us to adapt to changing environments. If we can bring our childlike imagination with us on our journey, no matter how old we are, we will be able to bring a new sense of enthusiasm and spirit to our lives as we navigate the waters with our own personal compass. Businesses need to wake up and realize that the old ways are fast disintegrating, even if not in the most obvious ways, and if they don't adapt, then they are unlikely to survive.

Being an adventurer is more aligned with valuing experiences over material possessions. In fact, for many Millennials, travel is starting to be seen as a vital part of their personal growth and life experience, and they also generally prefer to spend money on experiences than things.[62] In the US there are more than 1.6 million "volunteer tourists," those who prefer to help others, such as working in an orphanage, instead of having more typical vacations. These volunteer tourists, many of whom are from the younger generation, are spending over $2 billion a year, and they are not just traveling globally but re-imagining a more purposeful and meaningful travel experience.[63]

Our opportunity in the 21st century is to tell a different story, a story filled with so many souls creating and co-creating business with a humane-centered approach, with work being just one element of a meaningful life on the planet. We can stop trying to force people to pretend to be happy and optimistic all the time at work, and instead recognize that if we truly want to innovate, we need to be prepared for

---

[62] http://www.digitalmusicnews.com/2014/09/18/millenials-would-rather-spend-money-on-experiences-than-things/

[63] http://www.npr.org/sections/goatsandsoda/2014/07/31/336600290/as-volunteerism-explodes-in-popularity-whos-it-helping-most

a whole rainbow of emotions, such as frustration or sadness when our idea does not pan out as we expected. At the same time, by working out loud in open communities, we can share information and stories so much more easily and effectively.

Our Journey to Corporate Sanity: Running Purpose-Driven Lives and Businesses

As more people of all ages around the world align with their purpose, we will start hearing their bold voices through their ability to make a life instead of just a living. People will no longer wait for the change to happen as they realize that in their lifetimes, they can be the ones who choose themselves and work for organizations that place a premium on people—whether as employees, customers, partners, or any other group. They will also choose companies that care deeply about employee welfare, local communities, and commitment to the planet, and who have a strong sense of purpose. In thriving 21st century organizations, we will increase open conversations and share information. Information will become a key driver of maintaining shared purpose, and will start to flow more easily to the people who need it to be effective in their jobs.

Our Journey to Corporate Sanity started from the realization that it is time to let go of our false limiting beliefs, and instead imagine possibilities that can be transformed into practical opportunities by bringing people together around shared purpose. If we open our hearts and minds, we will tap into our strong desires to write our own stories on our own paths. Living in our open and connected world, we need to remember that what really matters is the quality of the relationships we build. Having a lot of followers on social media can be a great thing, but it is even more important to build trusted relationships.

This book shares the transformational stories of 21st century leaders, but with the recognition that these stories are meant to be inspiring, not simply copied. This is the beginning of our movement back to basics when it comes to business, to create new paths forward for all of us. As you lay down the foundations to help build thriving 21st century organizations, here are some views on the seven signposts.

#1 In Search of Conscious 21st Century Leaders

Conscious 21st century leaders recognize that life is for living. It is time to free ourselves from associating success with purely financial riches. When we awaken our consciousness and remember why we are here, we realize that we have the responsibility and the privilege of navigating our own lives.

Business should be a bridge to a more shared prosperity for everyone, not just for the few who control the shares. This is our opportunity to create a saner world by recognizing that organizations are made up of people—which is an obvious fact that is too often forgotten—and that we need leaders who design businesses that put people first. 21st century leaders know how to bring people together around shared purpose, and work without being constantly supervised or controlled. 21st century leaders share their work more openly, and they recognize that the sharing of information can have great mutual benefits (which is not to say that companies should give away all their secrets). We also value two-way conversations and spend more time connecting people than managing them. Empathy and leading from the heart matter as much as profit. It is a way of life for conscious 21st century leaders.

21st century leaders are pioneers who spring out of unlikely places to follow their own compass and make sense of the world, and they see business as a way to bring teams together and focus on key projects. While currently these leaders are often called innovators as they set a new course, many pioneers throughout history have been seen as being a bit mad during their own time. It no longer needs to be a lonely path; as we become more interconnected, more 21st century leaders are finding each other and connecting around shared and higher purpose.

#2 Uncovering the Beauty of Shared Purpose

Many of us have been conditioned to live in mental boxes, and we were meant to feel safe in them. But these so-called "safe boxes" have actually trapped us in harmful patterns and beliefs, and so they are not so safe after all. Many people today of all ages are seeking meaning and purpose beyond the confines of these boxes, either by asking new questions or remembering their own voices. We also have to proceed with caution, as we are at risk of purpose becoming commoditized like other flavor of the month initiatives.

Purpose should be integrated into the fabric of the organization in the 21st century. I recently met a woman who told me she had spent six months defining her company's mission and vision statements, but when I asked her what their purpose was, she could not tell me. Purpose has to be the fire inside every person and organization; it should spark something meaningful for people and the planet.

#3 A Mindset of Wholeness

It's time for each of us to become whole, as individuals and organizations. Societies often drive us into separation and segment us into parts, which can make us feel small or alone. Terms we use in business like "the war on talent" suggest a battle we must fight to get precious resources that are either insufficient or rare. It further divides us into working on separate goals in silos, when the opportunity is to share our knowledge and adopt a mindset of wholeness.

For the first time in the history of humanity, any person with a device, connectivity, and electrical power can connect with billions of people who are online. It allows us to see ourselves and each other beyond geographies, and do great and impactful work.

It is not a naïve utopian desire to strive after peace, love, and openness, but it is not realistic to believe that all of humanity will suddenly embrace and actualize such ideals. And with our technology wizardry and global connectivity, surely we could, at least in principle, provide material wellbeing for every person on the planet. So, what is stopping us?

It is time for harmony and wholeness as 21st century leaders bring people together around shared purpose to create something bigger than themselves. There is no doubt about it; an increasing number of people are starting to care deeply about their wellbeing and are no longer separating their physical, emotional, and mental health. The human spirit is seeking emotional and spiritual joy in life beyond material success.

On the journey to becoming whole, we want to reflect on ancient wisdom that elevates spiritual pursuits beyond mere material acquisitions. In business, too, we need to remember to heed nature's cycles, because no business exists in isolation from the rest of nature. When we act out of harmony with nature, we inevitably pay the price, sooner or later. We will also no longer need to rush to be the best at any cost, and instead we will value life more deeply—our own life, as well as the life of other people and organisms. Flow will become more important than ever as harmony and fulfillment drive us.

#4 It's Time to Integrate Ourselves and the Team

The most important currencies for a 21st century organization are trust, relationships, and community. When we have shared purpose, we see our humanity in each other, and we can have excellent relationships with all people—the people who work with us, the people who buy our products and services, the people who help us get our products and services to the market, the people who live in the communities we serve, and the people who care about what we create in the world. But we need to have a mindset that integrates our various parts into one person who lives and works with a goal of harmony and unity. We need to see our customers and employees as co-creators of our business and bring teams together to achieve our highest goals.

While the conversations about organizational structure will continue at the forefront until we have more 21st century leaders leading with shared purpose, it will eventually become secondary for businesses that drive human-centered design. The 21st century leader knows how to bring the right people into the conversation and enable co-creation.

As more people value themselves and the quality of their lives, the ability to create community will become much more important, and integration will move us away from our purely transactional work to having a compass that navigates us to co-create our work together. Our new metrics will be more focused on the depth of our relationships and unity, and how close or far we are from the heartbeat of the purpose of our business.

In this new century, it will become more common for work to be organized around small autonomous teams that come together as needed. As you will have greater access to people across the globe, you will be better able to build a team that will help achieve your purpose more effectively. An increasing number of people will choose themselves and see their working life as being structured around short-term, project-based teams rather than long-term jobs. There will be greater demand for open, two-way conversations in lieu of dogmatism.

#5 New Ways of Being

This journey allows us to be present to experience life in new ways. Living in an open and connected world requires more self-reflection and vulnerability as we share more openly and connect more easily. And while we recognize the extraordinary importance of technology, we will focus more on its value in helping to drive our purpose, where technology is in service to our higher shared purpose. And the definition of what "in person" means will be blurred, as we will spend more time virtually connecting with people from around the world and creating deep, lasting, purposeful relationships and experiences.

Many people are seeking environments that allow them to show up as themselves and let them connect with others in deep conversations. Someday soon, I hope, some brilliant heart will create new social platforms that connect us based on purpose rather than the old advertising paradigms. Status updates will then be replaced by deep, meaningful conversations that will connect us even more as we find like-minded souls in our connected networks and trusted communities

As we become whole, we will shed the internal and external organizational barriers that divide us. We will more easily find other people to work with on our projects and co-create with them. Organizations will need to change their back-end processes to accommodate a new way of being.

Working out loud will no longer be considered a separate process, as more people will share openly what they are working on, realizing that doing so is to everyone's benefit. We will no longer be rewarded only for being the smartest person in the room, as collaboration becomes a much more important way of being in the world of business. We will also recognize the value of communities and the increasing need of community management as a force for bringing people together in conversation and making an impact. Meetings will be places where we go to work in open conversations that lead to decisions and action.

#6 Co-Creating Possibilities with Connected Networks, Trusted Communities, and Unlikely Partnerships

The human-to-human purpose and experience driven adventure we are on allows us to find the artist and creator within each of us and co-create possibilities. In the 21st century, we start recognizing and celebrating ourselves and what we are creating in the world. While we may admire others, we will start admiring ourselves as well, and attract others who want to co-create with us.

Last year, I gave a keynote on connected networks, trusted communities, and unlikely partnerships at a senior executive offsite. A year later they had a person working on making connected networks a reality by working in new ways. In this new way of being, we treat each other with respect and dignity. This new way of co-creating allows us to find unlikely partners to go to market with and create something bigger than ourselves. When we focus on purpose, we connect with people who will help us enter new markets. We measure our ability to work in community and the depth of our partnerships and cooperation.

What if every time you used the word "audience" or "stakeholder," you paused to reflect on what you mean by the action associated with its higher meaning? Are you really just talking at someone or pitching someone with your messages? What happens if instead of using these terms in your work (unless you are about to perform on a stage with a band or a theatre troupe), you thought of it as a "community" that you are building, or "unlikely partners" who you can co-create with?

As the world gets more connected, we can no longer hide as easily. We need to look after each other. We need to recognize that we are each on our journey, writing our individual and collective stories. It is so important to remember that we are human and that we have this amazing imagination to co-create possibilities. It's up to each of us to reach out and touch the rest of the world. All it takes is a desire to find someone and connect your stories purposefully. Wake up to your purpose. We need you to create the ripples.

#7 LIFEworking Means Choosing Yourself

Life is one big adventure, and work is just a part of it. You can choose to be a workaholic (20th century scarcity mindset) or you can become a lifeaholic (21st century opportunity mindset). It's a choice. When I started LIFEworking, there was a high personal cost, and I needed to make important decisions about what no longer served me. Planting seeds for my path meant I needed to dig in the dirt, and I (re)learned that life can get messy. It was a shift from a scarcity mindset of being a workaholic and believing that my life was my work, to being a lifeaholic, where my life is my life and my work is what I co-create in the world with other pioneers as a part of my life.

You may have lived a life where other people's beliefs had inordinate power over you. By becoming a lifeaholic, you realize it's your story to write and create. External events no longer need to have such a devastating effect on you as you recognize your own power to pursue possibilities.

So many amazing things are possible when we leave the treadmill of conditioned fear, scarcity, and unnecessary competition behind. Instead of problems, you imagine possibilities and create opportunities to make your business thrive.

Creating a Saner and Healthier Planet for All Living Beings

What does love have to do with business? Everything. Love is the most powerful energy in the universe. As we have seen in many of the stories shared in this book, love and emotions have generally not been "allowed" in business. Despite talking about the love of what we do in a plethora of business books and mission statements, we have yet to allow the opening for love to penetrate our mindset in how business can be done. If there was more love in our work, could we be more conscious of how we treated people and our environment? Would we be able to bring cooperation and co-creation to drive our business, instead of fueling more and more competition between people and organizations in the race to be the best in the world? Imagine what could happen if we were to allow love and compassion into the world of business. It is not naïve to think this way. After all, you don't want to poison the people you love, so why do we accept the pollution of our air, water, and soil in the name of increasing profits, or beating the competition by being faster to market and using questionable practices?

For the first time in our collective history, people are starting to pay more to do business with companies that have higher ethical standards and pursue the wellbeing of society. In this emerging business world, when an organization demonstrates a clear purpose, people feel a connection to what the company creates. We will start seeing more people choosing the products and services of organizations that have a strong purpose, even if it is not the cheapest offering in the market. In this new world, value plays a higher role in how customers and employees assess whether they want to buy from or work for an organization. There will be greater scrutiny on whether organizations practice what they put in their mission statements and marketing. 21st century leaders will need to be present to bring these behaviors to life through their actions.

In a world where there is more to life than work, what will happen when we spend as much time taking into consideration all aspects of our life beyond our career track? Family, friends, laughter, theatre, music, sports, books, conversations, creating, being in nature, and so much more, are all a part of life. But without healthy organizations serving the social good, all of these are compromised by the appetites of private power, shareholder value, and pure greed. It's time for us to integrate ourselves and become whole again. No one else will do it for us. This is a fight for our lives, and how it ends is up to us. We need to be more conscious of the decisions we make regarding where we shop, where we eat, what we eat, who we spend time with and where we work.

We also need to stop leading with organizational development and structure in business, as if it will solve all our problems. Demoting organizational structure is not easy road, as it is how most of us have been trained to do business. A trigger for us, which could be helpful, is to catch ourselves every time we want to fix something by believing that the organizational structure or a framework will solve it. We need to move away from engineering solutions to every problem to bringing a 21st century mindset of questioning ourselves to find the higher meaning that will lead us to our purpose. We may build a house like our neighbors and find ourselves having rooms in it we rarely use, like a living room, that tells us what we are supposed to do once we are in it. More houses today are segregated by having a living room for guests and a den for family living. Imagine how houses will be built in the future when we integrate our lives and make them whole. Imagine a house built based on purpose versus following a floorplan like the cookie cutters of everyone else's house. What can happen when we break the mindset of sameness?

When we have clarity of purpose, the structure will follow, especially when we consider wholeness and integration in our design. While I know many of us have been conditioned to follow a framework or model that puts all the pieces on a PowerPoint slide, it too often shuts us out from our intuition and creativity. Instead of relying so much on the words and images on slides, let's remember our opportunity to dive into conversations that connect us heart to heart. It is part of our conditioning to quote the big thinkers, but the opportunity is not only to quote them but also have deeper conversations about what their thinking offers us and how we can apply it to our own opportunities.

Creating people-centered organizations can allow our humanity to prevail when we make it a value of our life and business. While it is obviously true that we have bills to pay, what would happen if we start questioning our own assumptions about success, and started thinking more seriously about the choices we are making in creating these bills in the first place? Our whole relationship with owning material possessions is shifting, and it will continue to shift over the next few decades as more people start making different choices about their consumption habits, such as learning more about the toxins that are in our food supply. All these changes and transformations can be scary, and it is harmful when some people falsely imply that change is supposed to be easy. Deep, lasting change is never easy.

For me, my trip to the Amazon rainforest was life changing, because I started facing my deepest fears head on. But my experiences on this trip also showed me what was already there before I arrived in the Amazon: I was un-conditioning from how I was told I was supposed to live my life. I had followed the manual, until one day I realized it was not written for me. I love working and making a difference in the world, and my path now is to do it with people who share this love and want to do it collectively. I also need the space to be able to bring my humanity and range of emotions on this journey.

It starts with each of us becoming aware of our purpose and living from our hearts. There is no reason to compete and take someone else down so that we can feel we are appreciated. It is not naïve to imagine a world where we practice compassion and cooperation instead of violence and destruction. This is why I am emphasizing in this book that the biggest change we need in the 21st century is one of mindset. It is about our own journey to explore why we are here, versus what we were told we were supposed to do with our lives. It is about understanding that we are whole people who can be professionals and have a fulfilling life.

When we start recognizing what our personal role is in what is happening around us, we create new opportunities to step up and make the shifts that are needed for us to regain our individual and collective sanity. It takes us convening and having open dialogue where we can truly listen and see. There is increasing information out there on every topic imaginable, which is so widely available. We don't need to have our heads stuck in the sand. A company that does not treat its people well will be found out in this connected world of ours. An organization that poisons our water supply will no longer be able to hide it as easily as even a decade ago. The people working in that organization may also start choosing to work for one that does not harm the planet.

A vital part of becoming whole requires understanding what our calling is in the world, and how much easier it is to connect with others when we have the courage to ask new questions, meet different people, and follow our greater purpose. I know this firsthand from my own journey, where the most amazing people keep appearing in my life who want to create a new path for business and are waking up to what is possible. We can create new stories, ones that are more grounded in reality and are better aligned with who we really are. The many stories shared so openly in this book by 21st century leaders can inspire us on our own journeys.

A significant part of creating a sane and healthy world requires us to recognize that we can step out and create a different path for business. Much changes when we can imagine how business can bring us together to live more in community and partnership. When we create thriving 21st century organizations that are people-centric, we will remember the purpose of our organizations, and prosperity will more easily flow to more people as part of co-creating with partners. We will also have access to more data that shows the correlation between profitable businesses that value people, because we will increasingly be asking for this level of accountability.

Unfortunately, we are not ready for the population growth that will hit certain parts of the world. According to the Guardian, it is "almost inevitable" that the number of people on the planet will rise from 7.3 billion today to 9.7 billion in 2050, according to the latest UN projections.[64] In some parts of the world, we are also facing an increased aging population that our systems will not be able to support. The cracks are already starting to show across European countries.

If you look at the recent Fortune 500 list of worldwide companies, you will see more Chinese organizations appearing on the list than ever before.[65] Some can view this as an increasing crisis and feel like there is

---

[64] https://www.theguardian.com/global-development/2015/jul/29/un-world-population-prospects-the-2015-revision-9-7-billion-2050-fertility

[65] https://www.weforum.org/agenda/2016/07/new-fortune-global-500-shift-business-landscape/

nothing they can do, while others can see this shift as an opportunity for business to bring us together in new ways to have conversations that are critical to our survival on this planet. We cannot afford to stay separated and believe someone else will take care of everything for us. We have seen how this story has played out throughout our history by replacing one conflict with another in the pursuit of transient power and the accumulation of material wealth.

We can—and we must—create a saner world, and because business has such an extraordinary impact on our planet and our daily lives, we need a significant focus on creating corporate sanity as a priority. Of course, since businesses are made up of people and serve people, then it is up to each of us to strive for greater sanity in our own lives. If we, the people who invest in, work for, and buy from corporations, are not very sane, then how can we expect to achieve corporate sanity? It is part of many ancient philosophical/spiritual traditions to seek greater self-understanding, greater wisdom, and better alignment with reality, and now such ancient teachings need to be brought in more explicitly into corporations and all our organizations. It is our biggest opportunity as we face this crossroads on our journey.

In the words of Aldous Huxley: "Today I feel no wish to demonstrate that sanity is impossible. On the contrary, though I remain no less sadly certain than in the past that sanity is a rather rare phenomenon, I am convinced that it can be achieved and would like to see more of it."[66]

Isn't it time for each of us to ask ourselves, and each other, this one question: What is our collective story on this planet?

---

[66] Brave New World / Brave New World Revisited (2005)

Exercises for Expedition 11

Thriving in the 21st Century

What would you like to focus on to thrive in the human-to-human purpose and experience driven adventure

34 **Internalizing the Seven Signposts**	Please capture what you need to do for yourself and your business to thrive in each of the following areas:		
		Me:	My business:
	21st Century Leadership		
	Shared Purpose		
	Becoming Whole		
	Integrating		
	New Ways of Being		
	Co-Creating		
	LIFEworking		

Crafting Your Story

Whatever you're experiencing, you are on a journey, one that is truly unique to you. We need to take the precious time we have been gifted and figure out our purpose first, and find the other leaders, creators, and organizations who will be delighted to work with us for a shared greater purpose.

35

Getting Clarity

Thinking about thriving, answer each of the following in terms of what it means to you personally, and what it means for your business

	For me:	For the essence of my business:
Why am I here?		
What is my story?		
Who can I create and co-create with?		

Making the Shift

Which stories no longer serve you, and which ones do you want to start living today? It's always a choice. A new story is available to each of us.

36 **Understanding My Stories**	What are the stories that you tell yourself, and what are the stories you tell others about yourself that no longer serve you? Are there new ones that need to be told? Why or why not?		
		An old story that no longer serves me:	A new story that lets me imagine new possibilities:
	Stories I tell myself		
	Stories I tell others about me		

Book Your Journey: An Open Invitation to the Architects of Humanity

A few months ago, I was driving across San Francisco's San Mateo bridge to a meeting. I was feeling frustrated. I passed accidents, and people cutting each other off in their need to get nowhere fast, while I was reflecting on an interaction I'd had earlier that day.

As I was driving in insane Silicon Valley traffic, this thought appeared: "I'd love to have a conversation with the architects of humanity." And then I started laughing when I realized what was so obvious, something that has always been here: In the 21st century, we all need to be leaders of our own lives, which is part of what it means to be an architect of humanity.

We have not yet fully awakened to the possibilities and opportunities that surround us. Many are still stuck in the programmed belief of fear, and everything that a fear mindset brings to our planet. Those who are stuck in these practices go to war every day, and try to solve problems by merely applying Band-Aids to stop the bleeding, without knowing how or why they got injured in the first place.

I am not sure how we have been programmed to believe that we must ask permission from some bigger body outside ourselves to live an authentic life. We have been conditioned to believe that someone apart from each of us is the architect of humanity, as if there is a special council that dictates how our humanity should manifest. It's always someone else who dictates how life should be experienced. That is the story I had been sold, and which I consciously no longer buy into.

There is no one else, apart from each of us that comes together to express our collective humanity. Wars break out, terrorist attacks occur, and crime proliferates throughout our cities. This is happening in our world and it is created by us. We can sit back and ask for a meeting with the architects of humanity, or we can reflect deeply on this one question of what our own role is in the world. If we lead together, humanity can find its deeper unity.

We have been given this precious gift called life to explore our purpose and create what is meaningful to us, with authenticity and a huge sense of responsibility, as the architects of our own human life. It does not need to be a burden. That is always a choice.

When you awaken to your voice and purpose in life, reach out and connect. You never need to be alone—unless you choose to be—despite all the stories our current conditioning tells us in this regard. Paint your canvass with beautiful colors and find the other architects and 21st century leaders who have given themselves permission to play on this abundant and beautiful planet with open hearts, a vivid imagination, and a belief that business is one of the biggest forces in the world that can start us on a journey to bring us together like never before. I hope that *Our Journey to Corporate Sanity* will help spark new conversations, and inspire you to greater understanding and enjoyment of your own amazing journey. This is just the beginning.

CPSIA information can be obtained
at www.ICGtesting.com
Printed in the USA
FSOW02n1212031116
26944FS